THE HISTORY OF THE
BRITISH FILM

1914–1918

D1103727

THE HISTORY OF THE BRITISH FILM

Vol 1 1896–1906
by Rachael Low and Roger Manvell

Vol 2 1906–1914
by Rachael Low

Vol 3 1914–1918
by Rachael Low

Vol 4 1918–1929
by Rachael Low

THE HISTORY

OF THE

BRITISH FILM

1914–1918

by

RACHAEL LOW

Published under the joint auspices of
the BRITISH FILM INSTITUTE and
the BRITISH FILM ACADEMY

Distributed in the United States by R. R. Bowker Company
(a Xerox Education Company)

First published in 1948
Second impression 1973

ISBN 0 04 791002 4   Volume 1
0 04 791008 9   Volume 2
0 04 791009 7   Volume 3

Distributed in The United States by R. R. Bowker Company
(a Xerox Education Company)

Printed in Great Britain
in 11 point Times Roman type
by Unwin Brothers Limited
Old Woking, Surrey

ACKNOWLEDGEMENTS

I did the research for this part of the History of the British Film Industry, and wrote it, under the joint sponsorship of the British Film Institute and the British Film Academy. I would like to thank the Directors of both organizations, Oliver Bell and Roger Manvell, for their co-operation. My thanks are also due to the many veterans of the film industry who have helped me in my research. Their names will be found in the Bibliography, but I would like to thank Cecil Hepworth and George Pearson in particular for their patience and understanding: Baynham Honri not only for the interesting Technical Notes (Appendix I) but for much helpful information: Ernest Lindgren and Karel Reisz for useful discussion of the sections on film technique: the Cinematograph Section of His Majesty's Stationery Office for making the official films and relevant documents available to me: Messrs. R. W. Proffitt for lending me their copy of *The Vicar of Wakefield*: the editors of *Kinematograph Weekly*: and Norah Traylen, for her help with the illustrations.

R. L.

Joint History Research Committee of the British Film Institute and British Film Academy

CECIL M. HEPWORTH (*Chairman*)

GEORGE PEARSON

DR. ROGER MANVELL

ERNEST H. LINDGREN

RACHAEL LOW

CONTENTS

PART ONE
THE INDUSTRY

PART TWO

THE FILMS

7

ILLUSTRATIONS

INSET I

JANE SHORE
London Film Company Studio
Cricks and Martin Studio
Alexandra Palace Studio
Gaumont Studio
THE PRISONER OF ZENDA

between pages 64–65

INSET II

A STUDY IN SCARLET, THE BETTER 'OLE
THE GREAT EUROPEAN WAR
KIDDIES IN THE RUINS
THE "ULTUS" SERIES
SALLY BISHOP, MY OLD DUTCH
THE AVENGING HAND

between pages 160–161

INSET III

Chrissie White
THE BOTTLE
THE ELDER MISS BLOSSOM
Billy Merson, Henry Edwards
TOWARDS THE LIGHT
MERELY MRS. STUBBS
BROKEN THREADS
THE SECOND MRS. TANQUERAY, THE WARE CASE
HER LUCK IN LONDON, FLORENCE NIGHTINGALE

between pages 224–225

PART ONE

THE INDUSTRY

CHAPTER ONE

The Industry and the Public

(I) EXHIBITION

Exhibition during the War.

Britain has engaged in a conflict which threatens to prove one of the most dreadful and far-reaching in all history, not with any sudden passion nor with a desire for greedy gain, but as the avenger of honour and the guardian of the rights of posterity. . . . The ultimate effects of the war no man can foretell, but for the time being, fortunately, they seem far less disastrous than was at first expected. . . . The picture theatre, which is at the basis of the industry, is likely to be the last form of entertainment to suffer by the war since it is the cheapest, the most easily carried on, and under current conditions, perhaps the most attractive to the public.[1]

The patriotic note of this editorial, written on the outbreak of war, was to find echoes in other editorials in film journals throughout the next four years. It was to inspire trade participation in many patriotic funds, as well as pride in the number of colleagues and employees volunteering for Kitchener's New Army; while enthusiasm for the cinema's importance to propaganda and morale was soon to supplant the flagging interest in the educational film. The optimistic view of business prospects, on the other hand, was short-lived. Early visionaries had claimed that the cinema had real value not only as recreation for the common people, but also as a wide medium of propaganda and information. Ironically, official recognition of this fact during the war took the shape of taxes, restrictions and inter-ference on a scale hitherto unknown. Both the increased consciousness of the trade as a group, vying with other groups in its war contribution of men, money and important work at home, and the mounting resentment of official action, led to a feeling that the film business was the "Cinderella of British industry." Every fresh restriction was met by more reproachful reminders of magnificent war services rendered. By the end of 1918

[1] *Bioscope*, August 13, 1914, p. 615.

direct resort to Parliamentary action, with an M.P. to represent the trade, was openly advocated.

Some of the greatest hardships were felt by smaller exhibitors, in spite of their brave protestations of Business as Usual. The Amusements Tax, although theoretically borne by the consumer in the form of more expensive cinema seats, was said by the showmen to fall largely on themselves through diminished patronage and a shift to the cheaper seats.[1] At the same time, the expenses of theatre construction were increasing, not simply because of war conditions but also because of a new trend at the beginning of the war towards sumptuousness in cinema architecture. Desperate longings for magnificence harassed showmen who already had to face rising costs of labour and electricity. In addition the expensive long feature film and a new tax on imported films raised the cost of providing programmes. The managing director of two well-known chains of cinemas[2] claimed that by the end of the war the increase varied from thirty per cent in some parts of the country to fifty per cent in others.[3] Even at the beginning of the war that very active exhibitors' spokesman, F. W. Ogden Smith, had written that although "business is undoubtedly good . . . the cost of working has doubled during the past two years."[4] It is clear that this trend was greatly accelerated during the war.

To Ogden Smith it seemed absurd that cinemas should provide the now greatly improved films and comforts at the same admission prices as before.[5] From threepence to ninepence or a shilling, however, continued to be the most usual admission prices. As a result, by July 1916 it was claimed that the damaging effects of the Amusements Tax, a fine summer, and increased operating costs were serious, at least as far as the smaller cinemas were concerned. The eventual closing of many cinemas was caused by this, rather than by the temporary slump in attendance at the beginning of the war, the disruption of foreign supplies of film or the agitations for the enforced closing of all cinemas—of which various unidentified killjoys were from time to time accused.

In view of the number of business failures during these years and

[1] No figures are available to test the truth of this assertion, or suggest how far such taxation may have contributed to the closing of many cinemas during the war.
[2] Provincial Cinematograph Theatres and Associated Provincial Picture Houses.
[3] *Bioscope*, July 11, 1918, p. 31.   [4] Ibid., August 27, 1914, p. 817.
[5] E.g. Ibid., July 6, 1916, p. 4; July 13, 1916, p. 90.

vigorous complaints about rising costs, the apparent reluctance of exhibitors to raise admission prices seemed strange to many contemporaries. One school of thought[1] accused them of apathy, deploring a tradition of easily-made fortunes which seemed to have killed adaptability. Another[2] suggested that the showman's constant demand for novelty led to wasteful competition. But one more articulate and intelligent protagonist of the showman's interests, Henry Bey, tried to explain that their attitude was not simply capricious. While they were not firmly enough united to act in concert, none dared put his prices up alone. Calling a meeting at the Holborn Restaurant,[3] scene of many early trade deliberations, Bey made a new attempt to arouse a sense of common interest amongst them. It was not Bey's fault that they proved, once more, that true individualists would rather sink separately than admit to being in the same boat as each other.

The agitation for higher prices grew slowly. The need became more and more obvious, but very little progress could be reported even two years later. From the beginning of 1918 onwards, however, it grew to a crescendo. It was through negotiations with the Chancellor of the Exchequer over the Amusements Tax that matters came to a head. For some time the trade had been protesting that to increase this tax would be to kill the goose that laid the golden eggs. They claimed that the tax was already such a burden on their patrons as to make the necessary rise in admission prices impossible. It was difficult to escape the Chancellor's conclusion, therefore, that if modifications in the tax increases were allowed, exhibitors would then be able to ensure their own prosperity, and consequently the tax returns, by making the desired price increase. By the end of the war, therefore, many showmen had been induced through the Cinematograph Exhibitors' Association to agree to the tax proposals, and with them a universal rise in prices.[4]

When war broke out, however, such developments had been far from the minds of film people as they complacently surveyed the rapid changes in their industry:

[1] E.g. E. H. Montague; *Bioscope*, August 12, 1915, p. 650.
[2] E.g. "Observer" in the *Bioscope*, March 29, 1918, p. 41.
[3] *Bioscope*, September 30, 1915, p. 1446.
[4] Ibid., August 1, 1918, p. 5.

Only a few years ago a film cost a few shillings, and was shown in a little shop. Now it may cost thousands of pounds, and is presented in a palace.[1]

The exact number of these "picture palaces"—the term was new—is as difficult to determine for this period as for the previous one. The two most widely quoted figures were 4,000 and 6,000, the choice between them depending very largely on the point to be proved. In the absence of any official figure, the most reliable estimate is probably that to be found in a very important document published in 1917 by the Cinema Commission of the National Council of Public Morals.[2] This report maintained that there were some 4,500 picture theatres in the British Isles.[3] How many of these closed during the course of the war and were not reopened is a matter of further doubt, but it was stated in the *Bioscope* early in 1918 that they numbered 700 or 800.[4]

There is, once again, even less indication of the size of the average picture theatre at this time. The report suggested that these 4,500 theatres held accommodation for one in every thirty-seven of the population;[5] on the assumption that the population of the United Kingdom numbered approximately forty-three millions in 1916–1917, there were thus some million seats. It was widely recognized at the time that there was more seating accommodation per head of population in America than in this country, and comparison with American figures suggests further that the individual British theatres were relatively small.

The fashion was changing in favour of the larger hall. The ideal was no longer the "cosy rendezvous" of previous years, but the more impressively decorated "super cinema." The Bijou gave way to the Majestic, red plush hangings to many shades of marble. The seating accommodation of 3,000 at one Majestic,[6] with its baronial entrance hall and a ceiling covered with allegorical design, was still considered "unusually commodious."[7] But, since competition kept admission prices low, much larger audiences were now needed to cover the increasing costs due to long feature films, and such desirable extravagances as organs and graduated lighting. Even before

[1] *Bioscope*, September 30, 1915, p. 1459.
[2] *The Cinema: Its Present Position and Future Possibilities*. Published in 1917 by Williams & Norgate. See Chapter II below.   [3] P. xxi.
[4] *Bioscope*, January 31, 1918, p. 4.   [5] P. xxi.   [6] In Clapham.
[7] *Bioscope*, September 3, 1914, p. 884.

the war many of the small theatres built about 1908 had already run into financial difficulty as a result of the rising cost of programmes.

Thus the Tower Cinema at Peckham—opened, like many others at this time, by a celebrated actress—seated over 2,000 and was designed with appropriate grandeur "in Neo-Grecian style":

. . . a handsome marble and mosaic stairway, with three gangways of ample proportions, leading to a crush hall quite equalling in size many an ordinary cinema. This noble place alone can accommodate 1,000 waiting patrons, and with its marble tiling, dadoes, and grand staircase, and with tapestry panels for the higher portions of the wall, presents a sumptuous effect, still further enhanced by leaded domes and the use of cornice lighting. Choice palms here and there, floral decorations, and, midway to the circle, a luxurious lounge, complete a remarkable *ensemble*. In one corner, under the terrace lounge, is an Otis passenger lift for the use on rush nights of circle patrons. From the lounge one ascends a panelled oak stairway to the circle, whence is gained an adequate idea of the huge proportions of the house.[1]

Gone were the white entrance halls with cosy red sofas, the dainty mirrors and the air of refinement, to be replaced by "black and white marble and ornamental pillars, with stained glass windows":[2]

The frontage, which is of very stately design, and possesses a great width, is built of carrara terracotta, and a wide flight of Biansola marble steps leads into a wide dome-roofed *foyer* with marble floor. An illuminated canopy overhangs the steps, and on either side of the approach is to be placed a huge marble lion. The appearance of the entrance is further enhanced by massive grey granite pillars and stones; the entrance *foyer* has been fitted with a large fireplace, and a swing door to the right, leading towards the ground floor opens out into a spacious café divided from the hall by a screen of decorative plaster and coloured windows, the whole forming an excellent feature.[3]

The careful efforts to attract "ton patrons" by cultivating an air of refinement seems to have been abandoned in favour of a policy, considerably more likely to succeed, of impressing the "cheaper sort of people" by their own idea of splendour. At the same time a great deal of attention was paid to the "new art of presenting the picture." Musical and other effects were a legitimate field for the showman's artistic talents, if any, but "presentation" was very largely a question of publicity. For:

[1] *Bioscope*, November 26, 1914, p. 899.   [2] Ibid., October 1, 1914, p. 75.
[3] Ibid., February 11, 1915, p. 530.

After all, the producer is only the creator—the manufacturer. The exhibitor is the salesman, and, if he wishes to get the best results from his material, he must employ the most powerful of all selling methods—which is Publicity.[1]

Film posters were the object of much criticism at the time as garish, crude and even in need of censorship, although we find one writer describing the hoardings as "art galleries"[2] and such posters as the Hepworth series of stock portraits were widely commended for their good taste.[3]

Hoardings were used only on the rare occasions when large-scale publicity was justified. At one time it was said that of five hoardings in London which were being used simultaneously by film companies one was advertising the company as a whole (Hepworth), two were for unusually important films (*Birth of a Nation* and *Cabiria*) and two were for serials (*Exploits of Elaine* and *The Black Box*).[4] More often, manufacturers' and renters' publicity took the form of house organs and the pseudo journalism of their publicity managers, who supplied the Press with "news items." Even front-of-the-house billing was supplied to the exhibitor. The practice of suggesting campaign "notions" to the latter was growing, too, and depriving them of the initiative in their *rôle* of beater of the big drum.[5] Contacts with the local Press, and "property displays"[6] in the front of the cinema, were at this time the chief outlets for the showman's own originality.

With the standardization of publicity, the film was growing out of its youthful habit of appearing in odd and unexpected places, heralded only the day before by gaily coloured handouts. The village hall was less frequently used, and the marquee picture palaces of the fairgrounds were fast disappearing by 1914,[7] for the towns visited by fairs had permanent shows of their own. Films were no longer an attraction exclusive to the fairgrounds. Their appearance in music-halls and legitimate theatres raised a new problem. The use of the film as a music-hall turn persisted only to a small extent, but a new practice grew up which was causing

[1] *Bioscope*, October 14, 1915, p. 165.
[2] *Kinematograph Weekly*, March 9, 1916, p. 3.
[3] It may be mentioned, incidentally, that the Hepworth Company put out a series of "get-the-pictures-habit" posters in 1915, an interesting use of advertising to popularize a type of commodity as a whole rather than a particular brand. See *Bioscope*, February 4, 1915, p. 395.   [4] *Bioscope*, September 23, 1915, p. 1319.
[5] Ibid., February 18, 1915, p. 595.   [6] E.g. Ibid., June 10, 1915, p. 1099.
[7] Ibid., October 29, 1914, p. 460.

growing concern amongst ordinary picture theatre proprietors from 1916 onwards. This was the renters' attempt to present their more important films in large halls or legitimate theatres. Even before the war such films as *Quo Vadis* had been shown for the first time at the Albert Hall and similar places, and it was at the Scala Theatre that *The Birth of a Nation* was first shown in London during 1915.[1] It seems that later, when exhibitors were reluctant to pay the high prices put by renters on their super films, the proprietors of theatres or variety houses—often short of players because of the war—would sometimes take the films on a profit-sharing basis.[2] Next year the premier of Cine's *Christus* at the Albert Hall, and similar cases, aroused very unfavourable comment.[3] Exhibitors had at first been in favour of the practice as a means of gaining prestige and attracting a new clientele to the cinema, but during the next two years they saw that if allowed to develop it would skim their audiences before they were even allowed to handle the pictures. As a result certain branches of the Cinematograph Exhibitors' Association sought during 1918 to boycott films which were first presented in this way.[4] In view of the traditional disunity of exhibitors, however, the *Bioscope* counselled moderation[5] and pointed out that the renters, backed by the manufacturers, were in a strong position. In this way began the controversy over pre-release and sharing terms, two issues over which many bitter struggles took place during the twenties.

Another form of cinema in the previous period, and one which had been given considerable weight in the film trade's protestations of good faith and social conscience, had been the specialized performances for other than purely entertainment purposes. Much had been made, in theory at least, of the film's possibilities for education and research. But during the war the industry's real or feigned sense of social duty was deflected from their disappointing struggles with the educational film to the more congenial task of stimulating recruiting, whipping up war fever, and generally maintaining morale by the simple expedient of giving the people the type of recreation they wanted.

In so far as the ordinary cinema programme still laid claim to any

[1] *Bioscope*, September 30, 1915, p. 151.
[2] Ibid., July 4, 1918, p. 10.
[3] Ibid., August 3, 1916, p. 374.
[4] Ibid., March 7, 1918, p. 4; July 4, 1918, p. 10.
[5] Ibid., July 4, 1918, p. 4.

specific educational value it did so mainly on the basis of a run of "moral problem" pictures of a somewhat doubtful reputation, disliked by many in the trade. These gave a superficial treatment, in the name of enlightenment, to socially-tabooed subjects such as birth control, venereal diseases and the drug traffic. These were not likely to charm the "ton patrons"; but then, as we have seen, these had proved rather too hard to please. The *bona fide* educational films, and even travel films, soon became deplorably scarce[1] in the ordinary programmes. There were isolated cases. There was the case of the Marylebone authorities who, in 1913 and 1914, arranged for the inclusion of occasional films "dealing with matters of importance in connection with hygiene" in the programme of a local cinema.[2] Apart from Ponting's famous lecture accompanying his film of the Scott Antarctic expedition, which he delivered for over a year at the Philharmonic Hall in Great Portland Street in London and then took on tour,[3] there was an even more conspicuous lack of shows consisting entirely of informational films.

Another early fad, the special children's show, had lost much of its popularity with the showmen, who had found it unprofitable without adequate co-operation from school authorities. The latter had not always taken their efforts very seriously, perhaps with reason. There were exceptions, of course, and it is recorded that when Ponting visited Northwood,[4] the Middlesex authority sanctioned the closing of the Northwood schools for an afternoon in order that all the children might hear him.[5] The Middlesbrough authorities, too, expressed themselves in favour of special children's shows once or twice a week, which were apparently to consist mainly of educational films.[6] But such experiments were clearly not widespread. The "schoolboy's educational matinée," like the children's films and yearly pantomime films, became very largely a thing of the past.[7]

Outside the cinema, the use of the film for education and research was

[1] See the pioneer J. D. Walker in the *Bioscope*, September 9, 1915, p. 1105.
[2] *Bioscope*, September 16, 1915, p. 1221.
[3] On behalf of the Belgian Fund—*Bioscope*, January 7, 1915, p. 12. The show returned to the Philharmonic Hall in 1916 for a second series—*Bioscope*, September 21, 1916, pp. 1077, 1141. Ponting returned from Spitzbergen in October 1918 after acting as photographer to the Shackleton Expedition—*Bioscope*, October 24, 1918, p. 6.
[4] In July 1915.   [5] *Bioscope*, July 1, 1915, p. 25.   [6] Ibid., July 27, 1916, p. 280.
[7] The Fox Company of U.S.A. announced the preparation of children's films in 1917, but little more was heard of them—*Kinematograph Weekly*, May 31, 1917, p. 3.

still so hampered by expense and the need for a sub-standard safety film that much of the hope with which it had formerly been regarded had disappeared. The firm of Pathé, still to the fore in the educational field, did indeed develop a special projector in 1914 which was to be sold only to school authorities and similar bodies. This was light and portable and could be stopped to give a still picture for as long as two minutes,[1] but it was for standard film again and little was subsequently heard of it. There were odd signs of interest in the idea of educating backward peoples by means of the cinema. Morley Dainow, formerly Hon. Secretary of the Educational Kinematograph Association mentioned in Volume II, wrote from the Army in India suggesting a "scheme for the use of the kinematograph in education in India,"[2] and Will Day was interviewed about a rumoured Government proposal to send a unit to make and show films in Ashanti:

"The object of this unique film mission," said Mr. Day to a *Bioscope* representative, "is to arouse in the natives of Kumasi a desire to improve themselves. They are a particularly ignorant and lethargic race.

"The present intention is to show them films of other neighbouring tribes, whose state of civilization is somewhat higher than their own, and to exhibit films of Kumasi as a contrast."[3]

Perhaps it is fortunate that this tactless proposal was indeed unique. But even the military training film found comparatively little support in this country. There were widespread rumours that it was being used extensively in Germany as early as 1914, and at a later period in the United States, where it was reported that the "knowledge of the service rifle is being taught by the moving pictures in 100 camps" and "drill is also taught by that means."[4] But when it was said in early 1918 that the new Air Board in Britain was likely to establish a cinematograph school for the training of airmen, this was described as the "first application of (this) intensive system of training in this country."[5]

Such serious discussion of the informational film as there was during

[1] *Bioscope*, September 3, 1914, p. 861.   [2] Ibid., August 17, 1916, p. 578.
[3] Ibid., September 28, 1916, p. 1208.   [4] Ibid., January 24, 1918, p. 5.
[5] About a year before the war, the Admiralty had begun to use film to record the effect of gun fire, and it was later used at the Naval Gunnery School on Whale Island to assist technical instructors. Some months before the war, too, a cinema target had been installed on the battleship cruiser *Queen Mary*—*Bioscope*, August 20, 1914, p. 753.

this period was, if anything, even further removed from action than similar discussion during earlier years. The L.C.C. controversies of pre-war years, for example, were not merely theoretical but centred on actual plans for the use of films in connection with school education. The idea was allowed to drop, however, and the most important signs of interest during these years were two investigations of the problems which were assumed to stand in the way of development. Education by film was treated as an academic question only.

The first of these was the work of the Authors' Society. Dr. Marie C. Stopes reported to the Cinematograph Sub-Committee of this body on the probable value of educational films early in 1915, stating it as her opinion that there was not much need for the film in the higher branches of science, where the expense of film production would in any case militate against its use, but that there was considerable scope for it in general education. The meeting decided to follow up her report by circularizing some thousand educational authorities with a questionnaire.[1] Many of these did not reply, and of those who did few actually used films, although many showed sympathetic interest. The reason given for this inactivity was expense, although there was also a considerable feeling that too little was yet known of the film's real effectiveness, how permanent were its impressions, or whether it might not actually discourage the student's own mental effort.

The state of affairs which Dr. Stopes had deplored in this Report was virtually unchanged at the end of the war:

The cinema is one of the greatest powers placed in the hands of humanity by scientific invention. Yet it is in the main a power prostituted. Myriads of lives are touched, and to some degree influenced by it daily: yet sociologists, scientists, authors, artists, all who have a serious or beautiful message to give to these myriads are scarcely represented on the films, or represented only by travesties. At the same time "penny dreadfuls" and sentimental romances have sprung up in thousands of varieties, and are more prolific than ever.[2]

Meanwhile the Cinema Commission of the National Council of Public Morals had made its own investigations into the educational use of film, among other things. (See below.) The work of this Commission was in

[1] *Bioscope*, January 7, 1915, p. 9. [2] Ibid., September 2, 1915, p. 1028.

general so successful that a further enquiry was planned, this time to deal simply with the educational film. The aims of the Education Committee were announced shortly afterwards. Remarkable for their clarity and restraint, they might well be the aims of any of the numerous investigations which have been made since. But like the recent enquiry, the terms of reference were no longer concerned with the immediate adoption of the educational film. They wished only to examine:

the psychological investigation of the durability of cinema impressions on school children, the measurement of the fatigue caused by instruction by means of the cinema, the carrying out of comparative tests of education by cinematographical methods of instruction, the direction in which the cinema would yield the most fruitful results, the possibilities of the cinema in cultivating the ideals of individuals in social conduct, tastes, and imagination, the best means of correlating the work of the cinema with that of the schools, and the most economical and effective methods of using the cinema for this purpose, and the collection of evidence with regard to experiments which have already been carried out or effected by using the cinema for educational purposes, and the best method of obtaining and using suitable films for school purposes.[1]

The Audience.

It is as difficult to gauge the size of the ordinary commercial audience (as distinct from scattered specialized groups) as it is to ascertain the number and size of the cinemas. According to the Cinema Commission of 1917 there were some 1,075,875,000 attendances a year in the British Isles[2] or approximately twenty million a week. Here again a comparison with North America, with its reputed daily attendance of over fourteen million, is interesting.

The effect of the war on the number of attendances was probably to increase it rather than to diminish it. There was an early period of confusion when many halls were emptied, particularly those in the summer resorts so quickly deserted in August 1914. But despite this and later difficulties with bombing and the Amusements Tax, audiences were maintained. A brief fall in attendances was reported in places where dislocation of industry and temporary unemployment occurred, but on the other hand wherever there was a concentration of troops they rose. Meanwhile many civilian families were drawn to the cinema, despite the

[1] *Bioscope*, March 21, 1918, p. 7.　　　　　　　　[2] P. xxi.

absence of the breadwinner, not only by the need for relaxation but also by the growing desire to see news films of the war. There are many indications that the benefits of this large attendance were reaped to an ever-increasing extent by the larger halls, which could best bear the rising costs of exhibition. It was not an absolute lack of patronage which ruined many a small man, but his own competitive stupidity.

As for the composition of this audience, there is little reason to suppose that any great change had taken place since the former period, although greater interest was aroused among better educated people by the war actualities and new, spectacular "super" films. The price of seats, it has already been pointed out, remained about threepence to a shilling in most cases; there were a number of halls with more expensive seats and one prominent exhibitor in the North referred to his two-shilling seats with some pride as evidence of the relatively high social level of his clientele,[1] but such prices were by no means unknown during the previous period. There was, in fact, a marked decline in the showman's preoccupation with the problem of attracting the *ton patrons*. It has already been suggested that the exhibitors, finding snobbery useless, devoted themselves quite openly after 1914 to the cultivation of the poorer people. With relief they abandoned elegance in favour of a more vulgar magnificence. There were fewer signs of the old reluctance to accept a humble position in society. This change of front may have been partly the result of bitter experience. But the war, with the obvious market presented by the mass of men in uniform and far from their homes may have contributed to it. The picture theatres in garrison towns were packed and in Morecambe, for example, where troops were billeted in large numbers, the 6,000 seats of the Winter Gardens were soon being occupied nightly.[2] The trade laughed as diehards in many such towns suddenly discovered the virtues of Sunday opening.

Before long commercial firms, often formed especially for the purpose, were opening Camp Cinemas in or near many large military camps in England. These were usually roughly constructed halls of corrugated iron[3] although there were more ambitious examples, like the one whose entrance received a "special treatment of stucco, and presents a sub-

---

[1] *Bioscope*, October 19, 1916, p. 231.   [2] Ibid., January 28, 1915, p. 319.
[3] E.g. Aldershot—*Bioscope*, April 22, 1915, p. 280; Cannock Chase—*Bioscope*, May 13, 1915, p. 609; Birmingham—*Bioscope*, July 8, 1915, p. 139.

stantial appearance in the Elizabethan style."[1] The provision of cinemas for the Army in France also received some attention, particularly from the Y.M.C.A., which had already provided free camp shows in England before the end of 1914.[2] As early as February 1915 reports were brought home of a cinema three miles behind the front[3] and films were now said to be "a regular feature on board a good number of warships,"[4] while by September of next year there were said[5] to be at least twenty fit-up cinemas, if not more, on the British front. Sentiment was stirred at home by the needs of the "boys at the front," and in a number of cases hard-headed renters were moved to provide free programmes. It is ungrateful to wonder what sort of condition films supplied thus can have been in, but renters were never known for their soft hearts.

Length of the Films.

Despite a gradual change in the state of the market there were still a very large number of films in circulation at any one time and the old evil of dilapidated copies was not yet fully under control. There was a tendency, however, for the number of new films coming on the market to decline as the length of the "features" increased. The only figures available to measure this tendency seem to be those relating to films put on the American market, figures compiled and quoted by the National Board of Review of Motion Pictures early in 1918. These may be given as examples of a world-wide movement, although the long film made a slower progress in this country than it did in America.

> Average length of film in 1915 1.65 reels
> „   „   „ „   „ 1916 2.23 reels
> „   „   „ „   „ 1917 2.77 reels
> (December 1917 3.28 reels)[6]

By the end of the war it was even said that the five-reeler was replacing the old one-reeler.

There was great opposition to the change, of course, and particularly in England. Pathé's new producer in Britain, the American G. Serrador,

[1] Belton Park—*Bioscope*, March 4, 1915, p. 787.
[2] E.g. Ibid., October 29, 1914, p. 433. [3] Ibid., February 4, 1915, p. 457.
[4] Ibid., February 18, 1915, p. 597. [5] Ibid., September 7, 1916, p. xv.
[6] Ibid., March 7, 1918, p. 6.

noted that the demand of the English market was for slightly shorter films than were normal in the United States.[1] Indeed, one renter was said to be "pruning" American films in deference to the wishes of English exhibitors. But in America, too, controversy raged over the question of length. Edison, evidently a better business man than prophet, was quoted as saying of the ninety-minute film:

"I do not believe in five-reel pictures. Three reels is the ideal length. With three reels, perhaps two, there can be no padding. For dramatic pieces the two- and three-reels picture will survive. The five-reel play is a fad, as slapstick comedy is a fad. Both will pass on.[2]

The standard argument that brevity and variety had always been, and would always be essential to the success of the cinema programme continued, as before, to ignore the possibility of change:

There is another reason why the "pictures" jumped into instant favour. They offered a programme of short pieces, and if one did not happen to please you the remainder did and, anyhow, you hadn't to suffer long. And you could "pop in" at any odd time to while away any period of time, say up to an hour and a half, and always be sure of relaxation.[3]

Such statements were apparently based only on the showmen's interpretation of box office results; and there is no indication that the public's preferences were tested in any other way. Wild attempts were made to justify the prejudices of backward showmen:

. . . nervous reaction is reflecting itself in every walk of life. Short stories requiring but a quarter or half an hour to read were never so popular as now. Poetry, which is after all but the drama of life condensed into more or less beautiful particles, is also tremendous (*sic*) popular. So it is likely to be with the pictures.[4]

Even more curious reasons were found in favour of the old one- or two-reelers lasting fifteen or thirty minutes. One Glasgow exhibitor, for example, contrasted them most unfairly with the "salacious big feature."[5] And although it is true that many films considered salacious at the time sought additional notoriety by their unusual length, there was no more

[1] *Bioscope*, October 24, 1918, p. 9.
[3] Ibid., September 16, 1915, p. 1266.
[5] Ibid., September 16, 1915, p. 1266.

[2] Ibid., January 11, 1917, p. 99.
[4] Ibid., August 8, 1918, p. 58.

reason to judge the long film as such by their standards, than there was to judge the short film by the many smutty little products put out for many years by one of the largest companies in the world. But many identified the future of the film itself with the open market system which they had built up, and on which their own existence depended. They saw the new fashion not merely as a threat to their own way of doing business, but to the whole future of the industry.

But although the expressed reasons were often weak the opposition itself was very real and at the General Council of the Cinematograph Exhibitors' Association in January 1918 showmen rose one after another to condemn the five-reeler.[1] Even the *Bioscope* was of the opinion that in this matter the exhibitors were simply reflecting a genuine and widespread hostility to films lasting over an hour. These and even greater lengths continued to appear, however, and the high prices were no sooner asked than paid. Knowing what happened later it is impossible not to feel, firstly, that fairly long films were in reality very popular with the public: secondly, that intelligent exhibitors were well aware of this: and thirdly, that the real reason for all this opposition was a competitive one. Most of the resistance came from the small showmen. The open market system of many short and relatively undistinguished films, with their prices kept down to the minimum by merciless competition, suited them better than the long, ambitious super film. This gained a world-wide fame and enabled prices to rise to heights which they could not possibly afford. When films were short, moreover, and a programme need last only an hour, a hall with four hundred seats could hold enough shows every day to cover costs, but programmes of two or three hours reduced the turnover to such an extent that even the cheaper "super films" were beyond their means. Their claim that the public disliked long films, too, should if true have benefited them at the cost of their richer rivals. In point of fact, however, even the avowed opponent of the long film sought to book it if he could.

The Programme.

Thus by 1916 lengths had so far changed that almost all dramas were at least three reels or more, while the one- or two-reelers were almost all

[1] *Bioscope*, January 3, 1918, p. 59

comic or actuality films. The average programme consisted of one long feature, one slightly shorter exclusive and perhaps one short film. The twice-nightly show was general in the suburbs in preference to the continuous performance, which by contrast thrived in localities where casual visitors were more numerous than the regular patrons.

It was among the latter that the serial films, also, found their best market.[1] This was, of course, the age of serials, which were believed by many to have come to stay. The first[2] had appeared in the United States in 1913. So great was its immediate popularity in both countries that by January 1915 there were at least four major serials circulating in Britain[3] and in 1916 it was estimated "that the 'Elaine' film has been seen by 10,000,000 every week in about forty per cent of cinemas of the United Kingdom."[4]

The success of the serial film, coming at the time it did, throws an interesting sidelight on to the development of film technique. During these years the "sensational," as it was called, was at the peak of its popularity. Old-style melodrama was flourishing. But neither this nor the other early favourite, the sentimental or "pathetic" story, nor yet the sophisticated stories of the future, were as attuned to the popular taste as was the "thrill-film," the film with "punch." As a result the serial form was ideal for the time. For it thrived on unresolved situations and provided an easy way of creating suspense by the simple device of breaking off the story at a crucial moment. In other films the average producer, not yet having learnt how to handle his medium and to build up tension by such means as the editing, was forced to rely on content alone. As a result new efforts to excite the audience brought forth a stream of stories with ever more unlikely plots which gradually surfeited the demand for sensations.

Maurice Tourneur, a visiting producer from America, said that "film spectators are like children. They demand different and unexpected toys all the time."[5] It is possible that producers, in their desperate efforts to find a new "punch," underestimated their audience's intelligence.[6] One friendly critic deplored the fact that so many films which were technically

[1] *Bioscope*, January 7, 1915, p. 3.   [2] *Adventures of Kathlyn*, Selig.
[3] *Bioscope*, January 7, 1915, p. 3—Edison's *Dolly of the Dailies*, Pathé's *Exploits of Elaine*, Thanhouser's *Million Dollar Mystery* and Pathé's *Perils of Pauline*.
[4] *Bioscope*, July 13, 1916, p. 91.   [5] Ibid., July 18, 1918, p. 17.
[6] E.g. *Bioscope*, July 27, 1916, p. 364. *Kinematograph Weekly*, November 1, 1917, p. 67.

worthy of the admiration of serious people, had plots so fatuous that they could arouse nothing but contempt:

I know several cinemas situated in well-to-do suburbs that have to rely for their main support on the low-class people on the fringe, simply because the present infantile type of film could never hope to cozen a sixpence out of the pockets of the more cultured residents.[1]

During the second half of the war the sensational, and its offshoot the vampire film, attracted less attention. The search for thrills seemed to have played itself out. Instead, the morbid found surreptitious enjoyment of social taboos an excellent substitute in the new "moral problem" films. Never had a trade show been so well attended by the public as that of *Shadows on My Life* (thoughtfully announced beforehand in the Press), a film which had previously been condemned by the Cinematograph Exhibitors' Association for its shameless exploitation of an actual lawsuit of great notoriety.[2]

Like sensationals, the war dramas began to pall after a short vogue. On the outbreak of war British companies rushed into the production of a large number of war dramas, searching their shelves at the same time for any news or interest films which could claim connections, however slight, with the war. Even before the end of August 1914 the Hepworth Company had issued an old travelogue of Belgium, a one-reel film called *Men of the Moment* dealing quite superficially with the forces and their leaders, and a short film about battleships.[3] Other firms issued similar actualities and also a number of rapidly-made patriotic dramas. Later, the feature-length official actuality films of the war did outstanding business. In its first two months *The Battle of the Somme* had the extraordinary number of two thousand bookings and raised about £30,000,[4] while the film of the King's visit to France had a record first run with no less than eighty copies showing in the Metropolitan area at the same time.[5]

One Hammersmith exhibitor placed a notice outside his hall, when the Somme pictures were being shown, which read:

WE ARE NOT SHOWING THE BATTLE OF THE SOMME. THIS IS A PLACE OF AMUSEMENT, NOT A CHAMBER OF HORRORS.[6]

[1] *Bioscope*, August 10, 1916, p. xii.
[2] Ibid., March 7, 1918, p. 39.
[3] Ibid., August 20, 1914, p. 702.
[4] Ibid., October 12, 1916, p. 117.
[5] Ibid., October 19, 1916, p. 223.
[6] Ibid., September 7, 1916, p. 869.

There was always some disapproval of war films, whether actuality or dramatic, and although the news films and official records continued to exercise an irresistible fascination over audiences throughout the war, military dramas enjoyed only a comparatively short period of easy popularity. The early mania for everything warlike gave way to the opinion that people should be able to forget the war when they went to the pictures.

The majority of us turn into the cinema for relaxation after the toil of the day. We go there to try and forget war and its horrors, but, instead of being able to do so, are continually reminded of the bloody struggle that is in progress, and have scene after scene flashed on the screen of happenings that may even at that very moment be occurring to those we hold most dear.[1]

At least for the first year or so, however, such dramas were booked in great numbers. Audiences apparently found that the phantasy world of faked war and mock heroics gave them as much of the relief they sought as any other type of phantasy. Presumably they sickened of it as the effects of real war made themselves felt more and more. There is no sign, however, that the actuality films which Dean Hensley Henson called "entertainment which wounds the heart and violates the very sanctities of bereavement"[2] ever palled, as did these lurid dramatizations.

Well-meant condemnations of repulsive war films which evoked the "ire of those with more refined and tender feelings"[3] demanded instead "good sparkling comedy . . . and comicality without vulgarity." It must not be forgotten that the most successful films of the time were not war films at all but the Chaplin comedies, for which there was an unprecedented vogue, and the great spectacular films from U.S.A. and Italy, including D. W. Griffith's *Birth of a Nation*[4] and *Intolerance*.[5] And in addition to these the vast output which fed the expanding market consisted mainly of war films, crude adventure stories, social problem pictures of cheap novelette standard and short comedies which, although not actually vulgar, had none of Chaplin's superb artistry.

One more type of production which deserves mention is the advertising film. It is clear that the audience, whether hoping for "sparkling comedy,"

[1] *Bioscope*, August 1, 1918, p. 41.   [2] Ibid., September 7, 1916, p. 869
[3] Ibid., August 1, 1918, p. 41.
[4] Specially reviewed in *Bioscope*, on September 9, 1915, p. 1114.
[5] Presented at Drury Lane Theatre in April 1917—*Bioscope*, April 12, 1917, p. 101.

news of the war in which their relatives were fighting, thrilling adventures or glimpses of social cesspools, could no longer be persuaded that what it really sought was instruction. The trade had ceased to pay even lip-service to their professed mission of elevating and instructing the common man. The disappearance of the educational film from commercial programmes has already been mentioned, and the once-popular "industrial film" also seemed to have come to the end of a lively career. The only comparable development during this period was the advertisement film, which became the subject of a bitter argument during the first part of the war. The compelling power of the screen, the size of its audience, and possibly the paper shortage and the example of the official propaganda films, all helped to turn the publicity man's attention to the film.[1] Kino-Ads, an offshoot of the early actuality firm of Kineto, specialized in advertising films throughout the early part of the war, producing mainly trick films.[2] For the most part, however, film people disliked them as a breach of faith with the public and even their supporters could hardly pretend that their reception was enthusiastic.[3]

I have seen the audience applaud advt. films as much as a Charlie Chaplin. At any rate, without exaggeration, I have heard a titter of laughter all over the house, and then seen the audience clap their hands.[4]

The Film's Place in Society.

Although most educated people still considered the cinema beneath them, few would deny its importance as a popular entertainment. It was even conceded that it might possess some influence over public opinion. The trade's reaction to this idea was entirely one of self-congratulation. Only the deliberate efforts to "do good"—by recruiting, by showing problem plays with moral endings—were remembered. The endless

[1] E.g. George Warrington in the *Advertisers' Weekly*—*Bioscope*, October 19, 1916, p. 229.   [2] *Bioscope*, December 14, 1916, p. 1103.

[3] Some people, while disliking advertising films in the commercial cinema, saw a future for them in a different direction:

"The time will surely come, when every important wholesale house will possess its own little private picture hall, where films depicting its activities can be shown to prospective customers. The future commercial traveller, too—especially when 'boosting' any sort of machine or apparatus—will carry a little cinematograph projector among his equipment, and his 'samples' will consist of films." *Bioscope*, September 10, 1914, p. 942.

[4] *Bioscope*, November 9, 1916, p. 601.

hidden ways in which films might distort facts or imply false values were ignored.

The cinema was already described as "the greatest social force in existence," and J. D. Best, Pathé's educational film expert, pointed out that despite the many prophecies of its impermanence it had not merely survived but even prospered in a time of great crisis, for "the popularity of the cinema is founded on some solid human need and appreciation . . . the satisfying of an indispensable human requirement." Films were described as an "entertaining, educative and often refining influence."[1] Refining they may have been to a small extent. One teacher tremulously admitted that the manners of the poorest class of children may have been improved by watching the example of their heroes.[2] On the other hand the claim that the films were doing society a service by popularizing literature completely ignored the type of literature upon which most adaptations were based. It is true that these did not usually live up to the lurid reputations of the originals. The films were perhaps slightly more "refined" than the posters seemed to suggest:

Those who go in expecting to see anything like a faithful rendering of the satyrs and *cocottes*, the dissipated supper parties and salacious sofa-scenes which greet their eyes on the posters must be grievously disappointed.[3]

But as for education, it was a film renter who said:

The weak link I have endeavoured to bring to light is that those in the film business, in their eagerness to make an immediate monetary success, have allowed the strong links of education and elevation to escape notice.[4]

A few of the more high-minded might agree with Best that this was an "age of intelligence, of educational development," and that the cinema, by freeing man from the "prison gates enclosing the mind in its narrow, monotonous circle of daily routine,"[5] was an instrument ideally suited to the age, and a great new civilizing force. But for the most part the trade was frankly preoccupied with the first and easiest of its functions, that of entertainment.

In this chosen field, the film industry found with delight that it could

---

[1] *Bioscope*, December 9, 1915, p. 1125.   [2] Ibid., July 13, 1916, p. 148.
[3] Ibid., November 4, 1915, p. 517.   [4] Ibid., November 18, 1915, p. 772*b*.
[5] Ibid., September 10, 1914, p. 973.

have things both ways. If it showed war films it was being patriotic by stimulating warlike feelings; if it showed films about anything else it was being patriotic by providing recreation, by taking peoples' minds off the war. The new idea of "morale" made it the patriotic duty of every citizen to enjoy himself. Not only business, but pleasure, must be "as usual." Films to keep peoples' spirits up, to prevent them from brooding, and to fill them with hatred for a ready-made new villain, the "Boche," were all socially justified.

It must be admitted that the film's place in society did not seem so exalted to some outsiders as it did to members of the trade. The official films gained a more general appreciation than many others. But it seems to have been realized by critics outside the industry that the film was capable of influencing people in a much more subtle way than the producers' superficial view of their power implied. The effects produced consciously and deliberately, such as the encouragement of war fever and the "popularization of literature," were merely the surface marks. For, although the film industry might lose interest in teaching, everything shown to the public was imparting or confirming ideas, moulding tastes and in fact provided an unplanned education. And the less interested showmen became in attracting the upper classes, the more dangerous this education tended to become.

One well-disposed clergyman, speaking to members of the cinema industry in Glasgow, said "you are a profession whose duty it is to inculcate ideals in a pleasing way."[1] A less patient fellow-clergyman suggested that by aiming at the lowest mental and moral standard to please the greatest possible number they were actually undershooting their mark, with the gravest consequences for society.[2] But reproof, whether in tones of disappointed hope or of outright condemnation, no longer sought to dismiss the cinema as a vulgar craze. For good or ill it was regarded as an established feature of modern life. The secretary of the National Farmers' Union may have thought it amusing to ascribe the difficulties of finding agricultural labour to the fact that there was not a picture palace in every village, but many would agree with the *Bioscope*

[1] The Reverend Marshall B. Skelland—*Bioscope*, October 26, 1916, p. xi.
[2] The Reverend Vivian T. Pomeroy—*Bioscope*, July 13, 1916, p. 148.

in finding this a "statement of peculiar interest."[1] Neither the sneers of its opponents nor the attacks which were still made upon it on old scores like Sunday opening and the alleged encouragement of juvenile delinquency found the film industry as sensitive as of old. After 1917, of course, critics were sharply referred to the unexpectedly favourable findings of the *Report* of the Cinema Commission (see elsewhere). But to a great extent the film industry no longer troubled to vindicate itself against such attacks. The security of its position had become such that it could afford to ignore them.

Official Use of the Film.

The trade was extremely proud of its efforts "to help forward the great cause for which we are fighting." Deliberate efforts to arouse a warlike spirit included not only the topical dramas, but many elementary "recruiting pictures," shown to the accompaniment of military bands with girls in khaki singing patriotic songs and pointing out the nearest recruiting office.

England's Call.—A good recruiting picture in which the portraits of Raleigh, Wellington, Nelson, Gordon and others leave their frames to utter a patriotic appeal. Some of our modern heroes are introduced.[2]

Very early in the war the cinema's enormous possibilities for much more far-reaching propaganda were realized:

The ever-increasing popularity of picture theatres might be turned to good account. Special films bearing on the war, its causes, its meaning, and its appeal, could be prepared, free of any suggestion of jingoism, bearing upon them the imprint of a simple, faithful rendering of facts. These, with suitable lantern slides, and accompanied by a thoughtful and reasoning lecture, should instruct, stimulate, and encourage.[3]

A digression on the use made of the film for official propaganda may, therefore, be of interest here.

The trade took action in the first place because of the difficulty of securing newsreels. At the beginning of the war cameramen, like journalists, found it hard to secure not only facilities, but even permission, to

[1] *Bioscope*, February 11, 1915, p. 493. [2] Ibid, July 20, 1916, p. vi.
[3] Ibid., September 3, 1914, p. 865.

visit the front. Those with sufficient initiative managed to send home some interesting films, but Geoffrey Malin's account[1] of his early work in France for Gaumont illustrated the difficulties faced by these unauthorized film journalists, carrying all their own equipment and arguing every step of the way with incredulous soldiers of the old school.

By October 1915 these inconveniences were so acute that a number of companies making newsreels had combined to form a Committee, the Cinematograph Trade Topical Committee, which consisted of the chief firms in actuality production and distribution: Barker, B. & C., Eclair, Gaumont, Jury, Kineto and the Topical Film Company. It negotiated with the military authorities for facilities to send cameramen to the front, agreeing to pay a royalty on the films so obtained to military charities. Similar arrangements were made with the Canadian Government in July of next year.

Geoffrey Malins and another operator, E. G. Tong, were among those sent over to France immediately. The first batch of films received, consisting of a number of short films taken in France and Flanders,[2] were shown here in January 1916. They were disappointingly like many behind-the-lines films already seen, and had a very poor reception.[3] A second series arrived in a couple of months which had a slightly better Press[4] but it was clear that all was not yet well. Attacks on the picture theatres appeared in the national Press[5] for having boycotted the films. The trade's reply to this was firstly that such films were "long sellers," not to be compared with the type of news film whose topicality was so short-lived that many copies had to be ordered for simultaneous showing: that the cost, thirty per cent more than that of other topicals because of the royalties due to the military authorities, was too high: and that since they had to be destroyed or returned after twelve months all but the best class of renters were reluctant to buy them.

About the same time the Foreign Office and Wellington House, the

[1] *How I Filmed the War*, by Geoffrey Malins, published in 1920 by Herbert Jenkins Ltd.

[2] *With the Indian Troops at the Front, No. I*, 540 ft.; *With the Indian Troops at the Front, No. II*, 500 ft.; *The Making of an Officer: With the Artist Rifles at the Front*, 680 ft.; *A Machine Gun School at the Front*, 440 ft.; *With Our Territorials at the Front*, 530 ft.   [3] *Kinematograph Weekly*, January 6, 1916, p. 3.

[4] Ibid., March 9, 1916, p. 3.

[5] *Kinematograph Weekly*, March 9, 1916, p. 13; March 16, 1916, p. 1.

centre of propaganda at the time, obtained permission for films to be made by various companies of Kitchener's New Army in training and of the Grand Fleet in the North Sea. The munitions firms of Vickers and Maxim lent films of their works, and together this material was made into *Britain Prepared*. This film was handled in America by Charles Urban and had considerable success overseas, a fact which must have pointed the way to the use of film propaganda among neutral countries.

It was clear that the Committee was not satisfactory and in 1916 a War Office Cinematograph Committee was set up to take over from the Trade Committee. When it was first set up Sir Max Aitken was Chairman, Sir Reginald H. Brade representing the War Office and William Jury the film trade. Sir Graham Greene, Secretary of the Admiralty, was added in May 1917, when it was arranged that films should also be taken of the Navy. It was decided that in future profits, should there be any, would be given to military charities while any losses would be borne by members of the Committee.[1] Operators were now sent to all fronts and included F. Bassil, Walter Buckstone, W. E. Davies, F. W. Engholm, Harold Jeapes, Geoffrey Malins, J. B. McDowell, H. Raymond, E. G. Tong and G. Woods Taylor.

The material filmed by these operators was sent home and made into both newsreels and longer films, which were distributed through Jury's renting organization and not credited to individual firms or cameramen. The regular newsreel was started in 1917, when the Committee first of all took control of, and later bought, the Topical Film Company.[2] But meanwhile the great series of long official actuality films which are described later had begun to appear. The joint use of film shot by many operators, to cover some major event in a feature-length film, was an idea which readily emerged from this form of organization.

Hence when the Department of Information was formed under Lt.-Col. John Buchan in February 1917, and took over Wellington House—already in touch with the industry—it was natural for it to be well-disposed to the film as a medium of information. Films were the concern of a Cinematograph Branch responsible to Buchan's assistant, T. Lennox Gilmour, with an Advisory Council consisting of such leading figures in

[1] *First Report of the War Office Cinematograph Committee*, September 1918.
[2] The Committee's interest was not sold until February 1919.

the industry as Hepworth, Barker, Paul Kimberley, and A. E. Newbould. After the early months under Percy Northey the manager was W. A. Northam, of Provincial Cinematograph Theatres, with a young member of the industry as his assistant, Adrian Brunel. The final steps in the official adoption of films was taken in the summer of 1918 after the Department was reorganized (in March) as the Ministry of Information with Lord Beaverbrook, already known to the trade as an explosive chairman of the War Office Committee, as Minister. The Ministry had a Cinematograph Department with Jury as Director; it had wider aims and powers than that of the old Branch; and, finally, the Cinematograph Committee was transferred from the War Office to the Ministry of Information, where it remained.

The Department of Information had first of all intended to arrange the distribution of suitable films in foreign countries, but its scope had been extended to include production and this was much increased when it became the Ministry. A small studio at Ebury Street was acquired, and many established film-makers and writers were employed to make films of various types. The only large scale dramatic feature films with official sponsorship of any kind were D. W. Griffith's *Hearts of the World*, made by agreement with the War Office Committee in 1917,[1] and the ill-fated "great national film" of Herbert Brenon. The latter, called *The Invasion of Britain*, cost £23,000 to make but, produced in the leisurely extravagant Brenon manner, was not finished until the end of the war had made it completely out of date, and it was never shown.[2] But films of various types were made or handled for many Government Departments, including the Service Ministries, Ministries of Food, Labour, National Service Pensions and Munitions: the India Office: National War Savings Committee, National War Aims Committee, Women's Land Army and Board of Agriculture. One of the most popular forms of film, made for many Departments, was the film tag. This, attached to newsreels, was intended for home audiences and was described as " a short film, taking about two minutes to show, and embodying, usually in story form, some useful moral such as 'Save Coal' or 'Buy War Loan.' " It was calculated that each tag was seen by about ten million people.

[1] It was shown in London on June 24, 1918. The Committee made over £13,000 out of it.   [2] *Fourth Report of the Committee on Public Expenditure During the War.*

37

The war was the first occasion on which films had been used on this scale for a serious social purpose, and the abrupt change in the official attitude towards them during these four years was part of a new approach to propaganda in general. When the war began public relations and information consisted mainly of pamphlets and displays, of pictures and reading matter, in shop windows. "State advertisement" was in any case somewhat vulgar. The need to counter German propaganda in neutral countries caused a revolution in this outlook, and once the principle of explanation and justification to neutrals had been established, it was extended to show the extent of the British war effort to ourselves, our allies and the British Empire, and later to prepare the ground for peace. Side by side with this development, attention had been concentrated on personal propaganda and wireless, cable and above all film as the chief means of conveying information and opinion. The outstanding success of the first full length war actualities contributed greatly to the film's prestige in this connection.[1]

(2) DISTRIBUTION

Britain's Position in World Trade.

During the war Britain's considerable foreign trade in films decreased in all its branches, whether of import, export or re-export. When the open market system was at its height London, as the nucleus of Britain's film trade, and at the same time the centre of an enormous international trade in all types of goods, had been well suited to act as the world's clearing-house for films. It soon became the commercial, rather than the artistic, centre of the film world's activity. But during the war transport difficulties and the general dislocation of European trade, official restrictions of one sort or another (See Chapter II, Section I), and in a different way the decline of the open market combined to reduce its advantages. By 1917 it was noted with concern that foreign buyers were gradually leaving the country. The value of films re-exported had fallen, in fact, from £61,000

[1] Material for this section has been derived from H.M.S.O. Cinematograph Section; Reports of the War Office Cinematograph Committee dated September 1918, August 1919 and December 1920; Adrian Brunel; and official sources.

in the first six months of 1915 to £42,000 in the first six months of 1917,[1] and since the price of films was increasing steadily. this implied a large decrease in quantity.

British manufacturers had profited from overseas sales in the early days of the film industry. But in the immediate pre-war years British merchants had found re-export of the better foreign productions more profitable than the export of the home output. The extremely important film-trading company of J. Frank Brockliss was a case in point. This firm had started handling films in 1908 or 1909 with exclusive British rights over the Méliès films from France. Imp, Powers, Thanhouser, K.B. and smaller American agencies had soon been added and in 1911 additional exclusive rights to two minor French brands (Monofilms and Pharos) and a German make (Bitascope, sic) were acquired. It seems that by 1911 Brockliss was convinced that America was "the home of progress in the cinematograph industry," and had secured the rights to Rex films of U.S.A. for the whole of Europe. He was able to bring the negatives over from America and do his own printing on the spot. Next year two more American agencies were added (Méliès films of New York and Solax films, made by Blache). Before long Brockliss, with various distribution branches all over Europe, was one of the two chief suppliers of American films on the Continent, being second only to the Vitagraph Company. In 1913 he acquired the European distribution rights of the very important Lubin films and also the smaller brands of Bison, Victor and Gem. At first Brockliss found American films hard to sell, and it was only by virtue of his very intensive publicity and sales organization that he managed to build up his large and thriving business. It is ironical that British firms should have worked so hard to popularize American films. During the war, many who rightly believed that the open market had gone for ever, and with it Britain's entrepôt functions, felt that our film dealers should have been paying more attention than they were to securing overseas markets for British films before the growing American export succeeded in dominating the world.

The few concerted efforts to improve the position were quite inadequate.

[1] Board of Trade figures. Early in 1915 it was announced that in future the Board of Trade annual returns were to include figures for cinematograph film—Bioscope, February 4, 1915, p. 369.

There was an interesting project in 1918, for example, to form a "British Screen Club" to influence the Press abroad in favour of British films,[1] a scheme which foundered on trade rivalries. The official films were backed by considerable pressure abroad, as they were largely designed to serve as British propaganda in neutral countries. A few British companies like the Ideal Film Company cultivated the export market more carefully than others. But relatively few of the ordinary commercial feature films had any great success abroad, Barker's *Jane Shore* being one of the few for which American rights were quickly sold.[2] But the British failure abroad cannot be ascribed simply to such wartime difficulties as transport. The poor quality of many of the films, which is discussed later, must have been largely responsible.

Thus it is not surprising that most of the films shown here continued to be of foreign make. At the outbreak of the war the dependence on imports was already so great that many showmen wondered whether, if supplies of American and Continental films were cut off, the whole film industry might not be ruined as a result. Trade was not cut off, and imports from several countries, particularly France, actually increased a good deal during the early part of the war. On the surface they seemed to be more than offset by the decrease of those from the United States. Since American films accounted for no less than 92 per cent by value of our imports in 1915 and 98 per cent in 1916, any decrease would have been of great importance had it meant a corresponding fall in the screen time occupied by American films. In actual fact, however, it simply meant that whereas previously all the circulation copies of a film would be printed in America and sent here, now only the show prints and a negative would be sent, for the printing to be carried out here. In point of fact the preponderance of American films in this country increased enormously, and one of the most noticeable features of this period was the stranglehold they obtained over the British market.

Changes in Methods of Trading at Home.

In the home market, the renters' troubles occupied the stage as the open market *versus* exclusives controversy drew to its natural end and possible abuses of the new system of distribution began to be felt.

[1] *Bioscope*, September 5, 1918, p. 4.   [2] Ibid., May 20, 1915, p. 717.

During the early part of 1914 it had seemed as if the coming of exclusive renting was inevitable, at least for all films of a thousand feet or more in length. Shorter films still seemed more suited to free sale, and when the Neptune Film Company was formed in this year it was with the intention of issuing some films on each basis.[1] After the outbreak of war there was a brief but noticeable tendency to revert to open market sale even for the longer films. This was partly because many foreign films (and therefore the majority of exclusives) were temporarily unobtainable; and partly because a wave of economy swept the exhibitors, who for a while feared a fall in attendances and were unwilling to take a chance on high-priced exclusives. But in February of next year the important Essanay Company at last decided to try the exclusive system, explaining that as few as four copies had been sold of one film in the last group of special three- or four-reelers which they had offered as usual on the open market; so well was the market now stocked that costs of production could not be covered if so few copies were to be sold at the low prices obtaining in the open market. In June of the same year the Hepworth Manufacturing Company, also, reluctantly entered the exclusives market. And next month one of the bigger renting firms, the Kinematograph Trading Company, announced that having built up a stock of forty exclusives they were now abandoning the open market altogether.[2]

All the same, the open market was by no means dead. When the Kinematograph Renters' Society was formed at the end of the same year it accepted as members only those companies which purchased or leased 20,000 feet or more of first release open market films every month;[3] and it is significant that at least a hundred firms were qualified to join.[4] But during the summer of 1915 the final trial of strength between the two systems took place, and after this the complete disappearance of the open market was simply a question of time. Extreme differences of opinion were argued hotly. One of the few who steered a middle course was F. W. Baker of Butcher's Film Service. Baker agreed that every programme should now have its four or five-reel feature which, if good quality, was likely to be exclusive; but he suggested that for ecomony's sake the rest of the show might consist of open market short films.[5] Most people were more vehe-

[1] *Bioscope*, October 15, 1914, p. 196. [2] Ibid., January 7, 1915, p. 8.
[3] Ibid., December 23, 1915, p. 1369. [4] Ibid., December 30, 1915, p. 1440.
[5] Ibid., October 26, 1916, p. 363.

ment than Baker. Each branch of the trade accused another of being the cause of trouble. Manufacturers were charged with foisting exclusives on the other sections of the industry because the elasticity of price suited them. Yet we have Hepworth and others, including Essanay, quite openly stating that they were forced to adopt exclusives by showmen who would no longer take open market films at any price, preferring to pay the high rentals and secure outstanding films on an exclusive basis. On the other hand, again, we find the exhibitors accused of acting as a drag on producers because of their preference for a standard price. And at a trade conference on the subject held by the Cinematograph Exhibitors' Association it was resolved:

That this Meeting is of the opinion that it is essential to the existence of the exhibitor that the Open Market for films be maintained, and that the exhibitor of this country should support the renter and manufacturer in every way in his power to make it reasonably profitable to maintain this condition; further that manufacturers and renters on their part should assist the exhibitor to the extent of their power in order to maintain the Open Market.[1]

Nevertheless it gradually emerged that the exclusive had come to stay. For although the system was hard on the greater number of exhibitors, whose finances were not adjusted to it, it was favoured by the powerful companies which could afford to pay high prices. In exactly the same way the difficulties felt by renters, the cost of buying an exclusive film from the producer and the risks of holding stock for the now spasmodic and incalculable open market, were felt most acutely by the smaller firms. The large *bona fide* renting companies had little trouble in adjusting their methods. By their side, too, grew up a host of small renter-agents whose practices caused great resentment among the older firms. The former benefited from exclusives more easily than did firms of the older type. Early in 1915 Williamson claimed that the number of renters had increased from eighty to about three hundred in the past two years, and we have seen that only a hundred of these carried on a large enough business in the open market to qualify for membership of the Kinematograph Renters' Society. Many of the new ones were the despised "ten per cent merchants" or others whose standing in the trade was little better.

A typical "ten per cent merchant" was described in a letter from Paul

[1] *Bioscope*, July 22, 1915, p. 411.

Kimberley as a traveller working on commission for a number of small firms, each owning one or two exclusives, probably·of a rather inferior description. In placing the films he might offer to split the commission with the exhibitors, and then represent himself to those handling more important exclusives as the sole booking agent for these exhibitors, thus building up a business of his own on very doubtful foundations.[1] Kimberley's chief objection to this seems to have been the harm done by booking films on considerations other than merit, but small local renters of the older type, who bought the films they rented, saw another side of the picture. For since the ten per cent man did not buy the films he handled he had an advantage over ordinary dealers; and moreover he need not worry whether the hire charges were ever paid, provided that he got his commission.

It was the new and sometimes disreputable renting practices, and in fact the whole position of the renter, that occupied the attention of trade circles during these four years. No sooner had the open market controversy begun to settle itself than a new bone of contention appeared, the practice of block booking, and with it advance booking and their joint corollary, blind booking. These were problems which did not become acute until after the war, but their initial appearance is interesting.

Block booking was the root evil of the new system. An interesting crystallization of the disputed aspects of renting occurred in 1915, when the English branch of the famous Essanay company of America announced that in future all Essanay productions were to be released directly to the exhibitor:

Because the Essanay Company are now devoting their enormous facilities to the production of long and important films, featuring world-famous photoplay stars, in stories by famous authors, it is impossible to place subjects of such importance and magnitude upon the open market. Nor will the occasional short films we shall continue to issue be sufficient in number for open market release. We shall therefore in future RELEASE THE WHOLE OF OUR OUTPUT DIRECT TO THE EXHIBITOR.[2]

This in itself need not have antagonized the exhibitors as much as it did other renters, for many exhibitors actually preferred to dispense with the

[1] *Bioscope*, August 26, 1915, p. 889.   [2] Ibid., August 5, 1915, p. 550.

middleman. But this statement, coming at the height of the open market controversy, was followed by the significant announcement that after November 1st all Essanay films, whether features or shorts, were to be issued as exclusives. To understand the anger with which this news was received it must be remembered that the Essanay output included the Charlie Chaplin comedies, which were at this time enjoying a prodigious popularity. An average of 170 copies of each were being sold on the open market in England alone, and these were proving goldmines to the exhibitors who secured them. Two things are clear. Firstly, that it was only by virtue of a phenomenal popularity that Essanay could make more profit by issuing fewer copies at a higher price, than by selling this unusually large number at open market prices; and secondly, that there was something else behind the exhibitors' frenzied opposition.

High principled reasons for this opposition were found in the "disgracefully" high prices and also, with a great show of indignation, in the third of the new conditions announced by Essanay. This was the decision to deal only with exhibitors who contracted to take a regular order of three reels a week from the firm.[1] It was felt that Essanay was seeking to exploit its temporary monopoly of Charlie Chaplin in order to force its other and less successful films on the market with a subtle form of block booking (a term not yet in general use):

> Showman of Britain! You are about to be seized in the grip of an American Company in an attempt to squeeze more money out of you, and at a time when money is none too plentiful . . . The Essanay Company have acquired a comedian (who by the way is an Englishman) and because of his popularity—a popularity that has been obtained by your assistance—they will apparently try to make you pay more for Chaplin films which they know you want, and try and force you to take other films which perhaps you do *not* want.[2]

The truth of this was denied, and the company took pains to point out that the weekly quota could if desired be composed entirely of Chaplin reels. This was a concession of doubtful value, however, since there were certainly not three reels of new Chaplin film put on the market every week of the year. In view of Essanay's experience in February of the same year, moreover (see above), when they had only been able to sell four copies of

---

[1] *Bioscope*, August 5, 1915, p. 569; August 12, 1915, p. 650b.
[2] Ibid., August 12, 1915, p. 650b.

one of their so-called "special" films, suspicion of their motives is understandable. A boycott of the scheme was considered, 'and some six weeks after the first announcement the trade was buzzing with anger. A meeting was held at the Holborn Restaurant which, instead of being a discussion of the open market and block booking issues as had been intended, turned into a vicious and absurd attack on the very films which meant so much to them. The meeting would be of little account did it not so clearly illustrate the low level of debate, stupid and vicious, which was to hamper every effort to organize the mass of ignorant small showmen during the difficult years to come:

. . . They were getting too much of Charlie Chaplin; a rest would do him all the good in the world . . . it was quite possible to be really humorous without being vulgar. As an instance one need only take Chaplin's great predecessor John Bunny . . . however good a man might be, he could be bettered. Let them remember that during the past three or four years there were several artists whose popularity nobody could question. Did one ever hear of them now? Popularity, in fact, is ephemeral. Too much Chaplin was nauseating . . . confessed he had been one of the earliest admirers of Charles Chaplin, whom he regarded as one of the greatest of humorists; but it was essential in the interests, not only of the Trade, but also of the public, that Chaplin should be held in check . . . Mr. —— said that the public was dead sick of the Chaplin type of comedy. (Hear, hear) . . .

. . . Let them once accept the Essanay scheme, and then, goodbye to freedom! . . .

Mr. George Henderson: . . . they had to face the fact that the open market which that meeting was asked to protect, had been destroyed long since. (No, no.) He said yes; it was destroyed, and instead of fixing upon the individual as they were doing, they should recognize that what that individual was about to do had been, and was being done by practically every firm in the Trade, not direct perhaps, but through others. How did they propose to fight Essanay? . . . He had imagined that the meeting had been convened to discuss the threatened danger to the open market, but up to the present, the open market had not been even mentioned. He had noticed one curious fact, however, that there had been a great deal of discussion on the vulgarities of Charlie Chaplin. Well, they had had a fairly good spell of Charlie, and it struck him as at least remarkable that it should have taken them so long to discover those vulgarities which the speaker had made so much of. Was it the open market that made all the difference to Charlie's vulgarities? How many exhibitors would refuse to show Chaplin films in future if they were placed on the open market. (Cries of "None," and "Yes, after using the scissors.") Using the scissors! Had they ever used the scissors on a Chaplin film? (Yes, several.) Will you give me the names? (No.) . . . he would ask the Chairman how it was proposed to carry out the resolution?

The Chairman: That is not the object for which the meeting has been called. We are discussing a certain resolution, not the procedure to be adopted. I cannot accept your addition.

The resolution set out above was then put to the meeting and declared "carried unanimously." Mr. Henderson did not vote.[1]

The solitary voice of reason was unable to stop the meeting adopting a resolution to boycott Essanay as long as it persisted in its new policy. As a renter, Henderson was if anything even more concerned with the issue than many exhibitors:

. . . the renter is now called upon to face the arguments of those who would see all films released on the exclusive principle, and instinctively he feels that once that principle is adopted, the third party will no longer be found necessary to the Trade—in other words, the logical sequence to the exclusive principle is to rent direct.[2]

It was as part of the readjustment to the exclusive system that block booking made its first appearance, and with it advance and blind booking. Trade shows, which were some six to ten weeks before release dates in 1915, were as much as four to seven months before release by 1917–18, and as the booking period lengthened the practice spread of booking films without seeing them. Complaints about advance booking were appearing by early 1916, when the *Kinematograph Weekly* noted that one exhibitor had some films booked for almost all his programmes for over a year,[3] and before long it was felt that this had been carried to dangerous lengths.[4]

By the summer of 1916 one particular exhibitor was known to have booked a block of as many as fifty-two films at once.[5]

During the summer of 1916, exactly a year after the last great battle for the open market and after Essanay's experiment, the issue was being argued on all sides. In October it was the subject of a bitter discussion by the Cinematograph Exhibitors' Association at Newcastle.[6] There were ingenious excuses for it, the most telling of which was that it saved the

[1] *Bioscope*, September 23, 1915, p. 1347.
[2] Ibid., May 20, 1915, p. 707.
[3] *Kinematograph Weekly*, January 27, 1916, p. 7.
[4] Ibid., April 19, 1917, p. 6.
[5] *Bioscope*, July 13, 1916, p. 160.
[6] Ibid., October 5, 1916, p. 5.

exhibitor the trouble of choosing film after film, in much the same way that the hire service of the old open-market renter had done; it was suggested that by this means the exhibitor could find and stick to a renter whose films suited his type of audience. In reply to this it was pointed out that the old system, whereby the exhibitor had little need to pick and choose between films, had deserved to die. The argument usually brought against the practice was that the exhibitor who booked in large blocks for the immediate saving of time and trouble would ultimately ruin the reputation of the cinema. Hiring for reasons of convenience rather than for quality, and perforce hiring films without seeing them, he would make it impossible for himself to act quickly when an unexpectedly good film appeared (cases in point were the official war films, whose appeal was largely topical). He would play into the hands of the powerful producing and hiring firms, who would be able to establish a Trust such as the Americans had only recently managed to destroy. Small producers (and this included most if not all British producers) liked the system as little as the better type of exhibitor. Firms whose output was too small to guarantee a frequent and regular supply of films could not secure contracts, and had additional difficulty in disposing of their occasional films to cinemas whose programmes were fixed for months ahead.

Seen from the renter's point of view, on the other hand, the system was merely a very necessary corrective to the uncertainty brought by the exclusive. For some years now the imminent disappearance of the renter had been a standard topic. Direct hiring by producers, started by Pathé in the early days of the exclusive, had been taken up by other important firms as well as Essanay.[1] But the renter was not dead yet, and by the end of the war block booking was flourishing quite as much as the exclusive system itself. In the words of the pioneer renter J. D. Walker:

... many of the producers are inclined to try and squeeze the renter out of the business. ... I am pretty certain that the producer who has an idea of squeezing the renter out of the business is going to be squeezed out himself. The renter absolutely refuses to submit to the process.[2]

[1] *Bioscope,* January 21, 1915, p. 231. [2] Ibid., September 9, 1915, p. 1105.

CHAPTER TWO

Production

(1) PRODUCTION IN GENERAL

Strangely enough, despite the many difficulties of production in war-time, the number of companies during these four years whose operations were of sufficient consequence to be noted in the trade Press actually exceeded that of similar companies during the previous eight years. It is true that several of the most important of the older companies suspended production for one reason or another, but several large new companies appeared to take their places. The war was certainly a time of difficulty for producers, but it was apparently not a time of such depression as to discourage new ventures, and British films appeared during this period under at least eighty brands and trademarks. For a time, at least, there were high hopes and great activity, rather than stagnation and decay. For since film imports were expected to fall, the beginning of the war seemed to offer British producers a big opportunity to expand and improve production, and capture their own home market. This expansion—or at least the improvement—proved hard to achieve. The possibility of capturing the home market became more and more remote as American film production grew. It has been stressed that the idea of Britain leading the world in film production until 1914, and losing its supremacy only because of American strides while Britain was preoccupied with the war, is false. The American leadership was bound to come, if only for economic reasons. And there is ample evidence of social factors, too, assisting cinema development in the United States. It is true that 1914 to 1918 were the critical years in this development and Britain emerged from the war with its film market indisputably dominated by American films. But to say that something took place during the war is not to say that it took place because of the war. There is no evidence that this state of affairs was caused, or even materially hastened, by Britain's war effort.

48

In general the key people in British production were not affected by mobilization. The greatest difficulty likely to be suffered by a luxury producing industry of this nature in time of war is a shortage of capital. But the shortage of capital for British film production, its fundamental weakness, dated from before the war. There is no reason whatever to suppose that, had there been no war, British production would have been able to withstand the irresistible growth of the American output.

Meanwhile, during these four years the proportion of films which were less than a thousand feet in length declined rapidly. The shorter films which did appear, moreover, were almost all actuality films (topicals, or the now much rarer interest films) or comics, and the companies still depending mainly on the production of these for their status in the industry were few. Thus it is convenient to trace the history of the production companies and individual film makers almost entirely with reference to their output of "feature films," of which for this purpose are defined as films of a thousand feet or more in length.[1] Many firms continued to regard the production of shorter films as a normal part of their activity but only in the few cases, like that of J. H. Martin, who specialized in trick films, did they rely on them either for the whole income or for the prestige of their firms; and even the several groups of music hall comedians who made films found it necessary to establish themselves with the one- or two-reel "comedy" rather than with the split-reel "comic" alone. At the same time feature production was being marketed more and more on an exclusive basis, and throughout the period the shift from the one- or two-reeler was accompanied by a shift from the open market to the exclusive system. During 1914 and 1915 the number of all films on the open market suffered a marked overall decline from 6,648 to 4,790; the number of films offered as exclusives increased from about 400 to 650.[2] The relative increase of exclusives was, however, merely part of an increased total world production which led to recurring complaints of over-

[1] The terms "feature," "exclusive," "super film," "longer film," etc., were used loosely in connection with any films considered worth "featuring" on the programme. Definitions such as that of the modern term "feature film"—i.e. a film of 3,000 feet or more—were not to be found, but for the sake of clarity 1,000 feet is taken in this book to be the lowest length of feature production at this time. The definition is not entirely arbitrary, for the difference between one-reelers and longer films on the one hand, and items of less than one whole reel on the other was in fact more than a difference of length.

[2] *Kinematograph Weekly*, January 6, 1916, p. 1.

production during the first two years of war (measured in footage rather than in numbers of films, since the growing length diminished the latter). Most of the British production activity was unfortunately of a very poor quality, and both the increasing number of companies in production and the mass of inferior films on the market were repeatedly deplored. On the staff of some of these struggling companies were technicians, good and bad, who were later to share responsibility for production during the 'twenties. Meanwhile, it should not be forgotten that there were several companies, and a handful of producers, releasing films which compared very favourably with the average American production.

Several features of the industry's changing structure emerge from the following account. Firstly, as a result of the war the threatened invasion of production by foreign firms did not take place. Secondly, it was no longer a compact little industry with a small number of dominant companies, a group of steady, medium-sized companies—several of them in the provinces—and a stable outside ring of firms making occasional actuality films. Some of the older leading firms were challenged by a large number of medium firms on a scale somewhat larger than those of the previous period. As for the members of the outside ring of small firms, this underwent constant changes. There were a number of individuals who from time to time engaged, or tried to engage, in independent production. But the early "part-time" producers of actualities disappeared early. So, with the exception of a group in Yorkshire, did the provincial firms. The problem of assuring distribution from the productions into which more and more money was reluctantly being put became a growing problem, and several companies such as Barker, B.A.F.C., Broadwest and Windsor secured regular agreements with renters. The tendency in the latter part of the war for new production enterprises to stem from large renting firms (Gaumont, Ideal, Harma, Butchers and Stoll) was evidence of this need, as well as of the growing demand for large and stable financial resources to back production.

A factor in the growing need for capital was the great length of time between production and release. This lengthened as the market was crowded with more and more American films, and the wait was very hard on British producers with little capital other than that locked up in films awaiting distribution. The rising technical level of films, too, made the old style of "cottage industry" production impossible. The registered capital of new companies during the war was usually in the neighbourhood of £10,000.

The cost of the studios themselves is indicated by the fact that Gaumont had put £30,000 into the construction of its new studio at Shepherd's Bush,[1] although this was admittedly one of the most ambitious in the country. But in comparison with similar figures in U.S.A. this was extremely small. The only two public companies in British production were the London Film Company and Broadwest, with £120,000 and £50,000 respectively at the end of the war. Much more frequent was the type of company, not necessarily having a registered capital at all, which started with a loan of one or two thousand pounds and carried on from film to film.

By 1918 this need for far greater capital and the difficulty of securing it in England, at least until the end of the war, was recognized as an important weakness in the British film industry. For the latter, although appearing at first to be stimulated rather than depressed by the abnormal war conditions, experienced an increase of quantity rather than that improvement of quality which had been sought with such anxiety during the months immediately before August 1914.

Nevertheless, for at least the first two years of war, production flourished. It was realized that far from emptying the cinemas the war would fill them to capacity:

Our friend "relaxation" will be seen at work. The money stringency will have been relieved; even those who have sent breadwinners and supporters to the front will have an assured allowance from the Government. Food prices will probably remain stationary; there will be no exceptional calls on the private purse—indeed, the few pence for the cinema will be available, and the people waiting, waiting, in their solitude, or comparative solitude, having nothing but the war in mind, will turn to the picture theatres for relief. The cinemas must be ready to cater for them with the proper "stuff."[2]

The spontaneous response to this situation was, for one thing, an outburst of newsreels and cartoon films and carelessly made war dramas. It was thought that exhibitors and audiences would "Support British Manu-

[1] *Bioscope*, July 22, 1915, p. 411.   [2] Ibid., August 27, 1914, p. 823.

facture"[1] for patriotic reasons, and moreover that by cutting off Continental film imports the war would force the market into the hands of British and American producers. In these discussions the interests of American and British producers were at first treated as identical. It was subsequently proved, of course, that although the French and small German output were cut off, Italian and Scandinavian films continued to pour into the country: and that a strengthening of the American position was the worst thing that could have happened to the British producer.

During the first year and a half of war the industry was enthusiastically joined by a large number of new producing companies and film output was large, if not particularly distinguished. Optimism still reigned, and it really seemed that fate had intervened on behalf of British producers, and that world catastrophe was going to secure them that supremacy at home which had been so hard to achieve when trade was free. It was not until the end of 1915 that fear of America's superiority began to strangle this new confidence in Britain's big opportunity. Friends of the British producer fell back on the plea that it was a patriotic duty to take more British films. An article in the *Bioscope* signed "Civicus Britannicus," in 1915, went so far as to suggest that:

the only possible solution of this situation appears to be the obvious one of levying a considerable tax upon all films imported into Great Britain. Such a tax would, of course, result at first in much disorganization and difficulty. The supply of British films is at present so inadequate that exhibitors would still be forced to rely largely upon American films for which they would have to pay much more. Had the import been created years ago while the industry was young, the British manufacturer would to-day be in a very different position.[2]

But the fact that so many British films were artistically and commercially disappointing does not mean that the structure and methods of the industry were not undergoing constant development, very similar to that in other countries. As usual the gauge of increasing complexity and elaboration of production was the higher price charged for major films. I have pointed out elsewhere[3] that *Rescued by Rover*, a British success of

[1] *Bioscope*, August 31, 1914, p. 644.
[2] Ibid., September 9, 1915, p. 1174. See elsewhere for a fuller discussion of tax and import problems.   [3] See Volume I.

the early 1900's, cost £7 13s. 9d. to make; *Jane Shore*, an outstanding British film of some ten years later, was sold for £6,000, and £4,000 seems to be an average production cost throughout the war. Prices varied a great deal, of course. In particular comedy films were usually made more cheaply, and the Homeland Company's expenditure of £1,000 on Billy Merson's first three-reeler, *Billy's Spanish Love Spasm*, was unusually lavish. On the other hand £20,000 was often quoted as the cost of the London Film Company's important production of Hall Caine's *The Manxman*. *The Second Mrs. Tanqueray* cost this in 1916,[1] and the Windsor Film Company at the end of 1918 planned to make ten films for £40,000.[2] Such figures, again, are very much lower than similar figures in America. £400,000, said at the time to be the cost of *Intolerance*,[3] was of course exceptional. But by the end of the war anything from £15,000 to £30,000 or even £50,000 was said to be normal for an American film.

Like the period between production and release, production time was lengthening considerably. In 1914 Charles Pathé was reported to have said:

Producers who heretofore have made it a rule to try to produce a film every week will soon learn that their idea is as false as would be the idea of a dramatic author who tried to produce half-a-dozen plays for the theatre in a year. Three or four films in such a period, properly studied, first from the point of view of the scenario, then carefully handled in the execution, such is the programme that must be followed in the future by the producer who wishes to earn really big money.[4]

It was mainly the preparation of a film which demanded this increased time and the actual shooting, although no longer a matter of a few days, seldom took more than two to four weeks. Many companies were able to release scratch war dramas within a few weeks—in some cases a few days—of the outbreak of war, and such a major production as *Brigadier Gerrard*[5] only took four weeks to make whilst the great crowd scenes in *Jane Shore* were filmed in three days.[6] The output capacity of the studios varied according to their size and the type and length of their films. In 1916 Broadwest, using the large Walthamstow studio, hoped to turn out

[1] *Kinematograph Weekly*, March 16, 1918, p. 6.   [2] Ibid., June 15, 1916, p. 21.
[3] Ibid., April 5, 1917, p. 2.   [4] *Bioscope*, November 26, 1914, p. 819.
[5] Ibid., September 23, 1915, p. 1321.   [6] According to W. G. Barker.

four or five reels a month.[1] Some time later International Exclusives, using the studios at Twickenham, planned to make one feature a month.[2] Harma claimed to be producing at the rate of twenty a year and Windsor had plans for ten a year, although these figures sound like publicity exaggerations. A number of sets could be erected at once, and frequently several films were in production side by side. Studios such as that of Gaumont at Shepherd's Bush in 1915, Clarendon at Croydon and Windsor at Catford in 1916 could take four or five sets; the Twickenham studio owned by the London Film Company, the largest studio in the country, could take as many as eight.

Frequent location work supplemented this studio capacity and reduced costs, although when the desert was optimistically reproduced for *The Life of Lord Kitchener* in 1917, together with a Sphinx twenty-two feet high, such items as twenty camels, a hundred negroes and a cavalry charge of 2,000 raised the cost of this desert sequence alone to the spectacular figure of £1,500.[3] The sets themselves were a matter of increasing difficulty. Painted backcloths were mercifully becoming a thing of the past, to be replaced by plywood sets, "thus avoiding the wobbling and fluttering of canvas so frequently seen on the pictures when a door is slammed or a window shut."[4] The use of plaster was apparently somewhat later, and when Percy Nash was in Italy in 1916 he wrote back with enthusiasm about the plaster sets used by Italian companies as though these were a distinct advance on most of those still found in England.[5] The size of the set increased. Period films such as *Jane Shore*, in particular, even required the construction of entire streets, although rather flimsy ones. The following passage describes a set built in 1914 for *Barnaby Rudge*, the riot sequence which employed 1,500 supers.[6]

"It is a wonderful piece of stage architecture, complete in every detail, and the illusion of solid realism, when viewed from the proper aspect, is quite perfect. The paved sidewalks, the cobbled roadway, the doors with their link-holders and extinguishers, the glazed windows with their neat white curtains—every

[1] *Bioscope*, July 13, 1916, p. 99.
[2] Ibid., December 6, 1917, p. 70; December 20, 1917, p. 54.
[3] *Kinematograph Weekly*, June 7, 1917, p. 36f.
[4] *Bioscope*, October 1, 1914, p. 17.
[5] *Kinematograph Weekly*, January 27, 1916, p. 73.
[6] *Bioscope*, September 20, 1915, p. 797.

tiny point has been remembered. . . . Behind the streets, moreover, there is a magnificent reconstruction of the facade of Newgate Prison—an immensely lofty structure, grey, drab, and forbidding, with a sinister gallows before its outer wall. The whole of this marvellous city, we understand, was designed by Mr. Warwick Buckland, and it is certain that he merits the very warmest congratulations upon what is without question a remarkable piece of work.[1]

The mention of a designer in the last paragraph brings us to the film makers themselves. Staffs, like everything else, became bigger. Like other things, they were not as big in this country as in America; in 1915 one American studio was said to have a staff of 250[2] while at about the same date the biggest English studio, that of the London Film Company, was said to employ only 130, with a wage bill of £750 a week.[3] The figures are impossible to verify and Ralph Dewsbury recalls the Twickenham staff, excluding the stock company, as much smaller. Other figures suggested by veterans of the industry[4] are interesting: twelve to fifteen for medium firms such as Cricks and Martin and the Martin Film Company, six to nine for smaller firms like Homeland or the staff of the studio at Ebury Street, and twenty-five to thirty for larger studios such as that of Clarendon or at Bushey. Barker remembers his staff as follows: stock company, twenty-two; carpenters, twelve; scenic artists, five; props, three; labourers, fifteen; cameramen, five; various, about a dozen more.

More and more specialized workers were becoming known by name, at least within the trade, and the growing distinction between producing and directing was accompanied by greater attention to writing, cinematography, design, and even research. For some time the studio buyer or the producer himself had in effect planned the sets. But the new company Neptune at one time boasted a "scenic designer," Edward Jones,[5] and in the case of some ambitious costume films publicity was given to their designers—Joseph Harker for *Kismet* in 1914, Buckland for *Barnaby Rudge*, and P. Mumford and F. Ambrose for *Jane Shore* in 1915, Lancelot Speed for *She* in 1916. John Everett was called "artistic adviser" for *All*

[1] *Bioscope*, September 24, 1914, p. 1160.
[2] Ibid., October 7, 1915, p. 15.   [3] Ibid., July 20, 1916, p. 234.
[4] Notes supplied by Ralph Dewsbury, R. H. Cricks, J. H. Martin, W. P. Kellino, A. T. Jones, L. J. Hibbert, Gerald Malvern, and W. G. Barker.
[5] *Bioscope*, October 10, 1914, p. 17.

the World's a Stage in 1917, and one of the best-known designers was Willie Davies, who worked on such plushy period pieces as *Masks and Faces* and *The Lyons Mail* for Ideal.

Strangely enough, despite their key position in the studio, cinematographers received less publicity on the whole than other members of the staff. Jack Avery, Frederick Burlingham, Cherry Kearton, G. H. Malins and E. G. Tong were mentioned from time to time in the trade news, although all were away at the war some if not all the time either as cameramen or in the forces. As cinematographers, moreover, all were best known for their actuality work. But within the studio the cameraman's work and importance was greatly increased meanwhile by the growing use of artificial light, and the contribution made by such men as Emile Lauste, Ernest Palmer, Groc, Balboni, Frenguelli, Pauli and others was of the utmost value to producers.

The most marked change among the producers themselves was the disappearance of that pronounced individuality which had previously distinguished one British production company from another. And this, despite the fact that several of the most strongly marked personalities of the earlier years remained in their previous positions. In fact production was in an intermediary stage, and such technical and artistic advance as was being made consisted of tentative movements which were almost unnoticed. The early formative stages with their crudity and colour were over, but the principles of the art had not yet been clearly formulated anywhere in the world. Both the former rough clash of personality and the later individuality of style were blurred, and despite recognizable characteristics in the work of the best companies British producers in general tended to favour the same things and to show, in particular, the same sentimentality. Almost all of them turned to contemporary or recent plays and novels for their stories. Before the war Barker had specialized in modern crime dramas in city surroundings, Hepworth in depicting the English middle-class scene, and even firms like B & C, with its rough adventure story film, had a character of their own. The newly formed London Film Company had been the only reputable firm to deal primarily in large-scale adaptation, and it is likely that the example of this large and powerful firm contributed something to the new trend. Moreover, the companies were larger now and functions more specialized, and it was becoming more difficult for the producer to impose a style of his own on all the work that left his studios.

Many producers still wrote their own scripts, including especially George Pearson, A. E. Coleby and Arthur Rooke, Henry Edwards, Cecil Hepworth, Sidney Morgan, Harold Shaw and Loane Tucker. There were some fifty producers who made one or more films at some time during the war, of whom the following are the most interesting: Thomas Bentley, Arrigo Bocchi, A. E. Coleby, Henry Edwards, Maurice Elvey, Cecil Hepworth, Will Kellino, Sidney Morgan, Percy Nash, Wilfred Noy, Fred Paul, George Pearson, Harold Shaw, F. Martin Thornton, Larry Trimble, George Loane Tucker and Walter West. Many of them, including Coleby and Rook, Henry Edwards, and Fred Paul took part in their own films. And Hepworth was one who usually acted as his own cameraman. Many were the "producers," too, who combined the functions of business executive and director on the floor of the studio, while it was the rule for the producer to design and furnish his own sets. But the tendency of the time was for him—still called the "producer"—to confine himself to the direction of players and technicians and only a few were able to impress any particular individuality on their films.

Of the actors, almost every one of them came originally from the stage, whether from that of highbrow or popular drama, or from the music hall,[1] whether as visiting celebrities:[2] as more or less successful stage actors who supplemented their stage work with film engagements: or as actors who took up films as their major occupation (even, in some cases, identifying themselves with particular film companies).[3]

[1] E.g. "Bella," Winifred Delevanti, Ella Shields, G. H. Chirgwin, Jack Edge, Brothers Egbert, Will Evans, Joe Evans and Fred Evans, Lupino Lane, Billy Merson, Sam T. Poluski, George Robey.

[2] Visiting stage celebrities: Dorothea Baird, Lilian Braithwaite, Lily Brayton, Hutin Britton, Gladys Cooper, Phyllis Dare, Alice Delysia, Sydney Fairbrother, June, Peggy Kurton, Hilda Moore, Ellaline Terriss, Ellen Terry, Vesta Tilley, Madge Titheradge, Irene Vanbrugh; Sir George Alexander, Oscar Asche, Donald Calthrop, Albert Chevalier, O. B. Clarence, Hayden Coffin, Sir Johnston Forbes-Robertson, Laurie de Frece, Sir John Hare, Martin Harvey, Leslie Henson, Seymour Hicks, H. B. Irving, Nelson Keys, Matheson Lang, Leon M. Lion, Gerald du Maurier, Owen Nares, Lennox Pawle, Milton Rosmer, Ronald Squire, Ernest Thesiger, Fred Volpe, Lewis Waller, Harry Welchman, Bransby Williams.

[3] Actors appearing regularly in, or known principally for their work in films: Eve Balfour, Ruby Belasco, Dorothy Bellew, Margaret Blanche, Ivy Close, Daisy Cordell, Mary Dibley, Edna Flugrath, Blanche Forsythe, Daphne Glenne, Odette Goimbault, Minna Grey, Mercy Hatton, Gwynne Herbert, Violet Hopson, Peggy Hyland, Joan

There were several stock companies or groups of players, but in general the two or three hundred actors who appeared in the films of this time formed a pool from which all companies drew, and there were a large number of free-lance artistes who appeared in film after film for every company. At the beginning of the period the emphasis was usually on the plot and the number of affecting situations into which the characters could be manœuvred, rather than on the acting. As time passed, stories which demanded more from the players came into favour. And although for the most part little more than a good appearance and fairly simple actions in front of the camera were needed still, there are indications of a shortage of satisfactory players. There were constant efforts to train film actors, although much of this was merely an exploitation of the film-struck, who pestered the studios for jobs after being fleeced by "bogus and unregistered concerns" which were all too numerous. More important was the use of successful stage actors. Apart from the publicity there is no reason to suppose that the additional expense of using the most famous stage players was justified, since the best stage actor was not necessarily the best film actor. But the marked preference for West End supporting players did ensure a certain competence which many, although of course not all earlier players had lacked.

But in any case the ideal of acting as such was still subordinate to that of stardom.

The play is no longer the thing. A hundred attractive titles and yards of superlative praise will leave a man quite cold. Baldly announce the name of a popular player, however, and you will at once gain his custom.

The reason for this is not far to seek. It is simply a question of ordinary human nature. A picture-goer is not interested in the cunning manipulation of circumstances by the playwright. What really holds his attention is the human

Legge, Ivy Montford, Joan Morgan, Christine Rayner, Elizabeth Risdon, Joan Ritz, Lily Saxby, Alma Taylor, Manora Thew, Queenie Thomas, Marjorie Villis, Chrissie White, Dora de Winton, Maud Yates; Henry Ainley, Gerald Ames, Edward Arundel, Rutland Barrington, J. H. Batson, George Bellamy, Trevor Bland, Langhorne Burton, Austen Camp, Arthur Cullin, George Foley, Basil Gill, Arthur Holmes-Gore, Fred Groves, Wyndham Guise, Campbell Gullan, Hayford Hobbs, Lionelle Howard, James Lindsay, Edward Lingard, H. Agar Lyons, Lyston Lyle, T. H. MacDonald, Norman McKinnel, A. E. Matthews, Percy Moran, Douglas Munro, Edward O'Neill, Fred Paul, Charles Rock, Stewart Rome, Edward Sass, Gregory Scott, Frank Stanmore, Aurele Sydney, J. R. Tozer, Charles Vane, Henry Vibart, Ben Webster, James Welch, Hubert Willis, Bert Wynne, Cecil Morton York.

effect of those circumstances as interpreted though the personalities of the principal players. . . . It must be remembered that the title of a play, nine times out of ten, means nothing to the average picture-goer, whereas the name of a well-known player means everything.[1]

Here lay a most important difference between English and American producers. It is fair to say that hardly any of the English film players were film stars on the American scale. There was probably as great a desire for the star system among British film makers as anywhere else, but little trouble was taken deliberately to build up the personality of native film stars by publicity, whilst their salaries never even approached those of the American favourites. According to Maurice Elvey[2] even established film players earned only about £5 a week in Britain, and comparative favourites not more than £10. This may be a low estimate (Charles Rock is said to have earned £25 a week at Twickenham), but on the other hand in America a comparatively minor star like fifteen-year-old Mary Miles Minter was said in 1917 to be earning £20,000 a year.[3] Mary Pickford and Charlie Chaplin were even more spectacular examples of such high-salaried players. Pavlova was paid £10,000 as well as a share of profits for her appearance in *The Dumb Girl of Portici*, or no less than a quarter of the total cost of the production.[4] The scale and continuity of production in the United States, with film after film rolling off the belt featuring the same players, made star-building a comparatively easy matter. But these figures were so high that by 1918 many believed that they would lead to the downfall of the star system itself:

If far-sighted opinion is accurate, motion picture stars are approaching days when their lustre may be dimmed. For several years now each successive season has witnessed larger salaries demanded by men and women of the screen who are regarded as box-office assets. But, as increase has followed increase, these salaries have at length crept up to a figure which producers, distributors, and exhibitors declare cannot be continued with financial safety.[5]

In the opinion of Herbert Brenon, the year will see the death of the star system. By this he says he means the centralization of all expenditure on the star, to the exclusion of everything else. In the making of the picture he is a

---

[1] *Bioscope*, April 11, 1915, p. 529.   [2] In an interview.
[3] *Kinematograph Weekly*, December 20, 1917, p. 58.   [4] Ibid., April 27, 1916, p. 31.
[5] *Bioscope*, January 31, 1918, p. 29.

firm believer in the story being first, last, and all the time of importance. In selecting a cast for production, he says, he does not look for a big name. Talent and suitability for the part are of far more consideration. No matter how great the drawing power of a star, it is, in his opinion, fatal for a producer to sacrifice the production as a whole just to include her or him in the cast.

The star system is dwindling already . . . to such an extent that 1918 is bound to see it disappear altogether.[1]

The payment of screenwriters in England was disproportionately low, and the subject of much complaint in the trade Press. The American firm of Famous Players caused a sensation by offering £250 for 1,000-word synopses in 1916.[2] Even later than this it was said that in Great Britain the writer of a scenario might get £20 if he was lucky, while only one or two screenwriters in the country could command as much as £100 for the script of a five-reel drama.[3] Other indications bear this out. £100 was offered for a scenario when C. B. Cochrane was seeking a starring vehicle for Alice Delysia,[4] but the normal price for a "fully worked out" plot was said by one producer in 1917 to be £5 to £50, and as little as £1 1s. for an idea.[5] It was the usual vicious circle of bad pay and bad prestige:

> The founder of the House of Lubin is credited with the assertion that, were he to give publicity to the authors of his plays, he would be compelled to pay whatever fees the writer demanded.[6]

There were some fifteen regular screenwriters known by name in the British film industry in addition to the producer-writers already mentioned, chief amongst them being William J. Elliott, Kenelm Foss, Reuben Gilmer, Blanche McIntosh, Bannister Merwin, Eliot Stannard and Rowland Talbot. But all told there were at least seventy who received writing credits during the period, and in addition to regular and occasional screenwriters and producer-writers this figure included a number of celebrities such as the playwrights Richard Ganthony, Louis N. Parker and Arthur Shirley and the novelists Rita and E. Temple Thurston, who accepted commissions for original film stories or scripts as well as allowing

[1] *Bioscope*, February 7, 1918, p. 31.   [2] *Ibid.*, August 3, 1916, p. 377.
[3] *Kinematograph Weekly*, July 12, 1917, p. 76.
[4] *Bioscope*, September 12, 1915, p. 988.
[5] *The Art of Photo Play Writing* by Harold Weston, p. 27.
[6] *Bioscope*, March 14, 1918, p. 47.

their other works to be adapted. Such commissions were an understandable development for, seeking name-value in their writers at a time when the cinema had no famous writers of its own, the producers found it easier to borrow the celebrities of other spheres than to build up their own.

But adaptation, whether by the screenwriters or the producers themselves, was very much more frequent than original work written for the films. It was suggested that as much as 95 per cent of all film stories were adapted,[1] and this can hardly have been an exaggeration. To employ writers accustomed to thinking in terms of the theatre or the novel was bad enough. To use works expressly written for them was worse.

All and every sort of book, whether suitable or not, is to be pressed into service. Now all books are not suitable for the screen. With a good many the interest lies in the brilliant or witty dialogue, in fine character drawing, or in the charm of the writing itself. . . .[2]

There was a marked preference in all this for adaptations from contemporary writers. Those drawn upon most frequently—with the exception of Dickens, whose popularity as a rich source of film material persisted—were all contemporary novelists and playwrights, especially the latter. The most popular (arbitrarily defined here as those upon whom English film-makers drew four times or more during the period), were Sir James Barrie, Robert Buchanan, Hall Caine, Marie Corelli, Charles Darrell, Charles Dickens, Tom Gallon, Charles Garvice, Ben Landeck, Leon M. Lion, Walter Melville, Sir Arthur Pinero, Arthur Shirley, George R. Sims, Andrew Soutar, E. Temple Thurston and John Strange Winter. It is noticeable that there was only one adaptation of the former favourite, Shakespeare, whilst other films based on what are regarded as traditional classics were a very mixed collection including isolated works by Mrs. Craik, Dumas, George Eliot, Fielding, Oliver Goldsmith, Thomas Hardy, Thomas Hughes, Longfellow, Lord Lytton, Captain Marryat, Charles Reade, Tennyson and Oscar Wilde. Other contemporary writers of repute whose works were also adapted, although less often, were Arnold Bennett, John Galsworthy and Somerset Maugham. But these were not favoured as much as Hall Caine, Charles Garvice and

[1] *Bioscope*, July 13, 1916, p. 19.
[2] *Kinematograph Weekly*, May 3, 1917, p. 84.

Temple Thurston and other writers whose novels have dated much more quickly.[1] Many were writers of crime stories or romantic adventures.[2] Others were sentimental woman novelists of the time.[3] But by far the most useful class of writers was that of the popular dramatists.[4]

This fondness for adaptation, which the screenwriter Eliot Stannard described as "at best . . . a cut-and-slash trade,"[5] became part of the vicious circle in which film writing was trapped. The comparative rarity of original stories for the screen was clearly both recognized and deplored, yet because of the ready source of second-hand material producers were not compelled to offer a real incentive to screenwriters. Relatively bad pay and prestige—despite occasional scenario competitions—continued both as cause and result of the loudly-lamented absence of a "film Shakespeare." The lack was not a new one:

Dearth of plots has been an ever-present source of worry to manufacturers from the earliest days of cinematography.; but, whereas hitherto, the novelty of the moving picture, the charm of its scenic variety, and the ingenuity of its original sensations have been sufficient in themselves to appease the public's appetite, it is no longer possible to satisfy an audience with such unsubstantial fare alone.[6]

But still no one managed to look like Shakespeare. During the years before the war the artistic importance of the writer had been valued highly in theory, and it was in his work, rather than in anyone else's, that the possibilities of development seemed to lie.[7] That this did not prove to be the case may have been inevitable. It may be that artistic leadership would have passed to the director even if the screenwriter had been as brilliant, and as unhampered, as his greatest supporter could have wished.

---

[1] Grant Allen, Marion Crawford, Jerome K. Jerome, W. W. Jacobs, E. Phillips-Oppenheim, Eden Phillpotts and many others.

[2] Guy Boothby, Victor Bridges, H. Bullivant, A. Conan Doyle, George Edgar, Nat Gould, H. Rider Haggard, Anthony Hope, W. J. Locke, Baroness Orczy, Edgar Wallace and Stanley J. Weyman.

[3] Marie Corelli and John Strange Winter, Ruby M. Ayres, Richard Dehan, Ethel M Dell, Elinor Glyn, Mrs. Hungerford, Lucas Malet, Helen Mathers, Allen Raine, Rita, Mrs. Humphrey Ward, Mrs. Stanley Wrench.

[4] Dion Boucicault, R. C. Carton, H. V. Esmond, Sidney Grundy, Monckton Hoffe, Walter Howard, Henry Arthur Jones, Edward Knoblock, Herbert Leonard, Henry Pettitt, Cecil Raleigh and Tom Robertson.

[5] *Kinematograph Weekly*, July 12, 1917, p. 108.

[6] *Bioscope*, October 8, 1914, p. 145.   [7] See Volume II.

One correspondent of the *Bioscope* felt that the real significance of the writer's work was bound to be small:

> While admitting that the picture play is a composite creation, I contend that the producer always has been and always will be its main progenitor. The author can supply only the basic idea; it is the producer who provides the treatment, and it is in the treatment not in the selection of material, that all forms of art consist.
>
> To cover in his scenario every detail of setting, business, character type, time and photographic technique, an author must possess the full knowledge of a producer. If he can supply all this, he should complete his work by producing the film himself.[1]

The earlier view persisted among the better type of writer, however. And by them it was held that, in so far as they were failing in their important task, it was because impatient producers would rather turn to rudimentary adaptations of tested literary works than wait for talented new writers to learn the techniques, now quite complicated, of film production. Bannister Merwin, one of a few film writers who later turned his hand to production, had maintained for some years that the writer should visualize his story from the start, and must therefore master the whole process of film production. The producers' lack of sympathy with the writers' needs in this respect had, he claimed, made it impossible for the latter to produce a satisfactory type of original film story:

> Gentlemen, did you give those writers as good a chance as you gave your producers? Knowing that their imaginations, though trained, were not trained in picture technique did you labour patiently and sympathetically to help them in evoking that precious thing, a good story? Did you let them come to the studio and practically live on the studio floor in order that they might master picture technique? Moreover, knowing that these men made their living by writing, did it occur to you to compensate them properly while they were learning picture work?[2]

Such imaginative producers as Edwards found a solution by writing their own scenarios, but naturally enough an antagonism developed in some quarters between writers and producers, and in 1918 this exploded in a *Bioscope* controversy about the relative importance of each. In a letter from Kenelm Foss it was suggested that one producer, Bentley, was

[1] *Bioscope*, November 30, 1916, p. 847.   [2] Ibid., November 23, 1916, p. 759.

taking an undue share of the credit for the scenario of his latest production, *The Divine Gift*. Foss claimed that he had been engaged to write "elaborate floor-scripts" for this and other films produced by Bentley, such as *The Labour Leader* and *Once Upon a Time*, and that the terms of his engagement entitled him to full public acknowledgement of this. Bentley's alleged infringement of this right was condemned as typical of the "increasing tendency of certain producers to claim every vestige of credit for pictures with which they are associated."[1] In a further communication the following week, which suggests that his views of the writer's significance were derived from the traditions of the stage, he claimed "the logical conclusion that it is the producer who is the parasite upon the author, not the author upon the producer."[2] A sharp reply followed a week later over the pseudonym "Duncan Keith," the gist of which was "Tut, tut! my dear Foss. How many scenarios are literally transferred to the screen?"[3] It is probably true that very few writers were sufficiently acquainted with film technique to be able to contribute as much as their protagonists had hoped. On the other hand the opposite view that the writer was of little account and that novels and plays, adapted by inexperienced writers, made good enough film stories, was full of danger to the British film.

The low standard of the scripts, indeed, was often mentioned as an important weakness in the British film. For by the end of the war the defects of the latter were once again being widely discussed, despite certain optimistic plans for post-war development. There seems to have been some difference of opinion as to whether British films suffered commercially because they were bad, or simply because, on their past record, they were suspected of being so. In 1914 Charles Pathé had expressed his opinion of British films:

"And what, Monsieur Pathé, is your opinion of things in England?"
"Ah, if you refer to the state of the art, I am compelled to say that film production here is still backward, and not what it ought to be. . . . I am afraid that the trouble is due to lack of enterprise. There is no true continuity of effort among your producers. They work too hastily and in too small a way."[4]

The fruits of the attempted revival immediately before the war, combined with the widespread activity on its outbreak, had seemed for a while to

[1] *Bioscope*, August 1, 1918, p. 58.   [2] Ibid., August 22, 1918, p. 15.
[3] Ibid., August 29, 1918, p. 15.   [4] Ibid., October 10, 1914, p. 241.

Jane Shore

Released in 1915, produced by Bert Haldane and F. Martin Thornton. Acting was clumsily theatrical and relied on sweeping gestures.

Pictorial composition was frequently careful, and even unusual, but our three bottom pictures show instances in which camera movement, or changes of camera set-up, could have been used to advantage.

Jane Shore

An outstanding feature of the film was its handling of crowds, and the use of pleasant exteriors.

One of the few change
of camera angle withi
a scene is this inter
polation of a shot
the army into tw
longer shots of a so
dier watching what
supposed to be th
same army—

Jane Shore

—and on another occasion an establishing shot is followed by a detail of the banqueting hall.

London Film Company studio, about 1918–19.

Cricks and Martin studio, about 1914.

Alexandra Palace studio about 1914.

Gaumont studio,
about 1915.

The same.

Henry Ainley and Jane Gail in *The Prisoner of Zenda*, released 1915, produced by George Loane Tucker.

Arthur Holmes-Gore in the same film.

be helping British production towards a new and more dignified position. By the middle of the war, however, output was falling and new companies had almost ceased to appear, while the relatively poor artistic quality of many of the films themselves was once more being openly discussed although perhaps with an unfair tendency to compare the average British film with the best imported ones. An article which appeared in 1917 (headed "Widen the Scope of the Home Industry. . . . But a Napoleon will be Required to do it") stated that "it would be fatuous to support the suggestion that the British picture-play is in a position to challenge the supremacy of its competitors, either at home or in the markets of the world."[1] Pathé's stricture of some two and a half years earlier was repeated, although in a slightly different form. It was admitted that the competitive advantage given to American producers by the existence of a vast home market was a serious obstacle to their British would-be rivals who, because they had to cover their costs in a smaller market, were forced to spend less on production or sell their films at a relatively high price, or both; but far from regarding this as a reasonable excuse the writer fell back on the old argument that there must be a singular lack of enterprise among British producers, that they should have failed to overcome their difficulties.[2] The hunt for Napoleons and Shakespeares continued.

A protective import tax on foreign films had been suggested as early as 1915, and throughout the war the purely economic aspect of the recurring problem of "British inferiority" received growing attention. It became less easy to appeal to bad weather for this inferiority as the use of artificial lighting and studio production increased. Many shades of opinion were crystallized in an interesting controversy in 1917 concerning a suggestion, made for the first time by the producer Sidney Morgan, that all British exhibitors should be obliged to show a certain quota of British films. Speaking at a trade luncheon Morgan claimed that American films, already deriving advantages from better publicity and a more successful use of the star system, received the greatest assistance of all from the practice of block booking, which made it difficult for even the best British films to get a showing in the home market. He accordingly suggested that cinema licences should in future include the condition that one third of the films shown should be British. He maintained that this would restore

[1] *Kinematograph Weekly*, May 29, 1917, p. 7.   [2] Ibid.

the competitive balance and estimated that English producers would be able to cut their prices by half, once such a home market was assured, and thus correct the present position in which English films cost from three to six times as much as American ones.[1] Two or three times as much was the ratio suggested by one of the directors of Butcher's Film Service, who agreed with his main contention but instead advocated an import tax as a more satisfactory way of bringing prices into line. Morgan later hastened to add that protection was to be accorded to British films not because American competition was in any way commercially unfair, but because it was culturally undesirable that English audiences should see nothing but American films.[2] A reply to this "extraordinary proposition" from the point of view of the exhibitor ignored Morgan's search for an economic explanation and repeated the earlier, more superficial view that the British film industry was suffering simply from a "lack of vitality inherent in itself . . . the poverty stricken imagination of its producers."[3] It was enquired whether the British public really wanted so many British films. To this Morgan replied that in the last month the Censors had passed for exhibition 27,000 ft. of new British film and 405,000 ft. of foreign films; since this was the proportion in which films were offered to the public, he asked, what chance had the latter to express any real preference?[4]

Thus suggestions for deliberately protective legislation were multiplying and discussions showed a growing body of opinion in favour of some form of help. But not everyone was yet convinced that it was wanted. Elvey, always the business man, said: "Why should the industry be protected? If it is not strong enough to grow up on its own accord, let it die as soon as possible."[5] There were some who felt that this was exactly what it was likely to do.

(2) CHIEF PRODUCTION COMPANIES

Barker Motion Photography

One of the oldest and most important production firms in the country was Barker Motion Photography. This company, with studios at Ealing,

[1] *Kinematograph Weekly*, May 17, 1917, p. 161.
[2] Ibid., April 26, 1917, p. 36.
[3] Ibid., May 10, 1917, p. 31.
[4] Ibid., May 17, 1917, p. 161.
[5] Ibid., May 24, 1917, p. 73.

had established its reputation by 1914 as the producer of few but important films of a sensational character, and a very large output of topicals. During the war it continued production with a comparatively small number of films which, although presented with a flourish which compelled attention, gradually ceased to be outstanding for quality.

Barker's studio, which he claims[1] to have run entirely on his own money, was busy immediately after the outbreak of war with a succession of military dramas, most of them fairly rough films of only one or two reels. These he hustled through with characteristic energy and contempt for detailed preparation. But by next year the novelty of war was diminishing and work returned to normal with some longer and more elaborate films. One of these, *Brigadier Gerrard*, was an adaptation of the play based on Conan Doyle's book and was produced by Barker himself, with a cast which included the stage favourites Lewis Waller and Madge Titheradge. Another, *Jane Shore*, was from a scenario by one of the better-known British screen-writers, Rowland Talbot, and was acted by such members of Barker's stock company as his chief woman star, Blanche Forsythe. This spectacular film, directed by Martin Thornton, was regarded as a very important British production. But although more lavish than most, it was not remarkable for its technique. (See below.)

During 1915 the scenario department under Irene Miller[2] announced that it was looking for "dramas containing unusual situations and sensations" for films of not less than 3,000 feet,[3] a length beyond which few British producers went at this time. Nevertheless, the number of the important releases during 1916 had fallen to three. Only one of these, *Trapped by London Sharks*, showed Barker's early flair for melodrama and the use of realistic local settings. The other two showed as much dependence on the London stage as did the work of other companies and were not even outstanding representatives of their type. *The Tailor of Bond Street* was a vehicle for two Jewish comedians Augustus Yorke and Robert Leonard: *She*, an adaptation of the Rider Haggard novel which featured Alice Delysia, was made in association with the theatrical impresario C. B. Cochran and H. Lisle Lucoque; whilst during 1917 only one feature film was released and this too was a stage adaptation, being based

[1] In a letter to the author.
[2] *Bioscope*, October 17, 1918, p. 83. [3] Ibid., July 15, 1915, p. 287.

on Cicely Hamilton's *Diana of Dobson's*. For although Barker states in a letter to the author that his stock company of former repertory players was extremely versatile, he frankly admits that he was attracted to the use of well-known West End players by the fact that he could "cash in on their popularity."

The company was one of many which found distribution a growing problem, and early in 1918 came to an agreement with a relatively young firm, the British Actors' Film Company.[1] A new firm was formed with Barker as Managing Director, National Cinema Productions, which was to provide joint office services whilst the two original firms retained their separate producing units. The appearance of this company, which was formed in March[2] with a much larger capital than that of the production companies, was symptomatic of widespread efforts to solve financial problems by some sort of integration. The arrangement did not last, however. And although the experienced director Percy Nash was connected with Barker during the year, and the company released three films in 1918 and two more in 1919, Barker himself retired from production at the end of 1918.[3] Events proved his shrewdness in doing so, for production was steadily becoming less profitable and the British film makers were at the beginning of a disastrous period of American competition. Known in his production days as rough and energetic, careless of dignity and cheerfully untroubled by artistic ideals, Barker showed in his earlier work a sensible if unimaginative grasp of the possibilities of the film medium. His importance had declined during recent years, as he failed to keep abreast of developments in technical equipment and the more serious conception of film content. Having neither artistic sincerity nor a flair for the type of showmanship that was to flourish after the war, he continued to film the type of stories popular before 1914, and became increasingly out of date. Several companies of more recent formation were doing equally significant work during his last three years in production. In so far as his position was retained it was probably more by virtue of his bounding personality and his achievements up to 1915, than because of any real contribution to the cinema since that date.

[1] *Bioscope*, March 28, 1918, p. 5.
[2] Registered March 6, 1918 with a capital of £100,000—*Bioscope*, March 28, 1918, p. 67.   [3] Ibid., December 12, 1918, p. 15.

British Actors' Film Company.

The comparatively young British Actors' Film Company, for example, was producing films which immediately became of as much importance as those of the older company. Unlike Barker, the new firm had no tradition of realism to sustain or half-heartedly abandon, for it had its roots in the new theatricalism and was deliberately formed to bring legitimate stage plays and players to the screen. Founded about a year after the war began[1] with Gerald Malvern as Secretary,[2] it took over the studio at Bushey built by the late von Herkomer. The intention of its founders was to form a group of well-known stage managers, producers and players, most of them as shareholders, and make films which would dazzle the world by sheer weight of recognized dramatic talent.[3] To this end Malvern and the West End actor, A. E. Matthews, obtained support from members of the Green Room Club, many of whom agreed to work for expenses and a share of the profits.

A list of some thirty stage people associated with the new company included in addition to A. E. Matthews such names, well known at the time or later, as Donald Calthrop, Fred Emney, Leslie Henson, Nelson Keys, Lionel Monckton, Owen Nares, Arthur Shirley and Godfrey Tearle.[4] Such a stock company was likely to encourage greater pride in the number and fame of the names attached to each production than in the quality of the film technique. Thus the type of drama favoured by the company was that with the largest possible number of small parts allowing scope for character acting. A fantastic number of the company were in the first film made by British Actors' Film Company, Walter Howard's own adaptation of his melodrama *The Lifeguardsman*. This was produced by Frank G. Bayly, a stage actor of some twenty years' standing who had already been associated with films as both actor and producer for some eight years.

The film was not trade shown until August 1916, and during this year the company still cherished hopes, never fulfilled, of obtaining original

[1] Registered September 18, 1915, with a capital of £5,000—*Bioscope*, November 25, 1915, p. 896.
[2] Later General Manager—*Bioscope*, October 7, 1915, p. 10; August 17, 1916, p. 587. Much of the material in this section was supplied or verified by Gerald Malvern himself and the actor J. D. Williams.
[3] *Bioscope*, October 10, 1918, p. 71.   [4] Ibid., November 4, 1915, p. 490.

scenarios by popular dramatists such as George R. Sims and R. C. Carton. Actual release was delayed until 1917, during which year the firm was joined by Thomas Bentley, producer of Hepworth's famous Dickens films, who had since been working for the Trans-Atlantic and Samuelson companies. The use of this stage material proved to have been financially successful. Three releases during this year included *One Summer's Day* from a play by H. V. Esmond, again adapted by the writer, with Owen Nares and Fay Compton: *The Labour Leader* with the same two players, from an original scenario by one of the more important regular screen-writers, Kenelm Foss; and one of the then popular "song-films," a sentimental five-reeler based on the song *Daddy*.

The Labour Leader was the first film made under an arrangement with International Exclusives which was in many ways similar to that later formed by British Actors' Film Company with Barker and National Cinema Productions.[1] Malvern states[2] that their first two films, *One Summer's Day* and *The Labour Leader*, proved that the company's capital was too small to be locked up in films awaiting, or in course of, distribution. As a result J. J. Sallmeyer of International Exclusives undertook to finance further production in return for contract rights over the films, and several more were made under this regime.[3] The only other films released by British Actors' Film Company during or just after the war were *Once Upon a Time*, also by Foss, and *The Divine Gift*, produced by Bentley. It was this period which was covered by the agreement with National Cinema Productions and Barker,[4] which superseded that with International. This, in turn, gave way to a distribution agreement with the film dealers Phillips Film Company.[5] Thus the history of the B.A.F.C. distribution arrangements is an early sign of the British producers' difficulties as the interval between production and release lengthened.

International Exclusives.

Meanwhile at the end of 1917 International Exclusives ceased to be simply a renting firm, and entered production on its own account. Asso-

---

[1] *Kinematograph Weekly*, February 15, 1917, p. 8.
[2] In an interview with the author.
[3] *Daddy, All the Sad World Needs, Les Cloches de Corneville.*
[4] *Bioscope*, March 28, 1918, p. 3.   [5] Ibid., November 21, 1918, p. 22.

ciated with Sallmeyer in this venture was Low Warren,[1] well-known as an early editor of the *Kinematograph Weekly* and the writer of several important Clarendon films of the previous period. International took over the now disused London Film Company studios at Twickenham, and announced that it would turn out one film a month,[2] beginning with a five-reel adaptation of a novel by E. Temple Thurston;[3] this was produced by Maurice Elvey, with Bransby Williams and a rising young film actress, Odette Goimbault,[4] in the main parts. Most of the 1918 films continued to be made by Elvey, who had become known as a prolific and popular producer with several companies since his work for B & C in the earlier period. His films for International included two adaptations from novels, but the most important was *Nelson*, from an original scenario, with Donald Calthrop and Ernest Thesiger as Nelson and Pitt. This was written by his colleague Eliot Stannard, the screen-writer son of an American woman novelist known as John Strange Winter, many of whose works were being adapted during this period. But International dropped out of production when in the latter half of 1918 Low Warren, with David Falcke and F. E. Spencer, founded a more important new company called Master Films.[5]

Master Films.

This used the old studios at Esher, which had previously been used as the first home of another major company, Broadwest. The first Master films[6] were produced by either A. V. Bramble, a rising actor-producer of mainly stage experience, or Geoffrey H. Malins, until a short while previously one of the Official War Cinematographers.

British Actors' Film Company and several other firms, including International, were alike in relying almost entirely from their outset on the legitimate stage for stories, actors and producers. Other companies which did this in a slightly different way included the Homeland and Sunny South groups of vaudeville artistes mentioned later, and such occasional small production enterprises as, for example, the British Photoplay Company. This sprang into brief prominence in late 1917 when

[1] *Kinematograph Weekly*, June 14, 1917, p. 38.
[2] Ibid., December 6, 1917, p. 70; December 20, 1917, p. 54.
[3] *The Greatest Wish in the World*.   [4] Later known as Mary Odette.
[5] Registered August 15, 1918, with a capital of £2,000—*Bioscope*, September 5, 1918, p. 62.   [6] Which were not released until 1919.

Edward Godal (later associated with B & C) persuaded the music-hall artiste G. H. Chirgwin to turn his famous "Blind Boy" sketch into a film.[1] Such companies existed solely because it was possible to transfer stage entertainment to the screen without too much difficulty. But many, if not all other companies did this in some degree during this period. We have seen how even Barker Motion Photography, an early company with years of experience of original film stories produced and acted by people of screen rather than theatre reputations, now started to borrow stage material to enhance its position.

British and Colonial Kinematograph Co.

Another such company was the British and Colonial Kinematograph Company at Walthamstow, known as B & C. This had become known as a reliable though not very imaginative firm in earlier years under its Managing Director, J. B. McDowell. During the war its history was uneven. McDowell himself was away a good part of the time as one of the Official War Cinematographers, and although a number of the more important film producers and writers were at times associated with the company it was for short periods only, while from early 1916 onwards there was very little activity. B & C, like most other companies, had started the war with some hastily-made topical dramas and one more important one, *It's a Long Way to Tipperary*. These and others were produced by Elvey, who had been with the company before the war and continued to be one of its main producers next year. He made a number of films with his star Elisabeth Risdon, the only British film actress who could be even compared in popularity with Hepworth's Alma Taylor and Chrissie White. At the same time Ernest G. Batley and his wife Ethyle Batley, one of the only women producers, made a number of their films for B & C before leaving early in 1915[2] to join the American Frederick Burlingham. (The latter was a travelling cinematographer associated before the war with first Charles Urban, and then B & C. At the outbreak of war he had been in Switzerland in search of mountaineering films for the M.P. Sales Agency,[3] the renting firm which handled all the B & C output. By October he had already made an arrangement with the Batleys, and his 1914 releases included not only his own

[1] *Kinematograph Weekly*, July 26, 1917, p. 75.
[2] *Bioscope*, January 28, 1915, p. 303.   [3] Ibid., March 18, 1915, p. 1035.

long interest film *Adventures on the Roof of the World* but several of their one-reel dramas. Next year the Batleys continued to produce, while by October 1915 it was said that "after three years of disappointment" Burlingham was getting good results in Switzerland,[1] results which were seen in his *Filming of the Avalanche*. From this time on his links with the British film industry became less, the agency for his Swiss films being taken up by the Charles Urban Trading Company,[2] and he settled in Montreux[3] until returning to the United States in 1918.[4] Meanwhile the Batleys started to produce British Oak films[5] on their own account as the "New Agency" at a studio in Ebury Street, Victoria. They released a large number of one-reel dramas of small importance during 1916 and 1917. Their only long feature was the patriotic *Boys of The Old Brigade*, based on the song "Boys of the Chelsea School," and when Mrs. Batley died in April 1917[6] the brand disappeared.)[7]

B & C itself continued to be busy after the departure of Burlingham and the Batleys, no less than twenty dramas of all lengths being released during 1915. Those made by Elvey were mainly his own adaptations of plays and novels, and included further works by Darrell[8] and John Strange Winter.[9] Sidney Morgan, a producer whose importance was gradually increasing, wrote and produced *The World's Desire* which featured the West End actress Lilian Braithwaite, but most of the films not made by Elvey were the work of a minor producer, Harold Weston. But in the middle of the war, B & C's output declined sharply. Only five long features were released in 1916 and 1917, including further sentimental dramas and melodramas and a five-reeler written and produced by Sidney Morgan, with Sydney Fairbrother in the lead.[10] But from now on the company was, in fact, more

[1] *Bioscope*, October 7, 1915, p. 10. [2] Ibid., November 16, 1916, p. 642.
[3] *Kinematograph Weekly*, May 4, 1916, p. 3.
[4] *Bioscope*, June 27, 1918, p. 6. [5] Ibid., July 13, 1916, p. 123.
[6] *Kinematograph Weekly*, May 3, 1917, p. 3.
[7] The British Oak studio at Ebury Street was later used by Lucoque Ltd., mentioned already in connection with Barker's film of *She*. This company was formed by H. Lisle Lucoque—registered January 30, 1915, with a capital of £6,000—mainly to deal in the film rights of works by such popular writers as Baroness Orczy, H. Rider Haggard, Jerome K. Jerome, Tom Gallon and W. B. Maxwell, but its activities included the production of a few large scale costume pieces. Early in 1916 Bentley left the staff of Trans-Atlantic, where he had been after leaving Hepworth, and filmed Baroness Orczy's *Beau Brocade* with Lucoque. Other films produced by Lucoque himself included *Tatterley* and *Dawn*. See *Bioscope*, October 24, 1918, p. 96 and March 11, 1915, p. 929; *Kinematograph Weekly*, March 16, 1916, p. 21.
[8] *The Idol of Paris* and *From Shopgirl to Duchess*. [9] *Grip*. [10] *Auld Lang Syne*.

or less out of the feature market, although it had plans for post-war production and in late 1918 announced that Herbert Brenon, the well-known producer from America, was to join it early in 1919.[1]

Charles Urban Trading Company.

The firm which took Burlingham's films over from B & C, the Charles Urban Trading Company, declined even more noticeably and by the end of the war had virtually ceased its important production of interest and scientific films. As in so many cases, it is difficult to determine how far this was due to war conditions and how far it was simply a personal matter. For Urban was an American and might well have returned to the United States in any case, although it seems likely that the difficulties of wartime production in this country and in France, where he also had interests, hastened his return. A number of actualities continued to be made. But Urban's attentions turned to America and the only longer British productions which were released by the company during the war were such films as the ten-reel *Building of the British Empire* and a two-reel official film, *Beer and Food.* Presumably the adverse decision of the Kinemacolor law suit also played its part in Urban's withdrawal. Until the case was finally settled against him in March 1915, when his appeal was dismissed in the House of Lords on the grounds of ambiguity in the patent, Kinemacolor remained in virtually its old position.[2] Trading as "Colorfilms Ltd.," for

[1] Brenon, who was brought up in Ireland and London but had made his name in the American film industry, had come to England early in 1918 to make a film at the London Film Company's studio, but was said to be contemplating independent production by the end of the year. See *Bioscope*, December 5, 1918, p. 7; June 20, 1918, p. 5; October 10, 1918, p. 16.

[2] See Volume II, and also *Bioscope*, March 25, 1915, pp. 1071, 1089.

The following account of William Friese-Greene's connection with the case may be of interest: Friese-Greene had invented a colour process called Biocolour, which had been bought by the Bioschemes Company backed by the millionaire financier S. F. Edge. Friese-Greene was called at the trial "to prove that he had, prior to the date of Mr. G. A. Smith's patent, taken films at Middle Street, Brighton, on the two-colour principle subsequently claimed by G. A. Smith," but this was not proved. Bioschemes Ltd. appealed (a) on the grounds that "the Smith patent was bad in that its claims were too wide. Mr. G. A. Smith had claimed that he could by his invention get all natural colours, but, as a matter of fact, he could not get blue by his two-colour (red and green) process. It was argued on behalf of Bioschemes Ltd., for example, that if a film had been taken of a man wearing the blue ribbon of the Order of the Garter, this would have come out green as if he was wearing a decoration of the Hibernian Association (b) for a new trial on the ground that Mr. Justice Warrington's decision as to the prior use was against the weight of evidence." The Court of Appeal decided that Bioschemes Ltd. were right

which purpose they had obtained a licence from the liquidator of the Natural Color Kinematograph Company,[1] the firm ran a collection of interest films in colour called *With the Fighting Forces of Europe* at the Scala for some months at the beginning of the war.[2] But after the early part of 1916 Urban spent most of his time in the U.S.A., where he handled the first official film *Britain Prepared*.[3] It appeared for some time that his interests in Britain were being retained, and when the C.U.T.C. took new premises in late 1916 it was rumoured that these included a new studio for the production of comic films.[4] But it gradually became apparent that Urban's headquarters were no longer in this country, and in 1917 the news was announced that he had taken a studio and was preparing for Kinemacolor production in America.[5]

London Film Company.

Even more conspicuous was the temporary collapse of one of the biggest companies of the previous period, the London Film Company. The large studios established by this firm at St. Margarets, Twickenham, had been opened in 1913 as an offshoot of a large circuit, Provincial Cinematograph Theatres, and were under the managing directorship of one of the leaders of the industry, Dr. Ralph Jupp. At the outbreak of war the company was in a very strong position, with a powerful stock company of players headed by two important American producers, Harold Shaw and George Loane Tucker, and their two American leading ladies, Edna Flugrath and Jane Gail. The staff included Ernest Palmer and the Danish Gustav Pauli as cinematographers, and Bannister Merwin and Frank Fowell as scenarists. Frenguelli, one of the best-known cinematographers of the period, had been engaged even before Shaw arrived from America in 1913 but had left the company with Percy Nash before war began. Nevertheless it was largely his excellent lighting and camera work in the company's first release in 1913, Shaw's *The House of Temperley*, which had set the standard

about the patent and revoked it, but did not go into the question of prior user. When Kinemacolor appealed to the House of Lords the validity of the patent could not be established, and once again the question of prior user was investigated. (Material from a letter from Bioschemes' counsel, Kenneth Brown Baker Baker, to Ray Allister, who kindly made it available to the writer.)

[1] *Bioscope*, October 15, 1914, p. 259.   [2] Ibid., April 29, 1915, p. 388.
[3] Ibid., January 10, 1918, p. 5.   [4] Ibid., September 21, 1916, p. 1175.
[5] *Kinematograph Weekly*, January 25, 1917, p. 1; April 26, 1917, p. 1.

for all London films. With their relatively large capital the L.F.C. could afford to work on a lavish scale, and the presentation of its first film had been preceded by expensive preparation and experiment. Their reputation, by the outbreak of war, was for well mounted and unsentimental drama, and the introduction of important literary works and legitimate stage players to the screen.

As in the case of other brands, London films at the beginning of the war included a group of one-, two- or three-reelers, many of them war dramas. All of these were produced by Shaw and Tucker, the first a steady producer of domestic and sentimental drama, and the second of stronger stories. With the help of Ralph Dewsbury, the young Joint Managing Director of the company, they continued during 1915 with a large output of feature films of slightly greater length. Apart from *Lil o' London*, specially written by Merwin, and an original scenario 1914 by the novelist "Rita," the films continued to be adaptations. They were of some importance, and included such popular works as novels by Anthony Hope[1] and Hall Caine[2] and a play by R. C. Carton,[3] as well as a famous play by Henry Arthur Jones, *The Middleman*, which contained the first screen appearance of the music hall celebrity Albert Chevalier.

But the company was already running into difficulties despite the number and importance of its films, and during 1915 had heavy financial losses. In addition some of the most important members of the company began to drift away, although this was due in almost every case to personal reasons and not to the war. By July Tucker's leading lady Jane Gail had returned to the American film industry[4] and next year Harold Shaw left England for African Film Productions.[5] This meant the loss of not only the lesser of their two producers but also their other chief woman star, Edna Flugrath, who was Shaw's wife and appeared in his films when he later formed the Harold Shaw Producing Company in South Africa.[6] Although conditions were unsuitable for film making and his work suffered, Shaw remained in Africa throughout the rest of the war.

[1] *The Prisoner of Zenda* and *Rupert of Hentzau*.
[2] *The Christian.* [3] *Liberty Hall.*
[4] *Bioscope*, June 17, 1915, p. 1163; July 15, 1917, p. 235.
[5] *Kinematograph Weekly*, March 9, 1916, p. 79. His first African film, *The Voortrekkers*, was shown here early in 1917—*Kinematograph Weekly*, February 8, 1917, p. 94.
[6] *Bioscope*, February 21, 1918, p. 36.

Meanwhile the London Film Company had found its troubles too much for it, although its financial position had actually improved in 1916. Once more during this year most of the films were adaptations, and included further works by Hall Caine and Henry Arthur Jones. But although the output continued to be of good quality and never failed to get a good Press, staffing and administration became even more difficult. Jupp's health was bad, and as he gradually withdrew from the industry the business management of the company was left to his cousin F. E. Adams[1] while Tucker was made Joint Managing Director for publicity reasons.[2] He was helped in the work of production by Dewsbury[3] and a new member of the company, Maurice Elvey.[4] Tucker was a masterly producer with a prodigious capacity for work, but these arrangements did not last. After 1917 Dewsbury could no longer secure exemption from the forces,[5] and many of the releases of this year were films which had actually been made in 1916. *The Manxman* by Hall Caine, one of Tucker's last films and also one of the last important films of the London Film Company, was well received both at home and in America, but production as a whole flagged. Rumours began to circulate of the company's impending collapse. These were strenuously denied, of course, and it was even hinted that its capital might shortly be increased. The tactless suggestion that the purpose of Tucker's rumoured visit to U.S.A. was to find assistant producers was met with another prompt denial. The company had always been careful to stress that it was entirely British. Nevertheless, later in the year Tucker did leave for America.[6] Moreover, although he was said to be making a short business trip, and it was later reported that he was making *The Prodigal Son* "for the company" in America, he did not return to this country and by 1918 had been engaged by the American producer Goldwyn.[7] The London Film Company did not long continue production after his departure, for it was on his work, more than on anything else that their success depended. The studio, with technical staff and equipment, was rented to other companies and the London

[1] According to Ralph Dewsbury, in an interview with the author.
[2] *Bioscope*, August 3, 1916, p. 373.   [3] E.g. *The King's Outcast.*
[4] E.g. *The Princess of Happy Chance, When Knights Were Bold.*
[5] *Kinematograph Weekly*, March 9, 1916, p. 9; *Bioscope*, July 20, 1916, p. 234.
[6] *Bioscope*, December 14, 1916, pp. 1054, 1056.
[7] Ibid., January 3, 1918, p. 25. Shortly after producing *The Miracle Man* in U.S.A. in 1919, Tucker was killed in a motor accident.

output was suspended until the end of the war.[1] This studio was one of the best-equipped in the country and was henceforth used by a variety of people. Dewsbury, still Joint Managing Director, was temporarily released from the R.F.C. to make *Everybody's Business* there during 1917.[2] This was a propaganda film issued for the Ministry of Food but actually financed by the renter Maurice Winnick. By November of the same year the studio was being used by the Ideal Film Company,[3] and later still by International Exclusives.[4] It was here, too, that the Fox producer[5] Herbert Brenon worked on the great "national film" in 1918[6] under the auspices of the Ministry of Information. As for the company itself, it changed character considerably before coming back into production after the war, and it never regained the position it held under Tucker and Shaw, above all under the brilliant guidance of Dr. Jupp. Early in 1918 Jupp sold his interests in Provincial Cinematograph Theatres to Sir William Jury.[7] As the result of a disastrous fire at the Twickenham laboratories and film vaults the company was forced to find another plant for their processing work and bought the Williamson Film Printing Company,[8] with works at Barnet. But although the company thus made ready for a post-war revival under the new leadership, its flair had departed with Tucker.

Hepworth Manufacturing Company.

The career of the next, and by far the most distinguished company both before and during the war, the Hepworth Manufacturing Company, is less depressing although it, too, shows the inevitable difficulties of wartime. One of the sadder features of this period was the disappearance of Turner Films. During the previous few years Hepworth's studio at Walton-on-Thames had been used by a group of associated producers who thus enjoyed the advantages of his stock company, laboratories and marketing facilities but were not actually under his direction. An experienced technician himself, Hepworth had much better equipment than most other producers and was quick to instal his own automatic developing

[1] *Kinematograph Weekly*, January 4, 1917, p. 53. [2] Ibid., June 7, 1917, p. 3.
[3] Ibid., November 22, 1917, p. 44.
[4] Ibid., December 6, 1917, p 70; December 20, 1917, p. 54.
[5] Ibid., January 25, 1917, p. 2.
[6] *Bioscope*, March 28, 1918, p. 3. See elsewhere.
[7] Ibid., May 9, 1918, p. 7. [8] Ibid., December 19, 1918, p. 50.

plant. Turner Films had been produced at Walton by the American Larry Trimble and starred Florence Turner, an American actress of exceptional talent. Production of successful three- or four-reel films continued during 1914 and 1915, the most interesting production being *My Old Dutch*, an immensely popular and nostalgic film featuring Albert Chevalier. But from now on the prevailing type of featured adaptation began to replace the simple comedies and domestic dramas previously characteristic of the brand. Thus Trimble's releases of 1916 included *Far from the Madding Crowd* from the novel by Thomas Hardy, *The Great Adventure* from Arnold Bennett and *Grim Justice*, adapted with the writer's co-operation from a novel by "Rita."

An important member of the Turner company at this time was Henry Edwards. Edwards was an experienced stage actor whose first film work was for the London Film Company, where he had been taken by Henry Ainley early in 1914 to play a small part in *Clancarty*.[1] Towards the end of the year he was playing in the West End in a spy drama, *The Man Who Stayed at Home*, when Hepworth decided to film it. After this was filmed at Walton he joined the Turner Company and became first their leading man and writer[2] and then, in 1915, their second producer. The first two films he produced were *A Welsh Singer* (1916), from an extremely popular romantic novel, and *Doorsteps*, a wistful story of a little waif which he wrote himself. The firm's last film was produced and adapted by him from a play called *East is East*, and was more like the homely sentiment of earlier Turner films. This was not released until 1917. But by the end of 1916 Larry Trimble and Florence Turner had returned to the U.S.A.[3] and Henry Edwards had joined Hepworth.[4] As in the case of both Charles Urban and George Loane Tucker, the two Americans were at first said to be simply visiting their own country. But although Ideal invited Florence Turner back in early 1918[5] neither she nor Trimble returned to Britain and the disappearance of their small but very important output, and in particular Florence Turner's great range and versatility, left a noticeable gap in British film production.[6]

[1] According to Henry Edwards, in an interview with the author.   [2] *Lost and Won.*
[3] *Bioscope*, December 14, 1916, p. 1097.
[4] Ibid., November 30, 1916, p. 935.   [5] Ibid., August 15, 1918, p. 5.
[6] By August 1917 Trimble had been engaged by Goldwyn, who later engaged Tucker also—see *Bioscope*, August 9, 1917, p. 567.

The main Hepworth company advertised that it would consider "anything strong and original,"[1] particularly anything with "strong heart interest."[2] Characteristically, it did not plunge rashly into the production of ill-prepared war dramas as did so many other companies. During the first quarter of 1914 a steady stream of some two dozen films was released, which continued as before to be mainly domestic comedy and romance. It was not until Albert Chevalier's original scenario, *The Outrage*, was filmed in 1915 that the even tone of the company's output was disturbed by the war. It is characteristic that when this did happen it was not by a simple topical drama made for its war interest alone, but a full-scale melodrama, linking the Franco-Prussian and current wars.

Another famous Chevalier film, *The Bottle*, was produced by Hepworth in 1915. A drink drama of the working class, it was longer and more ambitious than so many of the company's pre-war films although it had much in common with them. Many Hepworth dramas of only a reel in length continued to be made, as many as thirty or more being released in 1915. But the demand for multi-reel films was unmistakable. Thus more notable releases in 1914 and 1915 were the last two Dickens films made for the company by Thomas Bentley as well as another Pinero play, *Sweet Lavender*, and *The Man Who Stayed at Home*, both of which were produced by Hepworth. At this time Hepworth was being assisted by a minor producer, Frank Wilson, and scenarios were being written by W. J. Elliott, Victor Montefiore and Blanche McIntosh. His company was a strong and well-disciplined one, but there were losses during 1915. The business manager Parfrey had left, after ten years with the company.[3] Bentley, too, had left after the production of a somewhat spectacular *Barnaby Rudge*, to make his next Dickens film for Trans-Atlantic,[4] the European representative of the Universal Film Company of America.[5] He had been invited to join Universal, and although he did not cross the Atlantic it is interesting that his engagement by an American company aroused patriotic pride, rather than dismay, in the British trade Press. Another loss, although a less noticeable one, was that of Warwick Buckland. After the production in late 1914 of *Barnaby Rudge*, on which he had

[1] *Bioscope*, May 27, 1915, p. 624.
[2] Ibid., October 24, 1918, p. 97.
[3] Ibid., July 29, 1915, p. 436.
[4] Ibid., May 13, 1915, p. 624. *Hard Times,*
[5] Ibid., July 1, 1915, p. 171.

served as designer, Buckland went over to a new company called "M.L.B." after the initials of its three directors—Reginald Michaelson in charge of the business side, J. Welfear Lloyd for technical management and Buckland himself as producer.[1] This small company started in the small Pavilion Studios at Portsmouth Road, Esher,[2] with the ambitious plan of specializing in "high class society dramas." They assembled a group of players, several of whom were originally in the Hepworth Company with Buckland,[3] and engaged the scenarist Langford Reed to write and produce.[4] From May 1915 onwards the company released some half-a-dozen feature films, produced and sometimes written by Buckland and in one case[5] written by the indefatigable film enthusiast, "Rita." The company was of little importance, however, and did not last long.[6]

By 1916, the year in which Henry Edwards formally joined the Hepworth Company, the effects of national service were already beginning to tell on the industry. Such early members of Hepworth's as Hay Plumb[7] were in the forces, Stewart Rome was waiting to be called up[8] and their leading man Lionelle Howard had already been invalided out of the army during the summer.[9] There was still considerable feature production, however, most of it both produced and photographed by Hepworth himself. The high level of film technique and the standard of taste were maintained in such adaptations as his *Trelawney of the Wells* and *Iris* from Pinero, Mrs. Humphrey Ward's political novel *The Marriage of William Ashe* and Hepworth's first version of Helen Mather's sad love story *Comin' Thro' the Rye*. There were further important losses of staff during 1917, partly but not entirely caused by the war. Early in the year the scenario writer Victor Montefiore died during his first week at a training camp;[10] with the company since early 1912, when he had written an early script for the "Tilly" series for the sum of three guineas,[11] he had been responsible

[1] *Bioscope*, April 22, 1915, p. 275.   [2] Ibid., May 6, 1915, p. 488.
[3] E.g. Flora Morris, Harry Gilbey—see *Bioscope*, May 6, 1915, p. 488.
[4] *Bioscope*, July 29, 1915, p. 487.   [5] *A Park Lane Scandal*.
[6] Later in the year Buckland started to produce independently with some of the same players—e.g. *After Dark* from the play by Dion Boucicault—see *Bioscope*, August 12, 1915, p. 640. The studio was used by Broadwest and was the same as that later taken over from them by Master Films—see *Bioscope*, October 24, 1918, p. 98.
[7] *Kinematograph Weekly*, March 9, 1916, p. 74.
[8] *Bioscope*, October 12, 1916, p. 215.   [9] Ibid., July 13, 1916, p. 123.
[10] *Kinematograph Weekly*, March 1, 1917, p. 109.
[11] *Bioscope*, July 1, 1915, p. 87.

for a large number of original stories. During the same year, moreover, the producer Frank Wilson left the company after ten years and joined a new and distinctly less refined company, Broadwest.[1] Finally Lionelle Howard, one of the last remaining male leads from the original stock company, was called up once more.[2] This was especially hard as Howard, an actor who had been seen in all types of part but especially that of the smooth villain since his first film,[3] some three years before, had recently been lending a hand in production and other sides of the business as well.[4] At the end of the year the actor-producer A. V. Bramble was engaged,[5] but he stayed with the company for only a short while and most of the burden of production during 1917 and 1918 still fell on Hepworth himself, together with Henry Edwards.

In having two such considerable producers the firm fared better than its young rival the London Film Company. As a result it was never necessary for the Hepworth studios to suspend production as the other company had done. As late in the war as September 1918 the firm was sufficiently active to engage Paul Kimberley,[6] well known in business circles in the industry, to develop its own renting facilities. Meanwhile adaptations had become as prominent in Hepworth's output as they were among other companies. No less than three[7] were from stories by E. Temple Thurston, a writer who showed a great interest in film production. One of Edwards' films, too, was from a story by the same writer,[8] and another[9] was from a play by Tom Gallon and Leon M. Lion. But Edwards was also developing a characteristic style of his own in a number of original scenarios.[10] These were the "Edwards series," and although marketed under the Hepworth trademark were produced as a separate brand. In the first of these films Alma Taylor appeared, but in most of them Chrissie White was Edwards' leading lady, and together they became the most important romantic partnership in British films.

Although the brands were separate they had more things in common

[1] *Kinematograph Weekly*, February 8, 1917, p. 12.
[2] Ibid., May 17, 1917, p. 32.   [3] *The Bridge Destroyer.*
[4] *Kinematograph Weekly*, April 19, 1917, p. 32.
[5] Ibid., November 1, 1917, p. 41.   [6] *Bioscope*, September 5, 1918, p. 41.
[7] *The Refugee, Tares* and *The Nature of the Beast.*
[8] *His Dearest Possession.*   [9] *The Hanging Judge.*
[10] *Merely Mrs. Stubbs, Towards the Light, Dick Carson Wins Through.*

than the trademark. Excellent photographic quality, beautiful exteriors, restrained acting and unsensational stories were characteristic of the films of all members of the Walton group. Hepworth's influence is obvious, though he did not personally direct his colleagues' work. Another early brand associated with his studios was that of Ivy Close Films, most of which were short comedies, produced by Ivy Close's husband Elwin Neame. The last of these seems to have been *The Haunting of Silas P. Gould*, which was released early in 1915, and during the following year this English star was invited to join the Kalem Film Company of America. Her visit did not lead to further American contracts. On returning to England she joined Broadwest, a new company which the Hepworth producer Frank Wilson was also soon to join. After trying at the beginning of 1917 to reinstate Ivy Close as a light comedienne, Broadwest began to use her as a lead second only to another former Hepworth player, Violet Hopson.

Broadwest Film Company.

The mention of Broadwest brings us to the end of the major companies founded before the war—Barker, B & C, London and Hepworth. Started late in 1914[1] by Walter West, who obtained financial support from his fellow director G. T. Broadbridge, Broadwest production began at the small studio at Esher which had been used by Buckland. Their first four releases,[2] which included adaptations of daring popular novels by Grant Allen[3] and Mrs. Stanley Wrench,[4] were typical of most of their production. Broadwest films, which were usually unsentimental society dramas or melodramas of rather tough morals, were produced on a comparatively lavish scale and acted by an accomplished group of players. Beginning with pseudo-problem plays, they were best known for the films of racing life which followed these. But even these rarely missed an opportunity to present a "daring" situation, as long as it did not actually offend the trade.

After the production of *Burnt Wings* Broadwest moved to a larger studio. This was at Wood Street, Walthamstow, and had lately been

[1] Registered October 24, 1914, with a capital of £12,000—see *Bioscope*, November 19, 1914, p. 755. [2] I.e. in 1915 and the beginning of 1916.
[3] *The Woman Who Did.* [4] *Burnt Wings.*

used by Cunard Films,[1] a firm founded at the end of the previous period. This small company had been run by R. F. Gobbett, as Managing Director, with Wallett Waller as producer; it was backed by the considerable[2] wealth of the same S. F. Edge who had been behind the Kinemacolor lawsuit. Their over-optimistic aim had been to build up a firm with a reputation for "non-sensational," "refined" and "high-class" drama.[3] Gladys Cooper and Owen Nares were engaged, and a number of two- and three-reelers were released in 1914 and 1915, but most of them were made by Wallett Waller and the company ceased production after his death in late 1915.[4]

Thus in 1916 Broadwest acquired the freehold and contents of the Walthamstow studio, where Walter West began to produce his next film, *The Hard Way*. Six or seven three- or four-reelers were released during this year, most of them produced by West, although Harold Weston adapted and produced two popular novels by Andrew Soutar.[5] During this year West mistakenly tried his hand at Shakespearean production, *The Merchant of Venice*, with the well-known stage players Matheson Lang and Hutin Britton; but the technique of this film, which was substantially the same as that of many such adaptations before the war, was now out-dated. The film was widely condemned. Much more in tune with the prevailing fashion was *The Answer*, West's adaptation of a book by Newman Flower with the sensational title *Is God Dead?*

Broadwest built up a stock company which included such popular stars as Violet Hopson—one of the first stars who made a particular point of being well-dressed—and Gerald Ames, as well as Ivy Close. But it was one of the companies which considered the use of stage material their wisest course, and announced its intention of turning out four or five reels a month, "all known novels and successful plays featuring many well-known names in the stage world."[6] Because of the scale on which they were produced the films were amongst the most important being made in Britain at the time, but like other companies Broadwest found distribution a problem, and in late 1916 opened a joint renting department

[1] *Kinematograph Weekly*, August 23, 1917, p. 96.
[2] *Bioscope*, July 8, 1915, p. 124; December 9, 1915, p. 1095.
[3] Ibid., June 10, 1915, p. 1059; August 5, 1915, p. 576; October 14, 1915, p. 162.
[4] Ibid., December 9, 1915, p. 1095.
[5] *The Black Knight* and *The Green Orchard*.   [6] *Bioscope*, July 13, 1916, p. 99.

with the international firm Eclair.[1] During the next year they continued with a similar number of feature films. These were of the same type with the exception of a propaganda film[2] made at the request of the War Agricultural Committee and the first adaptation of the famous racing novels by Nat Gould.[3] These were of no literary merit, but contained just the action, suspense, society glamour and shocking complications to delight this company. As before, the producers were Walter West and Harold Weston, the latter sometimes acting as director under West's general supervision. In 1917 and 1918, during which period two more Gould racing stories were filmed,[4] West secured the help of the former Hepworth producer Frank Wilson,[5] who did much of his production. The stars were Gerald Ames, Ivy Close and Violet Hopson, and by the end of the war the company was generally recognized as one of the most important in this country.

Neptune Film Company.

Another firm which reached a position of importance during the war, although only for a short period, was the Neptune Film Company. Studios were built for this company at Boreham Wood, Elstree, by Percy Nash when he decided to break away from the London Film Company in the summer of 1914. A former stage manager with many friends in the theatre, he had introduced a number of stage players to the London Film Company but was not able to make a name as a producer until in command of his own company, to which he took several artists and the young cameraman Alfonso Frenguelli. He started production even before his studios were complete with some medium length comics featuring Gregory Scott and his own leading lady Joan Ritz, and by the end of the year had released five big feature films. Two of these were original dramas written and produced by Gerald Lawrence;[6] but the most important were Nash's own work, two of them being taken from popular melodramas by George

---

[1] This firm, with head offices in France, had been preparing for regular production in England when war broke out, but since then had restricted itself to distribution, actuality production and sponsorship of Lawrence Cowen's *Wake Up!*

[2] *The Women's Land Army.*   [3] *The Gamble for Love.*

[4] *A Fortune at Stake, A Turf Conspiracy.*

[5] *Kinematograph Weekly*, February 8, 1917, p. 12.

[6] *His Just Deserts* and *A Widow's Son.*

R. Sims and Henry Pettitt, *Harbour Lights* and *In the Ranks*, and one from Tennyson's *Enoch Arden*. Nash, with a personality almost as big as Barker's and a greater consciousness that entertainment was an art as well as a business, rapidly became one of the more important producers.

From early 1915 the company, by increasing the production of comics and interest films,[1] tried to keep up an output of three films a week. In addition it was the first of a number of English firms to issue cartoons during the war, for after two years of experiment in "trick drawing for the screen" Lancelot Speed had finished three cartoons which were being released by Neptune by the end of 1914.[2] During 1915 feature releases were numerous. Many of them were one-reelers, but in addition there were several three- or four-reel melodramas of the old style[3] and the "Royal Naval Division Film," an interest film made with official co-operation and distributed free for recruiting purposes.[4] Moreover the firm had obtained rights to Barrie's works as early as 1914, and made *The Little Minister* during this year. Later Neptune released *What Every Woman Knows* in 1917, as well as another production by Nash[5] and the work of a new producer, Fred W. Durrant.[6] But Percy Nash abruptly resigned from the company in August 1915[7] and although the Board of Directors tried to maintain the company[8] it was forced to give up production after his departure. On leaving it he joined Trans-Atlantic[9] and made their second film in this country,[10] afterwards going to Italy to produce two films[11] for an Italian company, Tiber, which planned to expand its British sales by using British stories and producers.

On Nash's return to England later in 1916 he announced that he had secured the backing of A. Bocchi and that together they were going to make a new brand of films under the trade name of "N.B."[12] Bocchi was an Italian who had been resident in England for some years[13] and who,

---

[1] *Bioscope*, December 24, 1914, p. 1305.
[2] Ibid., November 5, 1914, p. 499. For the history of cartoon production see Chapter IV, 2.   [3] *Romany Rye, Master and Man* and *The Trumpet Call.*
[4] *Bioscope*, April 22, 1915, p. 290.   [5] *The Coal King.*
[6] *Mrs. Cassel's Profession, The Picture of Dorian Grey.*
[7] *Bioscope*, August 19, 1915, p. 769. Some of this paragraph is based on information given to the author by Percy Nash in an interview.   [8] Ibid., July 4, 1918, p. 54.
[9] Ibid., September 9, 1915, p. 1094.   [10] *Royal Love.*
[11] *Fate's Decree*, finished by January 1916 and *Temporal Power*—see *Kinematograph Weekly*, January 27, 1916, p. 7 and *Bioscope*, October 5, 1916, p. 7.
[12] *Bioscope*, October 26, 1916, p. 333, and interview with Nash.
[13] Ibid., October 26, 1916, p. 335, October 12, 1916, p. 215.

like Nash himself, had experience as a stage manager.[1] Together they made at Barker's Ealing studio[2] a six-reel adaptation of a play by Louis N. Parker, *Disraeli*, with the stage actor Dennis Eadie.

Windsor Film Company.

After this, Nash continued working for Trans-Atlantic and Bocchi joined the Windsor Film Company. The latter had been founded in 1914[3] by another Italian, the Marquis Serra, who was a prominent film distributor in England. A studio had been finished at Catford by August 1916[4] and Rex Wilson and F. Martin Thornton (an American who had worked with Haldane on *Jane Shore*) were engaged as producers and Silvanus Balboni as cinematographer.[5] Films released during the first two years were not very important, although a six-reel film of *The Life of Lord Kitchener*, released soon after his tragic death, is interesting. During 1917, however, the company's status improved. It was during this year that management was taken over by Bocchi,[6] after which all the company's films were produced by him, with writing and adaptation by Kenelm Foss, whose reputation as a screenwriter was growing steadily. Bocchi's productions released during 1918 included *The Slave* from a novel by Robert Hichens and *Whosoever Shall Offend* from one by Marion Crawford. Films produced in 1918 but not released until 1919 included novels by Elinor Glyn,[7] Fergus Hume[8] and Lucas Malet.[9] Although from a newly reorganized company whose work was not yet known, these films, which might be summed up as sophisticated melodrama with a leaning towards sex and sensation, were of a sufficiently high standard of production to be patronized by one of the more important renters. During the year Windsor formed one of the now fairly common distribution arrangements with the old-established renting house of Walturdaw,[10] a close arrangement which was to include the joint discussion of production policy. The first three films issued under this agreement were highly

[1] For Alfred Hayes, according to Nash in an interview.
[2] *Bioscope*, November 2, 1916, p. 425.   [3] Ibid., October 24, 1918, p. 96.
[4] Ibid., August 17, 1916, p. 661.   [5] Ibid., October 26, 1916, p. 348.
[6] Ibid., October 24, 1918, p. 96.   [7] *The Man and the Moment*.
[8] *The Top Dog*.   [9] *The Wages of Sin*.
[10] *Bioscope*, October 24, 1918, p. 10.

successful and it was extended to cover at least ten films during the next twelve months.[1]

Eight other companies may be said to have reached a position of comparative importance by the end of the war. Of these, most had developed from large renting firms; and it is interesting that this was so at a time when the need for greater financial backing, and also some certainty of distribution, were becoming important problems for producers. A producer comparable in size was I. B. Davidson. Davidson had turned an old tram shed into a studio at Lea Bridge Road, Leyton, just before the war, and throughout the period issued a series of films produced— and often written and acted as well—by A. E. Coleby (a producer who had formerly been associated with first Cricks and later Pathé) and Arthur Rooke.[2] For a couple of years in the middle of the war their films were issued under the "Tiger" brand, several of them[3] being made at Shepherd's Bush, and throughout the period Davidson releases were well known among the trade for their unspectacular but reliable quality. Coleby himself, a former race-course bookie, is said by one of his contemporaries to have been tough but with the sentimental streak possessed by so many British producers. Spy stories, the adventures of Percy Moran (known for his performances as B & C's famous "Lt. Daring") and boxing films featuring the champion Bombardier Billy Wells[4] alternated with sentimental song-films[5] and equally sentimental films from Temple Thurston,[6] Marie Corelli[7] and Robert Buchanan.[8]

The Samuelson Film Company was similar in size, founded at about the same time by a young man from renting circles in Birmingham, G. B. Samuelson. His co-director was Mr. Engholm, who had been associated with him in sponsoring and marketing Barker's production of 1913,

---

[1] *Bioscope*, November 21, 1918, p. 6.

[2] One of Davidson's films, *Traffic*, was made by Charles Raymond, another early producer, who had been with the firm of Motograph. Another was by Charles Weston, who with Arthur Finn had previously formed his own company, the Regent Film Company, with studios at Queens Road, Bayswater. This firm had promised well and started the war with some topical dramas, but except for a very few films such as Weston's *Vice and Virtue* of 1915, little came from them during the next few years except the very popular "Piccadilly" comedies during 1916, featuring Fred Evans as "Pimple" and his brother Joe Evans as "Joey."

[3] E.g. *The Treasure of Heaven, The Secret Woman.*

[4] *Kent the Fighting Man, The Great Game.* [5] *For All Eternity.* [6] *Traffic.*

[7] *The Treasure of Heaven, Holy Orders, Thelma.* [8] *Matt.*

Sixty Years a Queen, which was the foundation of Samuelson's fortunes. The studio at Worton Hall, Isleworth, was opened immediately before the outbreak of the war. George Pearson, one of the most promising producers in the country, and until then working for the Union Film Publishing Company, was engaged as producer with Walter Buckstone as his cameraman. The first film made there was a six-reel adaptation of Conan Doyle's mystery *A Study in Scarlet,* produced by Pearson and starring Fred Paul and Agnes Glynne, but this was not released until the end of the year. In the meantime the company, like so many others, had quickly stepped in with a number of war dramas or reconstructions. The most important of these was *The Great European War,* which Pearson made in a week by re-enacting each day's news. During 1915 the releases were mainly two-reelers, still made by Pearson. The studio was enlarged during 1916 and the numerous releases during the year were longer, with the exception of *Nursie! Nursie!,* a two-reel comedy by Reuben Gilmer, who was already well known as a writer of comic films. By 1916 the company had achieved a reputation for well-produced dramas. In this year and after, its very varied material continued to be found chiefly in books and plays. By this time several different producers were working for it, for after making some thirteen films for the company Pearson had left late in 1915 for the Gaumont Film Company.[1] Fred Paul, until then an actor, tried his hand at production[2] and Thomas Bentley made the very important family saga film, *Milestones,* from a play by Arnold Bennett and Edward Knoblock before joining B.A.F.C.: a hitherto unknown producer Alexander Butler made several films:[3] Samuelson himself made some important ones:[4] and Maurice Elvey made his first film version of the Lancashire play *Hindle Wakes.*

When Pearson left Samuelson it was to join a Gaumont Film Company much changed since the first ten years of the industry, when on a much smaller scale it had produced so many interesting films. Premises at Shepherd's Bush had been acquired in 1911 or 1912,[5] but the large Lime Grove Studio was not opened until the end of 1915. And until then the

---

[1] *Bioscope,* September 8, 1916, p. 1104.   [2] *The Dop Doctor.*
[3] *The Sorrows of Satan, My Lady's Dress.*
[4] *In Another Girl's Shoes, The Admirable Crichton, The Way of an Eagle, Tinker, Tailor, Soldier, Sailor.*   [5] *Bioscope,* December 16, 1915, p. 1258.

firm had been acting simply as a distributor and as the British branch of the French parent firm, apart from a certain amount of actuality production and some early cartoons.[1] Consequently when the company under Thomas Welsh, its General Manager of many years standing, engaged Pearson and embarked on feature production it was in fact making a new start.

Feature releases during 1916 were few but important, including a thousand-foot news film *With the Kut Relief Force in Mesopotamia*, and the first two of a very important series, the "Ultus" films, written and produced by Pearson, and featuring Aurele Sydney as Ultus, a heroic adventurer who was to achieve immense popularity.[2] Aurele Sydney, who was of French descent, was a native of Sydney in Australia who had begun his stage career there, joined the Gaumont Company in Paris and thence had come to their English branch.[3] Of the Ultus films Pearson himself writes:[4]

Leon Gaumont desired a series of films to be made in his London studio that might achieve a popularity in Britain similar to the popularity in France of his *Fantomas* series. I was asked to create a character and the result was my series of original stories. . . . Aurele Sydney was engaged to play Ultus. He was a very remarkable personality and he quickly became news, and the film realised Leon Gaumont's hopes. The series became a world success.

Next year two more Ultus films[5] were accompanied by a four-reel adaptation by Pearson of Temple Thurston's novel *Sally Bishop*, with Aurele Sydney playing opposite Peggy Hyland.

But in company with Thomas Welsh,[6] Pearson left Gaumont at the beginning of 1918. Together they founded the important company Welsh-Pearson, with a studio at Craven Park. The company's first two films, which appeared during 1918, were *The Better 'Ole* from the play based by Bruce Bairnsfather and Arthur Eliot on Bairnsfather's own comic character "Old Bill," and *Kiddies in the Ruins* from the play based on the work of the French artist Poulbot.

---

[1] See elsewhere. A new brand of cartoons, the Louis Wain series was started in 1916.
[2] *Ultus the Man from the Dead*, and *Ultus and the Grey Lady*.
[3] *Kinematograph Weekly*, January 18, 1917, p. 12.   [4] In a letter to the author.
[5] *Ultus and the Secret of the Night, Ultus and the Three Button Mystery*.
[6] *Bioscope*, January 24, 1918, pp. 3, 5.

The Gaumont company continued to make films after Pearson's departure but on a much less important scale. During 1917 a member of the company, J. L. V. Leigh (previously with Cricks), had been helping in the preparation of scenarios as well as playing the master detective in the "Ultus" films and producing a brand of film known as "Brimstone" comedies.[1] When Pearson left, Leigh's importance as the latter's right-hand man was publicized and he took over the direction,[2] with Byron Webber as business manager and scenario editor.[3] Meanwhile the company was also being depleted in other ways. Their chief cinematographer, Emile Lauste, was at the war and Aurele Sydney had gone to Italy, where he was appearing in "Cines" films by March 1918.[4] Thus little was put on the market in 1918 except the "Eve" comedies with Eileen Molyneaux, which were based on the "Fish" drawings in the *Tatler*, although several more important films were produced which were not released until 1919.[5]

Foreign renters, or the English distributing branches of foreign producers, had seemed about to invade British production before the war, one incidental result of which was that Trans-Atlantic was the only American company which actually established itself in British production. Trans-Atlantic was the British agent of Universal Films of America. Starting to produce in England in 1915, it proceeded to draw important film makers away from existing British companies and opened in style with *Hard Times*, the first Dickens film which Thomas Bentley had made since his work for Hepworth. We have already seen that Percy Nash joined them on leaving his own company, Neptune, and made their second film with a number of former Neptune players, and the same producer also made the fourth Trans-Atlantic feature, *The Devil's Bondman*. These two and the third, Bentley's *The Woman Who Dared*, were all written by their newly-engaged scenario editor Rowland Talbot, who had been for two years with Hepworth and three with Barker and had written scripts for such important films as *Jane Shore* and *Brigadier Gerrard*.[6] At the end

[1] *Kinematograph Weekly*, December 13, 1917, p. 47.
[2] *Bioscope*, March 7, 1918, p. 15.
[3] Ibid., August 22, 1918, p. 59; October 24, 1918, p. 97.
[4] Ibid., March 21, 1918, p. 16.
[5] These included *Pallard the Punter* from a novel by Edgar Wallace, and *The Key of the World*, made by Leigh from the novel by Dorin Craig.
[6] *Bioscope*, August 19, 1915, p. 764.

of 1915 Nash had made his trip to Italy, which was followed by his venture with Bocchi, but he continued to be connected with the Trans-Atlantic Film Company[1] and after the middle of 1916 he made further films for them. These included three propaganda films, *Motherhood* for the National Baby Week Council and two films dealing with the Scout movement, *Boy Scouts, Be Prepared!* and *Boys of the Otter Patrol.*

An English renting company which entered production in 1915–16 was that of Ideal, which had been formed late in 1911. Simon Rowson, brother of the Managing Director Harry Rowson,[2] took charge of production[3] with Fred Paul as his producer[4] until the latter joined the R.F.C. in 1917.[5] Paul had considerable stage and film experience behind him; he had begun his film career before the war with parts in B & C's "Lt. Daring" films, after which he had become heavy lead in the Barker films and then acted temporarily as producer for Samuelson.

Ideal's first production was one called *Whoso is Without Sin,* from a prize-winning scenario by May Sherman; the competition had usefully advertised the firm's entry into production, but perhaps it is significant that before being produced the scenario required "adaptation" by Paul and the screenwriter, Benedict James. After this beginning most Ideal films, including two important productions by Paul—*Lady Windermere's Fan* and *The Second Mrs. Tanqueray*—were adaptations; *The Fallen Star,* the first film to be produced by Albert Chevalier, was also written by him and the scenarist Benedict James wrote a number of original stories. Paul did most of the production, including a *Vicar of Wakefield* in which the celebrated actor Sir John Hare appeared, and a costume drama called *Masks and Faces* with an "all-star" cast of distinguished players which was made to raise money for the Royal Academy of Dramatic Art Building Fund. During 1917 the favourite comedian, Fred Evans, also, returned briefly to the screen in an Ideal film, *Rations.*[6]

[1] *Kinematograph Weekly,* June 1, 1916, p. 23.
[2] Ibid., March 16, 1916, p. 5. [3] *Bioscope,* August 17, 1916, p. 601.
[4] *Kinematograph Weekly,* January 6, 1916, p. 22. [5] Ibid., December 6, 1917, p. 59.
[6] This comedian, famous before the war in Phoenix films as "Pimple," had volunteered for national service in August 1915, and was invalided out later in the year after a couple of months in a military hospital—see *Kinematograph Weekly,* January 4, 1917, p. 25. Meanwhile the Phoenix output had developed along other lines in 1915 and 1916, with Comedio films featuring "Arabella" and "Lynxeye the Detective," the latter played by the producer James Reed, and the Couragio series of adventure films which were made by Percy Moran until he joined the forces.

The firm had no studio of its own and had been operating at Worton Hall at the beginning of 1916,[1] and was at Elstree by the end of the year[2] and at Twickenham during 1917 and 1918.[3] These were all important and well-equipped studios and the very varied output from this firm was of considerable importance from the beginning, although none of its producers were of the same artistic standing as, for example, Tucker, Pearson or Edwards. By 1918 Ideal had lost Paul and several other producers[4] were tried out, but most of Ideal's films were made by Elvey, who had already made a successful version of *Justice* for them from Galsworthy's play. Several more were from plays[5] but most were from novels and most of these were adapted by Elvey's collaborator Eliot Stannard.[6] In addition Elvey produced a film about Lloyd George. The firm of Ideal had long wanted to make a film of national importance and in 1917 had prematurely planned a "peace film"; some time later Rowson was talking about a script which was to be written by Winston Churchill[7] and which it was hoped would form the "official case for the Allies in the War."[8] Finally, in 1918, Elvey produced *The Man Who Saved the Empire*, about Lloyd George, from an original scenario by the historian Sir Sidney Low.

Another renting firm which ventured into production without a studio of its own because of the difficulties of building one in war time[9] was the old-established firm of Butcher's Film Service. For some years this firm had engaged in actuality production in a comparatively small way, but as renters they had been important for some years, a major part of their policy being the presentation of good British films. Apart from the steady flow of Hepworth films which Butcher's distributed, the dearth of good English productions was claimed to be such that early in 1917 this firm, like others, decided to make its own.[10] Frank Butcher was put in charge of production with Elvey as producer,[11] and the first films were Kenelm

[1] *Kinematograph Weekly*, February 24, 1916, p. 12.
[2] *Bioscope*, August 17, 1916, p. 601.
[3] *Kinematograph Weekly*, November 22, 1917, p. 44; *Bioscope*, December 19, 1918, p. 37.
[4] Meyrick Milton—*Auld Robin Gray*, Edwin J. Collins—*God and the Man*.
[5] *The Gay Lord Quex, My Sweetheart, The Passing of the Third Floor Back*.
[6] *Red Pottage, God and the Man, Tom Jones, Dombey and Son*.
[7] *How the Great War Arose*.   [8] *Kinematograph Weekly*, August 9, 1917, p. 68.
[9] *Bioscope*, October 24, 1918, p. 97.
[10] Ibid., October 24, 1918, p. 97; *Kinematograph Weekly*, April 19, 1917, p. 15.
[11] *Kinematograph Weekly*, December 27, 1917, p. 39; April 5, 1917, p. 29.

Foss's *Grit of a Jew* with Augustus Yorke and *The Woman who was Nothing*, from a story by Tom Gallon adapted by Eliot Stannard. During 1918 Elvey continued to be Butcher's chief producer, using further adaptations by Eliot Stannard.[1] In addition Geoffrey Malins, late Official War Cinematographer,[2] and Bertram Phillips, previously associated with the small firm Holmfirth,[3] joined the company as producers. Moreover Wilfred Noy, another experienced producer, came from Harma (the firm which had acquired the earlier firm of Clarendon), and produced for Butcher's for a few months before being called up in October.[4]

The firm of Harma was originally a renting company also, and its entry into production was similar to that of Butcher's in that it, too, claimed to be impelled by the shortage of good British films. An important difference, however, was that by absorbing the early Clarendon Film Company, Harma had obtained a studio of its own at Croydon, with staff and equipment.[5] At the beginning of the war the proprietors of Clarendon were Percy Stowe and H. M. Sharpe.[6] During the last few months of 1914 some seven features were released, three of them[7] by their well-publicized screenwriter of the last few years, the Marchioness of Townshend. The company's dashing hero, "Lt. Rose," soon went on real active service[8] but for a while production was steadily maintained despite the war. The next year there were as many as fifteen feature releases. It was in September of this year that Clarendon was registered as a company.[9] During both 1915 and 1916 the output consisted of three- to five-reel romantic dramas or melodramas, usually based on books or plays,[10] with a further story[11] by the Marchioness of Townshend, and short comedies by their scenario editor Reuben Gilmer.[12] Production was by Wilfred Noy,

[1] *Mary Girl, Goodbye, Flames.*
[2] He wrote his own story for *The Girl from Downing Street.* It was in 1918, also, that Colour Movies Ltd. was formed to make use of Malin's invention for colour cinematography—see *Bioscope*, August 15, 1918, p. 9.   [3] *It's Happiness that Counts.*
[4] *Bioscope*, October 10, 1918, p. 71. He made *What Would a Gentleman Do? As He was Born* and *Spinner O'Dreams*—the last two not being released until 1919.
[5] *Bioscope*, March 7, 1918, p. 35.   [6] Ibid., November 11, 1915, p. 645.
[7] *The Family Solicitor, The Love of an Actress,* and *Wreck and Ruin.*
[8] *Bioscope*, April 8, 1915, p. 105.
[9] Registered September 27, 1915, with a capital of £15,000—see *Bioscope*, November 11, 1915, p. 645.
[10] *The Verdict of the Heart, Under the Red Robe, The Master of Merripit, Night and Morning, The Little Damozel, It's Always the Woman, The Queen Mother.*
[11] *When East Meets West.*
[12] *Bioscope*, April 29, 1915, p. 388; *Kinematograph Weekly*, November 23, 1916, p. 817.

who had been with the company since 1909. In 1917, when Noy was assisted by F. Martin Thornton[1]—recently working for the Windsor Film Company—Clarendon took the lead in the production of a number of extremely sentimental and melodramatic song-films,[2] but it was not until the company was absorbed by Harma that films of greater consequence was made. Then, with Martin Thornton as chief producer assisted by Harry Lorraine[3] and A. C. Hunter,[4] a series of long feature adaptations were put out, the first of which was the best-seller *The Happy Warrior* by A. M. Hutchinson, as well as further two-reel comedies by Gilmer. Thornton was a promising producer, and the reorganized company showed signs of becoming more important than its parent.

The last of the important British production companies which falls in this period was yet another renting firm, although as it did not turn to production until the summer of 1918 it did not actually release any films during the war. This was the Stoll Film Company, formed in April 1918 with the avowed intention of distributing British films on a large scale abroad as well as at home. Almost immediately Stoll, like other companies, found it desirable to produce on its own account[5] and engaged Elvey as the producer of its first film, *Comradeship*, in which the stage star Lily Elsie appeared. This was produced in a large converted house in Surbiton and on location in the South of France during the summer of 1918, but was not released until 1919, in which year the large Cricklewood studio was opened.[6]

(3) OTHER PRODUCTION COMPANIES

The companies described above, because of the scale or quality of their work and the personal importance of their staff and stars, constituted the bulk of the film producing industry. But there were a numer of smaller or less important companies, many of them old and well established and with reputations for good although unostentatious work, whose size

---

[1] *Bioscope*, October 24, 1918, p. 97.
[2] *On the Banks of Allen Water, The Lost Chord, Love's Old Sweet Song*, and *If Thou Wert Blind*.   [3] *The Big Money*.   [4] *Deception*.
[5] *Bioscope*, August 22, 1918, p. 4; December 12, 1918, p. 10.
[6] According to Maurice Elvey in an interview with the author.

or type of output during this period must place them in the category of minor companies. There were also, of course, the usual number of short-lived companies run by the shady, vulgar and small-minded adventurers who did so much to justify unfriendly criticism of the cinema. This is not to imply that all the more important producers were or pretended to be cultured, sensitive or idealistic. Bookies, commercial travellers, publicity men and rolling stones of all types could reach positions of real importance with a mixture of personality, commercial shrewdness and frank senti-mentality whose very opportunism, and all-embracing willingness to try anything once, made them strangely endearing.

Among the better secondary companies there was the group associated with Pathé, in former years the largest producing company in the world. Pathé had figured in several production enterprises in Britain, including that of "Brittania Films," two of which[1] were still to be released in the last quarter of 1914. The Union Film Publishing Company, also, had been started in 1913 by Pathé with a studio at Great Portland Street and had released some dozen "Big Ben" one- to three-reelers produced and written first by Pearson, then by H. O. Martinek and latterly by L. C. McBean. Shortly after the outbreak of war Union's new Alexandra Palace studio was disturbed by an influx of Belgian refugees and later by prisoners of war,[2] while at the end of 1915 the studio was burnt[3] and next year McBean was working for Barker.[4] Pathé, meanwhile, made no further attempts to make films in England until August 1918, when it was announced that production was to begin under J. Serrador, a South American with some film experience in California.[5] It was felt by many that if the firm of Pathé, with its world-wide connections, was to distribute English films the prestige of the whole of the British output would improve.

One of the oldest and most stable firms, although by the war a com-paratively small one, was that of Cricks and Martin at Croydon. This had been founded by G. H. Cricks and J. H. Martin, although by the outbreak of war the latter was operating independently at Merton Park, with Dave Aylott doing some of the production and Theodore Thumwood the camerawork. When war came Martin's output included a number of

---

[1] *The Boat Race Mystery* and *Peggy's Present.*
[2] *Bioscope*, June 10, 1915, p. 1045.   [3] Ibid., December 16, 1915, p. 1201.
[4] *Kinematograph Year Book*, 1916, p. 429.
[5] *Bioscope*, August 22, 1918, pp. 5, 9.

fairly short patriotics, the most interesting of which was Aylott's hastily made *War's Grim Reality*. But Martin, who had parted from Cricks over this question, was convinced that the future of the company lay not in feature production but in short comic and trick films, and continued to release a large number of these.[1] Meanwhile the original firm of Cricks and Martin continued to employ the producer who had joined them early in 1913, Charles Calvert.[2] Reuben Gilmer was acting as their scenario editor by early 1915. Many of their best productions were one-reel comedies produced by Will Kellino.[3] After a couple of fairly long patriotic dramas in 1914 the longest and most important film was a mystery-adventure called *The Avenging Hand* in 1915, written by W. J. Elliott,[4] but unfortunately Cricks found obstacles to the production of long features. From 1916 the position became more difficult and by the beginning of 1918 he had retired from production and was carrying on a printing business in his old laboratories under the name of the Croydon Film Company.[5] His studio was used during 1916 by Maurice Sandground, operating partly as a renter and partly as a producer-sponsor as the Gaiety Film Company.[6] In 1917 some two-reel Gaiety comics were released, produced by Dave Aylott and featuring Bob Reed (*The Walrus Gang*, *When the Heart is Young* and *His Uncle's Heir*), whilst the company's major films, *Russia—The Land of Tomorrow* and *Kilties Three*, were released as Sandground's own productions.

There is also a group of companies which were formed simply for the filming of stage productions. One of these, which apparently had no studio of its own and played a part more like that of a sponsor, was the Magnet Film Company. This survived from the former period with a strong melodrama, *The King of Crime* featuring John Lawson.[7] More important were the firm of Zenith and its later development, British Empire Films. The last film put out as a Zenith production was *Kismet* produced by Leedham Bantock from Edward Knoblock's famous play, and with the

[1] A number of longer "Martin Films," including Aylott's productions *Two Lancashire Lasses in London* and *It's Never too Late to Mend*, were made for A. E. Martin, who had no connection with the other firm.

[2] *Bioscope*, October 14, 1915, p. 125.   [3] Ibid., April 29, 1915, p. 388.
[4] Also *The Winner* and *How Love Came*.   [5] *Bioscope*, January 3, 1918, p. 13.
[6] Ibid., October 24, 1918, p. 98. His co-director was John William Hinks.
[7] Also *Mizpah*.

stage cast including Oscar Asche and Lily Brayton. The company was then taken over by British Empire Films,[1] which inherited both its studios at Whetstone and its policy of filming Lyceum Theatre productions. The first British Empire film was a two-reel comedy, *Always Tell Your Wife*, with Seymour Hicks and Ellaine Terriss, and the majority of films were still made by Leedham Bantock.[2] The link with the Lyceum type of drama persisted in 1915 and 1916 with a number of Melville adaptations[3] and others by Herbert Leonard.[4] By late 1915 and early 1916, also, a number of short comedies were being made at the British Empire studios by Will Evans, the comedian uncle of Fred Evans, but apart from two further features[5] nothing more was released by the firm and a receiver was appointed in November 1916.[6] By May of 1917 the company's effects were being sold;[7] and next year the studios were used by a new concern, Famous Pictures, to film a production of the operetta *Betta the Gipsy*. The producers associated with this latter company[8] were Bert Haldane, the pre-war producer Charles Raymond who had been associated with Bamberger and Davidson, and Willie Davies, who had hitherto worked as designer of a number of important British pictures.

Companies formed to film the productions of certain theatre groups had a parallel in those which were simply associations of well-known music-hall artistes, who added a certain amount of film production to their ordinary work. The Ec-ko Film Company, which had been formed in the previous period and which numbered amongst its associated artistes the Brothers Egbert, Blanche Bella of "Bella and Bijou," Sam T. Poluski and the Kellinos, was such a company;[9] the steady flow of Ec-ko comics by these and other comedians released during the early part of the war were all of less than 1,000 ft. in length. In the summer of 1915 its name was changed to Homeland, and its members now included Jack Edge,

[1] *Bioscope*, December 17, 1914, p. 1187.
[2] The Managing Director was Charles Reed, and George Alexander was made General Manager in late 1916—see *Bioscope*, October 26, 1916, p. 346.
[3] *The Beggar Girl's Wedding, The Girl Who Took the Wrong Turning, The Female Swindler, The Girl Who Wrecked His Home, The World of Sin, The Shop Soiled Girl*.
[4] *Girl of My Heart, The Safe Breaker, The Story of a Song*.
[5] *The Pleydell Mystery* and *The Veiled Woman*.
[6] *Bioscope*, December 21, 1916, p. viii.
[7] *Kinematograph Weekly*, May 10, 1917, p. 95.
[8] Founded 1918 by Edwin H. Wright, with a capital of £5,000.
[9] *Bioscope*, September 10, 1914, p. 949.

Teddie Gerrard and Winifred Delevanti as well as three comedians of greater interest, Charles Austin, Billy Merson and Lupino Lane.[1] A similar enterprise was that of the Sunny South and Sealight Film companies founded by F. L. Lyndhurst, a scenic artist, at Shoreham. The former company was started by Lyndhurst in conjunction with the music-hall comedian Will Evans (uncle of Fred and Joe Evans) in October 1914[2] and other artistes such as Arthur Conquest and George Graves were associated with it, their first releases being three of Evans' one-reel comedies.[3] Lyndhurst registered Sealight[4] in June of next year, but little more was heard of it. Homeland, on the other hand, grew steadily in importance. The success of this company, with studios at Kew Bridge, depended largely on the personality of Billy Merson and on the hope that he would become a world favourite as Chaplin had done, although much was due to the less publicized "Parker" series of Charles Austin and to the producer of both series, Will Kellino. It commenced with a flourish in 1915 with the release of an ambitious and well-advertised three-reel comedy featuring Merson, which was said to have cost as much as £1,000 to produce, *Billy's Spanish Love Spasm*.[5] This was followed by two more three-reel comedies, *The Man in Possession* and *The Only Man*, but this length proved to be unpopular for comedies and in 1916 three more films, *The Terrible 'Tec*, *The Tale of a Shirt* and *Billy's Stormy Courtship*, were released as two-reelers. All these films were written by Reuben Gilmer and produced by Kellino, as were the "Parker" series which were released later. Lupino Lane, who had made *The Dummy* about a year before, had already been fairly well known in his early twenties when he started making "John Bull" films[6] as "Little Nipper" for the Little Nipper Film Company.[7] Early in 1917 he and his wife, Violet Blythe, signed a contract with Homeland and later arranged to make a brand called Kinekature Komedies (the novelty of which depended largely on the use of distorted images) for Hagen and Double at the old

[1] *Kinematograph Weekly*, May 17, 1917, pp. 168b–g.
[2] *Bioscope*, October 1, 1914, p. 12.
[3] *Building a Chicken House, The Jockey* and *The Showman's Dream*.
[4] Registered June 15, 1915, with a capital of £10,000—*see Bioscope*, July 1, 1915, p. 58.
[5] *Bioscope*, July 1, 1915, p. 31.
[6] E.g. *His Cooling Courtship, Nipper's Busy Holiday, Nipper and the Curate*.
[7] Registered December 18, 1915, with a capital of £100. See *Kinematograph Weekly*, January 6, 1916, p. 21.

Phoenix studio on Eel Pie Island.[1] Lupino Lane was liked as a promising young comedian, but his films were considerably less spectacular than the Kellino productions featuring Billy Merson, which were remarkable in their day as the first well-mounted British comedies.[2] After 1916, however, wartime difficulties made it impossible to continue production of the latter.

Another group which must be considered of secondary rank during this period was that associated with Sidney Morgan. With John Melvin Payne, with whom he had previously made a feature film for Cherry Kearton, Morgan began to produce in the summer of 1915 under the name of Renaissance Films. During this year several films were released,[3] all written and produced by Morgan, and in March 1916 the company was registered.[4] Sidney Morgan had left the company about this time.[5] The company soon went into liquidation—this, according to Payne, being the result of maladministration by the Secretary.[6] Morgan, on the other hand, had joined a new firm called Unity Super Films,[7] which announced its readiness to make high-class productions adapted from the works of well-known authors. There seem to have been only a handful of releases,[8] all of them produced by Morgan and all appearing in 1917. These included *Derelicts* from W. J. Locke's novel and the "Dr. Nikola" stories from Guy Boothby. Morgan, however, did not stop, and in 1918 was producing and writing[9] for a new Manchester firm, the Progress Film Company.[10] Provincial companies, on the whole, were becoming less important. But one which was of some interest outside London was Aurora, which was formed in Brighton in 1915 for the production of

---

[1] *The Haunted Hotel, The Unexpected Treasure.*

[2] Some at least of these were made at the Cricks and Martin studio at Croydon.

[3] *Iron Justice, Light, Esther Redeemed.*

[4] With J. M. Payne, Joseph Braithwaite and Earnest Esdale as Directors. Registered March 30, 1916, with a capital of £10,000—see *Kinematograph Weekly*, April 13, 1916, p. 54.   [5] *Bioscope*, August 24, 1916, p. 763.

[6] *Kinematograph Weekly*, June 14, 1917, p. 66.

[7] Controlled by H. D. Marks and H. W. Townsend, both of whose previous experience of films had been as renters. See *Bioscope*, October 19, 1916, p. 238; October 26, 1916, p. 348.   [8] *Bioscope*, October 19, 1916, p. 238; October 26, 1916, p. 348.

[9] *Because* and *Democracy.*

[10] This was founded by Frank E. Spring, who had also founded Silent Dramas at the same address and during 1918 released one five-reeler called *Little Miss Optimist*. See *Bioscope*, October 24, 1918, p. 97.

films in colour by C. H. Friese-Greene, son of the pioneer inventor William Friese-Greene.[1]

But there was only one group of provincial companies which was really of more than minor or local importance, and that was the group associated with two Northern firms which were already in production before 1914, Bamforth and Captain Kettle. Bamforth and Company had studios at Holmfirth in Yorkshire, which were enlarged and improved just after the outbreak of war, and issued many comics in 1914. These included some by their own comedian "Winky," as well as marionette films ("Mario-Cartoons") based on drawings by A. K. Hazelden of the *Daily Mirror*.[2] Early in 1915 the company branched out under the guidance of its little-known producer and scenario writer A. Cecil Birch,[3] acquiring a new comedienne Lily Ward and a child star "Baby Langley"[4] and announcing a new brand of comics starring Bertie Wright.[5] They released several films of over a reel in length[6] but their most important film was a five-reeler based on a "daring" novel, *Paula*. Their output was handled by the Yorkshire Cine Company,[7] which also issued the films of another Northern Company, Pyramid Films.[8] This company had taken over the studios at Towers Hall, Bradford, towards the end of 1915 from Captain Kettle Films, a firm which after the outbreak of war had issued only a handful of one-reelers. The new firm had big schemes[9] for their own comedian "Captain Jolly," and in August 1915 secured the Bamforth comedienne, Lily Ward.[10] Their only film of any importance, however, seems to have been a four-reel "domestic" romance released in 1916, *My Yorkshire Lass*. Films from the Holmfirth studios, on the other hand, increased in importance after Bamforth was absorbed in October 1915 by a new firm, called Holmfirth Producing Company.[11] When it leased Cherry

[1] Registered February 3, 1915, with a capital of £5,000—*see Bioscope*, March 11, 1915, p. 929. William Friese-Greene himself is said by R. H. Cricks to have been experimenting with a colour process at the Cricks and Martin Studio some time during the period. Two one-reelers seem to have been put on the feature market by Aurora, *The Earl of Camelot* in 1914, and *The Pride of Nations* in 1915. [2] *Bioscope*, April 29, 1915, p. 401.
[3] Ibid., August 26, 1915, p. 401. [4] Ibid., March 4, 1915, p. 810.
[5] Ibid., August 26, 1915, p. 895; July 1, 1915, p. 69.
[6] Including *The Cripple of Ypres* and *Won by a Fluke*.
[7] *Bioscope*, December 24, 1914, p. 1310. [8] Ibid., November 4, 1915, p. 517.
[9] Under J. E. Pryde-Hughes. See *Bioscope*, September 30, 1915, p. 1433; November 4, 1915, pp. 5, 7. [10] *Bioscope*, August 12, 1915, p. 644.
[11] Registered October 15, 1915, with a capital of £7,500. See *Bioscope*, November 4, 1915, p. 593.

Kearton's studio at Clapham[1] shortly afterwards, however, this ceased in effect to be a provincial company.[2] Between then and the end of the war a number of moderately long dramas of a very varied description[3] were produced by Bertram Phillips, who was Managing Director of the company.[4]

In addition to these minor companies there were still, of course, a number of individuals who from time to time would undertake an independent production without big financial backing or studios of their own. Many of these were either remnants of companies formed in the previous period, or new ones founded early in the war on the wave of optimism about the future of British production.

The rise and fall of these numerous small companies means every kind of bad luck, bad management, and personal bad feeling. Some with big schemes which they did not have the money or the leadership to put into practice, and others with aims so meagre that they could hardly expect to succeed in an industry depending on showmanship, most of them are of little interest in themselves. But as the important lower level of an industry which was trying to become respectable, and as the breeding ground of many of the technicians of the 'twenties, these struggling companies should not be forgotten in a survey of the industry.

[1] *Bioscope*, July 20, 1916, p. 269.
[2] Cherry Kearton, with studios at Cranmer Court, Clapham, had taken over the assets of the Warwick Trading Company—see *Kinematograph Weekly*, March 23, 1916, p. 32—and arranged to take news films for the *Warwick Chronicle* in 1914. According to subsequent legal reports the new company soon entered into unwise contracts, and the profits from actuality films taken in Belgium at the beginning of the war soon disappeared in payment of debts. Nevertheless at the end of 1914 Rex Wilson was to be found on the staff as producer at the new Clapham studio—see *Bioscope*, December 24, 1914, p. 1304—and in the summer of 1915 J. M. Payne and Sidney Morgan made *Our Boys* for Kearton from a play by H. J. Byron. Kearton himself, however, was away at the war and in September 1915 a receiver was appointed—see *Bioscope*, December 30, 1915, p. 1439.
[3] *Ye Wooing of Peggy, A Week with the King, The Chance of a Lifetime, Meg o' the Woods, A Man the Army Made.*
[4] *Bioscope*, August 23, 1917, p. 863.

CHAPTER THREE

Regulation and Organization

(I) OFFICIAL REGULATION

During the war there was a sharp increase in the amount of official control exercised over the film industry. The position as regards the earlier restrictions, especially the Cinematograph Act and Sunday closing, underwent only minor changes. But a number of new measures came into being with a suddenness which left little time for discussion. In particular there was a tax on entertainment and one on film imports, both of which might have made a more gradual appearance before long even had there been no war. The resentment which was caused by this interference can be read between the lines of countless reproachful appeals to the morale-building performed by the film trade, its contribution to patriotic funds and the war work of its members, whether in the services or at home.

Continuation of Pre-War Problems.

Legislation which already touched the film industry was, of course, affected by the war in various ways. The most important early control was the Cinematograph Act of 1909. The question whether trade premises were subject to control under this Act had been exercising the trade and local authorities all over the country just before war broke out, and a test case brought by the L.C.C. against the Vitagraph company was heard in November. The decision[1] was given in favour of Vitagraph and established that local authorities were not empowered by the Act to regulate fire precautions, the amount of celluloid stored in one place, or such side issues as Sunday opening or censorship of films, in connection with trade showrooms. But the question of celluloid control, already the subject of a Parliamentary Departmental Committee and private Bills put before Parliament by the L.C.C. and Glasgow Corporation,[2] had been answered, for the time being, by the Defence of the Realm Act. This, a national

---

[1] See report in *Bioscope*, November 26, 1914, p. 836.
[2] *Bioscope*, August 13, 1914, p. 617.

measure of the widest possible scope, incidentally provided a temporary solution by limiting the amount of celluloid that could be kept on any premises without a licence.[1] The application of this was very strict, and many complaints of the inspectorship were heard from harassed film dealers.[2]

Apart from this the only new feature in the working of the Cinematograph Act was a changed policy in the issue of licences. In 1912 it had been suggested by the Fulham Borough Council that the issue of licences to all who complied with the regulations, regardless of the number of picture theatres already licensed in any one area, was unwise. The Theatres and Music Halls Committee of the L.C.C. had opposed a more restrictive policy, however, on the reasonable ground that the number of theatres an area required could best be decided by the proprietors whose profits depended upon it. But in November 1913 the erection of two cinemas which came up to licensing requirements, but were considered to be undesirably near churches, was marked by a complete change in policy. For the Theatres and Music Halls Committee's recommendation that in future every case should be considered on its merits was now approved by the L.C.C.[3] The aim was, however, not so much to judge the theatre requirements of a locality—a practice which would have created powerful vested interests in theatres already licensed—but to prevent hardship by taking into consideration before a theatre was built anything which might later be brought against it.[4]

Although these were the only aspects of the Cinematograph Act which came under serious discussion during the war it was confidently felt that revision would be bound to take place when peace returned. The mere fact that there was litigation under the Act encouraged the belief, at least within the trade, that it needed overhauling. When war had broken out the local authorities themselves had by no means been satisfied with the position in regard to either censorship or trade premises. Consequently by the end of 1918 the trade was gathering itself for the attack, and amendment of the Cinematograph Act was among the professed aims of the Parliamentary Committee of the Cinematograph Exhibitors' Association,

[1] *Bioscope*, October 22, 1914, p. 287.

[2] The most famous prosecution was that of the Power Feature Film Company, a *cause célèbre* of 1915—*Bioscope*, April 1, 1915, pp. 3, 26.

[3] *Bioscope*, October 29, 1914, p. 403.   [4] Ibid., November 12, 1914, p. 613.

which at the time was seeking to raise from five to ten thousand pounds to pay for a campaign for parliamentary and municipal representations.

The other major issue which had troubled both trade and local authorities before the war was Sunday opening. This had received more definitive treatment during the last four years and, although always a sore subject was more or less dormant by 1918. During the war the exhibitors were at last wholly defeated in Middlesex and other areas all over the country where Sunday opening was not allowed; and even the London County Council, representative of the more tolerant authorities, had allowed it only under the strict observance of the charity clause.[1]

Just before the war the Middlesex County Council had renewed its attacks upon Sunday opening and had announced that after August 2, 1914, all exhibitors opening on Sunday were to be prosecuted. Middlesex showmen, claiming that they were using non-flam film and therefore beyond the scope of the licensing authorities under the Cinematograph Act (which, it will be remembered, dealt only with exhibitors using inflammable film) banded together in common defiance and opened on Sundays, devoting that part of their profits which was required for charity to war funds.[2] The new issue was thus whether a licence issued to an exhibitor using inflammable film during the week could legally contain a clause stipulating Sunday closing, regardless of whether the film used on Sundays was inflammable or not. This was soon answered in the affirmative when the Middlesex County Council prosecuted Princes Electric Theatres Ltd. for opening on Sunday with non-flam film, although the penalty was made light as the profits had gone to the Middlesex Cinema War Fund.[3] Similar cases followed all over the country, with exhibitors counting heavily on the patriotic appeal of similar funds. In only one case[4] was the decision in favour of Sunday opening. As a result of it both sides lodged appeals. Early next year the matter was finally settled against the exhibitors, the *Bioscope* upholding the judgment as "the common sense view, as well as the legal":

In its judgment, however, the Court held that although the object of the Act

---

[1] Other districts in which Sunday opening was allowed included Brighton, Blackpool and one or two towns in the North and in Scotland.
[2] *Bioscope*, August, 20, 1914, p. 713. [3] Ibid., October 1, 1914, p. 45.
[4] At Tottenham—*Bioscope*, November 12, 1914, p. 653.

was to ensure safety at licensed premises, it had a much wider scope, and was not limited to the occasions on which inflammable films were used.[1]

To Gavazzi King, as secretary of the Cinematograph Exhibitors' Association, the decision was doubly bitter in view of the renters' recent victory in the Vitagraph test case.[2] However, there was no alternative but to abide by the decision. No glib promises to devote profits to patriotic or charitable causes were able to move the powerful groups which the *Bioscope* still dismissed as "a few local clergymen and religionists." Even the more lenient London County Council became suspicious of the enthusiasm which exhibitors showed for a system whereby 20 per cent of their gross takings was devoted to "charity" :[3]

That the abuses have been pretty bad at times is common knowledge in the trade—not a few of the "charities" being simply unsavoury swindles, formed, as it were *ad hoc*, and having little or no existence except as societies for the receiving of moneys from Sunday shows which the people at the head of them were running themselves "on the nod." Many are the Associated Leagues for Providing Walking Facilities for Postmen, or Brass Bands for the Stone Deaf, or Homes for Aged orphans that have suddenly sprung into life to give an air of legality to a Sunday cinema run without a licence.[4]

Consequently, early in 1916 the Theatres and Music Halls Committee of the London County Council suggested centralizing all dealings with charities in the National Sunday League,[5] and in July a list of approved societies was published.[6] After this there was an understandable lack of interest in the whole subject.

[1] *Bioscope*, February 4, 1915, p. 387.   [2] Ibid., February 11, 1915, p. 515.
[3] Sunday receipts in the London County Council.

	1913–14	1914–15
Total gross receipts	£169,069	£181,944
Rent, out of pocket expenses and films	95,619	103,012
Wages	40,806	45,901
Charities	32,644	33,031
	(19.3%)	(18.1%)

Bioscope, July 22, 1915, p. 334.
[4] *Bioscope*, August 17, 1916, p. 581.
[5] *Kinematograph Weekly*, February 10, 1916, p. 17.
[6] *Bioscope*, July 20, 1916, p. 118; August 17, 1916, p. 581.

New Problems.

Apart from the Cinematograph Act, Sunday opening and censorship (the last of which will be treated in a separate section), new regulations affecting the film industry during these four years were largely due to war conditions, although by no means all were removed when the war was over. The most important were the entertainments duty, and import and export restrictions.

The Amusements Tax was not wholly unforseen. In an editorial in September 1915 the *Bioscope* suggested:

... a small amusement tax. Such a tax has, of course, been in existence in France for many years.

This suggested amusement tax is, of course, by no means new or particularly novel. . . . Amusements taxes have been discussed at some length in the House but up to the present the idea has not been received with much favour. However, this year, in dealing with an abnormal Budget, we must be prepared to expect some new and strange taxes, and among them amusements may be included.

We do not think the introduction of such a tax will have an adverse effect on the Trade . . . the public—for naturally it is a consumer's tax—will quickly recognize that one of its luxuries, at least, is sharing the fate of its necessities.[1]

What was actually imposed by the 1915 Budget was an Import Tax. But early next year, before Mr. McKenna's April Budget, the rumour was alive once more. The film industry, making much of the social value of the cinema and the hardships it had already suffered, did its best to believe that nothing so unkind as a sizeable tax could seriously be intended.[2]

Sure enough, however, in April a new tax on theatres, cinemas, football and horse racing was announced, and said to be capable of bringing in £21,800,000 a year. Charges additional to the normal cost of admission to cinemas and theatres were to be imposed from May, at the rate of ½d. on prices up to and including 2d., rising to 1s. on 12s. 6d. seats and an extra 1s. on every 10s. or part of 10s. after that.[3] Only the lower grades of this tax, of course, affected the cinemas.

The immediate reaction of the film industry was confused but on the whole not particularly hostile. There were fantastic estimates of the

---

[1] *Bioscope*, September 16, 1915, p. 1203.
[2] E.g. *Kinematograph Weekly*, February 10, 1916, p. 22.
[3] Ibid., April 6, 1916, p. 1; April 13, 1916, p. 8.

possible yield and some very conflicting views of how the tax might affect exhibitors.[1] The extra work involved was naturally disliked by the latter but, as the *Kinematograph Weekly* noted shortly after the tax came into operation, there did not seem to be any immediate fall in cinema attendances.[2] It was even hoped that since the tax on the picture theatres was relatively light compared with that on the theatres, people might be driven into the cinemas in preference to other shows.[3] It was confidently believed, too, that unlike the patrons of some legitimate theatres where half the cost was to be borne by the proprietors, the cinema patrons would have to bear the whole tax.[4] In short the fact that the final incidence of the tax might not be on the consumer had not yet been fully realized, and exhibitors found that resignation to the hardships of others was a comparatively easy matter. Piously, the trade agreed that "the war has got to be paid for," and that they were sure the public would not mind making this involuntary contribution.

It was not long, however, before there was a movement to "Amend the Tax!" The method of graduation was gradually seen to be unfair or "actually unsupportable,"[5] For whereas the tax meant a 50% increase on the 1d. seats the more expensive ones—whose patrons could presumably afford to pay more—suffered only a relatively small increase. It was widely felt that the Amusements Tax had affected the "cheaper places of entertainment" most seriously,[6] and that cinema failures, now becoming quite frequent, were caused by the Tax more than by any other single cause. The 1d. to 3d. cinemas were most likely to be small companies in working class areas, where the slightest rise in prices meant a noticeable fall in attendances. The small exhibitors, moreover, could least afford a fall in receipts. One example of a penny show was quoted where the proprietor, who acted as his own projectionist, made a living of 30s. to 35s. a week for himself and his wife; at such a standard the slightest drop in receipts did indeed mean ruin.[7] A Bradford hall which reported the change of a weekly profit of £6 or £7 to a weekly loss of £5[8] was said to be typical of many small or medium-sized companies.

[1] *Kinematograph Weekly*, April 13, 1916, p. 51. [2] Ibid., May 25, 1916, p. 56.
[3] Ibid., April 13, 1916, p. 2. [4] Ibid., May 25, 1916, p. 56.
[5] *Bioscope*, July 20, 1916, p. 186. [6] Ibid., August 24, 1916, p. 669.
[7] *Kinematograph Weekly*, June 29, 1916, p. 2.
[8] *Bioscope*, August 24, 1916, p. 704.

Accordingly, protests were soon being organized. A meeting of exhibitors was held at Manchester and it was decided that a deputation should wait upon McKenna and suggest revisions. Under these (1) the highest price subjected to a ½d. tax should be increased from 2d. to 6d.; (2) 7d. to 1s. tickets should have a tax of 1d.; and (3) 1s. 1d. to 2s. 6d. should be taxed by 2d. only.[1] Moreover in the Budget debate the M.P. for East Edinburgh, J. M. Hogge, suggested that the Amusements Tax on all prices up to 6d. should be removed entirely. To this the Chancellor made the disarming reply that taxes usually did press hardest on the small man, and that this had been recognized and accepted when the tax was imposed. Claiming that the first six weeks' yield of £400,000 was very satisfactory, he promised nevertheless to watch for signs of hardship and to consider revision if any came to light.[2] When Hogge continued to press for modification McKenna demanded proper evidence of its need, which the Cinematograph Exhibitors' Association set about collecting. The *Bioscope* uncomfortably admitted that results were likely to be conflicting, and little more was heard of it:

There is one theatre—and there may be others—the receipts of which jumped up surprisingly even during the first week of the tax, and the manner in which receipts generally advanced during the past week of bad weather must have astonished those who had resigned themselves to a thoroughly bad time during this summer. One comparatively small theatre, last week, took £50 more than in the preceding week.[3]

After one year's operation it was still felt that despite a shift to the cheaper seats a good deal of the tax was being borne by the public. There had been brief hopes—real or assumed—that it might be dropped in the new Budget,[4] but to the Trade's fury proposals were made known in May for actually increasing it.[5] The usual deputations and discussions followed immediately. Percy Broadhead, A. E. Newbould and W. Gavazzi King represented the film trade in a protest to the new Chancellor, A. Bonar Law.[6] The Labour M.P.s F. W. Goldstone and Tyson Wilson

[1] *Bioscope*, July 20, 1916, p. 189.   [2] Ibid., July 20, 1916, p. 191.
[3] Ibid., August 24, 1916, p. 670.
[4] *Kinematograph Weekly*, April 19, 1917, pp. 14, 38.
[5] *Bioscope*, May 10, 1917, p. 494.
[6] *Kinematograph Weekly*, May 31, 1917, p. 89.

pressed for concessions[1] in the House of Commons. Mr. Stanley Baldwin, for the Treasury, assured the trade representatives that if the modifications they suggested were reasonable they would be adopted, and the Chancellor announced that the new arrangements had been postponed until October.[2] Next month the matter was discussed in the House of Commons and it was agreed to make concessions on the cheaper seats,[3] although according to Bonar Law 80 per cent of the revenue came from those priced 6d. or less. Despite this minor victory the trade was bitterly disappointed, for it had hoped to rid the lower-priced seats of tax altogether.[4]

Very bad feeling had been generated by the 1917 negotiations but next year it was once more hoped that the tax, by now regarded as an intolerable imposition, might be removed. In February the Executive Council of the reorganized Cinematograph Exhibitors' Association decided at Birmingham to press for its immediate abolition, a demand which was later changed to its reduction. But in April it was revealed that the tax was to remain unchanged. The *Bioscope* asserted that seven hundred cinemas had closed since its imposition,[5] but Bonar Law observed that despite such claims it was perfectly clear that the entertainment industry was far from ruined.[6] Certain concessions were made in June, however, in connection with the negotiations over a general rise in prices (see Chapter I). The trade's jubilation at the news that they were going to save £200,000 is chiefly remarkable for the light it throws on the diminution of patriotic generosity as the real meaning of "paying for the war" had made itself clear:

... has resulted in such concessions being made as it is calculated may cost this country, through loss of revenue, no less a sum than £200,000 during the coming year, an amount, in view of the necessity for raising every available penny for the national exchequer, of no small importance. . . . It is also a further proof that the cinema theatre and the work it is performing is looked at by the Government as of sufficient importance to warrant the possible sacrifice of a sum approaching a quarter of a million sterling in order that it may be maintained.[7]

[1] *Kinematograph Weekly*, June 21, 1917, p. 1.   [2] Ibid., June 28, 1917, p. 37.
[3] Ibid., July 5, 1917, p. 65.   [4] Ibid., July 5, 1917, p. 78.
[5] *Bioscope*, May 30, 1918, p. 4.   [6] Ibid., May 30, 1918, p. 4.
[7] Ibid., June 6, 1918, p. 4.

The second major issue of the time was the restriction of foreign trade. Even if there had been no war some sort of regulations might well have been introduced either during these years or shortly afterwards, as protection for the home industry. It has been mentioned elsewhere in this book that there were occasional suggestions of tariffs and even exhibition quotas for this purpose. But the war hastened their coming, and the restrictions which were actually introduced were designed simply to raise revenue, prevent trading with the enemy, and save both shipping space and foreign currency.

The first measure was the import tax imposed, somewhat unexpectedly, by that Budget of September 1915 which had been expected to introduce an amusements duty. The tax, hoped to yield £400,000 a year, was to be put into immediate operation. Duty was to be levied at the rate of 8d. a foot on negative, 1d. a foot on positive, and ½d. a foot on raw stock.[1]

There was great confusion as to its possible effects, the trade at first being inclined to resent it, particularly in view of the fact that films had been slightingly classed among the "unnecessary luxuries." Among the varied results which were forecast it was thought that film printing, which had been increasing lately, would suffer from the relatively greater tax on negative; this, especially in the case of exclusive films of which few copies were needed, would discourage the import of exposed negatives and on the other hand would increase the relative advantage of importing only prints. Particularly would that part of the film printing business decline which catered for the re-export trade, since there would be little point in paying duty to bring negatives and raw stock into Britain when the prints destined for other countries would thus have to be sold at an inflated price. The duty on raw stock also affected British producers, of course, and it was on behalf of both the production and film printing business that the K.M.A. sought reductions, which they secured at the end of the year.[2] These were comparatively slight, however, the duty on negative being reduced to 5d. and that on raw stock to ⅓d.[3]

The re-export business seemed to be specially hard hit, and a meeting of exporters sadly forecast the end of London's position as a world film

[1] *Kinematograph Year Book*, 1916, p. 21.
[2] *Bioscope*, December 16, 1915, p. 1193.
[3] *Kinematograph Year Book*, 1916, p. 21.

market.[1] A group of exporters[2] laying claim to a combined business worth over £500,000, wrote to McKenna asking for bond arrangements to help them keep it going.[3] The only reply was that drawback would be paid on exportation.[4] It was not until two years later that the Bonded Film Stores were opened in Endell Street, as a belated attempt to keep the world market in London. Here bulk could be broken and films screened, cut, titled or retitled without duty being paid.[5]

The immediate incidence of the tax was, of course, upon the importers and dealers, but they could pass some or all of it on to the exhibitors by raising their prices. The exhibitors' difficulty in raising admission prices and thus passing it on in turn has already been described. Consequently, to argue that in so far as the tax reduced imports it would do so at the expense of the inferior films, and thus raise the level of the usual programme,[6] was cold comfort for the exhibitor. This very fact, moreover, by encouraging features at the expense of the less worthy open market films, contributed to the death of the open market so dear to the smaller showmen. In any case, since the British produced so little—Hepworth said in 1916 that not more than 9,000 feet of new film a week were turned out by the home producers—the British exhibitor could not continue without imported films and had good cause for anxiety at any curtailment of the supply.

In general the results of the import tax, as distinct from import and export prohibitions, were mixed. Resented at first by members of the trade who had confidently expected only an amusements tax, which they hoped would be borne by the consumer, it had been accepted with comparative equanimity by other sections of the industry, particularly the producers, who found their market position improved and produced in great volume as a result. On the other hand, it aggravated the already considerable difficulties of the small exhibitor and contributed to the downfall of the earlier re-export trade.

[1] Bioscope, October 14, 1915, p. 117.
[2] Fifteen firms whose combined activities extended all over the world: Australia, Burma, Canada, Ceylon, Finland, France, India, Japan, New Zealand, Russia, South Africa, South America, Scandinavia, Spain.
[3] Bioscope, October 14, 1915, p. 219.   [4] Ibid., October 28, 1915, p. 357.
[5] Kinematograph Weekly, November 8, 1917, p. 16; December 20, 1917, p. 90.
[6] Bioscope, September 30, 1915, p. 1435.

The tax yield of the first six months was nearly up to estimates,[1] but by this time an even more alarming possibility had been suggested, that of the prohibition of film imports.[2] At the end of March, however, the trade was surprised to learn that it was export, and not import, which had been restricted. This was a shock to many who, recognizing the dangers of Britain's dependence on foreign films, had recently been advocating a greater export effort. The preliminary rumour was that the export of film was to be stopped completely under the Defence of the Realm Act, but this was corrected and feelings soothed when it was announced that export would be permitted to those with licences, readily granted through the War Trade Department to films passed and sealed by the British Board of Film Censors.[3]

The object of these regulations was simply to prevent trading with the enemy through neutral countries and they had little effect on the ordinary course of trade. Early next year, however, the threat of prohibiting film imports as unnecessary luxuries returned.[4] The war ended before anything was done. By the end of 1918 virtually all export restrictions were removed,[5] but by this time the fear of losing our overseas markets and of the world film centre shifting to America were all too near realization.

New Regulations of Wider Scope.

The application of the Defence of the Realm Act to the film industry has been mentioned in several connections. Other new regulations which were national in scope and touched the industry only incidentally were those dealing with conscription and daylight saving, and two which caused greater controversy, paper restrictions and the prohibition of trading with the enemy.

In the question of trading with the enemy can be seen the usual change of front as the financial consequences of patriotism were realized. Sentimental regard for Belgium at the beginning of the war was accompanied, of course, by a release of hatred of the foreigner concentrated on "the

[1] £184,142—*Kinematograph Weekly*, April 13, 1916, p. 7.
[2] *Kinematograph Weekly*, February 3, 1916, p. 17.
[3] Ibid., March 23, 1916, pp. 5, 14; April 13, 1916, pp. 1, 15.
[4] Ibid., February 22, 1917, pp. 7, 13.
[5] I.e. except to Switzerland, and except on raw stock—*Bioscope*, December 26, 1918, p. 6.

Boche." Actual trading with enemy countries was made impossible by war conditions, but there was at first some confusion as to whether "trading with the enemy" might not include doing business with those British firms whose capital was partly enemy-owned. The position was clarified later when Sir John Simon, then Attorney General, announced that money owing to enemies was to be paid to the Public Trustee.[1] But in the meantime, as one exhibitor complained,[2] "it's rather difficult to know the German firms from the British." A number of purely British firms were included in the victims of the first hysterical outburst. Among these were L. Kamm and Company and W. Heipel and Company, two old-established apparatus companies[3] and the film dealers A. E. Hubsch and Company.

But vilification of the Germans died away remarkably when it was seen that financial sacrifice was involved. On February 22, 1915, judgment was given for the London County Council in the Divisional Court of the King's Bench against London and Provincial Electric Theatres Ltd., establishing the London County Council's right to refuse licences to theatres in Notting Hill, Chelsea and Tottenham Court Road on the grounds that, although the staff was English, a majority of the shareholders were German.[4] The case aroused some interest, and an appeal was lodged against this decision, but failed. As the case unfolded the anti-Boche chorus sank into subdued silence and, on the whole, remained very quiet until the war neared its end. Rumours of a big film amalgamation in Germany which was likely to capture post-war world trade then led to a reaction and a fresh agitation against everything German. This was less concerned to improve and sell British films than to prevent by rule the showing of German ones. In October 1918 the Cinematograph Exhibitors' Association, which some eighteen months before had resolved to boycott films made in enemy countries for five years after the war,[5] lengthened this to ten years.[6] Later events were to prove commercial sense too much for this emotional gesture.

[1] *Bioscope*, November 26, 1914, p. 818.   [2] Ibid., September 17, 1914, p. 1070.
[3] Ibid., September 3, 1914, p. 862; September 17, 1914, p. 1071.
[4] Ibid., November 19, 1914, p. 782; December 3, 1914, p. 952; February 4, 1915, p. 396; February 18, 1915, p. 647; February 25, 1915, p. 751.
[5] Ibid., January 3, 1918, p. 35.   [6] Ibid., October 10, 1918, p. 19.

(2) TRADE ORGANIZATIONS

Between 1914 and 1919 trade combination, and the principle of joint action, made progress which was steady if not as conspicuous as it had been during the previous half-dozen years. In some ways this progress was stimulated by war conditions, but it was hindered by a narrow and ignorant individualism among many members of the trade. Towards the end of the war, as the trade came of age, the consciousness that in unity lay strength was joined by a new realization of the value of political action. But the small trials of strength which arose during the war were only big enough to provide useful spurs to combination, and not big enough to disclose the fundamental difficulty of securing enlightened co-operation in the film industry. Thus it was not until the 'twenties, with their crucial problems and the need for a solution which would benefit all three branches, that the underlying anarchy of the trade became apparent.

Authors' Society.

One instance of combination which was not significantly related to the war was that of the Cinema Section of the Authors' Society. The latter had been formed about 1885 by Sir Walter Besant. Even before the war, by which time it was under the Presidency of Thomas Hardy, the Society had found its functions leading it into the film world. The circumstances under which the Cinema Section was established in 1914 were described as follows:

At the beginning of the year, since many complaints of infringement of copyright and appropriations of title had come before the Dramatic Sub-Committee, they endeavoured to form a working Committee selected from the representatives of all those who deal with cinema property—authors, dramatists, theatrical managers, film producers, film renters and other trade bodies.

Accordingly, with some trouble a joint meeting was gathered together. Mr. Carton took the chair, presented agenda, and put before the representatives the purpose for which the meeting had been called. The following resolution was passed:

That the appointment of a Joint Board to protect the common interests of authors, film manufacturers, exhibitors, writers, theatrical managers and the film trade generally, would be to the advantage of all parties concerned, and it was decided that each association should appoint two members to sit on the Board, the dramatists being represented by the Dramatic Sub-Committee.

After the delegates of the various societies had been appointed two meetings were held. The attendance at both meetings was very unsatisfactory. It seemed clear to those present that the interests involved were so diverse, and in some cases so antagonistic, that it would be impossible for the new board to work on the lines originally proposed. The Dramatic Sub-Committee then suggested to the Committee of Management the appointment of a Cinematograph Sub-Committee.[1]

The Cinematograph Sub-Committee began to meet at the end of 1914, under the chairmanship of Edgar Jepson, and among the first questions to be discussed were the fees paid to authors for film rights and the terms of contracts.[2] In addition, a register of scenarios was established, to provide dramatists with evidence of their date of completion.

Much good work was done by the Committee on title registration, copyright and the disposal of film rights in America, and it was under these auspices that Dr. Marie Stopes conducted the investigation mentioned above into the educational use of the film. The efforts to secure better fees for writers were less successful. Authors of published works had by no means yet acquired such mastery of the situation that they could command the fabulous prices of later years, although it was already realized that whilst the "big cinematograph producing companies were unwilling to pay heavy fees in advance of royalties (they) were still willing to give large percentages on the gross takings."[3]

Kinematograph Renters' Society.

Turning to the traditional division of the industry into production, distribution and exhibition we find that in each of the last two a temporary failure of established combinations was followed by reorganization, and the eventual launching of a system which was to last successfully for many years. We have seen that towards the end of the pre-war period some sort of renters' organization had been formed in conditions of great secrecy, and had come to an agreement with the K.M.A. This agreement

[1] *Bioscope*, April 15, 1915, p. 185. [2] Ibid., December 10, 1914, p. 1061.
[3] Ibid., January 7, 1915, p. 8.

was not renewed,[1] and it was not until the end of 1915 that the new Kine-matograph Renters' Society of Great Britain and Ireland was formed. This was registered on December 10th[2] with the usual aims of trade pro-tection societies. H. Cluett Lock was its Secretary.[3] It had a hundred members but was never effective, possibly because it did not have the support of Pathé and Gaumont.[4] It seems, too, that it was an organization which looked backward rather than forward, for the membership qualifi-cation required a certain volume of open market business, a qualification which some more advanced firms would already regard as unnecessary and meaningless by 1915.

During the next few year the renters, many of whom thought that they were being squeezed out, were feeling immensely sorry for themselves. The uselessness of the new organization contributed to their feeling of oppression:

I, of all the integral parts that make up the industry, am the only man without a live organization to back up my rights and fight my cause.[5]

The result was the growth of a number of smaller provincial societies of a similar type but with little real power, and by early 1918 there was a strong feeling that the Society was in need of reorganization. During the summer there was a series of meetings to discuss reconstituting it on more attractive lines,[6] culminating on July 16th in an Extraordinary General Meeting. The attendance was said to be only moderately good but one encouraging feature of the new scheme was that it had the support of Pathé and Gaumont.[7] It had been decided to revive and revise the old society rather than to form a new one, but there were significant changes. The trend towards provincial grouping was recognized, and it was agreed that members of the Kinematograph Renters' Society were entitled to belong to the regional societies also.[8] The limiting qualification of a certain amount of open market business was removed, and although there was an initial distinction between the greater and the lesser renters, each of which groups elected their own representatives on the Council, the smaller firms were encouraged to join. The Council was under the

[1] *Bioscope*, January 27, 1916, p. 6.   [2] Ibid., December 30, 1915, p. 1440.
[3] Ibid., December 23, 1915, p. 1369.   [4] Ibid., July 25, 1918, p. 7.
[5] Ibid., July 18, 1918, p. 58.   [6] E.g. *Bioscope*, July 11, 1918, p. 58.
[7] *Bioscope*, July 25, 1918, p. 7.   [8] Ibid., August 22, 1918, p. 5.

chairmanship of E. G. Turner—a veteran with twenty-one years in renting behind him—and consisted of an equal number of representatives of each group. But it is very significant that the dividing line between these two groups was not open market business, but the number of exclusives handled every year.[1] The new organization was showing signs of life by the end of 1918, negotiating for a long overdue meeting with the Cinematograph Exhibitors' Association to discuss a standard form of contract.[2]

Cinematograph Exhibitors' Association.

The Cinematograph Exhibitors' Association[3] had, of course, been formed in 1912, but the centrifugal tendency of exhibitors had been almost too much for it. Throughout the war it was necessary to continue the uphill work of persuading them to unite for common objects. It was generally believed to represent only 2,000 out of 4,500 cinemas, and although this was a very substantial number there was inevitable resentment that the defaulting 2,500 should reap the benefits secured by members. One fundamental defect of the existing association was one felt by the officers themselves most acutely, and that was the fact that it was a company with liability limited by guarantee under the Consolidation Act, whereas what was really required was something nearer a trades union. Thus the mounting agitation for a "National Union" in early 1916 was aimed at more than mere expansion. It was Gavazzi King himself, Secretary of the Cinematograph Exhibitors' Association, who made the following proposal at the annual meeting of the existing body at Newcastle in July, 1916:

> That this conference is of the opinion that the C.E.A. as at present constituted is inadequate for the full protection of its members, and the accomplishment of its ultimate ends; that the constitution of a National Union as framed under the rules already registered embodies principles of action which meet the interests of the business; and that the Executive Committee be and is recommended by this conference to proceed with the organization of the Union, to the rules of which all the members should be asked to subscribe pending the official winding up of the Association.[4]

By the end of 1916 the movement for a national union had made great

[1] The greater renters were those handling at least twenty-six exclusives a year—*Bioscope*, November 7, 1918, p. 10.

[2] *Bioscope*, November 14, 1918, p. 7.   [3] President: T. P. O'Connor.

[4] *Bioscope*, July 20, 1916, p. 253.

strides,[1] thanks largely to the energy of J. A. Seddon, an M.P. and former President of the T.U.C.[2] and a worthy successor to pioneers like Ogden Smith and Gavazzi King in the work of bullying recalcitrant exhibitors. Hence the conference at Birmingham in June 1917 marked the death of the Cinematograph Exhibitors' Association in its old form, and the birth of a new "national association" of the same name with the chairman of the old one, A. E. Newbould, at the forefront of the welcome to the new.[3] The latter[4] had been registered under the Trades Union Acts[5] and, according to Gavazzi King, had possibilities for both the democratic structure needed in so large an organization, and an agressive policy to secure the members' interests without overstepping the law.

Much of the discussion at the inaugural meeting was about the super-film. The super-film issue was causing important cross-currents. It seemed to many showmen that despite the reorganization of the Cinematograph Exhibitors' Association such objects as the remission of the amusements tax would be more easily secured by joining an organization such as the "Provincial Entertainments Proprietors' and Managers' Association,"[6] which was open to all branches of the entertainment industry. But the antagonism between the cinemas and legitimate theatres over the exhibition of super-films in the latter acted against any such combination. Nevertheless, there was for some time a considerable lack of confidence that the new Cinematograph Exhibitors' Association would prove any better a fighting organization than the old one. Thus an even greater provincialism than that which had impeded the K.R.S. was seen at work among the exhibitors. In July a number of showmen in Cheshire, Yorkshire and Lancashire announced that they would join the Provincial Entertainments Proprietors' and Managers' Association in preference to the Cinematograph Exhibitors' Association,[7] and a month later a Provincial Cinematograph Exhibitors' Federation was launched at Manchester.[8] But after these somewhat abortive moves many Northern exhibitors began to announce

---

[1] *Bioscope*, November 2, 1916, p. 425; November 16, 1916, p. 1.
[2] Ibid., August 2, 1917, p. 481.   [3] Ibid., June 14, 1917, p. 1048–9.
[4] Registered January 25, 1917, rules registered May 3, 1917.
[5] *Kinematograph Year Book*, 1918, p. 31.
[6] *Bioscope*, July 26, 1917, p. 337. Secretary: P. Percival—*Bioscope*, August 2, 1917, p. 459.
[7] Ibid., July 26, 1917, p. 337.   [8] Ibid., August 23, 1917, p. 804.

themselves in favour of the new Cinematograph Exhibitors' Association[1] and by the time its big meeting was held at Liverpool in December it was firmly established. Here the Temporary Council appointed at Birmingham handed over to the newly elected Council, of which A. E. Newbould was made President. J. A. Seddon, who had been acting as Organizer, was made Parliamentary Representative. Sixteen branches had already been formed and by the middle of next year the association was sufficiently well established, and had achieved enough in regard to contracts and the remission of entertainments duty, for its leaders to feel some satisfaction. But exhibitors still appeared to have remarkably little sense of solidarity, and appeals to "slackers" continued.

Labour Combination.

The K.R.S. and the Kinematograph Manufacturers' Association (of which there was little or no published news during this period) were solely employers' groups. On the other hand both the Authors' Society and the Cinematograph Exhibitors' Association were professional associations with a good deal of the labour union about them. But in general the organization of labour in the usual sense played little part in the developments of the time. Even before conscription was introduced there was an acute shortage of almost all types of labour, which led to the use of many very young and untrained projectionists. The unionism which had been emerging among cinema employees suffered accordingly.

In point of fact labour problems of any kind seem to have attracted but little attention until nearly the end of the war, when discussion of how to make a land fit for heroes to live in turned on the recommendations for joint industrial councils contained in the Whitley Report. Thus in June 1918 G. H. Roberts, M.P., adjured exhibitors at a Cinematograph Exhibitors' Association meeting to recognize the right of their employees to join labour unions, and asked them to co-operate with the Whitley scheme after the war. The only field in which labour organization was active, however, was that of the cinema musicians. Here again, as in the case of the cinema proprietors, the interests held in common with similar workers in other branches of the entertainment world threatened to cut across those within the film industry. This was carried much further among

[1] E.g. *Bioscope*, August 30, 1917, p. 938.

musicians, who were apparently able to bargain inside the trade with greater strength by virtue of their representation in both the Amalgamated Musicians' Union and the National Orchestral Association (the latter being mainly confined to London).[1]

The first important sign of activity was in 1916, when the Amalgamated Musicians' Union, which had had a joint committee with the other organization since the previous year, began to press for a minimum standard of pay. Naturally enough the proposition received no sympathy from the exhibitors and in any case the musicians were hampered by having no strong centralized body of showmen with which to deal. The Amalgamated Musicians' Union continued its activity in various parts of the country.[2] By 1918 it had made such progress that a meeting between it and the now reconstituted Cinematograph Exhibitors' Association was held in Newcastle, to form a conciliation board to deal with the wages and conditions of cinema musicians in the North. This was successfully negotiated, although a further project to drive other musicians and other exhibitors into the scheme by a two-way boycott was deferred.[3] The Glasgow and West of Scotland Branch of the Cinematograph Exhibitors' Association, too, had recently agreed to the Amalgamated Musicians' Union's demand for a 25 per cent rise in wages.[4] Since this 25 per cent increase meant only an extra 7s. 6d. a week, the light this throws on the remuneration of cinema musicians at this time of steadily rising prices goes a long way to explain their anxiety to have a strong union.

Unity of the Industry.

Sectional joint action was an accepted principle by 1917. The joint conciliation board of the Cinematograph Exhibitors' Association and the Amalgamated Musicians' Union was a reality. One of the first activities of the two reconstructed trade bodies, the K.R.S. and the Cinematograph Exhibitors' Association, was to be a conference to devise a model contract. Of even greater importance than this was the development of a consciousness of the trade as a whole, and even of joint action.

[1] *Bioscope*, July 6, 1916, p. 44.
[2] E.g. *Bioscope*, September 28, 1916, p. 1238.
[3] *Bioscope*, March 28, 1918, p. 10.
[4] Ibid., March 14, 1918, p. 87; March 21, 1918, p. 3.

This had been conspicuously absent at first:

I think that most of the discord at present existing in the industry is due to the apparent inability of the three Trade Associations to work together for their mutual benefit.[1]

Each part of the industry accused the others of making difficulties by failing to co-operate, while retaining its own position. Ogden Smith and others like him, of course, had been explaining the benefits of combination in general, and of certain groups in particular, for years. But the worse conditions became, and the greater the motive for combination, the louder instead became the cry that only a Leader could find a way out of such a labyrinth of difficulties. Both *Kinematograph Weekly* and the *Bioscope* set up an irritating whine for a superman:

What the Industry needs to-day is a leader—one who is able to make order out of disorder, to organise agreement and concord with a strong hand, tactfully and helpfully, yet with a stern repression of pettiness and ignoble motives.[2]

No such ideal leader appeared. But a growing awareness that many needs were common to all members of the trade was noticeable, as well as a growing ability to work together, if at first only in small ways. The Trade Conference on the open market in 1915, although it was held on the initiative of the Cinematograph Exhibitors' Association, was actually a conference of all three branches of the trade.

It is more than likely that the increasing attention paid to the cinema as a body by official quarters contributed to the feeling of solidarity. The growing restrictions, as well as the official use of the film, have been described. But there were other, almost symbolical, recognitions of the cinema as a factor in modern society. When Hepworth's *Comin' Thro' the Rye* was shown at Marlborough House to Queen Alexandra the event was heralded as the first time an individual film play had been given a Royal command performance, and the gesture was appreciated as a compliment to the trade:

This mark of Royal interest and appreciation is particularly gratifying at the present moment, in view of the many accusations made against the industry by narrow-minded, ignorant and malicious critics.[3]

[1] *Bioscope*, September 9, 1915, p. 1105.
[2] Ibid., August 26, 1915, p. 875.　　　　　[3] Ibid., August 10, 1916, p. 463.

More gratifying still was the knighthood conferred on Jury, a prominent member of the trade whose humble beginning twenty-one years before as one of the fairground showmen made this honour a fitting symbol of the changing status of the industry. A renter of the rough old school, W. J. Jury, head of Jury's Imperial Pictures, was knighted for "services rendered to the state in connection with War Charities, the War Loan, and the Organization of the Supply of Cinema Films of the Operations on the Western Front." The *Bioscope's* view of the significance of this was characteristic:

The inclusion of his name in the roll of knights proves the importance that the King attaches to the cinema as a means of propaganda and entertainment, and in whatever capacity we are connected with the industry we are justly entitled to feel to-day a little taller than we felt in 1917.[1]

Volumes of praise and sentiment poured forth as though Jury, by no means the most popular man in the industry, were the father of the trade. It is ironical that the English pioneer inventor, William Friese-Greene, on whose grave it was later inscribed that "his genius bestowed upon humanity the boon of commercial cinematography," was suffering such poverty during these war years that the trade was called upon to help him, which it did with pitiful inadequacy.[2]

Another example of concerted action, which sprang from the new maturity as well as from disagreeable experience of the power of the legislature, was the attempt to break into politics.

In July 1918 the Leeds Branch of the Cinematograph Exhibitors' Association wrote to the General Council remarking that the latter's success in securing some remission of the entertainments duty "proved the high value of political action," and recommending representation in Parliament and on municipal bodies. A. E. Newbould, President of the Cinematograph Exhibitors' Association, was suggested as the prospective M.P. J. A. Seddon, of course, already watched over the trade's interests in the House of Commons and a handful of other M.P.s were beginning to take up its defence. Newbould informed the Cinematograph Exhibitors' Association at Blackpool that in any event he was going to stand for an

[1] *Bioscope*, January 3, 1918, p. 18*a*.
[2] Ibid., December 23, 1915, pp. 1306, 1369. *See also* biography by Ray Allister.

Essex constituency, and that if elected he would "sit . . . as a direct representative of the Trade."[1] The C.E.A. Council resolved to support him financially, and even considered the possibility of subsidizing others. A couple of months later it was decided to raise a Parliamentary Fund of at least £1,000 for candidates, and a Parliamentary Committee of the Cinematograph Exhibitors' Association was formed to administer it and prepare amendments to the Cinematograph Act, the latter being one of the aims of all this activity. Later still, branches were asked to raise as much as £5,000 or £10,000. It is understandable that there was some confusion as to how a candidate for a political election in one small constituency could "represent" the trade in any but an honorary sense. Whilst the *Bioscope* admitted (rather ambiguously) that Newbould obviously "could not have stood on a cinema ticket," constant reference was made to him as the "exhibitors' candidate"; in the same way it was loftily declared that the trade must "be kept clear of the maelstrom of Party Politics,"[2] although no candidate would stand much chance of election simply as the film trade's representative, and Newbould stood in fact as an Independent Liberal. The war ended suddenly and the election was upon them in November, and although Newbould did in fact stand for the West Leyton division of Essex he was defeated by a Coalition Unionist and the *Bioscope* observed without a trace of humour:

The sudden incidence of the General Election at a moment when all business men are preoccupied with the great changeover from war to peace conditions, has found the cinema industry not fully prepared to play that major role in national politics which should be its ultimate destiny.[3]

Cinematograph Trade Council.

The heroic Leader failed to appear, but by the end of the war there was in effective existence a joint bargaining instrument of the whole trade which, perhaps more than anything else, stands for the cinema's commercial coming-of-age in Britain. This was the Cinematograph Trade Council. Admittedly, accounts of the C.T.C.'s negotiations betray a brusque and even insulting tone which seems clumsy and immature

---

[1] *Bioscope*, July 11, 1918, p. 46.
[2] Ibid., November, 28, 1918, p. 4. [3] Ibid., November 28, 1918, p. 4.

beside the formal politeness of Ministerial replies. But in view of the early apathy and antagonisms it is sufficiently remarkable that even this degree of development had been achieved.

The first stimulus was given by the outbreak of war itself. In this crisis the Executive Councils of all three Associations forgot their differences, met on August 10th, and resolved themselves into a Trade Council. So great was the panic that the pooling of films and even profit sharing was rashly suggested.[1] Such ideas of co-operation could hardly be expected to last, however, and it was not long before the absence of a real "Trade Defence" was a matter of concern.

Throughout the early part of 1916 rumours of import and export restrictions were exploited to urge an effective trades council.[2] But it was not until the Home office proposals for an official censorship that the necessary spur to action was present. These proposals will be discussed in the next section. But is may be mentioned here that, as a result of them, a Joint Trade Conference of the whole trade was called "to concert measures for an active propaganda against the undesirable features of the proposed 'official' censorship"[3] and in November the C.T.C. was formed. This was to be a standing Committee of the three associations, its aims being "the protection and betterment of the Cinematograph Industry."[4] The scenarist Frank Fowell was engaged as Publicity Officer[5] and later Secretary.[6]

The Council's first actions were naturally in connection with censorship, and it was owing to its recommendation that T. P. O'Connor was invited to the office of Chief Censor after the death of G. A. Redford. It was also on the C.T.C.'s invitation that the National Council of Public Morals undertook the commission of enquiry which was of such importance in vindicating the cinema's reputation. More important still, it was the C.T.C. which acted for the whole trade in criticizing the Home Office proposals, and eventually had them dropped.

But it did not thereupon cease to exist. For one thing, censorship was by no means a settled question, and even before the Commission had

---

[1] *Bioscope*, August 13, 1914, p. 627.
[2] *Kinematograph Weekly*, March 30, 1916, p. 3; June 29, 1916, p. 19.
[3] *Bioscope*, November 16, 1916, p. 63.
[4] Ibid., November 16, 1916, p. 630.   [5] Ibid., December 7, 1916, p. 952.
[6] On the departure of the first Secretary, Mr. de Lacey, for the Army.—*Bioscope*, January 11, 1917, p. 93.

finished collecting evidence it was suggested that the B.B.F.C. should be in the hands of the new joint body:

> The point for him (*the exhibitor*) to consider is that his Censor, in whom he has confidence—who works for his protection—is employed, not by any official trade organization, but by a few private individuals belonging to one section of the industry. . . . If the trade censorship is to have the respect and confidence of the public—as we believe it deserves to have—the time has come when it must be put on a proper footing. The British Board of Film Censors has done good work in days gone by. But it has outgrown its usefulness, or, rather, it has ceased to be in any way representative of a great and growing industry, with official institutions of its own.[1]

The suggestion was not approved. But censorship was not the only question which required the attention of a body representing the whole trade and by this time the C.T.C. had been reorganized along more general and permanent lines. Its terms of reference were wider, making it, in the words of the *Bioscope* "a real Cabinet of the industry . . . a Cabinet for war—war on the trade's enemies." The temporary executive ceased to exist, but some of its members[2] remained on the new Council, which was to consist of ten exhibitors, five renters and five manufacturers, each appointed by their own Association;[3] A. E. Newbould was re-elected Chairman.[4] By the end of the year the Council was active in many matters relating to the welfare of the whole industry, and its status is characterized by John Buchan's request for help in providing an Advisory Council for the Cinematograph Branch of the Department of Information in 1917.

(3) CENSORSHIP

British Board of Film Censors.

In 1912 the British Board of Film Censors had been set up to protect the trade from harassing local variations in the definition of an "undesirable" film. Its aim was to help the trade by ridding it of its own worst elements, and thus gaining the confidence of the local authorities.

[1] *Bioscope*, April 26, 1917, p. 282.
[2] Sidney Bacon, R. C. Buchanan, Arthur Cunningham, A. Davis, A. J. Gale, F. R. Goodwin, C. M. Hepworth, A. M. Kay, Paul Kimberley, A. C. Lovesy, F. H. Montague, A. E. Newbould, E. W. P. Peall—*Bioscope*, March 22, 1917, p. 1207.
[3] *Bioscope*, March 22, 1917, p. 1200.   [4] Ibid., March 29, 1917, p. 1297.

Publication of the Board's Reports for 1914 and 1915 showed some progress in their double struggle with refractory film makers on the one hand, and even more refractory local authorities on the other. Between January 1st and December 31st of 1914 some 6,881,614 feet of film had been examined, or roughly 140,000 feet a week; this had been submitted by 84 film publishers and was said to comprise almost the whole supply of films for that year.[1] In the Report for 1915 these figures had fallen to 6,273,924 feet and 65 publishers,[2] probably because the early effects of the war on production and imports were making themselves felt; but on the other hand, the number of local authorities recognizing the Board's certificates had risen from 23[3] to 35,[4] this being the number of authorities stipulating that licensees should only show films certified "A" or "U" by the Board. Confidence in the latter, moreover, was growing in Whitehall as well as among these local authorities. At the outbreak of war the Home Secretary had chosen the Board to censor topicals for security reasons,[5] while some time later the War Office asked it to assist in the censorship of films for export.[6]

Despite these marks of respect a stream of complaints showed that the Board was not making enough progress to silence the film industry's more outspoken critics. The C.E.A. still supported the Board, but included among its members little more than half of the existing 4,500 picture theatres (1917 *Report*, page 23). It had been hoped that the system would be extended as more and more of the local authorities accepted the Board's ruling and insisted on its certificate for all films shown in their areas, thus eliminating the local variations which kept producers, renters and exhibitors alike in a state of uncertainty. But on the contrary, the exhibitors in many parts of the country found local authorities becoming steadily more, rather than less active. Many magistrates, justices and Chief Constables exercised a censorship whose incalculable prohibitions were the more harassing in that they were frequently announced after the film had not merely been booked and announced, but actually started its run. Little wonder if exhibitors in Liverpool, to take a district frequently troubled by this type of interference, ceased to place much

---

[1] *Bioscope*, January 14, 1915, p. 91. [2] Ibid., July 6, 1916, p. 13.
[3] Ibid., February 25, 1915, p. 705. [4] Ibid., July 6, 1916, p. 13.
[5] Ibid., September 10, 1914, p. 935. [6] Ibid., July 6, 1916, p. 12.

confidence in certificates which did not guarantee their right to show the films.[1]

The aim behind most of this interference was the protection of children. There were at this time many attempts, partially successful in some areas, to restrict the hours during which children might be admitted to cinemas. It was the fact that this was not practicable which gave many educationists, social workers and others a greater interest in the question of censorship in general than they would otherwise have had. The very widespread belief that a recent increase in juvenile crime mentioned by the Home Secretary was, as he suggested, partly due to the type of film being shown[2] redoubled this interest. Since it was not seriously suggested that pornographic films (of whose existence rumours were heard from time to time) were likely to appear in the public cinemas the censorship question hinged rather in the indefinable effect of vulgarity, the depiction of crime, or the excessively stimulating treatment of sex than on obscenity. And it was the effect of these things on young people which gave rise to the greatest anxiety. Consequently, the fact that the admission of children was never prohibited outright in this country is of the greatest importance in the history of film censorship.

The subject of the most notorious of many tussles was a film of the novel *Five Nights*. This film had a varied career. Given an "A" certificate by the Board, it was shown with impunity in such places as Liverpool, Cardiff and Bristol, but encountered opposition from the police and justices of Preston, Weston-super-Mare and Bath and from the Watch Committee in Leicester,[3] as well as Walsall, Brighton, and finally London.[4] The case was taken to the courts by the National Film Company, which fought the justices of St. Helen's in Lancashire,[5] maintaining that although licensing authorities were legally entitled to stipulate that films shown should not be objectionable, indecent or likely to exercise a harmful influence on young people, they were not justified in using this right to establish a local censorship.[6] The judgment, however,[7] was that "the

[1] *Bioscope*, November 12, 1914, p. 658.   [2] *Kinematograph Year Book*, 1917, p. 513.
[3] *Bioscope*, September 9, 1915, p. 1079; September 16, 1915, p. 1211; October 7, 1915, p. 13; October 21, 1915, p. 319.
[4] *Kinematograph Year Book*, 1916, p. 21.   [5] Ibid., p. 141.
[6] *Bioscope*, September 28, 1915, p. 392a.
[7] Finally upheld in 1916—*Kinematograph Weekly*, April 27, 1916, p. 77; May 25, 1916, p. 43; June 8, 1916, p. 106.

British Board of Film Censors was not a statutory body, and whatever might be the meaning of the affidavit" (i.e. the Censor's) "it was not enough to set against the honest opinion of the justices."[1]

The outcome of this unsatisfactory decision was that both the trade and the local authorities, although for different reasons, began to favour the idea of a centralized official censorship. The trade had no respect for the local authorities:

The most careful, reputable and experienced exhibitor may find himself at any moment at the mercy of some hare-brained "General Purposes Committee," absolutely incompetent, in nine cases out of ten, to form an intelligent opinion on any subject of larger importance than the redecoration of the parish pump.[2]

But they were losing respect for the B.B.F.C. also, and many regarded it as a dead letter after the *Five Nights* episode:

. . . we have to recognize the fact that little, if any, real importance is attached to the certificates, and that with many authorities the decisions of the Board are entirely disregarded, and they themselves act as censors. To add to this, we have a Divisional Court judgment to the effect that the Board of Film Censors, not being a statutory body, has no *locus standi*, and its statements are not sufficient evidence to set against the opinions of licensing justices.[3]

Another solution was sought:

. . . the censorship to-day is practically useless. It lacks the support of the industry which was responsible for its birth, its decisions are ignored by a certain section of the Trade, and the authorities, even those who at first were favourably disposed toward the Board and its work, are now acting as if they had never heard of its existence. . . . The Trade has got to make a move—a big combined move—to obtain Government approval and recognition of an Official Censor Board, to secure the appointment of an Official Examiner of Films.[4]

Ogden Smith, too, had suggested efforts to get "our censorship officially recognized by the Government . . . let us call upon the Government to give Mr. Redford official powers, that no L.C.C. or Borough Council can question."[5]

This ingenuous plea for official backing of the trade's own censor, far

[1] *Bioscope*, November 11, 1915, p. 643.   [2] Ibid., July 20, 1916, p. 186.
[3] Ibid., November 11, 1915, p. 605.   [4] Ibid., November 25, 1915, p. 849.
[5] Ibid., October 21, 1915, p. 245.

from meeting the local authorities' wish for an official censor, was a bid to undermine their power. During late 1915 and 1916 many of these authorities, as well as the Chief Constables' Association of England and Wales, expressed themselves in favour of an official censor. A scheme was suggested by the Home Secretary, but it was found that many local authorities wished to retain the right to differ from the official decisions if they felt so inclined. It was this final discretion, however, permitting local variation, to which the trade objected most of all and which was in fact the crux of the problem. When in late 1915 the L.C.C.'s Theatres and Music-Halls Committee recommended the adoption of the usual clause in their licences, saying that it would "strengthen the authority of the Board to give official recognition to the work done by it,"[1] the *Bioscope* retorted that the reservation of the right to override the Board invalidated the whole concession.[2]

Home Office Proposals.

In April 1916 the trade, inspired by the vision of acquiring official status for the Board and thus laying its enemies low, sent a deputation to the Home Office.[3] In due course a circular letter was sent by the Home Office to the local authorities on May 16th to discover their views on a centralized official censorship.[4]

Councils all over the country made it known that they were in favour of some such scheme.[5] Their vision of it, however, was rather different from that of the trade. Seeing it as a Government alternative to the British Board of Film Censors, rather than as the Board transformed by official backing, many of them were nevertheless still not prepared to make that surrender of final discretion which alone would have made the change worth while for the trade. Foreseeing the rout of the trade censorship, its critics were able to jeer:

Yes, we know a great deal about that censorship committee in London! It is appointed by yourselves, but the Government is taking into consideration the appointment of a different kind of censor![6]

[1] *Bioscope,* December 23, 1915, p. 1368.
[2] Ibid., December 9, 1915, pp. 1089, 1108.
[3] *Kinematograph Weekly,* April 20, 1916, p. 6.
[4] *Bioscope,* October 19, 1916, p. 262a–g.
[5] E.g. *Bioscope,* July 6, 1916, p. 4; July 1, 1916, p. 182.
[6] *Bioscope,* July 27, 1916, p. 281.

The County Councils Association wrote to the Home Secretary, Herbert Samuel, asking to be allowed to consider the scheme. Samuel replied on June 26th that this was not yet ready,[1] but on August 23rd a set of model conditions were sent out for consideration by the local authorities[2] and the trade.[3] The plan was for a National Censorship Board with an Advisory Committee which was to represent authors, dramatists, educationists, local councillors, the general public and the industry, with a President chosen by the Home Secretary.[4]

There was an immediate outcry in the film trade Press. "Samuel Tries to Please Everybody" was the headline of a hostile editorial in the *Bioscope*[5] whose theme was that Samuel had tried to please everybody but the trade. On September 18th the three trade associations met separately and, with the Authors' Society, together at the Connaught Rooms. Disappointed that their idea had backfired, they achieved wholehearted union of the entire trade for the first time. The objections voiced here continued to be the basis of opposition throughout the negotiations. They were in two main parts. Firstly, the composition of the Advisory Committee was criticized for representing too many groups hostile to, and ignorant of, the trade and not enough of the trade itself—which was promised only two representatives;[6] the Council, moreover, had too little power and should have been allowed to appoint the Censors. Secondly and most important, the trade was dismayed to find that the local authorities would in effect have the same power to differ from the new Board as they had from the old.[7]

A Sub-Committee of seven (including W. G. Barker, C. M. Hepworth and A. E. Newbould) was appointed to prepare the observations for which Samuel had asked, and to form a Deputation. This group met several times and on September 22nd sent a letter to Samuel signed by one member of each of the four associations[8] claiming among other things: (1) that a test case was still required to establish whether the local licensing authorities had in fact any legal right to exercise censorship; (2) that the Home Secretary had gone back on the original circular letter, which had

[1] *Bioscope*, August 17, 1916, p. 580.   [2] Ibid., November 16, 1916, p. 635.
[3] Ibid., August 31, 1916, p. 772.   [4] Ibid.   [5] Ibid.   [6] Ibid.
[7] Ibid., November 16, 1916, p. 635. Most of this paragraph from *Bioscope*, October 19, 1916, p. 262a–g.   [8] J. F. Brockliss, E. Jepson, A. E. Newbould and H. Wood.

implied a certain amount of finality for the Board's ruling on films, whereas the model conditions perpetuated the uncertainty and lack of uniformity which had been the worst feature of the old system; (3) that the appointment of the Board by the Home Secretary was "bureaucratic"; and (4) that the four organizations should together have a representation at least equal to that of the other group, and that the chairman should be a permanent official of the Home Office.[1]

Following this letter a deputation visited Samuel on October 13th, its ten members including F. W. Baker, C. M. Hepworth, Edgar Jepson, W. Gavazzi King, H. Cluett Lock, A. E. Newbould and J. Brooke Wilkinson. After two members of the deputation had elaborated their objections at some length the Home Secretary replied. He agreed that the representation of the industry might be increased, although not to the fifty per cent suggested in the letter, since the greater attendance among industry representatives would make this a virtual majority. To other criticisms, however, he replied: (1) that in the official view the rights of the local authorities required no further proof; (2) that in any case only nine out of the 126 authorities which had replied to the proposals had shown the least desire to exercise these powers; finally (3) that the alternative to the proposals, a Bill, would not be popular in a war-time Parliament with more important things to consider.[2]

On October 27th a reply was sent to Samuel which refused co-operation with a dramatic flourish typical of trade action at the time:

> The Committee is confident that films would not be submitted to a censorship constituted in the manner proposed; nor would the trade provide the funds to maintain it. . . . War has changed many things, but it has not yet brought it to this pass, that outside a statute a trade can be compelled to pay for its own execution.[3]

A further conference was then held at the Connaught Rooms early in November, as a result of which was formed the Cinematograph Trade Council described in the previous Section. The activity of this body has already been mentioned; a campaign to arouse public interest was launched by it, and provincial meetings were addressed by the M.P. J. A. Seddon.[4]

[1] Most of this paragraph from *Bioscope*, October 19, 1916, pp. 262a–g.
[2] *Bioscope*, October 19, 1916, pp. 262a–g.   [3] Ibid., November 9, 1916, p. 584.
[4] Ibid., November 30, 1916, p. 869.

But before a solution had been reached the Censor, G. A. Redford, died[1] and early in December the politician and journalist T. P. O'Connor, for the last three years President of the C.E.A., succeeded him and became the second chief Censor.[2] Samuel was shortly replaced by Sir George Cave, and before long the Home Office proposals were abandoned.[3] Further negotiations had met with nothing but prevarication from the trade,[4] and on January 24, 1917, a letter from the Home Office stated:

> As it is evident from your letter that no useful result would be achieved by further discussion, Sir George Cave will not proceed with the scheme, but will postpone the question of a central censorship until there is an opportunity for dealing with the matter by legislation. . . . accordingly he proposes to inform the local licensing authorities of the withdrawal for the present of the scheme for a central censorship, and to recommend them to exercise to the full extent the powers of control which they possess under the Cinematograph Act.[5]

By this time, however, the centre of interest had shifted to the commission of enquiry into the cinema set up by the National Council of Public Morals. But before discussing this, a word is necessary about the trade reaction to the official proposals. The mixture of belligerence and pertness which is to be found in verbatim reports and correspondence, tends to obscure the real strength of this single-minded opposition.

A fundamental issue, the possibility that an official censorship might be more subject to the pressure groups already demanding such restrictions as the exclusion of children, was almost ignored in the general resentment that the trade had failed to acquire official blessing. The real dangers of abuse inherent in an official censorship were hardly mentioned by the trade. Apart from indignant but not very explicit references to "bureaucracy," the opposition seemed to be based on little more than childish resentment at finding that an official, centralized system need not make use of the trade's own machinery at all. The industry had sought centralization, claiming that the smaller the locality the more narrow-minded the prevailing opinions; it had sought officialdom, recognizing that the more official the central body the greater its chances of being accepted by local authorities as arbiter. Yet fantastically enough it seems

[1] *Bioscope*, November 16, 1916, p. 653.
[2] Ibid., December 14, 1916, pp. 1054–5.
[3] *Kinematograph Weekly*, February 1, 1917, pp. 1, 7.
[4] *Bioscope*, February 1, 1917, p. 428.   [5] Ibid., February 1, 1917, p. 428.

to have expected—or at least professed to expect—that complete official status, overruling local powers, would be given to its own Board. The fact that the central instrument was not to be one of their creation, and that officialdom was not synonymous with centralization but could actually mean a confirmation of local powers, seems to have been a shock to these inexperienced politicians.

The Cinema Commission.

The National Council of Public Morals was a large unofficial body of religious, scientific, educational and political leaders under the Presidency of the Lord Bishop of Birmingham. Its motto was:

"The Foundations of National Glory are set in the homes of the people. They will only remain unshaken while the family life of our race and nation is strong, simple and pure."[1]

Its professed object was the "Regeneration of the Race—Spiritual, Moral and Physical."[2]

This body was in the limelight in the summer of 1916 because of its recent National Birth Rate Commission. Known for some time to be interested in the influence of the cinema, especially on young people, the Council itself showed a film on the question of birth control called *Where Are My Children?* early in November. By this time it was already in touch with the trade, the Government and educational authorities concerning the need for an impartial enquiry into what evils there were in the cinema and how best to remove them, and for "the establishment of a censorship which would give legitimate freedom for the proper development of the cinematograph while rigorously cutting out undesirable films."[3] Many meetings were held before the newly-formed Cinematograph Trade Council eventually wrote, on November 24th, inviting the National Council of Public Morals

to institute an independent inquiry into the physical, social, moral, and educational influence of the cinema, with special reference to young people.[4]

[1] *Report,* p. vi. [2] Whole paragraph from the *Report.*
[3] *Report,* p. vii. [4] Ibid.

The National Council of Public Morals undertook the enquiry only on the understanding that the trade would not allow it to affect their negotiations with the Home Secretary.

As a result a Commission was set up with the following terms of reference:

(1) To institute an enquiry into the physical, social, educational, and moral influences of the cinema, with special reference to young people; and into

(2) The present position and future development of the cinematograph, with special reference to its social and educational value and possibilities.

(3) To investigate the nature and extent of the complaints which have been made against cinematograph exhibitions.

(4) To report to the National Council the evidence taken, together with its findings and recommendations, which the Council will publish.[1]

The Secretary of the Commission was the Rev. James Marchant, Director and Secretary of the National Council of Public Morals. The twenty-four other members included not only representatives of religious, educational and social welfare groups but three very able members of the trade (W. Gavazzi King, A. E. Newbould, and Sidney Lamert, director of the London Film Company) and the new Censor, T. P. O'Connor.[2] The skill, and extensive knowledge of the industry, possessed by the last four enabled them to make the best of the evidence for the trade. The latter, however, although the Commission had been of its own seeking, felt that the personnel was weighted against it. Members of the industry cautiously reminded each other that their position was

. . . not that of a criminal on his trial, but of an innocent man seeking the vindication of his honour.[3]

Latent hostility to the Commission can be read between the lines in issues of both the *Kinematograph Weekly* and the *Bioscope* until late in the year.

But before long the trade perceived that a surprise was on the way for its critics.[4] The Commission sat from January 1917[5] to July,[6] examining some forty witnesses. These included such prominent

[1] *Report*, p. ix. The rest of this paragraph also from the *Report*.
[2] Ibid., p. ix.   [3] *Bioscope*, November 30, 1916, p. 845.
[4] E.g. *Kinematograph Weekly*, August 30, 1917, p. 76.
[5] *Kinematograph Weekly*, January 4, 1917, p. 1.   [6] Ibid., July 12, 1917, p. 85.

members of the industry as Cecil Hepworth, Brooke Wilkinson, A. E. Newbould, Gavazzi King and T. P. O'Connor, and a number of teachers, local magistrates, social and religious workers and school children, and as a result of their evidence a valuable and largely favourable mass of information on many aspects of the cinema was collected. The Report was taken to Sir George Cave, now Home Secretary, at the end of the year.[1] In addition to certain regulations for health, safety and good conduct in picture theatres its recommendations were chiefly notable for including an official censorship to supersede all local regulations.[2]

Feeling that the trade did not, and could not, have the machinery to solve its many problems, the Commission was sympathetic:

We want to place it in a position of real dignity. We want it to be something more than a trade; in fact, we wish it to be one of the assets of our national entertainment and recreation.

We are anxious that the cinema should be beyond all suspicion in the mind of the average member of the public.

We deeply regret that the negotiations between the Home Office and the trade proved abortive, and we do not think that fault attaches to the trade because of the failure of these negotiations.[3]

Accordingly, while commending T. P. O'Connor's work, the Report suggested that the Censor should in future be appointed by the King in Council. This Censor, who need not necessarily be a Civil Servant, should appoint the examiners and be assisted by a broadly based Advisory Council and a small executive formed from it. Perhaps the most important recommendation from the point of view of the trade, however, was that the virtual censorship of the local authorities should be completely swept away.

The film industry was naturally overjoyed at this, as well as the generally favourable tone of the Report, and after its publication anyone who attacked the morals or influence of the films was promptly referred to it. The people whom *Kinematograph Weekly* was accustomed to call "busy-bodies and meddlers" were so suspicious of the Commission's tolerance that the trade was accused of having financed the investigation, but this

[1] *Kinematograph Weekly*, December 20, 1917, pp. 45, 50.
[2] *Report*.   [3] Ibid., p. xc.

was strongly denied[1] and James Marchant emphasized in the Report itself that the Commission was appointed by, and solely responsible to, the Council. Many other critics realized that they had been hasty and F. R. Goodwin, for example, as chairman of the London Exhibitors' Association, received a handsome apology from the Church Army:

DEAR SIR,—On giving due consideration to the very excellent report of the Commission of Enquiry on the question of Cinema Theatres and their influence on the young, we have come to the conclusion that there are no grounds for general condemnation, and that the adverse reports were much exaggerated.

Numerous statements as to the evil influence of some theatres reached us from various parts of the country (some, no doubt, mistaken and others unduly magnified), but sufficient in volume to cause much anxiety to our Probation of Offenders Homes Department. We were naturally anxious to eliminate such influences as far as possible, hence our attitude in the matter. That we took a much too narrow view of the whole of the circumstances we are now convinced, and our only excuse was our fear for the youth of the land.

May we assure you that we do realize the great value of the cinema and its possibilities for the highest educational purposes, and we feel assured that the high standard of pictures you are so keen to present will be maintained.

With sincere regrets for any annoyance we may have caused you and the Cinema Trade generally, etc.[2]

Thus to some extent the trade benefited from the *Report* even though its recommendations were not implemented. Sir George Cave postponed action:

when receiving the deputation which waited upon him to present the report of the Commission, referred to this as an interesting event, and one which represented a notable advance. The suggestion of the Commission that the Official Censor should be assisted by an Advisory Committee he regarded as a very wise step, and on that Committee he thought the representatives of the Trade should have seats. From the manner in which the Home Secretary received the report, it seems obvious that he will at least be guided to some extent by the suggestions contained therein when framing new conditions for the government of the Trade *après la guerre*.[3]

During 1918, therefore, the British Board of Film Censors' troubles with both the local authorities and parts of the industry continued almost as

[1] *Kinematograph Weekly*, November 15, 1917, p. 7; December 6, 1917, p. 51; *Report* p. viii.　　　　　　　　　　　　[2] *Bioscope*, January 31, 1918, p. 9.
[3] *Kinematograph Year Book*, 1918, p. 21.

before. When the Famous Players film *Sapho* was banned at York the *Bioscope* thought once more of a central official censorship:

I suppose that if we had State Censorship we should be able to circumvent these self-constituted custodians of the public's right. . . .[1]

It had also been suggested that the Board, although its Committee included four members of the C.E.A. as well as four of the K.M.A.,[2] gave too little weight to the opinions and needs of exhibitors.[3] Now, early in 1918, a notorious English film of an actual murder case, *Shadows on my Life*, was condemned by the General Council of the Exhibitors' Association although passed by the Board, a circumstance which stung the distributors of the film to an angry denunciation of this form of double censorship.[4]

Censorship in General.

The number of films banned by the Board was very small in relation to the number submitted.[5] The fact that the proportion banned in the first year of operation was actually smaller than that two years later seems to suggest that, unless the standard was made progressively more strict (and there is no indication that this was so) there was, in fact, no large output of "objectionable" films existing at the time when the censorship was set up, to be discouraged thereafter. It was established, in fact, not so much to rid the cinemas of films to which the better elements in the trade objected, as to forestall various pressure groups and prevent them from ridding the cinemas of the films which they considered undesirable. Of

[1] *Bioscope*, January 10, 1918, p. 7.
[2] The chairman of the Committee was the chairman of the K.M.A., and the K.M.A.'s four nominees constituted the finance committee—*Bioscope*, June 10, 1915, p. 1049.
[3] *Kinematograph Weekly*, January 4, 1917, p. 18.
[4] *Bioscope*, February 28, 1918, p. 38.
[5] *Report*, p. 214:

	Subjects passed			Subjects to which exception was taken	Subjects entirely rejected
	A certificate	U certificate	Total		
1913	627	6,861	7,488	166	22
1914	416	5,866	6,282	148	13
1915	372	4,395	4,767	214	22

course, this is not to deny that many behind the Board were acting with very high motives. But the issue was not explicitly one of ideals, any more than the bitter fight against official censorship was fought on general grounds of the freedom of expression from Government restriction.

It was in keeping with its opportunist beginning that the British system of film censorship should have had no predetermined set of rules, its character and development being left in the first instance in the hands of G. A. Redford. Principles were naturally evolved in the course of its operation, but even these were broad and flexible and for private guidance rather than for publication as a final code. Experience soon taught the Board that it was necessary to judge each film on its merits, and that although consistency was desirable it was not always possible to be strictly logical. Some theme or incident which was not harmful in itself might become so by repetition, for example, the cumulative effect being to suggest that some undesirable state of affairs was not merely normal but acceptable. In such a case the Examiners might feel justified in banning further examples of a theme which they had previously passed. When asked by a member of the commission of enquiry whether he thought set rules were possible, an anonymous Examiner from the Board replied:

You must consider that in one year we had something approaching five thousand subjects, and therefore I think we should have to have someone with quite exceptional powers to lay down rules.[1]

The Board was influenced by the knowledge that its decisions affected "an average audience which includes a not inconsiderable proportion of people of immature judgment."[2] The fact that it had no real power to prevent the witnessing of "A" films by children, too, would presumably make it more anxious to secure alterations in these than otherwise. As a result of several years' experience with these considerations in mind, however, one Examiner was able to outline certain guiding principles:

The examiners, therefore, have been guided by the broad principle that nothing should be passed which in their opinion was calculated to demoralize an audience or any section of it; that could be held to extenuate crime or to teach the methods of criminals; that could undermine the teachings of morality; that tended to bring the institution of marriage into contempt; that lowered

[1] *Report*, p. 110. [2] Ibid., p. 104.

the sacredness of family ties. They have refused their sanction to incidents which brought into contempt public characters acting in their capacity as such; i.e. officers wearing H.M. uniform, ministers of religion, ministers of the Crown, ambassadors and representatives of foreign nations, judges, etc. They have objected to subjects calculated to wound the susceptibilities of foreign peoples, or members of any religion. And, especially recently, they have rejected films calculated and possibly intended to foment social unrest and discontent.[1]

The attitude grew stiffer towards the treatment of controversial social problems, including these "calculated . . . to foment social unrest" but "we considered scenes depicting conditions under which people live, or the hard life in the slums to be perfectly legitimate." It also included the "moral problem" films which leapt into prominence during the war, for although several sincere treatments of controversial social questions like *Where are my Children?* were accepted, such serious propaganda fell into disrepute on account of the many less worthy productions exploiting prurience in the name of enlightenment. The Report for 1914 expressed anxiety over the wave of films dealing with "applied eugenics,"[2] and next year the *Bioscope* said of the new fashion for films about the drug traffic, represented in their publicity as films intended to correct a social evil:

. . . there being no reason to suppose that this habit was prevalent in this country to any serious extent, the evils of arousing curiosity in the minds of those to whom it was a novel idea, far outweighed the possible good that might accrue by warning the small minority who indulged in the practice.[3]

It was admitted that the films which seemed daring from their publicity and titles were frequently innocuous. But in 1916 the practice of capitalizing the reputation of notorious books had reached such an extent that the Board decided that "no film in future shall be passed of the same title as a book which is generally acknowledged as objectionable."[4]

Apart from the special class of moral problem films, the main questions which occupied the attention of the examiners at this time can be roughly grouped as those of brutality and crime on the one hand, and general sexual morality on the other. What was considered objectionable was obviously based on contemporary standards, and liable to change. Decorum

[1] *Report*, p. 104. [2] *Bioscope*, February 25, 1915, p. 705.
[3] Ibid., July 6, 1916, p. 13. [4] Ibid.

dictated cuts if costumes seemed intentionally indecent—girls in bathing suits for swimming were permissible, but in bathing suits for "displaying their shape (was) regarded as prohibitive."[1] Convention also decided the point at which passion became lascivious, "the efforts of the actors, and still more the actresses, to obtain dramatic effects leading them sometimes to proceed to lengths which are quite prohibitive."[2] The Board objected to "manifestations of the pursuit of lust" and clear signs of the intention to rape; and it was said that the Board had succeeded in stopping the introduction into this country of "first night subjects" and "repugnant" stories based on the theme of unwitting incest, both of which had been unhealthily numerous at one time.[3] But it must be admitted that there was no suggestion in this witness's evidence that these standards were held to be absolute. Throughout the evidence the emphasis was plainly on the immaturity of a large part of the audience and their inability to withstand bad example if this was presented in an attractive light. The Board had objected to seduction when the treatment was such as to suggest that "a poor girl is morally justified in succumbing to temptation in order to escape from sordid surroundings and uncongenial work,"[4] while stories showing "women leading immoral lives" were condemned because as a rule they presented an attractive picture of gaiety, luxury and admiration with a final debacle whose powers as a deterrent were usually insignificant. In the same way a distinction was made between stories in which crime was the sole interest and was treated in such a way as to familiarize people with methods, and accustom them to its existence to such an extent that it seemed the normal: and stories in which crime was simply used as a dramatic motive, or "costume crime" stories which it seemed were "regarded by the young as simply dramatic and thrilling adventures, with no connection with their own lives or probable experiences."[5] The assumption was that the majority of the audience was immature, and, in view of the great influence the cinema could have on them, in need of paternal guidance.

[1] *Report,* p. 66.   [2] *Report,* p. 105.   [3] Ibid.
[4] Ibid.   [5] Ibid., p. 106.

PART TWO

THE FILMS

CHAPTER FOUR

Film Content

(I) FACTUAL FILMS

Elementary factual films before 1914, whether of topical, travel or general interest, had almost all been short. During the war period the actuality film developed in structure and content but in a much expanded form, and as the open market disappeared both the number of the simplest type, and the importance accorded to individual examples, diminished. Some companies continued the old form of production longer than others. Loving care for photographic quality and camera angle enabled Hepworth, for example, to dispose not merely of travelogues but even of a number of simple scenics at least until the middle of the war, and he developed with considerable success his "stereo-scenics," films using ordinary photography to present as nearly as possible a stereoscopic effect. Burlingham's *Winter in Marseilles* shows the elementary travel film at the beginning of the war:

> BURLINGHAM. *Winter in Marseilles.* (Released November 5, 1914, 435 ft.) Probably the most cosmopolitan port in the Mediterranean, this city, with its famous cathedral, is seen to furnish a capital "scenic." Views of the great transporter bridge are well shown, there is some remarkable tinting, and a very beautiful sunset makes a most artistic *finale.*[1]

But such brevity now seemed inadequate, and more characteristic of the period were Burlingham's two longer travel films, *Adventures on the Roof of the Earth*[2] and *The Filming of the Avalanche on Mont Blanc.*[3] The actual structure of these films seems from the written accounts to have been of equal simplicity, but as they were longer and had been secured with some difficulty, they were put out as productions to be featured by exhibitors. Kineto, too, released a film called *The Building of the British*

[1] *Bioscope*, October 15, 1914, p. vii.
[2] Two reels, released 1914.
[3] Released 1915.

Empire (1917) in ten reels, which reads like an expanded travel film containing historical information in map form.

But travel films, or interest films of any type not connected with the war, were of little importance. The pre-war voyages of exploration which had promised the film a new field of development ceased. And the only new film of this type was *Lion Hunting in East Africa*, a two-reel film released in 1917 of Sir Thomas Dewar's expedition in British East Africa. Some short interest films continued to be put out throughout the war, of course, particularly by Kineto. Their *Kill that Fly*,[1] a short film openly intended to influence people's behaviour, was an early example of the propaganda film. But the scientific film[2] was now comparatively rare and when *Floral Favourites*[3] attempted to revive the first interest in speed magnification it was observed that this was "no longer a novelty." Gradually interest films shorter than a reel became of very minor importance.

The virtual disappearance of the half-reel interest film could be attributed to the decline of the open market. But it was the war which was responsible for the simultaneous decline in the great variety of subject matter which had previously been such a pleasing feature of actuality production. For a while film people, like everybody else in Britain, could think of hardly anything but the war. It was felt that even the most obtuse could hardly fail, now, to realize the film's value as a record of real life. Firms that had specialized in melodrama or comics suddenly took to topical or interest production, while old hands like W. G. Barker, Kineto and Jeapes were in their element. Few were above stretching a point to give their films a war flavour. At one time all Kineto's interest films, from *Airmen and their Craft* to *Peasantry Round Smyrna*, were listed as "war films." And Hepworth's scenic of the Meuse was a timely release while interest in Belgium was at its height.[4] An ordinary film about trawling was connected rather awkwardly with the war by means of a title *In the Mine Strewn North Sea*.[5]

Many films about the armies of our Allies, our enemies and ourselves

[1] 455 ft., released June 10, 1915.
[2] E.g. *Wonders of Static Electricity*, 330 ft., released July 8, 1915.
[3] 405 ft., released July 29, 1915.
[4] *Bioscope*, August 13, 1914, p. 640.   [5] 799 ft., Yorkshire Cinematograph Co.

appeared immediately, and were popular until the end of 1915. Hepworth's one-reel *Men of the Moment* about the forces met the sudden demand with startling speed for, together with the Meuse film, it was advertised nine days after the declaration of war, for release two days later. "Everyone is wanting Army and Navy films,"[1] and Kineto put out *Ready, Aye Ready* (690 ft.) and *With the British Forces* (770 ft.) by the end of August. Much of the material used was old, as for example in Kineto's *Germany's Army and Navy* (1914). But it was not long before there were big changes in military organization, and "any other army film is now out of date," stated Dreadnought[2] in the announcement of its three-reeler *Lord Kitchener's New Army*. The public's desire to see films of the new army, and the new life led by so many of their relatives and friends, was met by a run of films such as Captain Kettle's *Backbone of England* (1914) showing army training, Kineto's *Britain's New Army*[3] or Kinemacolor's *With the Fighting Forces of Europe*.[4] Even Clarendon, a firm not usually fond of actuality, did *A Day with Our Territorials in the Field* and *Training our Volunteer Constables*. Neptune's *The Royal Divison at Work and Play*, a one-reeler subsidized by the Admiralty for recruiting purposes, shows little advance on the early army and navy films:

The film opens with a general view of the Crystal Palace grounds, kiosks and other relics of the days when it was a great entertainment centre, looking a little out of place amongst the squads of men being drilled. A group of recruits is shown; also men who have had nineteen days' training and already look considerably smarter. Some interesting displays of physical drill follow; it is evident that naval recruits go through a more arduous and varied course than do soldiers. The 5th Battalion is seen on parade; this is the battalion of which Lord Tredegar is president. Bayonet practice with dummies as adversaries, wrestling and boxing are demonstrated. Then is shown the training of selected bluejackets for officers, and the title mentions that all these men have since received commissions. Instruction in signalling and shooting is illustrated, and the men are seen assembling for parade. They stream past the camera in thousands on their way to the parade ground, and this makes a very effective picture. A fine march past before the Commodore is shown, and one or two humorous scenes conclude. The men are seen indulging in light-hearted pranks while waiting for dinner,

[1] *Bioscope*, August 20, 1914, p. 720.　　[2] Ibid., October 1, 1914, p. xvi.
[3] 625 ft., released May 17, 1915.　　[4] *Bioscope*, September 10, 1914.

and following the sub-title "Won't you come and join us?" two or three of the men wave a pointed appeal to the spectators of the film.[1]

Such films formed the majority of the more important interest films of moderate length until 1916. It was not until much later that the interesting Kineto film *What We are Fighting For*[2] appeared.

This may, without exaggeration, be described as the Greatest Short Film ever put out. Hundreds of newspaper columns have been filled with the articles and reports of speeches, the object of which has been to make the public understand what we are fighting for. But the essential fact has not yet been driven home. Words have failed. But the motion picture will succeed. The film brings to life President Wilson's stirring pronouncements: (1) That the Allies are fighting and will continue to fight until the peoples of Central Europe are freed from the sinister dominations of Prussian Militarism and have control of their own destinies. (2) That any nation of free peoples that compounds with the German Government compounds for its own destruction. The principal instrument in the German plot for World-Dominion was the Baghdad Railway. The nature of this plot is literally ploughed into the minds of all who see the film by the series of maps and pictures covering the three thousand miles or so from Hamburg to Baghdad. The concluding picture —The Power Behind President Wilson's Words—a fine view of American battleships steaming line-ahead gives a fitting touch of grim determination.[3]

There was a time when it seemed possible that the once-popular industrial film might make a partial recovery by using war material. Films such as Edison's *Manufacture of Big Guns*,[4] made with the permission of the United States War Department, aroused a certain amount of interest. Despite its title Palmer's *Fighting the German Air Raiders* (1916) was virtually an industrial also:

It contains many interesting and unique photographs taken inside Messrs. Vickers' works, where military aeroplanes are in course of construction. We are shown female workers covering the wings of aeroplanes with fabric, to enable them to withstand the great strain put upon them; bench hand fitters working overtime to speed up deliveries of vital parts; workers preparing and fitting wings to biplanes; and many other details relating to the production and manipulation of our aircraft.

The second part of the film shows us some of our aviators engaged in a trial

[1] *Bioscope*, April 22, 1915, p. 291. [2] 500 ft., released May 2, 1918.
[3] *Bioscope*, March 21, 1918, p. 56. [4] 586 ft., released August 19, 1915.

flight before taking up their active duties at the Front; two German Taube machines scouting for their prey; British anti-aircraft guns in action; and a fight in the clouds between English and German airmen. This last is particularly exciting, and ends in the German being brought down, his machine landing on the ground a complete wreck. As a wind-up to the film, we are shown some portrait studies of British aviators, including Mr. Harry Hawker, the daring Australian, Flight Commander Mari, who received the D.S.O. for his exploits at Dusseldorf . . . (etc. etc.)[1]

Nevertheless the day of the industrial film in its old form was gone, and by 1916 it had given place, like other short or medium-length interest films, to a new type of topical feature film.

Topicals, unlike other short factual films, had been establishing themselves as an indispensable item on every programme before the war. Between 1914 and 1918 the position of the newsreel was naturally very much strengthened by public interest in the war. In addition the topical drama described later, the now revived interest film, and the short news film all combined to form the long actuality feature film, a purposeful presentation of reality which was chiefly associated with the official war films.

The heightened popularity of the factual film during war-time, whether based on morbid or sentimental curiosity, was exploited by both trade and government for propaganda purposes. A number of official and unofficial propaganda films were dramatic, rather than factual, and are mentioned elsewhere; but one produced for the War Office may be described here by its maker, Joseph Best:

I myself went into the army in 1916 and was released in 1917 to make the first government film ever made. It was for the War Office—a film to show the evils of venereal disease. I wrote the story in twenty-four hours, had it approved next day, produced, did all the camera work, edited, made the titles, joined them in, and finally projected it myself to the Army Council—a one-man job if ever there was one. It was well liked, and some hundred copies were sent to all British and Allied fronts for showing to the troops. I made most of it at Richmond Park, using army huts, soldiers, calling and filming at hospitals, etc. . . . (It) was called *Whatsoever a Man Soweth*.[2]

A number of the "topical dramas" which producers made early in the war

---

[1] *Kinematograph Monthly Film Record*, January 1916, p. 107.
[2] Extract from notes by J. Best, January 14, 1949.

show the desire to present a slightly dramatized form of the reality around them. Pearson's *The Great European War* (1914) was a rapidly-produced representation of the events leading up to and immediately following the outbreak of war, and the company planned to bring it up to date from time to time with new sequences. More fictional were Frank Newman's *The Great North Sea Tunnel* (three reels) and *The Terrors of the Great European War* (1,000 ft.); which was packed with "thrills" not yet available in reality.

Vividly depicting Germans in armoured motor cars, entire village on fire, inhabitants flee, British soldiers fighting, shells explode around them, marvellous escapes, thrilling rescues, barbed wire entanglements, digging trenches, thrilling aeroplane flights. Rheims cathedral before the war, German prisoners, hospital van on fire, territorials entraining and many other terrific scenes.[1]

The desire to film battles as yet unfought led to Regent's *Called to the Front* (three reels), advertised as soon as August 13 with the announcement that "this great film shows Britons fighting, Belgians fighting, Frenchmen fighting and Germans fighting." Three biographies of contemporary heroes were further signs of the new dramatic interest of contemporary history. Samuelson's *The Life of Lord Roberts* (1914) was released shortly after Roberts's death and consequently had great emotional appeal. Windsor's *The Life of Lord Kitchener* (1918) was an ambitious film treating of Kitchener's career in Egypt, South Africa and India and finally showing the Great War, Kitchener's part in it and his eventual death. It was not an intimate personal biography but rather a six-reel reconstruction of certain events during the past thirty years, stressing the greatness of the British Empire, and particularly its military greatness. The third film of this type, even more scholarly in tone, was Elvey's film of Lloyd George, *The Man who Saved the British Empire* (1918); this was written by Sir Sidney Low, then lecturer on Imperial and Colonial History at the University of London.

But these long dramatic reproductions were only one manifestation of the increased market value of fact. Every form and length of war film can be found, from short items in the regular newsreels or actuality shots in dramas[2] to the full length feature film. From the start the large

[1] *Bioscope*, October 1, 1914, p. xvi. [2] See elsewhere.

international firms Pathé, Gaumont, Eclair and Eclipse continued to put out regular newsreels, sending their cameramen as near the front as they were allowed to go. Both Jeapes and Cherry Kearton, who was releasing a twice-weekly newsreel by the end of August[1]—the "Whirlpool of War" series—did as much as they could with the material:

The film opens with a procession of armoured cars, then a number of London omnibuses carrying supplies. The British Navy and Army men are seen in force and fraternizing with Belgian soldiers. The Royal Marines also make a fine picture, and cross the now famous bridge of boats. A corps of civilian trench diggers provide a somewhat tragic note, then follows the arrival of the Naval Brigade. Actual work in the trenches as shown at close quarters, and the wily Belgian snipers give an illustration of guerilla warfare. After a glimpse of the military field kitchens, and the men at their leisure, comes a remarkable length devoted to the "47 express," or armoured train, actually engaged on the outskirts, the huge Naval guns making the heavy train fairly rock upon the lines.
Views of blazing ruins under shell fire conclude a really enthralling "topical" feature.[2]

But cinematographers, like journalists, were at first denied access to the battlefield. Since the film industry now scorned the faked "incidents" of the Boer war, undisguised dramatic reproductions were for a time the only answer to the demand for battle pictures. The handicap to war reporting was attacked outside the film industry. An early letter to *The Times*[3] protested that to keep the public in ignorance of the life and conditions experienced in the army was a mistake, and that a greater frankness would stimulate recruiting. It even advocated the appointment of at least one official cinematographer. Nevertheless the difficulty of obtaining facilities at the front persisted despite protests for a considerable time.

There was an abundance of news material without pictures of the front. Farewell marches gave greater opportunities to the local lad with a camera than he had been given for many years, whilst the public activities of royalty and many celebrities acquired new significance. Films on the occasion of the sinking of the *Lusitania* were represented as a scoop, although their appeal was based on public interest in the disaster rather

[1] *Bioscope*, August 27, 1914, p. 793.   [2] Ibid., October 15, 1914, p. 274.
[3] Quoted in the *Bioscope*, September 3, 1914, p. 859.

than on the value of the pictures themselves, which necessarily consisted solely of library shots of the ship and shots of survivors returning to safety.[1] Fight films retained something of their old power, still appearing as long individual films rather than as newsreel items. It is interesting that attempts to elaborate the style of these films and bring them into line with other modern productions of similar length were not welcomed. The film of the Willard–Johnson fight in Cuba (1915), for example, at which the negro Johnson lost the title, was criticized for including shots of the locality and of ringside celebrities. The Harma film of the Wilde–Conn fight,[2] also, showed the contestants in training and spectators filing in and out of their seats as well as all rounds of the fight.

The trade and its supporters continued to press for permission for cameramen to visit the front. This was ultimately secured, although not until almost a year after French cameramen from Pathé, Eclair, Gaumont and Eclipse had been able to take and show films of the front with the sanction of the French War Office. This was in May of 1915. It was towards the end of this year that the group of topical producers in Britain was regularized as the War Office Topical Committee, and the first official British cinematographers sent to France. Early next year action pictures were sent home.

It was in September 1917 that Jeapes' Topical Film Company was taken over by the War Office Topical Committee,[3] and from November an official one-reel topical was released regularly[4] under the name of the "War Office Topical Budget and Pictorial News."[5] But it was becoming more and more obvious by 1916 that the short news item was not able to do justice to "history in the making," and the *Bioscope* printed an article which openly condemned the weekly or twice-weekly topicals for whisking so quickly from one subject to another. Any tit-bit of reality had been able to fascinate audiences when films were a novelty, but the novelty had gone. Now, however, there was magnificent material on every side, and strong motives for bringing it to the public notice. Both the wish to exploit commercially the widespread interest in the war, and the wish

[1] *Bioscope*, May 13, 1915, p. 623.   [2] 2,500 ft., released 1918.
[3] *Bioscope*, September 27, 1917, p. 23.   [4] Ibid., October 11, 1917, p. 26.
[5] Known as the "Pictorial News (Official)" from February 1918—*Bioscope*, February 28, 1918, p. 7.

to stimulate recruiting and build up morale, encouraged strenuous efforts to develop the topical film.

One interesting but isolated venture in film journalism was the *History of the Great War* started by Pathé in 1917. Using material taken since the beginning of the war, of which some had already been shown, this firm announced a weekly series of half-reelers dealing with events during the past three years.[1] An attempt to make slightly more of the usual Royalty item was Bertram Phillips' *A Week with the King* (1917), a one-reeler which combined the usual tours of inspection with semi-domestic scenes. An interesting symposium of topical interest was the project for a film of Cabinet Ministers assembling in the Cabinet Room, a project which was the centre of a mild storm during the summer of 1916. A. E. Newbould had been persuaded to suggest that such a film might be produced by the trade for charitable purposes, and when permission was granted (somewhat to his surpise, according to Hepworth's account at the time)[2] a committee consisting of Hepworth, W. G. Barker and George Loane Tucker met to discuss production. Hepworth wrote "It was at the first meeting of this committee that I let drop a bomb, which kept the said committee quiet for a considerable number of minutes."

All the time these negotiations had been going forward, I had been nursing a guilty secret which I could no longer keep to myself. It was this. For many months I had been quietly taking a series of what we technically call "close-ups" of these very cabinet ministers, who it was now proposed to photograph *en masse*. I had, in fact, already got this Cabinet picture in detail, and in far better detail at that, than could possibly have been obtained in the conditions that would be involved in the Cabinet Room itself.

Nearly all of these ministers, as well as a number of other distinguished people, had sat specially for me in a studio I had fitted up in one of the Government offices, and naturally, working on conditions of my own choosing, I had obtained good results. This series of "Kinematograph Interviews" was an old idea of mine, started as far back as five years ago, when such people as the Right Hon. F. E. Smith and the Right Hon. A. Bonar Law came down to the studios at Walton to be "kine-interviewed" on the subject of Tariff Reform. I had similar interviews about this time last year, but I found that the numerous engagements of these important people made it too difficult to get them out into the country for photographing, and so I postponed further pictures until

[1] The first was announced for September 10 and the second, a set of nine, for October 3.
[2] *Kinematograph Year Book*, 1917, pp. 43–6.

last winter, when a Government office was placed at my disposal, and specially fitted up as a studio.[1]

Hepworth agreed to merge his film with the new one and satisfaction was felt in the industry, for the charity seemed likely to add to both their profits and their prestige. But over-enthusiastic publicity aroused widespread ridicule and official agreement was suddenly withdrawn. Hepworth's thirty-six film interviews at Winchester House remained, and from September 1916 these were issued in three one-reel films consisting of close-ups interspersed with extracts from the sitters' speeches; 25 per cent of the profits were devoted by the producer to the Sportsmen's Ambulance Fund.[2]

Turning now to official production, this was not started until there had been public demands for an answer to the German official films which, shown here privately as early as January 1915,[3] were said to be in great demand in neutral countries.[4] The band of cameramen sent abroad by the War Office Topical Committee in 1916 and after have already been mentioned but perhaps the names of Jeapes, in the Middle East, and Malins, McDowell and Tong in France and elsewhere are best remembered. Jeapes and McDowell, running the Topical and B & C film companies respectively, and Tong—formerly Jury's factory manager[5]—received less publicity than Malins. If more is said of the latter (formerly cinematographer with the Clarendon Company), it is not because he took more or better films than the others, but because his book *How I Filmed the War*, vain and badly written as it is, gives a rare picture of the life of a war cameraman at that time. The job was a new one, evolved by the initiative and courage of men with few precedents to guide them. Filming the Boer War had established no tradition of heroism. It can hardly have seemed reasonable for non-combatants to risk their lives carrying heavy cameras into dangerous hiding places thirty yards or so from the German snipers, filming soldiers running out into no-man's land, falling, lying in heaps or returning with bleeding, limping prisoners. Development of

[1] *Kinematograph Year Book*, 1917, p. 44.
[2] *Bioscope*, August 31, 1916, p. 791.   [3] Ibid., January 14, 1915, p. 98.
[4] Ibid., April 15, 1915, p. 179; April 22, 1915, p. 278. French official war films were shown at the Scala in early 1917, and later the American official four-reeler *America's Answer to the Hun* and the Italian two-reelers *Amid Ice and Snow on Mt. Tonale* and *The Other Italian Army*.   [5] Ibid., November 4, 1915, p. 520f.

the scope of the record film depended on their own sense of what was possible, and their capacity to convince or override the often incredulous people on whom they depended for information, transport and many other forms of help. The qualities needed were those of a journalist rather than of an artist, and determination and nerve in the securing of pictures rather than subtlety in their presentation were characteristic of official production. It is rarely possible to attribute the finished films to individuals, for although the name of the cameraman is often known the assembly and titling was rarely done by him, and in fact much of the footage was used several times in different combinations and credited simply to the Topical Committee.

The films fall into seven main groups: ordinary topical issues and minor feature films, films of the Middle East, Royal tours of inspection, naval films, films of particular battles, and a couple of general or interpretative treatments of larger themes. The regular issues, especially at first, were very largely of scenes behind the lines, and showed training and the life of the troops, inspections and the presentation of medals or troops entering towns that were in the news at the time. *Allenby's Historic Entry into Jerusalem*,[1] a famous film taken by Jeapes which was shown all over the world, occupied the whole of one issue of the *War Office Topical Budget and Pictorial News* early in 1918. Slightly longer and more important were films such as the two- or three-reelers *The Men Ludendorf Fears*,[2] *The British Offensive, July* 1918,[3] *Ribemont Gas School*,[4] *With the South African Forces*[5] and *Woolwich Arsenal*.[6] Films from the Middle East formed a very important category taken chiefly by Jeapes, the Australian Frank Hurley and American A. L. Varges. Examples were *Palestine*, one of Jeapes' films; a four-reeler *With the Australians in Palestine*; *The British Occupation of Gaza*; *The Advance in Palestine 23rd–27th September*, 1918, a six-reeler taken by Jeapes; *With the Forces on the Palestine Front*, a three-reeler; *The 44th Remount Squadron on the Egyptian Coast*, one reel taken by Jeapes; another of his called *The New Crusaders*, a very important film of some 2,500 ft.; *The Occupation of Es Salt on May 26th*, 1917; and a four-reeler *With the Forces in Mesopotamia*[7] which was mainly the work of Varges.

[1] Half-reel, released February 23, 1918. [2] Two reels. [3] Two parts.
[4] Two reels. [5] Three parts. [6] 3,000 ft., released May 6, 1918.
[7] Released January 7, 1918.

Royal visits to various spheres of operation provided a convenient focus for several more films. Malins tells how he had been collecting shots of British soldiers in France and was searching for some "thrill" or "punch" to knit the film together, when he heard that the King was to visit the Army in France. The result was *The King Visits his Armies in the Great Advance*,[1] composed of material shot by Malins and McDowell. The desolate scenes of the battlefield aroused more comment than the tour itself, but the film was followed by *The King's Visit to the Fleet*[2] and *The Royal Visit to the Battlefields of France*.[3] Other naval films besides *The King's Visit to the Fleet* were *Our Naval Air Power*[4] and *The Way of a Ship on the Sea*.[5] More important was *The Empire's Shield*;[6] this was Admiralty material showing training, shipbuilding, the merchant navy, bringing food to Britain, the bombardment of Zeebruge, minesweepers in harbour and at sea, the Royal Naval Air Services, the building of a seaplane, the King's visit to the Fleet, the exploits of the H.M.S. *Vindictive*, and the Grand Fleet in harbour and at sea.

It is probably for the four great films of single battles or their aftermath that this phase of production is best remembered. These films, of the Somme, St. Quentin, Ancre and Arras, were shot by Malins and McDowell. The first and most famous was *The Battle of the Somme*, a five-reel film shot early in July 1916 and shown in August. It aroused overwhelming enthusiasm, and was expected to do much to raise morale at home and encourage greater efforts among the industrial workers. In Malins' own words:

The Somme Film has proved a mighty instrument in the service of recruiting; the newspapers still talk of its astounding realism, and it is generally admitted that the great kinematograph picture has done much to help the people of the British Empire to realize the wonderful spirit of our men in the face of almost insuperable difficulties; the splendid way in which our great citizen army has been organized; the vastness of the military machine we have created during the last two and a half years; and the immensity of the task which still faces us.

His Majesty the King has declared that "the public should see these pictures";

[1] 2,500 ft., released October 1916; alternatively *The King on the Somme Battlefields*.
[2] Released July 1917.
[3] Four parts, released July 1917; alternatively *The King's Visit to France in* 1917.
[4] 2,000 ft., released January 21, 1918.   [5] 4,200 ft., reviewed in March 1918.
[6] Eleven parts. Alternatively *Rule Britannia*, five reels, reviewed in December 1918.

and Mr. Lloyd George, after witnessing a display of the film, sent forth the following thrilling message to the nation: "Be up and doing! See that this picture, which is in itself an epic of self-sacrifice and gallantry, reaches every one. Herald the deeds of our brave men to the ends of the earth. This is *your* duty."[1]

St. Quentin[2] was similarly constructed, with batches of titles (sometimes heavily loaded with emotion—"The 'mark of the Beast.' Damning evidence of the German's disrespect of the dead") to introduce groups of more or less unrelated shots. *The Battle of Ancre and the Advance of the Tanks* was in five parts, released in January 1917. Malins had been present at Martinpuich in September 1916 when the first tanks had gone over the top, and these films, described as "Malins' Triumph,"[3] thrilled the public as the few still photographs which had been released to the Press never could have done. *The Battle of Arras*[4] was made by McDowell and Malins, and was slightly more developed in continuity, with a title for one item at a time. Its more connected character was noted by the trade, together with the finer photographic quality. Its content was less sensational:

In the first part our engineers are shown counteracting the endeavours of the enemy to hamper the advance by blowing up the main roads. Then we get a pathetic scene of Arras Cathedral, now a total wreck, followed by views of the work of the artillery, depicting every scene of the advance, from the taking of the Vimy heights to the capture of Monchy. We see a tank moving up to attack the German trenches, and watch the South Africans carry out a raid and bring back three prisoners. Then the enemy shells begin to burst and the bombardment of Arras commences. We next witness the King's Liverpools and King's Own Shropshire Light Infantry advance to the attack, and note the wounded being carefully tended by their comrades. Towards the end of the film we obtain a view of the Middlesex Battalion occupying an old German trench, and of the first Allies' train to arrive at Arras, after a lapse of two years (only four days after the advance). The Gordon Highlanders celebrate the event with pipes and drums. Then we see the Queenslanders and Tasmanians in front of Bullecourt, and finally some of the "immortal 29th Division" going out for a well-deserved rest.[5]

These four films conveyed to the public an entirely new understanding

[1] *How I Filmed the War*, p. 177.   [2] Three reels.
[3] *Bioscope*, December 28, 1916, p. 1261.
[4] Alternatively *The German Retreat and the Battle of Arras*, in four parts; released June 1917.   [5] *Kinematograph Monthly Film Record*, July 1917, p. 68.

of the complexity of modern warfare, and a picture of mud, cheerfulness and death in the trenches. Of them, the *Bioscope* said:

The release last Monday of the great "Tanks" film has resulted in a sudden blaze of publicity for the cinema of the most desirable possible kind. London daily newspapers have devoted whole columns to chronicling the event with an enthusiasm and fullness of detail rarely accorded even to the greatest of theatrical or literary achievements. With complete unanimity the entire press of the capital has urged the public to the picture theatres to witness a cinematograph film, the appearance of which has been heralded as an affair of national importance. ... These great war films, and such similar production as Mr. Ponting's wonderful Antarctic pictures, are doing more good to the whole industry than thousands of pounds' worth of advertising.[1]

The success of these films must have been due to the material itself rather than to its arrangement. The editing was very elementary. The order in which shots followed each other had little meaning, and the structure of the films seems to have depended almost entirely on the titles. The question of film continuity, and the confusion of literary and film editing, is discussed more fully elsewhere but it is interesting in this connection that the two films whose intellectual approach most nearly approximated to latter-day documentary relied largely on titles for the integration of their material and its interpretation. These two films, *Sons of the Empire* and *Our Empire's Fight for Freedom*,[2] tackled larger themes than usual. *Sons of the Empire* dealt in five weekly parts of two reels each with the winter of 1916–1917 in France: preparing for the spring offensive: the fall of Bapaume on March 17th: pictures of the Navy after Jutland: the arrival of transports in France: aerial photography: preparations for battle: and the aftermath. *Our Empire's Fight for Freedom* was in seven reels and covered the first two years of war—the declaration of war: its beginning: workers at home: a naval section: the great offensive: and after. Production of both these films implied considerable care in the selection of material from all that had been shot and both, particularly *Our Empire's Fight for Freedom*, were built into connected stories by elaborate titles. Those of *Sons of the Empire* were short until the climax of the film. But *Our Empire's Fight for Freedom* was welded together with

[1] *Bioscope*, January 18, 1917, p. 203. [2] Both early 1917.

very long titles giving the political, social and military background of the times and including quotations and speeches.

The *World's Greatest Story*,[1] a film made after the war by the commercial firm British Famous Films, should be included in this account of the official war films for two reasons (although it must be stressed that it was not a production of the War Office Topical Committee). Firstly, it was made from the same War Office material; secondly, it is a particularly bad case of the dangerous dependence on titles. Completely reorganizing the material shot by the official cinematographers, the makers of this film attempted no less a task than to tell the story of the whole war. This it did in fifteen two-reel episodes: (1) Preparations for the Great Struggle, (2) the First Winter in Flanders, (3) the Battle of the Somme, (4) Organization and distribution of Supplies, (5) the Tanks and Mining Operations, (6) and (7) the Great Offensive, (8) Munitions, (9) the Attack on the "Mole" and Allenby's campaign in Palestine, (10) In the Far North—Our Armies in Russia, (11) the work of the Archangel Relief Force, (12) the Regiments who comprised our Armies, (13) and (14) the Great Final Offensive, and (15) the liberation of the captured territories and the Peace Procession. The professed motive for this recapitulation was patriotic; at the box-office it offered satisfaction to the morbid curiosity of the bereaved as well as the solace of glorification; to the demobilized it offered an opportunity to relive fear and discomfort as heroes; while underlying the whole was the gratifying suggestion that the war had been worth while. Scorning the long, but sober and factual, titles of *Our Empire's Fight for Freedom*, the film attempted to take wing. "We show you . . . the brave men who went with throbbing hearts and tuneful lips to face the slaughter and carnage"—"Then all hearts beat in Unison with the Demand for Right"—"The noblest manhood of our race responded to the divine impulse which sought in sacrifice to prove that they who lay down their lives for the Right do not die, but pass to immortality"—". . . those sterling qualities which in War or Peace shall lead this Nation to a greatness which shall crown her as the mightiest Empire that history ever knew"—"Since the beginning of civilization War has been one of the great agents contributing to progress"—". . . yet in the far off years the loud thunderings of War shall sink into the tender cadences of Peace"

[1] Alternatively *The Greatest Story in the World*.

—". . . the first stone in the Temple of Ultimate Civilization was laid."
Words and phrases such as "bedizened," "myriads" or "the welkin rings"
were characteristic of the clichés and florid prose with which it was sought
to put epic qualities, nobility and poetry into an inadequately edited
collection of film material which had become out of date, but not yet
"historical."

All the known technical resources of straight cinematography had
been devoted to recording trench, desert and naval warfare. The films,
often of superb photographic quality, had to overcome limitations such
as the absence of sound, the impossibility of filming after dark, and the
extreme difficulty of aerial photography. Many years later soldiers still
wave and smile from the screen, smoke as they sit on the ammunition
dumps, wait in tense groups for the attack, or hang their clothes out to
dry in muddy encampments. Lacking sound or a truly interpretative
approach, and relying largely on such devices as tinting and titles to supply
the sense of drama which scripted films were learning to derive from their
structure, nevertheless the material is moving as only the factual film
can be. The fascination of such historical material is so great that it seems
to overcome all deficiencies of technique, and Malins' confession of faith
may be quoted in tribute to the spirit of the pioneers of this branch of
production:

My leave is fast running out, and I am nearing the end of my story. In all
the pictures that it has been my good fortune to take during the two and a half
years that I have been kept at work on the great European battlefield, I have
always tried to remember that it was through the eye of the camera, directed
by my own sense of observation, that the millions of people at home would gain
their only first-hand knowledge of what was happening at the front.[1]

(2) HUMOROUS FILMS

The humorous film[2] can be seen during this period, as before the war,
at several distinct stages of its development at more or less the same
time. Firstly, as in the previous period the simpler forms lingered longer
in comedy than in drama or the factual film, and were to be found at

[1] *How I Filmed the War*, p. 303.
[2] For detailed credits, lengths and dates see Film List at the end of this book.

A Study in Scarlet

Released in 1914, produced by George Pearson.

The Better 'Ole

Released in 1918, produced by George Pearson.

The Great European War

Released in 1918, produced by George Pearson.

The same.

INSET II

Kiddies in the Ruins

Kiddies in the Ruins

Released in 1918, produced by George Pearson.

The "Ultus" Series

Released in 1915 and 1916, produced by George Pearson.

The "Ultus" Series

Sally Bishop

Released in 1917, produced by George Pearson.

My Old Dutch

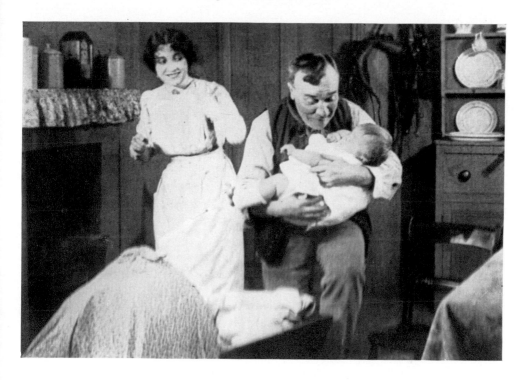

Released in 1917, produced by Larry Trimble, with Florence Turner and
Albert Chevalier

The Avenging Hand

Released in 1915, produced by
Charles Calvert.

least until 1917, especially in the work of the smaller or less important companies. Secondly, leaving the early impersonal "comic" behind, the development of personality on the one hand and of plot on the other progressed separately for a time—personality in the films of the music-hall comedians, and plot in the short story-comedies. Thirdly, at the same time, the two lines of development were fused in what was widely regarded as the highest form of comedy so far achieved, the filmed play with a known comedian from the legitimate stage.

The short comic with no particular plot or characterization continued to be a standby of many producers until the decline of the open market made more important "feature" comedies essential. In 1914 and even 1915 "an unpleasant surprise" still seemed to many producers sufficient of a grand climax; and many a "bustling farce" of less than a thousand feet was dismissed by bored reviewers as a "slight story, a sufficiently entertaining string of incidents." Even the "naughty boy" comic still had some life in it:

> CLARENDON. *A Day of Rest.* (Released February 8, 1915, 540 ft.) Comedy of chaos, caused by an exploit of little Johnny, who has been cautioned as to a propensity for noise. Grandpa is tied by the leg to a huge boar-hound, who follows Johnny all over the house. A trail of broken goods and chattels follows grandpa, and Johnny has an exciting time until he receives condign punishment.[1]

The trick comic, too, was still hopefully presented as a novelty and continued to exercise a fascination over a few producers, notably J. H. Martin. "Pimple's" skits continued to appear in great numbers and were immensely popular, and although in these the element of personality was becoming important, the style was still comparatively simple. Short mock melodramas were so common during the first two years of the war that by 1916 the trade press was becoming almost contemptuous of them.

Even these short elementary comics did not disappear at once, however, and there were many examples of films whose length had been increased without comparable development of content and style. Many of the "Pimple" skits or even the "Winky" comics of the Bamforth Company were over a thousand feet without being noticeably more elaborate than

---

[1] *Bioscope*, December 31, 1914, p. i.

the shorter ones. Clarendon's *Five Wishes* (1916) was another film which ran for as long as fifteen minutes on a theme which would have been suitable for a five to eight minute film. In this story a husband and wife, given an idol which will grant them five wishes, find themselves in many predicaments when their thoughtless wishes are granted literally. The simple device which brought this film to its close was for the last wish to restore normality. And this absence of plot was not unusual in films of even greater length. Martin's *All Stars*,[1] which was pure slapstick, was another 1,000 ft. film with the simplest possible construction:

> MARTIN. *All Stars*. (Released December 11, 1916, 1,108 ft.) The dressing rooms of the Grand Music Hall are alive with merriment. The famous big boot dancer, Wonwiff, has not yet arrived. Why not, it is suggested, play a practical joke upon the old fellow and hide his dancing boots? The great Wonwiff arrives. Where are his boots? Searching high and low, he at last sees them, nailed to the ceiling. He tugs and tugs, at last they come down and with them much of the ceiling, through which also slip Miss De Vere's shapely legs. Her mother dashes down. "My daughter! Oh my daughter" she cries and straightway faints in the arms of the stage carpenter. The fat is now well in the fire. The call boy dashes into the manager's office, "There's murder," he says, "ring up for the police." Meanwhile Miss De Vere is dragged from her dangerous position and the dragging breaks a gas pipe, and fire is seen fiercely flaming. As the boys in blue arrive, Wonwiff, hose in hand, lets fly upon the police and then turns the water upon the audience with drowning effect.[2]

Many films of approximately the same length and almost equally lacking in story emphasized the element of personality important in a film with a music-hall comedian. Unlike the early comics which created lay figures like Winky, whose brief but violent adventures left little time for characterization, the newer type of film, being longer, was able to give more scope to the comedian in this respect. As for the stories, these were little more than music-hall sketches giving the usual scope for knockabout. One of Lupino Lane's first films, *His Cooling Courtship* (1915), illustrates the importance of a funny personality and at the same time the short-comings of plot and setting often found in such films:

[1] Reissued in 1916.
[2] *Kinematograph Monthly Film Record*, December 1918, p. 98.

Of facial make-up, in fact (other than, we suppose, the necessary grease paint), he is entirely destitute; while his antics consist of very little more than a few stock acrobatic "stunts" (including the "splits" and an extremely laughable limpness under pressure), a dude-like preoccupation with a monocle and "the nice conduct of a clouded cane" . . . the chief actor is often right out of the picture altogether. The full effect of several comical wheezes is lost, on account of Lupino being stationed a long way "up stage" and once, when somebody pitches him off a landing stage into the water, his actual splash (with, we presume, acrobatic "effects") takes place about three inches *outside the screen*. Then again, the attempts of the producer to improvise a plot would have been entirely ludicrous if it had not been for Lupino's resourcefulness every now and then in coming to the rescue.[1]

From these films the more lavish comedies, with stories as well as comedians, were a logical development; and the most famous humorous films of the time were a series of ambitious productions featuring three famous music-hall comedians. The first and most important of these was Billy Merson, in 1915 and 1916. Bigger films were made by Lupino Lane after 1916 and by George Robey, who appeared in two films in 1916 and a further one made in 1918.[2] Of the three Billy Merson, working at the Cricks and Martin studios, was the first in this country to turn out comedies almost equal to dramas in length and cost. His first, which was a three-reeler, was much admired for the attention which had been paid to sets and costumes, for its script, and for its many supers. It would be reasonable to expect such films to have real stories. On examination these prove to be somewhat elementary, however, and it is obvious that farcical situations and the comedian's own genial personality and gift for mime and "business" were of more importance. In the first film, *Billy's Spanish Love Spasm*, Billy goes to Spain for his health; leaving his *fiancée* behind him he flirts gaily, eventually fighting a bull and discovering at the climax of the film, that this is his suspicious *fiancée* in disguise. This was, in fact, an expanded version of his music-hall sketch *Serenata*, and certainly sounds slender material for a film lasting three-quarters of an hour, although of course it contained subsidiary adventures. *The Man in Possession*, another "mirth-compelling farce" with titles which were said to be "as funny as a stage comic's asides," showed Billy

[1] *Kinematograph Monthly Film Record*, October 1915, p. 152.
[2] Released 1919.

as a baliff who was persuaded by his embarrassed hosts to dress as a guest at their fancy dress ball, and ended in a chase. In *The Only Man* he is a shopwalker; discouraged by bitter experience with a flirtatious girl friend he tries to bury himself in a seaside resort, but is somewhat hampered by the fact that he is the only man in the place; a chase over the sands and a resort to female impersonation are the culmination of the film. These *dénouements* are so simple that it is not surprising to find the *Bioscope* saying on the appearance of his next film, *Billy's Stormy Courtship*, that "what the story is about matters very little."[1]

In the same way Lupino Lane's films can hardly be called comedies in any developed sense. In *Who's Your Lady Friend* (1917) he played a husband who had to invent a twin brother to take the blame for his behaviour during his wife's absence, while in *Nipper and the Curate* (1916) the old idea of the chase provided the climax to a string of incidents about the flirtatious curate and a troublesome lad who dressed up as a girl and flirted with him. On the other hand George Robey's first film seemed to have more promise of the humour inherent in a plot rather than a situation. As the offensively virtuous chairman of the *Anti-Frivolity League* (1916) he sets out to convert a public-house gathering; here he is given a violent reception, as a result of which he has to be given a blood transfusion. Since this is given by his tough assailant, he awakes a changed man indeed, and returns to convert his own League to a more robust way of life. But Robey's next film did not repeat this neatness of plot. Called £66 13s. 9¾d. *for Every Man, Woman and Child* (1916), it was a skit on the redistribution of wealth. The theme, one of great possibilities, was not developed into a plot and was simply used as the basis for a string of amusing incidents; the *finale* was simply the old device of the dreamer awakened. His next film[2] was described simply as "two reels of Mirth," the avowed absence of plot actually being greeted by the *Bioscope* as a new approach to film comedy, and it seems that Robey, like Merson, treated the "story" simply as a vehicle for amusing behaviour or business.

Meanwhile genuine plot-comedy had been attempted in films not relying on music-hall personalities. The short romantic comedy with a

[1] *Bioscope*, November 30, 1916, p. 931.
[2] *George Robey's Day Off*, released 1919.

complete plot had appeared before the war, often worked out on the theme of confused identities or other temporary misunderstandings through which the audience was allowed to see. During the first half of this period a number of such films were made, principally by Turner and Ivy Close Films, with Ivy Close and Florence Turner as light comediennes in a very different vein from that of the music-hall artists. The Ivy Close film *Two Elderly Cupids* (1914) is a good example of this type of film. A young couple, suspecting that their marriage is desired by their fathers, perversely make up their minds to hate each other; but they are quickly reconciled when their cunning parents pretend to be opposed to the match.

Such a plot was suited to the one-reel film. But the desire to increase the length of comedies to something approaching that of dramas made it difficult, if not impossible, to provide humorous plots with similar unity. The one-reel plot-comedy was in fact the film equivalent to the "funny story" told in a few sentences, with a final *dénouement* to the whole. A film of three or more reels could not rely so completely on the story, and in the search for something more elastic a new form of film appeared around 1917 called variously "comedy-drama," "dramatic-comedy," "tragi-comedy" or "pathos-comedy." Two well-known films will serve as examples. In Hepworth's *The American Heiress* (1917) a young heiress falls in love with a local boy when visiting the country. Wishing to avoid a snobbish dinner party, she lets her maid impersonate her. After many embarrassing moments the maid falls into the hands of jewel thieves, from whom she is rescued by an admiring butler; when he learns that she is not the true heiress he dares to declare his love and the film ends with a double wedding. Samuelson's *In Another Girl's Shoes* (1917) is about the bride of an army officer who, returning to the front immediately after the wedding, is later reported dead; compelled to visit his parents, the bride is so bored by the idea that she induces another girl to change places with her on the way. The latter temporarily loses her memory in a railway accident; taken to the parents' home she is assumed to be their daughter-in-law, and when she recovers her memory no one will believe her story. The son returns unharmed, to everyone's surprise and the girl's dismay. He soon falls in love with his new "wife" and the film ends happily when the other "wife" returns, and admits that she was really married to someone else all the time. This was by no means only a comedy, but was interspersed with patriotic visions of "historical incidents" and even contained a close-up of Kitchener pointing at the audience. It will be seen that these films hinge on considerably more than a single comedy situation, and have much in common with serious drama, the difference being largely one of treatment rather than of substance.

It is not surprising to find that in their search for a suitable form for film comedy, many film makers turned to that tempting but treacherous source of inspiration, the stage. Adapted stage comedies include a tragi-comedy by H. J. Byron, *Our Boys* (1915), adapted by Kearton: a romantic comedy by MacKay and Orde, *Dr. Wake's Patient*, adapted by the Samuelson company: Barrie's social satire *The Admirable Crichton* (1918), also by Samuelson: as well as Ideal's *Lady Windermere's Fan* (1916) by Wilde and *The Gay Lord Quex* (1918) by Pinero, R. C. Carton's *Liberty Hall* (1915) adapted by the London Film Company and the popular comedy by Grundy, *A Pair of Spectacles* (1916), made by Samuelson. And although Turner's *The Great Adventure* (1916) was said to be based more closely on Arnold Bennett's book than on the play, it is worth noting that it had already been adapted for the stage. (Many other semi-humorous works are dealt with more conveniently under the heading of drama.)

If the loss of speech had presented difficulties in the adaptation of stage drama, the problems involved in the loss of verbal humour were even greater. The difference between legitimate comedy and slapstick appeared, after several experiments, to reside more in the dialogue than in the story structure, and the latter seemed to have little similarity to the plot-comedy possible in one-reelers. As a result the trade reviewers tended to give a cool reception to these films, particularly those in which the dialogue was well known and its loss deplored.

Among the attempts which were hopefully made to solve these problems were several films in which a famous comedian from the legitimate stage supplied an element of personality similar to that in films with music hall comics. An important example was B & C's *Honeymoon for Three* (1915), a romantic farce with Charles Hawtrey, which had a story typical of many stage comedies. Prince Ferdinand and a pretty dancer flee from the restrictions of the Court and hide in a mountain resort; here they

meet an American millionaire with his young bride and the latter, feeling
rather bored with her rich but unattractive husband, flirts with the Prince;
Ferdinand plays a joke on the millionaire by assuming his identity and
signing his cheques, but when the American retaliates by pretending to
be the Prince he is arrested by the sleuth who has come to take the latter
back; the film ends with Ferdinand and the dancer escaping in a taxi
chased by the Grand Duke, the sleuth, the millionaire and the whole
guard. But although the situations were in this case genuinely farcical
and gave much scope for "business" the verbal aspect had once more
proved important. A solution had been sought as usual in joke-titles, which
proved entirely satisfactory to the *Bioscope* reviewer at least, who described
as "absolutely *screaming*" such titles as

> Prince Ferdy to her room has toddled,
> But Molly refuses to be Molly-coddled.

Next year another comedian, James Welch, was filmed in two of his
plays, *The New Clown* (Ideal) and *When Knights Were Bold* (London
Film Company). Once more titles were used with some success:

Who, for instance, could help laughing at sub-titles such as this: "What is
the number of my dressing room?" "Dressing room! It's the second flap on
the right behind the camel." And again: "Oh, you're the camel are you? (seeing
the animal's head appear over the top of the canvas screen) Well, I've got the
hump!"[1]

It began to look as if the future of film comedy lay in the development of
neither story nor personality but in the comic title.

By the end of the war the humorous film had made important progress
from some points of view. It had acquired an entirely new dignity, for
production was now carried on with much greater care and at greater
expense; and better taste was usually shown in the choice of subject.
Emerging from the lower class domestic circle to a less restricted and less
familiar field, with the American millionaire replacing poor old Pa as the
favourite figure of fun, the increase of romantic comedy had brought a
more chivalrous note to laughter. A certain antagonism to women was
still to be found, now matched by a wave of female impersonation. But

[1] *Kinematograph Monthly Film Record*, July 1916, p. 130.

unselfconscious mirth at physical discomfort or humiliation was now concealed and subjects of greater subtlety were necessary as vehicles for such cruel jokes.

But this more dignified type of production was not accompanied by a corresponding advance in technique, and future lines of development were certainly not clear in this country. The most successful humorous films here, as in America, were those of Chaplin. It is true that the economic conditions of the industry militated against a similar world-wide success on the part of any British comedian, but it is also only too obvious that there was no British comedian deserving of such success. Perhaps it is unfair to compare British comedians to Chaplin, for he had few rivals anywhere. But lesser American comedians, too, were favourably compared with their British counterparts at the time, and the scarcity of British talent in this sphere did not go unnoticed. It was sometimes attributed to the lack of plot-comedies, for too many of the films were said to require no greater acting power than the ability to fall downstairs. But it is unlikely that the form of the short plot-comedy was capable of simple expansion when longer films were in demand. A further trouble was that the obvious need for more compelling personalities and acting were met in the usual way, with material from the theatre. On the one hand longer stage comedies—which in point of fact were loosely-knit farces rather than plot-comedies—brought with them a quite unsuitable school of acting which, poor in mime, was driven to rely heavily on titles. On the other, a short cut was optimistically taken to the development of mime by the use of music-hall comics accustomed to knockabout. Of these George Robey, Billy Merson, Lupino Lane and perhaps Charles Austin were the only ones of much consequence. Lupino Lane, then a cheeky youth whose dexterity and timing were much appreciated, made films of insufficiently high technical quality to become best-sellers in a market now crowded with more expert productions. Little came of the new films made by Robey, whose effect depended too much on his rich and husky voice, delivering the prim and pedantic remarks so strangely out of keeping with his robust appearance. The only one of the three with anything of the wistful appeal of Chaplin was Billy Merson, and it was significant that he was the most successful British comedian on the screen during the war. Even for him, however, the future seemed uncertain.

Cartoon Films

The animated cartoon was a new form of humorous film[1] which in this country was first produced during the war, and indeed was bound up with it. Few producers cared to make humorous films about the war, for such a theme "is not, as a whole, a laughing matter"—although this remark comes from the review of a war comic by "Pimple" which was admitted to be:

... ever kindly, free from bitterness, and inspired solely by the true spirit of mirth.

Pimple Enlists may be described as a skit on the German Army and the Kaiser, who are unmercifully satirized in this excellent film. Every weak spot in the enemy's armour is pierced by the keen wit of Pimple, and the result is a burlesque which (is) . . . pure and legitimate fun which can be painful to no one. . . . It is simply a merry joke at the expense of our foe.[2]

But "Pimple" (to whom, in any case, few things were sacred) was unusual in regarding hatred of the Germans as a source of "pure and legitimate fun," and for the most part comedy, unlike drama, was not topical. Only in film cartoons were current affairs the subject of laughter.

Animated film cartoons had appeared abroad some six years previously and American examples, particularly the Edison cartoons which were being released here shortly after the outbreak of war, were shown in this country before any of English make. There were also so-called film "cartoons" which were simply drawings, usually with topical reference, shown on the screen for a few moments as slides had been in earlier days, or with the artist's hand at work. Some "Ensign" cartoons towards the end of 1914 by the Anglo-Indian artist Frank Leah, for example, were described as "Lightning Sketches," and to all intents and purposes were merely film records of this established music-hall turn. They exploited the admiration so often felt for artists not because their work is good, but because it is done quickly. Harry Furniss, too, made *Peace and War Pencillings* which were shown at the London Coliseum for some weeks at the beginning of the war, and his *Winchelsea and its Environs*[3] was a combination of scenic photography and lightning sketches.[4]

[1] For convenience all film cartoons, including the few serious ones, will be included in this account.   [2] *Bioscope*, October 1, 1914, p. 79.
[3] Released November 12, 1914, 430 ft.   [4] *Bioscope*, November 22, 1914, p. iii.

The first British animated cartoons were made by Lancelot Speed, hitherto a conventional illustrator and painter. The first of his "Bully Boy" series, topical lampoons some three or four hundred feet in length each, was released on October 12, 1914. Some half-a-dozen numbers had been released by April 1915 and the series, made with the backing of Percy Nash and the newly-formed Neptune Company, had been applauded for their wit and skill. Typical subjects were *French's Contemptible Little Army*[1] and *Sea Dreams*,[2] the latter ridiculing the Kaiser's dreams of sea power.

The method of production was different from the separate-drawings system of later years, although both depended on stop-motion cinematography. There were actually two techniques in use at this time, usually employed together. In the first of them, the film began by showing an apparently blank sheet of paper; on this a figure had previously been drawn in blue so faintly that it was not visible to the film spectator. A hand would then appear to draw the figure with magical speed, each frame of film actually showing the pencil line more advanced than would have been the case if the film had been exposed at the usual rate. This, of course, was the method used in many of the "lightning sketches" and was really speed magnification rather than the animation of drawings. Animated cartoons, although not in the sense of drawings that appear to move (just as "animated photographs" was an early term for photography giving the appearance of movement), were made by the "cut-out" technique, and used what were in effect flat puppets. A little figure was made of cardboard or thin paper with the separate limbs, eyes and so on jointed at the back by paper fasteners which were invisible from the front. A separate half-tone background was then made, sometimes a very elaborate one, and a series of frames exposed showing the puppet in various stages of movement against it. A common practice was to begin the cartoons with rapid-drawing; when the character was drawn the artist would find some pretext to cover it entirely with his hand; a clean sheet of paper and the puppet would then be slipped under his hand so that when this moved away it would seem to the audience that the figure

[1] No. 2, released November 9, 1914, 375 ft.
[2] No. 4, released December 21, 1915.

sprang into life. Several items with cut-out figures would complete a four or five hundred-foot issue.[1]

Speed did little more, although some interest was aroused as late as 1917 by a cartoon of his about the tanks.[2] But others had immediately begun to enter the field. Shortly after Speed's work was announced Anson Dyer, hitherto an ecclesiastical artist with an interest in the theatre, was engaged by J. B. McDowell to make cartoons for B & C.[3] And in November the renter Davison advertised under the name "Tressograph Films" a series of War Cartoons by Dudley Buxton,[4] an artist who was well known, although of lesser calibre than Speed. Both Buxton and Dyer made a few films for these sponsors. Meanwhile in December the Gaumont Company announced "Studdy's War Studies" by G. E. Studdy, "Humorous Cinema Sketches by the Famous caricaturist."[5] Even such a small firm as Bamforth claimed to have a cartoonist.

Kineto, too, started its famous War Maps in November. Although they contained nothing elaborate in the way of animation these films, in their modest way, were an original achievement and carried on the tradition of the Urban companies in the sphere of the factual film. The first one was described in a review as follows:

The Kineto War Map is just an ordinary map of the war area, the positions of the various armies on which are marked in the usual manner by flags. But, instead of having to be contented with the fixed position of the forces on one particular date, we are enabled by the Kineto map to watch their progress backwards and forwards all over the huge field from the very commencement of the campaign. It is, that is to say, a war map in animation.[6]

This review suggested that too large a field of operation was shown at once, and that the movements were too quick to be followed with ease. In the second issue[7] the field was shown in sections with better results, and the *Bioscope*, now carried away by enthusiasm, made the further suggestion that animated diagrams might be employed to convey statistical information. The series was extremely popular, and continued at approximately monthly intervals for nearly two years with such items as *The*

[1] Technical information supplied by Anson Dyer.   [2] Handled by Jury.
[3] No. 1, released October 18, 1914, 541 ft.
[4] No. 1, released November 19, 1914, 511 ft.
[5] No. 1, released December 28, 1914.
[6] *Bioscope*, November 22, 1914, p. 377.   [7] Released November 30, 1914, 305 ft.

Exploits of the "Emden"[1] and *The Jutland Battle,*[2] explaining military and naval moves with a clarity which wrung this tribute from the *Bioscope*:

The achievement of the Kineto Maps is to place before one in concentrated form the true significance of various intricate and extensive operations. In a few minutes, they make absolutely clear and comprehensible important facts which the average reader finds it difficult to grasp fully from the muddle of official *communiques* and unofficial comments. Better than any verbal explanations these animated diagrams assist one to gauge the exact value and meaning of involved military evolutions which are often so perplexing to the lay mind when dealt with in the ordinary manner. It may almost be said, indeed, that these Kineto Maps are essential to a proper understanding of the War.[3]

Kineto, like many other firms, also released a few ordinary cartoons. Their imaginative version of the new tanks, which were still wrapped in some secrecy, was actually delayed for nearly a month by the War Office, and only released when the title had been significantly altered from *Tanks* to *Tank Cartoons*.[4] More important, however, was the work of Buxton, Dyer and E. H. Mills. Quite early in 1915 Dudley Buxton and Anson Dyer had amalgamated to do *John Bull's Animated Sketch Book*, a series of half-reel films nominally made by the "Cartoon Company"[5] which were sponsored and distributed by the renting firm of Ruffell's. Each artist working separately was able to finish one cartoon in eight weeks, one being released each month. This continued until September 1916. Broadwest announced at the end of 1916 that they had secured their services[6] and later released cartoons by them and by Ernest Mills as "Kine Komedy Kartoons." The first two of these, *The Devil's Little Joke* by Buxton[7] and *The Romance of David Lloyd George*[8] by E. H. Mills were considerably longer than hitherto for single subjects. Mills, already known for a cartoon of the Zeppelins called *What London Saw*, later did *The Entente Cordiale* for the same company. Meanwhile Anson Dyer's films were also increasing in length, his *Old King Cole* of December 1917 being as long as ·800 ft. In May of 1917, too, Film Booking Offices (another renter) announced twelve cartoons by Bruce Bairnsfather of

[1] No. 3, released January 7, 1915, 410 ft.
[2] No. 14, released August 17, 1916, 580 ft.   [3] *Bioscope*, July 1, 1915, p. 103.
[4] Ibid., October 12, 1916, p. 131; November 2, 1916, p. 425.
[5] No. 1, released May 3, 1915, 500 ft.   [6] *Bioscope*, December 28, 1916, p. 1260 .
[7] Released February 19, 1917, 750 ft.   [8] Released January 22, 1917, 750 ft.

the *Bystander*, creator of "Old Bill," which were to be 1,000 ft. each. These, however, were not specially drawn by the artist for the screen but were simply well-known examples of his work "redrawn" by another artist, and the same applies to the twelve sets of war cartoons by the famous Dutch cartoonist Louis Raemaekers which were done by the same firm from September 1917.[1] Each of the films in these two series consisted of from six to eight cartoons, and apparently were of the drawing-hand type. According to one source Raemaekers himself did at one time during the war go to the B.A.F.C. studio and draw cartoons in front of the camera.[2]

Only British film cartoons have been described in this account, and of these, only the more successful. But a number of other attempts had been made in this country to seize the cartoon market, notably with "Say's" *Topical Sketch* in 1915.[3] American cartoons, too, both important and unimportant, had come to the British cinemas in such numbers that, according to Anson Dyer, it soon became difficult to find a market for even the famous Essanay cartoons and Fox's *Mutt and Jeff*.[4]

At this time British film cartoons were exclusively concerned with the war. But unlike newspaper cartoons they were simple lampoons rather than political or social satires, and this not only because of the immaturity of the audience but also for two other reasons, probably connected with each other. In the first place, the length of time required for production was already a serious bar to topicality in any but the most general sense. Secondly, the artists attracted to the new technique did not include the important political cartoonists of the day. To some extent this was to be expected, for there was little temptation for successful artists in one medium to try a new one, especially one linked to the humble cinema. On the other hand it would be reasonable to expect more serious graphic artists, at least those primarily interested in capturing movement, to take up the new technique and develop it along their own lines. There are several cases of important black-and-white artists—Charles Dana

---

[1] *Bioscope*, October 24, 1918, p. 108.
[2] According to Gerald Malvern in an interview with the writer.
[3] No. 1, released July 5, 1915, 316 ft.
[4] *John Bull's Animated Sketch Book* was sold at £4 a copy; a 670-foot film by Buxton was hired in 1918 at £5 for the first six days after release, descending to £1 10s. by the fourth week

173

Gibson in America, for example—who did attempt to do this. But the demand of the time was for topical items and contemporary satirical artists, accustomed to daily or at least weekly publication, were probably discouraged by the inevitable loss of topicality. Thus, with mature political cartoonists unable to make use of the new medium and other types of artist not encouraged to do so because only topical cartoons were commercially profitable, the animated cartoon promised to fall between two stools. The appearance of movement so far achieved was still so rudimentary as to offer little aesthetic satisfaction or even the hope of a better future.

(3) DRAMATIC FILMS

The photo-play is a means of national expression. Art, Religion, ethics, and philosophy are carried in the shadow-drama of each country; the national code of honour is stamped on the film as surely as is the action of the player.[1]

This was written in 1917 by Harold Weston, a prolific producer, and certainly a study of early film drama yields more material for the student of psychology than for the student of film technique. For whereas few of the films are still in existence, many reviews and synopses are available to indicate themes, and often plots as well. It is true that accounts of the plots must be treated with caution, especially those published after 1917, when it became fashionable to write in a much more mannered "literary" style which makes both synopses and reviews less useful for the present purpose. But on the whole there is ample information on film-content and the way in which it reflected reality. This it did at two removes. For the picture of life given in these films is a deliberately selective one, showing the world as film makers believed their public wished to see it. Both the interest in reality and the nature of the distortions are significant. To trace them in operation it is necessary to consider the stories of a large number of films, some of them important at the time but most of them totally unimportant; it must be stressed that films are not necessarily included in this account for their merit, or even for their importance, but only for the significance of their themes and because sufficient relevant

[1] *The Art of Photo-Play Writing*, p. 72.

information on them is available.[1] It is largely for the latter reason that films under a reel in length are not discussed although they were still being produced in some numbers; the picture would in any case not be materially altered by their inclusion.

A very large proportion of these film dramas were adaptations of novels, serial stories and stage plays, but it is dangerous to classify the film simply according to the characteristics of the original writer, so changed did many of the works appear. Thus one dramatist or novelist known for his social themes may have contributed to film categories as far apart as sensational melodrama and sentimental romance. These categories, incidentally, are not always mutually exclusive and many films are of interest in several different connections.

Apart from the work of a few producers—chiefly the Hepworth group working at Walton, and the London Film Company—most British films of the period, when examined for artistic merit, seem better forgotten. But in so far as it reflects the ideas of the public and those who sought to please it, even poor and tasteless work is of immense interest. The content of the films represents a complex interaction of influence amongst which may be mentioned the development of popular literature in general, the logical development of earlier film-types and the freer social atmosphere which came with the war. A factor of obvious importance was the background of the people who made the films and their reasons for entering the film world. Examples among the better companies are many of the London Film Company players and producers, who came from the stage and who carried much of their stage tradition and theatrical connections into film work; members of the Hepworth company on the other hand were largely new to the entertainment world, and were very much influenced by Hepworth's own interest in the purely photographic aspect of cinematography and his innate artistic sense; while yet another influence was at work in the case of Pearson, a lonely figure from the unlikely field of education, who was inspired by a passion for films not simply as photography or as drama but as something unique and full of poetic possibility. Not the least interesting question is whether it is possible to gauge the integrity of the makers of various films from this

[1] See Film List at the end of the book for a record of British feature production during the war.

examination; in some cases it is painfully obvious that their motive was not a sincere desire for artistic self-expression but a calculated intention to exploit the weaknesses of their public.

It is in keeping with the premature sophistication of the early cinema that there was never a true film equivalent of either the penny dreadful or the later *Gem* and *Magnet* form of schoolboy serial literature, despite its very large circulation from the 1850's onwards. The only clear case of the adaptation of this type of story in Britain seems to have been Samuelson's series of separate *Adventures of Deadwood Dick* (1915), made by arrangement with that famous source of boys' stories, the Aldine Publishing Company. Next year Windsor put out a goody-goody *Tom Brown's Schooldays* but this was no substitute for Jack Harkaway or Tom Merry, whilst any demand for the serial form itself was met by the great American examples. The only true British serial was Nash's *Boy Scouts! Be Prepared*[1] which, however, was simply made to popularize the Boy Scout movement and although sufficiently successful to warrant a sequel[2] was not truly comparable to the hair-raising adventures of earlier schoolboy desperadoes of the magazines. The heroes, two plucky and right-minded little chums, had several adventures with wandering horse thieves upon whom they had such a remarkable effect that, according to the *Bioscope*, one of the latter finally became a Scout, remarking:

"I've had more excitement and fun since I became a scout than I ever had as a wastrel, and, better than all, it has made a man of me."[3]

Nor, for that matter, did the British film go through an early phase of morbid thrills comparable to the "Gothic" tales of the early nineteenth century. It is true that vampire stories from abroad had a short vogue during 1916, but weird and exotic British films were few and for the most part mild. Several stories of hypnotism, among them Hepworth's original story *The Basilisk* (1914), give early examples of a beautiful girl in the clutches of a man with occult and irresistible powers. The staple figure of the later horror film, the Being that seems to be a man and yet is disconcertingly beyond ordinary human methods of persuasion, made a comparatively inoffensive appearance in *The Man Without a Soul* (1916),

[1] Eight one-reel parts, released in 1917.   [2] *Boys of the Otter Patrol*, 1918.
[3] *Bioscope*, August 30, 1917, p. 922.

as a man brought back from the dead totally lacking in moral sense. Similarly the supernatural element in Crick's *The Avenging Hand* (1915), a story in which murder is committed by the stolen hand of an Egyptian mummy, was that of hostile action by something that could be neither understood nor controlled. Magnet's *The Monkey's Paw* (1915) contained a situation of genuine horror with its betrayal of human confidence, in the twist that makes the long-sought joy horrible when granted. This famous story by W. W. Jacobs had already exerted its ghastly fascination as a short play featuring John Lawson, who retained his original part in the film. On the other hand there was a more pleasant eeriness in several films of soul-barter. Probably the most interesting of these was Butcher's *Flames* (1918), a comparatively sophisticated story from the book by Robert Hitchins about a mystical exchange of souls between a good man and a corrupt one. Few British film makers at this time, however, could have conveyed much of the minutiæ of mental and spiritual change which absorbed this very popular author. Little can have been left, either, of the atmosphere of *The Picture of Dorian Gray*,[1] except the morbid associations aroused by the title:

To all those familiar with the book itself the film should be a revelation, so skilfully has the producer avoided the incidents that critics have taken exception to. The love that Basil Hallward (Sidney Bland) and Lord Henry Wooton (Jack Jordon) both manifest for Dorian Gray cannot be construed as otherwise than that of firm friendship, engendered by the boy's frank and open character, the only difference being that whilst one takes a fatherly interest in his welfare the other sets himself out to win the boy's affection through imparting a knowledge of the world to him. Dorian Gray's gradual deterioration through coming in contact with the worst things in life is wonderfully well masked, and there is not a scene throughout that is not a work of art.[2]

And whilst atmosphere was sacrificed for melodrama in such films, the exposure of social corruption, too, was sacrificed in the film of Marie Corelli's famous novel *The Sorrows of Satan*,[3] leaving only an eerie melodrama with a prologue and an epilogue in Hell. On the whole, however, the supernatural was not used to any great extent for sensational films and

[1] *Neptune*, 1916.   [2] *Kinematograph Monthly Film Record*, June 1916, p. 110.
[3] Samuelson, 1917.

visualization of the ghoulish horrors loved by early exponents of popular literature was rarely attempted.

Possibly the Lucoque films of H. Rider Haggard's *She* (1916), filmed by Barker, and later *Dawn* (1917) and A. E. W. Mason's *The Four Feathers* (1918), were the best among the few outright adventure stories chosen for adaptation during the war. But the plain adventure story was almost as rare as the old "sensational," or loosely connected string of incidents filmed solely as an excuse for some breathtaking stunt. For with the war as a ready-made background for all the "punches" the showmen could wish, the sensational easily outgrew its early story difficulties and, like the adventure story, became localized in France and Belgium.

A promising field was opened for film producers by the "spy menace," and the market was glutted with spy films until about six months after the beginning of the war, when they abruptly faded away. With great unanimity German spies were represented as cads, with an habitual tendency to assault English girls; sly but fortunately extremely clumsy, they were kept busy tracking down numerous secret inventions and deadly explosives upon which the outcome of the war depended, while their honourable British Secret Service antagonists toiled to outwit them, thereby saving such items of national importance as troop trains, London's water supply and even the Houses of Parliament. Many medically-unfit victims of the white feather were able to "win their spurs" in this way, although not all had the good fortune of one hero[1] who, walking down Whitehall one day, chanced to overhear a group of spies discussing their plans to blow up Parliament. Black or White Cross, Triangle or Circle Gangs flourished, and although their aims were obscure their connections with the enemy were suspicious, and on one occasion[2] they so entangled an indiscreet British diplomat that he was forced to seek the help of Marcus Plane, detective, to whom the most distressing adventures were mere trifles:

Shot at from behind, trapped in burning houses, stabbed in the dark, and finally "gassed" in a barred and bolted room, these are only a few of the thrilling situations from which the detective and his boy emerge triumphant.[3]

[1] *The German Spy Peril*, 1914.   [2] Martin's *The Crimson Triangle*, 1915.
[3] *Kinematograph Monthly Film Record*, September 1915, p. 95.

Detective Rex Omar,[1] too, was nearly beaten when his head was fixed in the top of a huge clock, giving him one hour before he would be beheaded by the knife hand. The "usual orgy of ridiculous and impossible sensationalism"[2] had its milder side, however, and many were the smart little Boy Scouts or even Girl Guides who were able to trick German spies of quite incredible stupidity.

The few spy dramas which appeared after the first vogue was over were more carefully constructed, with espionage as simply one element in a more closely integrated plot. Characteristically, it was when the spy film was no longer a novelty that the Hepworth Company turned their attentions to it, with films of greater individual importance. The theme of *The Man Who Stayed at Home* (1915) was the unmasking of a group of enemy agents by a detective masquerading as a shirker; a stage adaptation produced by Hepworth himself with the stage actors Dennis Eadie and Henry Edwards in their original parts, it was a long way from the crude and sensational spy films which had been streaming from the studios during the past few months. Broadwest's *A Munition Girl's Romance* (1916) was another more developed story attempting to derive interest not only from espionage but from its actuality shots of aircraft in flight and during manufacture, and from its treatment of the war-time development of women's work in munition factories and the partial breakdown of class barriers.

A number of Sexton Blake spy films struck the topical note,[3] but theft was a more lasting favourite and the possibilities of violent action continued to fascinate producers of the ordinary crime film. It did not pass entirely unnoticed that one of the greatest charms of detective literature was the sustained mystery and the final detailed solution, and that adequate representation of this in a silent film would require a very high standard of technique. But the ordinary crime melodrama continued instead to rely on mere thrills as heavily as did the ordinary spy melodrama. Car chases and last minute rescues were commonplaces with burning houses, cars diving over cliffs, drugged flowers, and such variations as the sliding bed on which Sexton Blake was tied[4] in front of a revolving saw. At the

[1] Crick's *Guarding Britain's Secrets*, 1914.   [2] *Bioscope*, October 1, 1914, p. 78.
[3] E.g. *Britain's Secret Treaty*, 1914; *The Kaiser's Spies*, 1914.
[4] *The Stolen Heirlooms*, 1915.

same time, however, the crime film was deriving much from lurid society melodrama, and with the advent of the gentleman cracksman or "swell mobsman" crime rose above the humble surroundings of petty burglaries and turned, like so many other types of drama, to High Society. Here the focus of attention shifted from extraordinary and sensational "punches" to human passions, and by the latter part of the war settings were becoming more varied and the personal relations slightly more subtle.

The law continued to triumph, however, and perhaps the only famous character who finally outwitted the police was George Pearson's creation Ultus, the Man from the Dead. Pearson's version of Conan Doyle's *Study in Scarlet*, made for Samuelson in 1914, had been a drama of revenge and was a detective story only in that Sherlock Holmes was called in towards the end of the film to clear up the mysterious death of the two Mormons. The "Ultus" films which he made later for Gaumont, however, were out-and-out thrillers and among the most important of the period. *Ultus: The Man from the Dead* (1916) starts with a prologue in the Australian desert in which the villain steals his partner's diamonds and leaves him to die; but five years later the wronged man returns as "Ultus the Avenger," traces his now prospering partner and takes an elaborate revenge, escaping at the end of the film from his admiring adversary, the master detective Conway Bass. The latter pursues him further in *Ultus and the Grey Lady* (1916), in which Ultus returns and leads the Grey Lady's confederates to settle an old score with the man who betrayed Ultus himself in the previous episode. In *Ultus and the Secret of the Night* (1917) he is found hiding in Devon where, with the aid of the Grey Lady and her followers, he rescues a child from a villainous old couple in a mystery house. This time he is caught by Bass, but in *Ultus and the Three Button Mystery* (1917) he escapes from prison while awaiting trial, rescuing a kidnapped Cabinet Minister as he himself flees to disappear, as it proved, for ever. "Master of a thousand disguises," the fascinating, elusive, daring and ingenious hero of these adventures may have been outside the law, but was inspired only by noble motives; ever careful of censorship, the publicity pointed out that the stories were so unlikely that they would never encourage crime or teach criminal methods. Written by the director himself, they were crowded with more "punches" per reel than many more lurid films, and yet had well constructed plots with none of the incongruities and absurdities with which less skilful writers enlivened their slender stories.

In addition to the spy film and the crime film there was another type of action picture which was fashionable for several years. This was the sporting film, parallel to and in many cases adapted from the popular sporting novel. Boxing and horse racing were the sports chosen, and in several of the films famous boxers or jockeys were starred. An early Hepworth example[1] simply used the ring as the background for a normal drama of marital jealousy played by their stock actors; but later the same year the negro boxer George Gunther appeared as Stewart Rome's adversary in *The White Hope*. Shortly after this Clarendon put out a one-reeler[2] built around boxing "fought strictly according to National Sporting Club rules," and late in 1916 a further step was taken by Tiger Films with *Kent the Fighting Man*. This was a long feature film produced by Coleby from a sporting novel and this time the part of the hero was played by a real boxer, the champion Bombardier Billy Wells. Next year Coleby used this idea again with Jimmy Wilde in *A Pit Boy's Romance*, a film with a similar story of a villain losing all when his *protégé* is beaten in the ring by the hero. Harma's *The Happy Warrior* (1918) was made by Martin Thornton. Taken from a novel of the best-selling author A. M. Hutchinson, it was about an orphan whose fond aunt's hopes that he would claim his rightful title were unfulfilled because the boy was quite happy earning his living as a prize fighter. The search for boxer-actors seems to have been abandoned, and this engaging part was played by the professional actor Harry Lorraine, while in the next boxing film[3] the young boxer seeking revenge for his father's death was once more played by an actor, Ronald Colman.

Coleby's *The Great Game* (1919) from a new story by Andrew Soutar, another author with a wide circulation, gave the public not only Bombardier Billy Wells, but also "the sport of kings," as reviewers persistently called racing. Racecourse scenes, described or ingeniously faked in so many stage melodramas, had long been a triumph of the melodramatic film; but with Barker's *By the Shortest of Heads* in 1915 the racing film came into its own. In the years that followed several ambitious feature

---

[1] *They Called Him Coward*, 1915.　　　　[2] *The Winner*, 1916.
[3] Broadwest's *A Son of David*, 1919.

films were made with High Society racing stories, of which no less than four[1] were from novels by Nat Gould, a famous popular author of exciting stories easily made visual. These racing stories, which were extremely elaborate and usually included a comparatively large number of characters and several sub-plots, followed a set pattern reaching its climax in a race on which depended a fortune and the heroine's hand. A necessary element in the plot was the attempted nobbling of the hero's horse, although usually by simpler means than those used in one film[2] in which it was bombed when out practising.

Although many of the extremely numerous war dramas also contained strong action, for the most part they were melodramas and romances rather than action dramas, and had far heavier emotional tone than these sporting films, for example. Their vogue, similar to that of the spy film although considerably longer, ended with equal abruptness. For the first eighteen months of war, however, innumerable war stories of every length and description were released. A few were sentimental episodes or stories with titles such as *Christmas Without Daddy*,[3] clearly descendants of the earlier "pathetic." Many, of course, simply took over the stunts of the pre-war sensationals and there were large numbers of films whose chief reason for existence was an explosive battle scene.

Most of the hundreds of war dramas were so similar that few need be described. Many were almost plotless incidents set in Belgium. In others a limited number of plot elements were combined and recombined so frequently that their abrupt disappearance at the end of 1915 must have seemed a welcome relief. "Outwitted by a child" proved a useful theme once more, with German officers or sometimes whole German companies playing the foolish part once assigned to criminals and being foiled not simply by children but by the old and infirm or even by animals, all of whom could fetch help and thus prove themselves equal to at least ten of the enemy. B & C's *Saving the Colours* (1914) may be quoted in detail, as one of the first films to use a number of situations which were soon to become familiar. A "nob" marries a nurse, Ruth, but her "ignorance of social usages and her *gaucherie* make her a laughing stock among the

---

[1] Holmfirth's *The Chance of a Lifetime*, early 1917; Broadwest's *A Gamble for Love*, 1917; *A Fortune at Stake*, 1918; and *A Turf Conspiracy*, 1918—all produced by Walter West and with Violet Hopson and Gerald Ames in the leading roles.
[2] *The White Star*, 1915.   [3] B & C, 1914.

ladies"; feeling bitterly humiliated, she quarrels with her husband, whereupon he "enters the billiard room and tries to drown his disappointment in liquor." Comes the war. Ronald leads an "idle dissipated life," and Ruth, "disgusted with (his) . . . apathy as to his country's call," herself joins up as a nurse. The now shamefaced Ronald plunges into the fray to redeem himself; he falls, honourably wounded and lo! by a happy coincidence the nurse who brings him back to health is none other than Ruth. Sweethearts, families, direst enemies, all were united by these chance encounters on the battlefield. The nurse who nursed the wounded hero almost always happened to be his long lost sweetheart, the leader of the enemy detachment was the German cad who had mistakenly been taken for a gentleman at that house-party just before the war. "The heroism and grit of the British soldier" was always a pleasant contrast to the insufferable caddishness, the "brutality, stupidity and drunkenness" as well as the "savagery and contemptible behaviour of the common enemy," whose main occupation or at least preoccupation seemed to be the pressing of unwelcome attentions on English girls—attentions pressed so hard in one film[1] that the lady was actually choked into insensibility, whilst in another[2] the heroine met the usual advances by promptly stabbing the despicable enemy with a paper knife. Nor was the hero of *Saving the Colours* alone in finding regeneration in the war. The air at home was full of white feathers, and bad brothers belatedly followed good brothers to the front: drunken husbands and even embezzling sons found salvation in honourable wounds, which, happily, were rarely fatal. Driving them to such desperate measures more often than not was the scorn of their women, who broke marriages as easily as engagements in their patriotic frenzy and set a remarkable example when they themselves went over to Belgium or France; for there was a frightening class of athletic heroines, regular good chums, who briskly saved many a village or company from destruction and rescued their heroes with repulsive efficiency. The Belgian setting became slightly more varied as the war progressed and the atrocities and romances took place in the towns and villages whose names were in the news at the time. But producers, at least, seemed to have felt the need to bring the war a little nearer home and imagined many

[1] *The Gurkha's Revenge*, 1915. [2] Phoenix's *In the Clutches of the Hun*, 1915.

invasions of Britain, although these were prudently limited to small portions of the coast.

Both during and after this first phase of war drama there were, of course, a few less routine examples. Companies such as Barker[1] and Clarendon[2] tended to use the war simply as the locale for a melodrama of theft and disgrace, romance, inheritance or any of the other usual ingredients, for which more or less any setting would have been equally satisfactory. As usual it was from the London and Hepworth film companies that there came more thoughtful work. The London Film Company's *1914* and the Hepworth–Chevalier film *The Outrage*, for example, both in 1915, were developed personal dramas integrally related to their war background. But after 1915 the battlefield seems to have been regarded as box office poison. Three years later there were a few more productions which might be described as war films, but these were isolated and of a rather different type. One was Sidney Morgan's *Democracy* (1918), in which the war was of interest not so much because of its possibilities for dramatic action as because "class prejudices are broken down, and real democracy is a recognized factor." Others were Pearson's two important films *The Better 'Ole* (1918) and *Kiddies in the Ruins* (1918), based respectively on Bruce Bairnsfather's cartoons of "Old Bill" and the French artist Poulbot's newspaper drawings of children in the devastated parts of France. It cannot be said, however, that contemporary fiction films in this country drew on the war for anything more than "thrills."

There were, of course, a number of military dramas not connected with the current war, of which John Strange Winter's novels *Bootle's Baby* and *Beautiful Jim* were rather sentimental examples. Many of the comparatively few costume dramas, in fact, were in uniform of one sort or another. Important historical dramas were Thomas Bentley's version of *Milestones* (1917) and Percy Nash's *Disraeli*. The former, from a play by Arnold Bennett and Edward Knoblock, was an early example of the industrial family saga, three generations of rebellious youth becoming old and conservative in turn; Bentley was resolved to make it a picture of changing times at all costs:

Thus we behold Dickens and Disraeli walking the streets of old London; Queen Victoria with Prince Albert at the launch of the first ironclad; a wonderful

[1] E.g. in *A Sister's Honour*, 1915.   [2] E.g. in *The Seventh Word*, 1915.

old omnibus and the first motor-car, the latter with its flag-man walking solemnly in front; an ancient high bicycle; the first telephone and the first typewriter; not to mention a typical modern picture theatre.[1]

The "gentlemen of the road," whether gipsies or highwaymen, were the subject of a small number of costume films, of which Baroness Orczy's *Beau Brocade* (1916) and Eden Phillpott's *The Master of Merripit*[2] were the most elaborate and important. Most were adaptations. A wistful desire to turn highwaymen films into the British equivalent of the American Western was repeatedly expressed and such stories, with swift action in the open countryside, may well have sounded attractive film material. But except in the case of racing films British producers had almost forgotten their old liking for the open air, and moreover their choice suggests that in the case of costume stories it was prestige, rather than action, that they sought.

Much was made of the literary and theatrical associations of the original work in all these cases. Particularly was this so in the case of classic novels, and this even when they reached the hands of film makers by the way of stage adaptations. Before the war, films of contemporary stage productions had been greeted with some respect; but now the few prestige films were more likely to be taken from novels of very varying merit. Shakespeare had been abandoned, and the only Shakespeare film of the period[3] was a disappointment. On the other hand a number of films were made from Dickens, as well as versions of George Eliot's *Adam Bede*,[4] Goldsmith's *The Vicar of Wakefield*[5] and Fielding's *Tom Jones*.[6] Apart from their fame it is sometimes hard to see why these particular books, rather than any others, were chosen. Certainly the qualities considered outstanding in them were frequently dropped by the way, and we find *Barnaby Rudge*[7] appearing simply as a historical spectacle, while Elvey's modern-dress *Dombey and Son* (1918) was but a shadow of its Victorian self; *Adam Bede* acquired a happy ending and was summed up as a "great heart story of old English life," while Goldsmith would have been surprised to find that a "quaintly pretty old English story" was all that remained of the *Vicar of Wakefield*. Grappling bravely, Ideal could make nothing of *Tom Jones* but a more than usually complicated inheritance romance.

[1] *Bioscope*, December 14, 1916, p. 1059. [2] Clarendon, 1915.
[3] Broadwest's *Merchant of Venice*, 1916. [4] International, 1918.
[5] Ideal, 1917.   [6] Ideal, 1918. [7] Hepworth, 1915.

Although it is convenient to classify these films according to their content as costume, spy, war stories and so on the classes are not always mutually exclusive. Moreover, many of each class could be described as melodramas and many others as dramas, and a more fundamental division than that between subject categories is that between these two different methods of treatment. The use of nineteenth-century melodrama[1] became very fashionable about 1915 and then began to give way to a more sophisticated form of drama. While at the same time the emphasis was shifting from events as such to personality and character; for the drama of circumstance was beginning to give way to "psychological" drama, the drama of thought and feeling and of personal relations. There is a possibility of confusion here. For, since melodrama tended to rely heavily for its emotional appeal on events, it is tempting to conclude that the two movements were in fact one, and that "drama of personality" was simply the logical development of "melodrama of action." But although the two developments took place side by side and were closely connected they were in fact separate—for example, many of the new psychological dramas employed that exaggeration which had been one of the chief characteristics of melodrama. In point of fact the shift of interest from external behaviour to internal thought and feeling probably made more progress during this period than the shift from melodrama to drama.

The characteristics of nineteenth-century melodramas were everything the merchant of "strong stuff" could desire, making a violent appeal to the emotions by way of exaggerated behaviour and forced situations, and usually ending happily with justice satisfied. They tended to have a fairly large number of stereotyped characters, of whom the chief and most obvious were the rough-hewn hero, the worldly "heavy" villain and his rough confederates, the wronged maiden and the adventuress. Sympathies were aroused and tension created not by representing these as individualities with subtle interrelations, but by using them as lay figures in whose action was embodied the righting of prodigious wrongs. In the course of the action many lands and social settings were encompassed,

---

[1] "Melodrama" refers throughout to the particular brand popular on the stage in this country during the nineteenth century and lingering on until the war. Dramatists of this school adapted for the cinema included Robert Buchanan, Charles Darrell, H. V. Esmond, Walter Howard, Ben Landeck, Herbert Leonard, Walter Melville, Arthur Shirley and George R. Sims.

with a fire, a shipwreck or a train-crash, rather than an emotional crisis, as the climax. There was a limited range of wrongs, however, of which vastly the most important were disputed inheritance and the betrayal of innocent girls—usually country girls—with wrongful imprisonment a popular alternative. The importance of seduction and disputed inheritance cannot be stressed too much, for they were the predominant themes not only in melodrama but in every type of film drama during this period. No subject category was free of plots based on them. It may even be said that the distorted reflection of the contemporary social pattern showed anxious preoccupation at this time with firstly the possession of wealth and rank by birth, and secondly the slippery social path trodden by women. The theme of the drunkard's ruin had recurred in films before the war so often that it looks as though the producers knew how much it meant to their public. But during this period the drunkard was a figure of minor importance in comparison with those two casualties of society, the innocent maid seduced and the man tricked of a social position which is his birthright. But to find these themes of social significance is not to suggest that they were regarded in this light by producers, or filmed for this reason. Both disputed inheritance and seduction were treated simply as private calamities. And when producers deliberately made social evils their theme, which they sometimes did (with much show of enlightening their public), they still showed a significant preference for Vice. This now included a few cases of drug-taking[1] and white slavery[2] as well as the old favourite, drink. The latter continued to be the subject of a very few special films, of which only the Chevalier film *The Bottle* (1915) and Fred Paul's film of Richard Dehan's novel *The Dop Doctor* (1916) were of importance as first-class productions. And, of course, it continued to be used as an element in many films of other types until at least the end of 1915. But it was gradually declining in importance and after 1915 was superseded as a social theme by class barriers and to a much greater extent marriage and sex problems.

Melodrama characterized by exaggerated behaviour, and moreover by easily understood conventions of behaviour, was obvious material for silent films of elementary technique. But they were made in very great

---

[1] E.g. Hepworth's *Morphia: The Death Drug*, 1914; B & C's *London's Yellow Peril*, 1915.   [2] E.g. *The Slavers of the Thames*, 1915.

numbers and the constant search for some new event to heighten the audience's excitement led to many absurdities. This fact alone might well have led to the decline of melodrama even had it not been for other influences such as the growing interest in social questions, the film makers' search for higher artistic repute and the progress of psychological drama on the stage. Thus it is not surprising that towards the end of the war a subtler type of drama increased in importance relatively to frank and lusty barnstormers. In the case of original scripts, still largely modelled on melodrama, the more successful were not those in which ever more impossible situations were devised. They were instead those in which the writer, perhaps unconsciously and perhaps even to his regret, approached once more the infinite variety and doubtful issues of real life. There were still signs of "that air of imaginative optimism which distinguishes true drama from squalid realism," as one member of the trade described it. But on the whole the simple antitheses of right and wrong and its inevitable outcome became more and more out of date. The famous old melodramas might live on their past reputations, but new and often inexpert imitations were increasingly recognized as inferior. A group of films purporting to be about the underworld of London,[1] for example, were received with a certain coolness even in 1915. And by the end of the war such films as Coleby's version of Marie Corelli's novel *Holy Orders* (1918), or Barker's *On Leave* (1919), were clearly seen to be lagging behind more sophisticated productions.

There was thus a marked tendency to adapt a more mature type of play and above all to adapt contemporary or recent novels, with their greater emotional range and subtlety. In such films the action tended to be less diffuse. For the stories could only become more complex emotionally when fewer people and incidents were included, and those given fuller treatment. In some cases the film shrank to an almost plotless intimacy. An extreme instance was the Turner film *My Old Dutch* (1915), which was written by the dramatist Shirley and Albert Chevalier around the songs made famous by this great music-hall artist. A slender and largely extraneous story was woven through scenes in the life of a Cockney couple, and such was the skill with which the appeal to sentiment was made

---

[1] E.g. W. G. Barker's *Rogues of London*, Regent's *The Underworld of London*, and Martin's *The Vultures of London*—all 1915.

that for once the absence of a "strong" plot aroused no trade hostility to the film, which had an outstanding success. A later Chevalier film, Ideal's *The Fallen Star* (1916), was based on his monologue about an old actor and had a considerably more defined story although still a slight and uneventful one. A greater demand was made upon the actors in these films, as it was in all the so-called "psychological plays." Some of these hardly deserved this description. *Esther Redeemed*,[1] which was about a girl "full of animal instincts and a predilection for crime" whose moral nature was completely changed by a surgical operation, was typical of the emphasis on the external results of psychological changes. Nevertheless even here the intention was clearly to portray a character rather than simply a pattern of events.

At the same time this type of film showed greater variety of both theme and plot. It is true that a new theme almost as stereotyped as the old lost inheritance drama was that in which romantic wooing took place after a marriage of convenience, as in a Garvice adaptation, *Just a Girl*.[2] But drama was beginning to show a greater elasticity. The London Film Company, for example, put out a version of *The Christian* (1915), a more serious novel. There were several stories which touched, however lightly, on political life, including Hepworth's *The Marriage of William Ashe* (1916) from a twenty-year-old novel by Mrs. Humphry Ward, a more intellectual writer with social and religious interests. Nor was the alignment of right and wrong crude and clear any longer in such films as *The Strange Case of Philip Kent*,[3] in which an attractive scoundrel set to work to swindle an insurance company. *Traffic*,[4] from a novel by another best-seller, Temple Thurston, included a fire and an attempted suicide by way of incident, but was more concerned with the problem of a Roman Catholic woman barred by her religion from divorcing her drunken and faithless husband.

Together with simpler action, greater emotional complexity and considerable variety of theme and plot such films gradually acquired a certain degree of probability, although many of the situations remained as unrealistic as those of earlier melodrama. In Hepworth's *The Confession* (1915), for example, an innocent man is saved from execution because his

[1] Renaissance, 1915. [2] Samuelson, 1916.
[3] Neptune, 1916. [4] I. B. Davidson, 1915.

fiancée, who happens to be nursing the real murderer, secures the latter's confession by preying on his mind. But although the central situation is unlikely, the film is significant in its deliberate use of psychological factors to create suspense. This short[1] film was an early and isolated movement in this direction. For the most part manageable plots and better motivation were found in later adaptations from the less grandiose of recent dramatists. Pinero's *The Profligate* (1917) supplied a well integrated drama worked out of the comparatively simple and credible relations of a guardian, his beloved ward and the unworthy young man she marries, and later in *The Gay Lord Quex* (Ideal, 1918), the same playwright entangled and disentangled a web of human relationships with great finesse.

Probably the greatest refinement of this new treatment of emotions was in the films of tender sentiment associated above all with Henry Edwards. These are discussed later. But first we must examine a group of films which accompanied this emergence of human passions, the "daring" sex films. These, which appeared in the guise of problem plays, were on the one hand an exaggeration of certain elements in melodrama and the new psychological play, and at the same time part of a general interest in social justice, showing itself in rather sentimental moralizing.

While melodrama was seeking more outrageous thrills to shock and excite, the new emphasis on feelings and human contacts was naturally bringing sex relations into prominence. Many of the popular novelists on whom film makers drew for the new, more intimate and more exciting material yielded anything from provocative light romance to properly disguised lasciviousness. The resulting films were of two main kinds: stories of marital infidelity or compromising situations; and stories of loveless, or conversely frustrated, sex relations.

Almost always presented as problem plays they ranged from old-style melodrama, with a new emphasis, to films whose publicity and literary associations were much more "suggestive" than censorship allowed them to be themselves. There were a few films which fall in this class inasmuch as they treated sex with greater freedom than of old, but which were free of prurience and were clearly expected to raise the artistic and intellectual level of the cinema. Such were two earlier Pinero adaptations, Hepworth's *Iris* (1916) and Ideal's *The Second Mrs. Tanqueray* (1916), as well as

[1] One reel.

Pearson's film of the novel *Sally Bishop* (1917) by Temple Thurston. But more numerous were films like Eve Balfour's *Love* (1916), which was said to be very little more than a string of love scenes. The two Broadwest films *Burnt Wings* (1916) and *The House Opposite* (1917) illustrate respectively the infidelity theme and the compromising situation theme. The key situation in the latter, which was from a play, was a man's inability to clear an innocent person of a murder because by doing so he would have to reveal that he had at the time been in the boudoir of the Home Secretary's wife. *Burnt Wings*, adapted from a novel by Mrs. Stanley Wrench with her help, was about a wife who decided to forgive her husband his unfaithfulness and even to adopt his illegitimate son because she, too, had been unfaithful—in thought. To one reviewer this film seemed to have irresistible appeal:

Man or woman, you never know but what you may find yourself in a similar situation. . . . This it is which constitutes the principal claim of *Burnt Wings* to the consideration of all who like their film dramas to deal with experiences which may fall the lot of any one of us. . . . It is sufficiently conventional to be recognized at first sight, and yet fresh enough to start a new train of thought. It raises several points of conduct and morality which cannot be settled offhand —which doubtless never will be settled—and spicing it all, there is, as in the novels of Thomas Hardy (to which in some respects, it bears more than a casual resemblance) the attractive flavour of sex.[1]

Loveless marriage was an even more popular theme, whether it was for money, social position or more obscure gains involving the honour of fathers, scapegrace brothers and suchlike. In Bamforth's *Paula* (1916) an ambitious lady playwright married that her play might be produced. This film, from a novel by Victoria Cross, is a good example of the stories which dwelt with relish on loveless unions and frustration. Since the unfortunate woman was refused by her virtuous lover when she returned to him after her marriage, she returned to her sick husband and nursed him until his death; by this time the lover, too, was so ill that only a blood transfusion could save him; this she gave, dying instead of him, presumably feeling that this sort of union was better than none. Victoria Cross was one of a group of popular writers including Elinor Glyn and Hubert Wales which exploited the growing freedom in contemporary

[1] *Kinematograph Monthly Film Record*, March 1916, pp. 94–5.

discussion of sex in novels which, probably intended as serious treatments of the subject, were of little literary merit. But they were full of situations which were appreciated by a certain section of the film trade, and Elinor Glyn's *The Man and the Moment* (1919) was another of a number of films which began by marrying the hero and heroine and spent most of the next few reels toying with the possibility of consummating the marriage. One of Hubert Wales' novels, *Cynthia in the Wilderness* (1916), was also used. One reviewer sounded resigned:

We have not read the novel, and so we take it that the above is a fair summary of the story which it sets forth to tell. . . . Candidly, we do not care for the story, for it deals with a phase of life which is anything but pleasant. . . . It does not follow that . . . it will not find favour with many picture theatre patrons. Personally we have no doubt that it will do so, and we merely speak of the story as unpleasant because that term to our mind exactly describes it. . . . We must take the story as we find it, however.[1]

The Woman Who Dared (1916) found its title in the fact that the heroine had lived openly with a lover, but the film was a melodrama rather than a problem play, seeking an undeservedly shocking reputation from its title. *The Woman Who Did* (1915) which preceded it, on the other hand, was a genuine problem play whose film treatment was significant of the whole attitude to unconventional themes. Written by Grant Allen, a novelist with a considerable reputation as a sincere social reformer, the original story told the fate of a young Girton girl who lived with the man she loved, but refused to marry him because she considered marriage was incompatible with feminine emancipation. The girl's views, considered nonsense by the *Bioscope* reviewer but at least not ignored, were actually omitted from Broadwest's film: instead her refusal to let her sweetheart leave her, followed by the suggestive title "some time later," put the story back on the level of other melodramas.

More popular than such tests of sincerity were ordinary marital or triangle dramas, which were produced in great numbers, not only from famous popular novels[2] but also from many original scenarios. Wives and best friends were betraying husbands on all sides, and many rival lovers

---

[1] *Kinematograph Monthly Film Record*, July 1916, p. 139.
[2] E.g. Mrs. Augusta Evans-Wilson's *Infelice*, filmed by Samuelson and released in 1916; Andrew Soutar's *The Green Orchard*, filmed by Broadwest and released in 1916.

hit on the senseless scheme of drawing lots for the women they loved. Motivation was frequently obscure and much trouble would have been avoided if more characters had heeded the advice of one film title, *Why Not Speak Out?*[1] But the reason for secrecy and misunderstanding on the part of the producer, on the other hand, was clear enough. For bitter and tangled situations had to be so devised that neither hero nor heroine was in the wrong. And although characters might behave unconventionally from time to time the implied social attitude of most films was strongly in favour of respectability. In one, for example,[2] the conflict was one of maternal duty and illicit love; to this it was unhesitatingly concluded that a child will be happiest if its mother cleaves to her husband, brutal and drunken though he was in this instance. In Harold Weston's own story *Shadows* (1915) a destitute girl leaves the young man who loves her and has been keeping her, and slips into the shadows to free him for a conventional marriage. Girls must be decorous—"he was a hot-tempered, but an upright man, and as soon as he suspected his daughter of departing from the narrow path"—she returned late one night—"he acted quickly, and turned (her) out of the house."[3] In another instance when "little Melissa, . . . sacrificed . . . on the altar of marriage to a dissolute man" flies to her friend Adrian Lovberg for help, the latter's mother forces her out on the streets rather than let her contaminate Adrian, although it is clear that she has no particularly hard feelings for the girl and is ready enough to welcome her after the dissolute husband's timely death.

The attitude to problems of nationality, similarly, was implied rather than expounded and showed an even greater acceptance of current prejudice. The simple assumption of countless war films was that the French and Belgians were heroic, while the Chinese rarely appeared except as members of some sinister secret society. It is unnecessary to add that Germans were represented without exception in the worst possible light and, as the war ended, exposures of the "dangers" of naturalization and Germany's commercial aims[4] took over the theme of foreign villainy.

Thus complacency about conventions, or at least acquiescence in them,

---

[1] Ideal, 1917.   [2] Hepworth's *The Call*, 1914.
[3] *Kinematograph Monthly Film Record*, September 1915, p. 89.
[4] E.g. *It is for England*, 1919; Broadwest's *Yellow English*, 1919; Davidson's *World Power or Downfall*, 1918.

was found even in "social problem" films. The fascination which the latter had for many producers certainly lay in the surreptitious delights of convention outraged, rather than in the opportunity of preaching reform. It is understandable that film makers should have been wary of Puritanical opposition to the discussion of sex and marriage. But even in the discussion of class can be seen the idea that audiences always wanted morals to be pointed in favour of established custom. Once more, as in the case of sex and nationality, a definite attitude to class was implied in countless films not raising it as a controversial issue. For example, men might marry their social inferiors and in melodrama were actually more likely to do so than not: women, never. The question of class was clearer, but still incidental to the theme, in films as different as Nash's adaptation of the old melodrama *The Coal King* (1916) and Elvey's film of *Hindle Wakes*. *The Coal King* was simply an inheritance story about two babies who were exchanged at birth, the coal king's son growing up a fine manly miner who rose to be manager while the wet nurse's son, brought up by the coal king, proved to be a waster and a cad. The play *Hindle Wakes*, on the other hand, was by a realistic playwright of the Lancashire school, Stanley Houghton, who had died a few years previously at the age of only thirty-two. In this refreshing film the mill-girl heroine turned down the chance of marrying her socially superior seducer for the very good reason that she did not feel like doing so. Such common sense was not usual. More typical were the sentimental satisfactions of Tom Robertson's famous play *Caste* (1916), adapted by Larry Trimble, in which grief over the reported death of a young soldier united, for the first time, his aristocratic mother and his wife—"beautiful and noble, but a commoner." And more explicit treatments tended to teach the folly of disregarding class barriers. Henry Edwards's production *East Is East* (1917) was the story of a Cockney girl who inherited a fortune and left her humble lover on the hop fields for the treacherous places of the West End; here she learnt that Home—the lover's strong young arms, still down in the hop fields—is best.

This pleasant complacency did not mean that social injustice was never used as a theme, but only that very few films, if any, were inspired by genuine indignation. Instead, the few films about social inequality seem to have been made for two main reasons. One was a lingering idea that the humble majority would like to see their own lives dramatized on the screen. The other was the same literary impulse that led to the adaptation of so many costume dramas.

The idea that the public would get most satisfaction from stories about people like themselves had been behind many a film of lower class life before the war. Its more sophisticated recent manifestation was the belief that triangle and drink dramas would have an unfailing appeal because they "might happen to anybody." But recent practice was for the producer to let his audience identify themselves with superior people, rather than to reverse the procedure and identify his characters with the audience. The latter's pleasure in royalty, for example, was recognized in a number of Ruritanian-type romances.[1] But the older idea died hard and in several films made by the Walton group, in particular, it was carried further than before. In *For Her People* the labour movement was symbolized in the romantic triangle of the mill girl, the manager's son and the honest young workman devoted to the cause of labour. The film, which was neither a love story nor a social problem play, was set in the cotton industry and was expected to do well in the industrial areas of the North. In 1914, also, *The Life of a London Shopgirl* was produced and billed by Motograph as "depicting the evils of the 'living-in system.' " This was in reality the usual melodrama of a poor working girl, but next year a more deliberate cultivation of this particular group of the population can be suspected behind *Shopgirls*. It was put about that this film had been written by Florence Turner, and that she had worked in a large American store in order to get the correct atmosphere for a "social document," and although the story was little less melodramatic than the Motograph film it seems to have achieved an effect of greater realism and sincerity. Once again, it was to the shopgirls themselves that this story of their oppression was expected to appeal. In 1915, too, W. J. Elliott's original scenario *The Sweater* was filmed by the Hepworth company. About a girl who falls into the clutches of the Master Sweater, according to reports it had been written after a stay in Bermondsey and Poplar, where Elliott had "studied conditions." It was said to be a "plain unvarnished tale of life revealing

[1] Anthony Hope's *Prisoner of Zenda* and *Rupert of Hentzau*, London Film Company, 1915; *For Love and the Crown*, Anchor, 1914; *A Royal Love*, Trans-Atlantic, 1916; Walter Melville's *The Lifeguardsman*, B.A.F.C., 1917; Tom Gallon's *The Princess of Happy Chance*, Elvey, 1916.

the hideous realities of sweating . . . of slow murder by the worst form of capitalism . . . the ghastly crime of the whole system is laid bare, and no one could say that the fact has been distorted in any way."[1]

The rarity of such films suggests that audiences did not care for even this degree of realism in the depressing matter of social inequality. This did not prevent the filming of a number of works famous as expressions of social indignation. But once again, as in the case of the costume films based on novels, the quality on which the fame of the original work rested was usually reduced to a shadow in the process of adaptation. Once more the story and the prestige were borrowed but not the meaning. Defects in the prison system no longer emerged from Galsworthy's *Justice*[2] or *It's Never Too Late To Mend*,[3] the latter made from Shirley's thirty-year old play of the book by Charles Reade. *Red Pottage*, a satirical attack on the middle classes by Mary Cholmondeley, appeared simply as a love story; and Sims' song of twenty years before showing the hardships of the poor, *Christmas Day in the Workhouse* (1914), was a novelty for patrons who "enjoy a spell of lachrymation." Dickens fared worse than usual. *A Christmas Carol*[4] omitted

those vexed social questions which, however excellent as a means to point a moral by force of contrast, may be considered by many to hamper the novelist's delightful humour and playful fancy.[5]

As a result it became "so Christmasy," ". . . breathing the very spirit of the Christmas season as everyone would wish it to be. . . ."[6] *Hard Times*,[7] too, lacked "the writer's own peculiar charm and quaintness of expression," and moreover:

Some of the worst of the evils of Lancashire life prevalent in Dickens' time have now been remedied, and perhaps Mr. Bentley was right in toning down these elements of the story. At any rate, the sense of bitterness and indignation

---

[1] *Kinematograph Monthly Film Record*, August 1915, p. 60.
A curious item in the film industry's very limited crusade against social injustice was a film made in 1916 by a small Birmingham company and treated with some contempt by others in the trade. This was *Truth and Justice*, six episodes dramatizing glaring social abuses which were interspersed with shots of Horatio Bottomley, the much-publicized editor of *John Bull*, demanding—with as much emphasis as a silent film of immature technique could afford him—"Is this justice?" [2] Elvey, 1917.
[3] Martin, 1918. [4] London Film Company, 1914.
[5] *Bioscope*, November 5, 1914, p. 509. [6] Ibid. [7] Trans-Atlantic, 1915.

and biting satire left by the book has almost entirely disappeared in the film.[1]

Despite this apparent unwillingness to face any but the spicier social problems there were a number of avowed propaganda films, all of which, however, were on more or less uncontroversial subjects. Some were inspired or sponsored by interested bodies, but not all. Most of them, of course, were connected in varying degrees with the war, and therefore of particular interest to the public at the time. The officially sponsored war films included not only factual material but fiction or semi-narrative films such as Dewsbury's well-known "food film" *Everybody's Business* (1917) and others which have been mentioned elsewhere. But in addition there were very many ordinary commercial films, ranging from fully developed drama to simple scenes or incidents pointing a moral, whose much-publicized mission was to encourage recruiting or drive home the results of strikes and slacking in munition factories. But this was not all. Clarendon's *If Thou Wert Blind* (1918) and Elvey's *Comradeship* (1919), the respective profits of which were to be devoted to St. Dunstan's and the Red Cross, were connected with the war only in so far as both had blind heroes at a time when wounded ex-servicemen were attracting more and more attention. While the scout subjects mentioned above, filmed by Nash as an ordinary commercial venture although with Baden Powell's approval, were deliberately chosen by their producer because he felt that the Scout movement was worthy of encouragement.[2] *Motherhood*[3] was simply social propaganda in story form; written for the National Baby Week Council by Dorothea Baird, it contrasted a slut whose baby dies with a good mother who takes full advantage of infant welfare services, and was not related to the war.

These films were welcomed on principle by some sections of the trade. But appeals to the spectator's social conscience, especially those tiresomely exhorting action, were probably only acceptable when they dealt with the emotional focus of the time, the war. On the other hand it was commonly felt that picture audiences enjoyed a little sermon, and films which allowed them to feel sentimental satisfaction with the established code of personal morality were as frequent as those vindicating social convention. In a way,

[1] *Kinematograph Monthly Film Report*, October 1915, pp. 113–5.
[2] According to Nash in an interview with the author.   [3] Trans-Atlantic, 1917.

most melodramas and many more advanced dramas did this; for "right" always triumphed and few heroes or heroines were half-heartedly pure. But such stories simply accepted the code and the need for it to prevail in the end. There were in addition a number of films in which a moral generalization was the theme itself. For this was the age not only of *Intolerance* but a number of lesser films with equally accusing titles: *Greed, Sin, Infidelity, The Sins of Man, Love and Hate, Selfishness*. Griffith's own moral tone may have been emulated by other film makers. But his use of the film in this respect seems to have been in keeping with the spirit of the time rather than ahead of it. Two British treatments of similarly universal themes were Broadwest's film of Newman Flower's book *Is God Dead?*[1] and Bentley's *The Divine Gift* (1919), in which an after-dinner discussion of the greatest gift with which a human being could be endowed formed the prologue to a set of stories representing different human virtues. Several more films[2] taught the comforting philosophy that worldly wealth was dust and ashes. The tone of most of these films was extremely sentimental, many of the titles dreary: *If Thou Wert Blind* (1918), *One Shall Be Taken* (1914), *All the Sad World Needs* (1919), *Whoso is Without Sin* (1916). Needless to say, death was *The Wages of Sin* (1919) in the version of the Victorian best-seller by "Lucas Malet," a serious novelist of some literary merit and the daughter of Charles Kingsley. In general the theme might be moral teaching—"do as you would be done by"; or practical justification of moral behaviour—"virtue pays"; or simply moralizing in the manner of the old pathetics, which had always tended to be priggish—

> Just the art of being kind,
> Is all the sad world needs.

But if these films took over the sentimental moralizing of the pathetics, their sentimental search for beauty turned up once more in the "song films." Productions based on poems or songs were not new in 1914, when Neptune and Clarendon respectively made *Enoch Arden* and *The Gardener's Daughter* from two of Tennyson's poems; in previous years they had provided

---

[1] *The Answer*, 1916.
[2] *Tatterley*, Lucoque, 1916; *Profit—And the Loss*, Ideal, 1917; *The Treasure of Heaven*, Tiger, 1917.

such moral little scenes as Paul's *Ora Pro Nobis* of about 1900. But it was in 1915 that the Chevalier film *My Old Dutch* gave a new impetus to the idea of integrating films with their musical accompaniment by basing them on songs. During the next few years a stream of these song films[1] added a well-known musical accompaniment to the advantages of ready-made stories and fame, which songs shared with all other forms of adaptation. It was, in any case, merely a new manifestation of the "pictorially illustrated" songs which had once been a feature of lantern slide entertainments. The songs chosen were sentimental ballads, and although the stories were sometimes extremely melodramatic the intention to capture lyrical beauty was clearly to the fore. But before long the severe limitations of the form, in which excerpts of verse were usually alternated with pictorial illustrations, began to irritate reviewers. It was also noted with growing disapproval that in many cases the story of the song was either unsuitable or non-existent, the title and music being simply exploited to attract audiences to an otherwise inferior film. This they certainly did for a while. Hepworth writes:

Annie Laurie was an utter failure as first made—I forget what it was called —until we renamed it *Annie Laurie* and put the verse on the screen. It sold well then but was still very bad.

Thus we finally come to a small number of purely sentimental films. Neither moralizing nor amazing, exciting nor spectacular, their stories are conspicuous for the comparative skill with which they played on the tenderness and sensibility of the audience. With a truer aim, they could afford to strike more gently. And it is among these films, and above all in the type of hero found in a number of Henry Edwards's films, that the most subtle appeal of the period is to be found. As usual, several were from plays and novels of tested powers. At least one was filmed by B.A.F.C.,[2] a company known for its sentimentality, and others were made by producers such as Barker[3] and Nash,[4] who were usually busy with stronger stuff. Hepworth, as might be expected, was much at home in

[1] 1916: *Abide With Me*, Hepworth's *Annie Laurie*; 1917: Clarendon's *Asthore, Home Sweet Home, On the Banks of Allan Water, Queen of My Heart*; Windsor's *Ora Pro Nobis*; 1918: Progress' *Because;* Davidson's *For All Eternity*; Ideal's *Auld Robin Gray*; Monarch's *Master of Grays.*   [2] *Once Upon a Time*, 1918.   [3] *Diana of Dobson's*, 1917.
[4] *The Little Minister*, 1915; *The Elder Miss Blossom*, 1918.

this field. *Sweet Lavender*[1] was from Pinero's play of a bachelor who took under his care a poor woman and her child; *Molly Bawn*[2] was an adaptation of Mrs. Hungerford's uneventful romance of Victorian Ireland; and *Comin' Thro' the Rye*,[3] from the novel by Helen Mathers, was a simple love story with a sad ending. These three important films, produced by Hepworth himself, were all adaptations. On the other hand, most of Henry Edwards's films were from his own scenarios. Producing and playing in them himself, he deliberately developed a hero who, sensitive and gentle, was at a touching disadvantage in some important respect. *Lost and Won* (1915), during the course of which the hero was reduced to beggary, was written and acted by him with Florence Turner as co-star. It was one of his first appearances and was produced for Turner Films by Larry Trimble.[4] *East Is East* was a play adapted, produced and acted by Edwards which has already been described, and in which the patient humility of the hero was beginning to take shape. This was further developed in *Merely Mrs. Stubbs*, for which he acted as writer, producer and star. The story of this film, of a newsboy who marries an heiress and proves himself worthy of her, hangs on the familiar devices of a conditional will and a marriage of convenience followed by love, and it would be easy to laugh at it as improbable and extremely sentimental. His next films *Dick Carson Wins Through* (1917), *Broken Threads* (1917) and *Towards the Light* (1918), in which Edwards played in turn a social failure, a sad and gentle lunatic and a hunchback of conspicuously tender feelings, were possibly even more improbable and sentimental. Nevertheless, their plot construction was deft and their sentimental appeal made with rare skill. In Henry Edwards the British film industry had at last acquired a hero of full "star" status, and it would be a superficial analysis that overlooked the part his own stories played in building this reputation. All the films of this group compare favourably with any of the hundreds of melodramas in at least two important points of development. Their relatively simple stories depend on the interplay of character and situation for effect; and, moreover, they enlist sympathy not by the creation of perfect people but by the

---

[1] Made in 1915.   [2] Made in 1916, released in 1918.   [3] Made in 1916.
[4] *A Welsh Singer* (1915) later in the same year was from an immensely popular romance by the woman novelist "Allen Raine," and was a more melodramatic film which Edwards produced and in which he again starred with Florence Turner. In 1916 he adapted a short and sentimental play of his own about a little waif, *Doorsteps*.

creation of appealingly imperfect ones, of whom Henry Edwards's heroes are representative examples. At last audiences, accustomed to an overwhelming succession of incidents, were to participate in the emotional experiences of the characters.

In so far as it is possible to discover the film technique used in these films, it will be considered in the next two chapters. It is reasonable to hope that the technique was better than most of the stories on which it was exercised. For the very nature of most of the people who entered the film world made it inevitable that technique should develop more rapidly than the intellectual content of films. It is unlikely, for example, that the typical film maker of the day set himself to master the technique because he was driven by a desire to say something so much as that, mastering the technique, he found himself obliged to discover something to say. And while he could learn the use of his medium by experience, he could not so easily learn to have anything worth saying; a fact which the use of novels and plays, too often chosen and adapted without discrimination, was unable to conceal.

Harold Weston complained in 1917[1] that few writers[2] bothered to learn how to construct a film continuity, with the result that their original contribution to film technique was correspondingly limited. But that part of their work which lay in the theme and in the construction of the plot (as distinct from the construction of the assembled film), and which can be judged from the material in this chapter, does not suggest great originality either. Inheritance and fallen women; the underworld of London with its night clubs and gambling hells; the superiority of honest poverty, with class acting as a one-way barrier to marriage; the regenerating effects of war, the worthlessness of shirkers, the savage and drunken stupidity of the "Hun," and death-defying feats by which people won their spurs— these were the materials of not only the undistinguished majority but a number of the more important films as well. Perhaps it is true that no theme, reduced to its simplest terms, can be original. But in these films plot devices or even whole plots recurred with depressing frequency. Villages invaded by the Germans are saved when help is brought by juveniles, athletic heroines or old people; Germans met before the war

---

[1] *The Art of Photo-Play Writing*, p. 54.
[2] "Writer" in this connection refers to the person who originally conceived the film.

at house parties reappear as spies or brutal enemy officers; honest people are caught in incriminating situations with dead bodies, or mistakenly imagine they have killed their dearest friends; heroes and heroines take the blame for scapegrace brothers, suffering unjust punishment and often being involved in serious misunderstandings with their lovers through such quixotic behaviour; wills contain clauses which make unconventional marriages necessary; betrayed country girls come to London to make a living (often by selling flowers) but in the end usually marry respectable young men after precarious careers in the well-mapped underworld.

Admittedly almost any plot can be made to sound ridiculous when it is summarized. Admittedly, too, many commonplace themes and even commonplace plots have been transformed by brilliant treatment, and made the basis of reputable or even great works of art. Abandoning the search for originality, therefore, we may look simply for stories which were intelligently conceived and skilfully executed. But before they are seriously considered as anything more than mere assortments of situations, we are surely justified in asking for these to have two qualities; firstly, that they should have a genuine emotional appeal; secondly, that they should have a certain inevitability of their own. As Weston said:

It is such a simple matter to think out a series of "blood and thunder situations" and to write them in such a manner that a cheap picture palace audience shall be thrilled by them, but this is the work of a hack-writer, not of a self-respecting artist who desires to see the screen play reach its zenith.[1]

And in these two respects some progress, not very great but still progress, can be seen. Firstly, the changes appear on analysis to consist of a movement away from a string of situations which were striking in themselves but linked only loosely by a plot, towards an integrated plot whose situations, often fewer and less sensational, derive from each other through the characters of the people involved. The logical development was from an incident, to a string of incidents held together as it were by force, and finally to incidents with a seemingly spontaneous and inevitable pattern. And this was clearly the trend of all types of dramatic film. Secondly, films relying on a string of situations tended to make them hot and strong since they could not very well arouse sympathy by the use of

[1] *The Art of Photo-Play Writing*, p. 53.

character or emotion. But gradually the people to whom interesting things happened were superseded by interesting people, and attention began to centre round their emotions, their emotional relationships, and primarily the all-conquering theme, romantic love.

The British film cannot be singled out for praise in these developments. But the cinema as a whole did reach this degree of maturity with remarkable speed. The striking fact is not so much that most of the stories were banal, as that by its twenty-first year film drama as a whole had achieved so high a degree of story development. This, of course, was largely because it was not doing pioneer work, and was so greatly influenced by the contemporary stages of popular drama and the novel. In Britain, especially, the overwhelming majority of films were adaptations of stage plays and novels. It is easy to see why this is so. To increase the number of good screenwriters would have cost more than British producers were willing to pay. And the number of writers who knew enough about film technique to conceive their stories in a suitable form for filming was few. Consequently most stories submitted by outsiders were presented in the wrong form and it was little more trouble to adapt a novel or play of proved success with the public, than to adapt an untried draft scenario.

But there is more to consider. Why should the works that were actually adapted have been chosen? There does not seem to be much evidence in contemporary writings that the qualities which make a story suited to visual representation received serious thought. Naturally considerations such as the availability of players and locations, or the extent of set construction necessary, would weigh heavily. As we have seen, the British companies' preference for inexpensive production militated against spectacle films. But it is clear from accounts of the films that, once filmed, their stories frequently proved too long, too complicated, too short and thin, or to have too much action or too little. In point of fact it seems that the choice of story was strongly influenced by entirely different considerations.

The three chief motives seem to have been large circulation, literary snob value, and theme values. To give a film the title of a famous book or play gave it two important advantages: people might be curious to see how it had been adapted, and in any case would almost certainly pay more attention to its name, displayed outside a theatre, than they would to the mass of other names which meant little or nothing to them. The same considerations account for the vogue for song films. Moreover, regardless of the differences of medium it seemed reasonable that a story which had already been able to charm a large public would be able to do it again. Thus, to take only novelists, films were based on the works of some acknowledged best-selling writers of the nineteenth and early twentieth centuries; some dozen of these films were from novels of immense circulation by Garvice, Hichens, Hutchinson and two women writers, Lucas Malet and Allen Raine. They were for the most part stories about the upper middle or middle classes, and were read mainly by the middle class. Aiming at the same public, the cinema could no more be expected to outstrip its level of culture than could the popular novels of the day, and stories written especially for the films were as near to the usual pattern as the skill of the writers could contrive. But at the same time it was felt that the public "likes its melodrama mellowed by a little literary tradition."[1] Thus the second motive, literary snob value, led to the adaptation of a number of works which in their original state were of greater literary or dramatic merit. Many books were from writers[2] whose works had figured as Yellow Backs. The appearance of those with the greatest prestige was often the signal for a display in the trade Press of high-minded contempt for trash (although the supply of the latter was prudently maintained by some producers). References to the original ranged from a nonchalant appearance of familiarity to a reverence which sometimes strangely missed the point. But whatever their reception, such films usually made more of their parent's prestige than its content.

Coming finally to a recapitulation of content, we find that the range was wide although the films within each theme group followed a limited number of formulae. They ranged from the extreme action film to films of neat sentimentality. Action films included few adventure stories which did not depend on some particular theme value; a small but important group in the middle of the period were sporting films; there was a fairly steady flow of ordinary crime films which latterly tended to become less

[1] *Kinematograph Monthly Film Record*, June 1915, p. 53.
[2] Grant Allen, Robert Buchanan, Hall Caine, Mrs. Craik, Charles Dickens, A. Conan Doyle, Alexandre Dumas, B. L. Farjeon, Henry Fielding, Nat Gould, Thomas Hardy, Fergus Hume, Mrs. Hungerford, Lord Lytton, Helen Mathers, Charles Reade, Rita, Dora Russell, G. R. Sims, J. S. Winter.

sensational and more like other dramas; and, as might be expected, a very large number of spy and war dramas which flooded the market for about two years and then almost disappeared. Films with greater emphasis on personal relations ranged between the melodrama of society, which gradually shed its reliance on sensational incident, through strong romance and the social problem film to sentimental romance. Many war and costume films placed more emphasis on personal relations than on action; many melodramas and romances treated sex with such pretended frankness that they overlapped the important group of films of social interest. These, with varying sincerity but almost universal shallowness, treated anything from morality to social justice, and included a number of propaganda stories. Grand-scale moralizing brings us back finally to the sentimental films, with a small group of "pathos-comedies" and gentle romance.

CHAPTER FIVE

Analysis of Two Films

JANE SHORE

Produced by B. Haldane and F. Martin Thornton for Barker Motion Photography and trade shown in March 1915. 5,500 ft. By Rowland Talbot. Design: P. Mumford and F. Ambrose. Cinematography: Fred O. Bovill, L. Eveleigh.

Jane Winstead	Blanche Forsythe
Edward IV	Roy Travers
Matthew Shore	Robert Purdie
William Shore	Nelson Phillips
Lord Hastings	Tom Macdonald
Richard, Duke of Gloucester	Rolfe Leslie
Master Winstead	Tom Coventry
Garth the Bard	Frank Melrose
Warwick the Kingmaker	Fred Pitt
Margaret	Dora de Winton
Queen Elizabeth	Maud Yates
Dame Winstead	Rachel de Solla

THE VICAR OF WAKEFIELD

Produced by Fred Paul for Ideal and trade shown in October 1916. Five parts. Adapted by Benedict James from the novel by Oliver Goldsmith.

The Vicar	Sir John Hare
Olivia	Laura Cowie
The Vicar's Wife	Marie Illington
The Squire	Ben Webster
Sophia	Margaret Shelley
Hon. Miss Skeggs	Mabel Twemlow
Lady Blarney	Jess Dorynne
Jenkinson	A. E. George
George	Martin Lewis
Moses	Lambert Terry
The Squire's Uncle	Frank Wolfe

This analysis should not be regarded as an account of film technique in general. For although it is illuminating to examine the film making of the period in practice, examination of two films would not by itself justify generalizations about technique. There is no guarantee, even, that the copies used are complete.[1] To the ordinary hazards of age we must add the possibility that these copies may have been stripped of footage and even whole shots dear to their producers, but dismissed by the renters as padding. Thus analysis of the details of their structure must in the end be tentative. Although useful as a demonstration of the film technique seen on the screen at this time it is valid only as an adjunct to, rather than as the basis of, the treatment given in Chapter VI of the principles of film making.

The fact that these two films have been chosen for scrutiny does not mean, either, that they were the best or most important British productions of their time. Very few of the many films made in Britain during the First World War have survived, none of them made by producers whose work might have stood comparison with the best American films. *Jane Shore* was a spectacle film famous in its day and the *Vicar of Wakefield* a consciously "prestige" film of a literary classic and featuring a celebrated stage actor, and neither Martin Thornton nor Fred Paul were unknown within the trade as producers. But nor were they in the same class as Tucker, Hepworth and a few others.

In many ways the less ambitious, and certainly the less famous of the two was Ideal's version of the *Vicar of Wakefield*. Goldsmith's novel underwent some curious changes during the course of adaptation. The film opens with a sequence apparently devised to strike a domestic note and establish the Vicar's character, in which he insists on giving his wife's dress away to beggars. After this we see the family's banker abscond with their money. His departing note is found by the Vicar's eldest son George, who returns to tell the family. Sir William Thornhill is then shown hearing of the Vicar's misfortune. He writes a letter presenting him with the living

[1] The copy of *Jane Shore* was made available by the National Film Library and that of the *Vicar of Wakefield* by R. W. Proffitt, Ltd. Both copies are recent prints in which the original tinting has not been reproduced. Hence, for example, scenes which the sense of the story requires to represent night appear in full daylight, a fault which dark blue tinting presumably corrected in original prints. It is most unfortunate that the National Film Library has been unable to make provision for the reproduction of tinting in the early films which it reprints.

of Thornhill, at the same time making his own rakish nephew Ned steward of his estate in the same neighbourhood and telling him to mend his ways forthwith. Thereupon Sir William sets out incognito on a "walking tour" to watch developments at Thornhill. The family is shown leaving their old home, meeting "Mr. Burchell" (whom we know to be Sir William) on the journey. All arrive together at Thornhill, where Ned later meets and is attracted to the Vicar's daughter Olivia and Mr. Burchell himself to her sister Sophia. We see the unscrupulous Ned plotting with some friends, visiting the Primrose family, flattering the women and lending the Vicar enough money to buy George a commission. There follows the incident of the Vicar's little son Moses selling the colt at the fair and being cheated by Jenkinson, a crony of Ned's, who then enters into the latter's plot to seduce Olivia. During a party at the Vicarage Ned persuades Olivia to elope with him. She does so and they are married, as Ned thinks, by a sham priest. The audience, however, has learnt from Jenkinson (in a sub-title) that he has tricked Ned in this respect and that the marriage is a real one. We see the Vicar setting out to find his daughter, the marriage of the runaway couple, and the arrest of the Vicar, who cannot pay off the bond he gave to Ned and is therefore thrown into gaol. Here he preaches to his fellow prisoners, greatly impressing Jenkinson, who for some reason not explained is found in the same prison. Meanwhile George meets the banker abroad and retrieves the family fortune by force. At home, Mr. Burchell pays the Vicar's bond and gets him out of prison. The Vicar continues his search. In the meantime Ned tires of Olivia and brings his old disreputable companions to his rooms, whereupon she learns that he has cheated her. She leaves him, and we see her falling exhausted by the wayside, rescued by some country people, and eventually found by the Vicar. We are shown Ned in London yearning for her, and Mr. Burchell at Thornhill proposing for the hand of Sophia and being refused on account of his apparent poverty. Returning to the prison he learns from Jenkinson that the marriage was in fact a real one. Meanwhile the Vicar comes home with Olivia, who is reluctantly forgiven by Mrs. Primrose. Ned arrives on the scene and pleads with Olivia in vain until Sir William appears, revealing his own true identity and the fact that Ned and Olivia are really married, and thus reconciling the parents to both matches.

The film is a romantic melodrama bearing little relation to either the spirit or form of the book. Many of the story changes were omissions—the reasons for selling the colt, the Vicar's own visit to the fair, Farmer William's suit, and George's travels in Europe. But in addition motives were altered and time reversed. In the book the Vicar did not go to prison until a much later point in the story: indeed, until after the family had lost their house in a fire and endured much poverty. The whole balance of the story was altered by making the Vicar find Olivia after his imprisonment, not only because it cut out the Vicar's travels when looking for her but because it made their homecoming the climax of the story. The basic reason for these changes, of course, was to single out, telescope and "improve" the romance of Olivia and Ned, with that of Sophia and Sir William as a sub-plot. The tone of the film was significantly set by using as the opening title a verse which did not occur in the book until well after Olivia's homecoming:

> When lovely woman stoops to folly,
> And finds too late that men betray
> What then can sooth her melancholy,
> What art can wash her guilt away?

This concentration explains why both Ned and Sir William, as principal characters, are introduced earlier in the film than in the book. Incidentally, by letting the audience meet the latter first as Sir William and then referring to him in titles as "Mr. Burchell," in quotes, the film clumsily loses the slight air of mystery which surrounds him in the book. By this, and by letting us know throughout that Olivia's marriage is a real one, it wastes its few opportunities of arousing our interest.

In the exigencies of compressing, or trying to compress, a leisurely and discursive book into a tight dramatic plot it is not altogether surprising that the atmosphere of country life and the peaceful suggestion of passing time was lost. Less excusable was the complete disappearance of all the little absurdities of character which gave point to the novel. The actors did their best with limited insight into film acting and an even more limited script, Miss Laura Cowie displaying coyness, and Mr. A. E. George cunning, at long distance with the greatest determination. Sir John Hare gave a spry and businesslike impersonation of piety, but his exaggerated and oversimplified reactions did not succeed in making the Vicar anything but a tedious prig. Along with personality there disappeared much of the purpose of the action. Motivation was obscure and in many cases the opposite of that intended by the writer. The dislike the Primroses had for Burchell, and their conviction that it was with him that Olivia had eloped, vanished as unnecessary subtleties; the daughters' little ambitions and schemes were smoothed out of existence, and Olivia was provided with a runaway marriage to make her fit to be a heroine.

Having lost the atmosphere and the spirit of the book and robbed the people of the foibles which gave them life, the producers were left with a slim romantic melodrama and the problem of telling it in pictures. This they did without prejudice against words. There were actually more shots (200) in this five-reel film than in either of the pre-war films of the same length analysed in Volume II. But a shot is here defined as a picture which not only was taken, but also appears on the screen, without interruption. Hence when anything such as a title or the end of a reel occurs in the middle of a picture actually filmed as one shot, it makes it two shots according to this definition. Thus, since sixty of the hundred titles are speech titles and these are normally cut into the middle of scenes filmed as one, the figure of 200 shots conceals the fact that the number of pictures actually filmed as one shot was very much less. The proportion of titles to shots in this sense, in fact, was extremely high.

The speech titles, usually called dialogue titles, sometimes convey soliloquies or thoughts; in general, however, they do convey dialogue, each bearing the remarks of one or two speakers prefaced by their names. In so far as they are an integral part of the action before the camera, speech titles are an advance on those which merely summarize or explain it. In some instances in this film, however, they do not seem necessary to the progress of the action. In such cases they seem to be used rather to ease the cut from one angle on a set to another, softening the visual jar which was so much feared at the time. The same intention must also lie behind many explanatory titles, some of which still anticipate action as they did in earlier films and many of which would appear redundant were it not for three things, one of them this desire to avoid a sharp cut from one shot to another within an action; another was the need for emphasis from time to time, the titles being a more obvious—as well as a more congenial—way of achieving it than cutting to a detail; and a third being the inadequacy of the mime. But the result of using so many explanatory titles in addition to the numerous speech titles, and a number which introduced the characters as they first appeared, was to weight the film very heavily with words. It is clear that the producers did not share the new feeling against titles. On the contrary they probably felt that an almost equal combination of written words and pictures was a proper way of visualizing an important literary work.

As for the pictures themselves, their appearance was not exciting. There was some theatrical domestic grouping of an attempted prettiness but the dark, flimsy sets have a gloomy and mean appearance out of keeping with the original work and little is made of the English countryside, notwithstanding an incongruously "artistic" shot of silhouettes on a skyline which is used as the Vicar sets out on his search and again as he returns with Olivia. But the most noticeable and consistent effort to obtain pictorial effects is to be found in the frequent use of irising and the several shots held in a circular mask.

Irising was used throughout the film to introduce or round off phases of the story. Close shots were held in a circular mask, moreover, on several occasions when they were cut into longer shots to represent thoughts. Both may have been used in preference to dissolves or straight cuts on the one hand, or ordinary close ups on the other, for their pictorial qualities. But their function was primarily a continuity one, in that both implied a definite relationship. The masked shots were in a subordinate relation to the main theme, and the irising between phases of the story denoted changes of time and place. It is one of the marked characteristics of this film that there are many separate phases of the action and that there is no attempt to join them by bridging shots or continuity passages in the story, the iris (alone or with a title) being used for this purpose instead.

In its discontinuity of action the film bears every resemblance to a stage play of numerous scenes. It is also like a stage play in that, within the phases of action represented by each scene, the actors usually remain within the limits of one set. Thus within phases hardly any cutting is necessitated by the movement of one piece of the action from one position to another. Nowhere, for example, is there moving action such as a fight starting in one room, continuing downstairs and ending in another room, with the camera following it. Actions in the *Vicar of Wakefield* almost always take place entirely within range of the original camera position. With this impetus to cutting within an action removed, and with very few passages into which one or two shots of another action taking place at the same time are cross cut, the structure of the film as a whole is extremely simple. A single static long shot was normally used, and there were few single actions which continued out of range of the original camera position. In all, there were some nine instances of cutting to closer shots of a detail of the previous picture and back again, and only one of cutting from one part of the setting of the action to another part not included in the previous shot. When the position best for most of the action was too far away or wrongly directed for a significant part of it, the need for adjustment was more likely to be met by movement of the actors in relation to the camera, or even by slight camera movements, than by multiplying the number of shots. Although few and very short, the slight panning movements are well timed to follow someone, or to take in something not of sufficiently lasting importance to justify the whole shot being taken in a wider angle. There is one instance, too, in which the camera moves very slightly to ensure that Olivia is in the centre of the picture after the departure of Ned, who has previously occupied half of it. But despite the ease with which these movements are used the camera technique as a whole is very undeveloped for a film made two years after the *Birth of a Nation*.

The whole conception is still so near that of a stage play that it is frequently disjointed and always slow. To some extent, of course, a leisurely pace may have been intentional, and might have captured that atmosphere of the novel which the distortion of the story did so much to destroy. And to this extent the use of the iris and a minimum of cutting, like Hepworth's preference for dissolves, could claim some justification in the type of subject filmed. It is significant, in this connection, that the cutting is more advanced in the spectacular *Jane Shore*, although this was made some two years earlier. The more massive conception, with more people doing more things in more places, required a greater number of shots combined in more varied ways than the slower story with its more circumscribed action.

The story of this five-reel film is considerably more complex than that of either the *Vicar of Wakefield* or the films analysed in Volume II, and a bare outline of the action, in the order in which it is seen on the screen, is necessary to an understanding of the film's correspondingly more complicated construction. It opens with the routed Lancastrians streaming over the hills after the battle of Mortimer's Cross, and Edward of York sending word of his victory to London. The Lancastrian William Shore is then shown in a prison cell, from which he sends word by an aged bard to his brother Matthew, whom we first see entertaining his *fiancée* Jane Winstead. He and the old man retire to a secret vault and plot William's escape with other Lancastrians while news of the rout is spreading through London. Matthew and two other conspirators then steal into the Tower while the Yorkists are celebrating their victory, and rescue William. Back in the vault they make further plans. When King Edward rides through London in triumph he catches sight of Jane and is attracted to her, and he later arouses Matthew's resentment by gazing at her as he walks masked through the streets.

Matthew tells his cousin Margaret that Jane has promised to marry him. In the town, Jane is rescued by the King from a drunken assault. He is still in disguise, but he later meets her again and courts her openly at a ball. Margaret takes this opportunity to arouse Matthew's jealousy and he quarrels with Jane, but on the way home they decide to marry immediately. Margaret vainly declares her own love to Matthew but is unable to stop the wedding, and in revenge denounces him to the King as a Lancastrian. Meanwhile William has actively urged rebellion and the King, now knowing of Matthew's treachery, visits Jane and persuades her to be his mistress in return for her husband's life. She is distraught, and consents. He carries her off, and before Matthew's return Margaret destroys Jane's letter explaining her action. When he returns she is triumphant and takes him to spy on Jane, who is with the King. At the Palace Jane is wretchedly miserable. Meanwhile Matthew fights his way through the soldiers to whom Margaret has denounced him, and flies to his brother and the rebels. Richard, Duke of Gloucester, is then seen watching the King and Jane sitting in a garden. He seeks out the Queen and leads her to the garden, where she reproaches the King for his behaviour. Later Jane asks Hastings, who loves her, to help her escape. A royal banquet is broken up by the news that the Lancastrians are assembling, whereupon the King joins his own forces and leaves Jane in the Palace. The Yorkists lose the battle and Edward escapes by sea with a few of his followers Matthew, too, survives the battle and takes refuge in Flanders. Meanwhile Jane, believing him dead, accepts Edward's love. When the King lies dying, poisoned by Gloucester, he commends Jane to Hastings' care and they plight their troth at the foot of his bier. Matthew, hearing of the King's death, decides to return. During the marriage of Jane and Hastings the latter is arrested on Gloucester's orders and is executed. Jane is tried for witchcraft, and hounded through the streets, and finally collapses in the snow, where she is found by Matthew.

Thus in a little over an hour action ranging back and forth with six main characters of almost equal importance, together with battles, processions, crowded street scenes, banquets, and so on move towards what should be a tragic climax. Jane, plump and ordinary, bounces or glides with uncomfortable stateliness through a part which demands charm and dignity whilst venomous cousin Margaret leers, points and chuckles with a will, but most of the cast have little more individuality than members of the well-disciplined crowds. But it would be unfair to blame the actors alone for not inspiring conviction or sympathy, since once more both action and motivation are grossly oversimplified.

We may suspect that superficial treatment of character and emotion was the price paid for the scale of the action. For although the way in which the story was broken down into shots was flexible enough to keep the various strands in movement at the same time, it was not sufficiently advanced to make the audience feel intimately concerned with them. As a result the film has a faint air of the tableau about it, although in point of fact its construction is by no means simple.

Little indication of the greater complexity of construction can be found in the number and length of the shots, as it could at earlier stages of development. There were about the same number of new shots as in the word-bound *Vicar of Wakefield* of two or three years later. They varied from short shots of two or three feet to several of well over a hundred, not differing much in this respect from earlier films. Nor were there any signs of imaginative advance in the physical nature or timing of the cuts. Neither the iris nor the dissolve, soon to be used so extensively for variety and for their suggestion of a time relation, were employed. The cuts themselves, moreover, were made meticulously at the beginning and end of each action. This was done with smooth regularity and even with dramatic effect in one case, that of Hastings' execution, where the cut occurs two frames after the fall of the axe. But in most instances there was nothing to be gained by waiting until the action was finished. For example, on many occasions when a character is seen in movement the shot is laboriously continued until he disappears, whether through a door or out of frame. The cut might well have been made here at any moment after there had been enough movement to show that he would eventually leave the picture, the exact place to be decided in each case by the dramatic tempo required. A quicker cut occurs successfully when we see William kill his gaoler, for we cut to the sunlight immediately after seeing him begin to climb out of his dungeon. But the more usual practice was to tailor the shot very carefully to the whole of the action within its range, with an effect on the pace of the film which can be illustrated by an example. First we see a long shot of Shore addressing a street crowd; we cut to a closer shot, fifteen feet long, of soldiers advancing through an arch to within a few feet of the camera, turning to the left and slowly marching out of the picture; and then we cut back to the street, with the same soldiers appearing at the back and dispersing the crowd. Here the length of the middle take and the fact that we see the soldiers turn and go off left considerably lessens the sense of movement, and especially the sense of approaching movement.

Although the same lack of imagination is to be found in the position of the camera in relation to the actors, much thought was clearly given to pictorial values. No masks were used to enhance or vary the effects, but sunny natural exteriors, in particular, include a number of pleasing shots of the hills, the palace gardens and round about the castle. The interior sets are adequate for the time, the large and spectacular ones painted and the more homely ones built. Certainly the exterior sets are far less successful, whilst much of the grouping is better suited to the stage, but even so the general level of composition and a few especially interesting shots show a greater consciousness of the importance of camera position than is suggested by the *Vicar of Wakefield*.

Some of the many unconventional shots—a vista of hill slopes which shows no sky, several crowd shots taken from a rostrum, the battlefield strewn with bodies and Jane lying in the snow, both of the latter taken from slightly above—were probably taken in this way simply because it was physically difficult to take them in any other. But several others imply a voluntary choice of the unusual, a measure of experiment however small and tentative. There is a shot looking out to the country beyond from the castle battlements, over which the escape rope is flung by an unseen hand behind the camera; one in which the escaping Matthew backs diagonally away from a position close to the camera, his back to a wall running from front right to back left of the picture; another of the King, seated at the banquet between Jane and his outraged Queen, which is taken from a corner and slightly below the level of the table (another shot proves that the table was not on a dais and could easily have been taken from the conventional angle); and Jane's final trial is seen from above, in a circular clearing in a dense crowd of people which parts right down the screen to make way for her as she is driven out.

These very modest deviations are only worth noting because of their rarity. The placing of the camera remained for the most part straightforward and functional, with a marked preference for shooting the players fairly near the camera. There are no large close-ups, but nor was the action of a small number of people now filmed in long shots, which were usually restricted to cases where large vistas and crowds were the main focus of attention.

Where, as was bound to happen, the major part of a shot required to be taken in long shot but certain players required closer attention during part of the time, the most frequent solution was for them to move in towards the camera. Throughout the film there is constant movement to and from the camera, which remained immobile. Not only did it not track, it did not pan or tilt either, although these types of movement were by no means unknown in 1914. The limitations of this technique are evident in several shots, including the last one, in which the camera is trained on the ground to make the best of Jane when she falls in the snow and consequently presents a rather strange appearance while she enters it feet first.

An alternative solution, of course, was to cut to another angle of the same thing. It is important to remember that the film's capacity to record movement not only within range of a fixed camera point but from one point to another, either by moving the camera or cutting, was not generally realized spontaneously but emerged as the solution to specific difficulties. Cutting within single phases of action, as distinct from the inescapable cuts between the phases, is comparatively frequent in the present film. But it is not so frequent as to suggest a new theoretical approach to the question. The basic assumption still seems to be that of a fixed camera for every scene, and every change is a deviation requiring exceptional justification. The advance is in a more liberal interpretation of what constitutes a justification, rather than in a radically different idea of the camera's function.

We have seen that the characters constantly moved in and out of close mid shots, and in so far as they could do this the need for cutting within a phase was less urgent. But there are cases when this is not a possible solution. Most obvious is that when the participants in a single action move out of range of the original camera angle, however wide this may have been. Thus in *Jane Shore*, when Matthew fights his way from a ground-floor room, up the stairs and into an upstairs room, the camera could only treat it as one action by cutting, and did so. Again, there may be a physical barrier which makes two places, for the camera, of what is only one place from the point of view of the action: thus William in his cell talking through a narrow window to the old man outside had to be shown in six alternating shots of first William and then the old man. A different type of case is that in which all the action is within range of a single long shot, but, since most of it takes place in a smaller area, the camera is put close to this and the part left out of the picture is shown when necessary by cutting momentarily to another angle. Both types of cut are used frequently in *Jane Shore*, demonstrating a great advance on the early theoretical technique in which the longest shot needed was that used throughout, regardless of the resulting difficulty of seeing details, and if there were a physical barrier one part of the action only would be shown. Both types are entirely functional and spring from the desire to show only what is significant at any one moment, and show it as clearly as possible. Slightly more sophisticated is the case in which the close shot merely shows in greater detail something which was already distinguishable in the previous long shot. Here the aim is simply emphasis. Thus two shots of the King's scout watching the assembling army enclose a closer shot of what he is watching, although this is easily visible in the original shot. Perhaps the best example, however, is Hastings' execution. In an establishing shot we see Gloucester hobble to the window of a large room. A quick close shot over his shoulder as he looks through the window enables us to see quite clearly the crowded courtyard with a scaffold in the centre and Hastings being led up to it; nevertheless, we cut to a much closer shot of the foot of the steps, with Hastings kissing Jane goodbye, after which we return to the window and see the fall of the axe from over Gloucester's shoulder (presumably we cut back because it is Gloucester's interest in the execution which is significant at this point, or possibly just because by retiring within the window frame we could witness the fall of the axe without actually having to see a head fall). Finally, the fight on the beach as Edward escapes to his boat is shown in six shots which alternately look out to sea or face the sandhills at the beginning of the beach. The long duration of each take, and the lack of imagination in the actual choice of each angle, fail to make this sequence exciting. But here at last is a sign of real elasticity in the number of camera positions considered necessary to one phase of action, and a sign that dramatic requirements as well as intelligibility might play a part in determining them.

Just as cutting within an action ranges from that forced on the producer by consideration of space to that with deliberately dramatic intent, the extent to which the frequent cross cutting between two sets of action is dictated by considerations of time or of dramatic effect varies. All of it is fairly elementary. Rarely are more than one or two shots of any one part of the story cut into another, and there is nothing like the continued parallel cutting of classic film chases or rescues. Nevertheless, the principle is frequently used in a modified form, both for different actions that converge and for those that do not. Some of the latter, it is true, are interlocked to remarkably little purpose. For example, a shot of the old bard wandering past some soldiers and hearing that Henry V is to be taken to the Tower is pointlessly cut in between two shots of Margaret seething with fury at Matthew's marriage. The only reason for its occurrence at this point seems to be that it was happening at roughly the same time and had to be fitted in somewhere. More satisfying, because the juxtaposition itself has dramatic meaning, is the intercutting of Lancastrian conspirators with the announcement in the streets outside that the Lancastrians have been routed; or the shot of Matthew hearing of the King's death and deciding to return from Flanders, a shot which is placed between the death-bed scene in which the King charges Hastings to look after Jane, and that of Jane and Hastings plighting their troth.

Thus various types of sequence are used to piece together an ambitious story. The widely separate activity of several people fall into a proper time relation, and contiguous or simultaneous incidents converge or run parallel in a more or less intelligible, if not an exciting, whole. Certainly it is hard to imagine any audience being stirred by the film, for the script was too impersonal and the editing too literal and unimaginative to counteract the vile acting and arouse a little excitement. We have seen, moreover, that the tendency to wait until an actor left the screen before cutting made for slowness, and that the possibility of creating tension by continued parallel cutting was ignored. Nor was the story always completely intelligible, partly, perhaps, because the use of titles was less advanced than other aspects of technique. The story depends less on its titles, and uses proportionately less of them, than either the *Vicar of Wakefield* or *East Lynne*. But they included very few of the new speech-titles, and none of those briefly introducing new characters, badly needed as these were in view of the number of people and their complex historical background. Some even gave explanations in advance of the shots in the now antiquated way of the early filmed stage plays.

Nevertheless the film is an attempt at large-scale story telling which, besides often being pleasant to look at, does show some advance in construction since the earlier films. How much this is due to a difference between the producers' styles and how much to a general advance it is difficult to say. Unfortunately the fact that *Jane Shore* was deliberately conceived as a "spectacle film" encouraged a certain pompous pageantry and acted against that intimacy with the characters which was necessary to arouse the audience's sympathy. On the other hand, it is interesting to speculate on the connection between the scale of the theme on the one hand and the nature of the cutting on the other. It is possible, for example, that the very size of the sets made possible a greater variety of angle from which they could be taken than the little two or three-walled rooms, the whole of which could be clearly shown from one camera position; while at the same time the size of the sets and the crowds made emphasis of detail a more pressing problem. In a similar way it was clearly the scale and complexity of the action which demanded the greater elasticity of cutting.

Although the technique of the film compares favourably with others we have analysed, its relation to that of contemporary British production as a whole can only be deduced from the various sources used in the rest of this book. Everything indicates that from this point of view it was a creditable though not an outstanding achievement, however remarkable as a rare and much-publicized piece of pageantry. But for a comparison with the best film making of the day it is only necessary to think of the *Birth of a Nation*, which was being made at the same time,[1] for the technique we have discussed to fall into its own very humble perspective.

---

[1] *Birth of a Nation* was made during the summer of 1914, shown in America in February 1915 and trade shown in this country in August or September 1915. *Jane Shore* was trade shown here in March 1915, and since the exteriors at least were obviously shot during the summer it was most probably also made during the summer of 1914.

CHAPTER SIX

Film Technique

Big changes in the film technique and theory discussed in Volume II are not to be expected in so short a period as that of the war. But the period, although short, was enriched by the production (in this country, the showing) of *The Birth of a Nation* and *Intolerance*. Such indications as we can find of the trends of film theory are therefore doubly interesting in their relation to the standard of achievement of these two films.

Before the war there was a marked divergence between those who saw the film as a pictorial art and those who concentrated on its story or time structure. There was no appreciation of editing as the point at which the two elements met. The film's dual nature was symbolized by this time in the difference between American films on the one hand and Italian films on the other. For the obvious and successful exponents of the pictorial school were the Italians, with their photography, which was considered superb, and with the sets, costumes and mass effects of their spectacle films. The Americans, on the other hand, were developing the story-telling element of the film, and in doing so were developing a sense of intimacy beyond anything in the Italian films; to quote a book written by a little known but enterprising British producer which may be taken in this chapter as a representative primer of film technique of the time:[1]

One views an Italian production as one would view actions looked at through the wrong end of a telescope; the characters seem to be too distant for us to feel deeply about them.[2]

Griffith, of course, is the most obvious example of a producer who could make his audience feel deeply about his characters, although it will later appear that his mastery in this respect was less appreciated in this country, and certainly less tempting to imitate, than the scale and magnificence of his conceptions.

[1] *The Art of Photo-Play Writing*, by Harold Weston.   [2] Ibid., p. 69.

It was a time when large sets were greatly admired in most film-making countries and properties and *décor* were being given much more attention than before, as well as more money. It has been seen that a handful of British films were even credited with designers. The term "art director" was beginning to be used here, as it was in America, and more careful designing showed a conscious desire "to interest through the senses as well as by the intelligence."[1] This purely visual appeal through the sets was sought largely by using them on a grand scale, and even in America such experiments in stylized *décor* as the large black and white patterns in a Vitagraph film, *The Yellow Girl* (see the *Bioscope*, October 12, 1916, p. 195) seem to have been rare. In England, although such films as *Jane Shore*, *She*, *Dawn*, and *The Lyons Mail* had comparatively large and lavish sets and crowd scenes, on the whole producers who sought pictorial values found lovely scenery and lighting both more congenial and more economical. The Walton group, especially—Hepworth, Neame, Trimble and Edwards—received considerable praise for their choice of exteriors, grouping and lighting, and it is significant that Hepworth, son of a lantern lecturer and a one-time lantern lecturer himself, should have excelled above all in pictorial composition and photographic work rather than in the pace of the film. In any case reviewers, and so far as can be ascertained film makers themselves, seem to have been guided by the conventions of pictorial beauty which applied to static art.

Of much more immediate interest was the realism of the effect created by the separate images. Because of the preoccupation with pictorial beauty the use of trick work was for the most part somewhat restricted during this period. A certain amount of double printing or double exposure was used in such films as *The Avenging Hand*, *The Christmas Carol* and *The Chimes*, although it was less important here than in a run of dual-role films[2] in 1916 and 1917. But anything savouring of trickery came uncomfortably near to breaking the golden rule of letting the audience forget the camera, and energy was spent in giving the films a realism out of all proportion to the probability of their stories.

Realism was in some cases achieved by the use of actuality shots or

---

[1] *The Art of Photo-Play Writing*, p. 76.
[2] E.g. *The Princess of Happy Chance*, *The Girl Who Wrecked His Home*, *Arsene Lupin*, *Face to Face*, *Why Not Speak Out?*, *The Lyons Mail*.

location work. For example, in *Kismet* a travel film of Baghdad mingled curiously—but to the satisfaction of trade reviewers—with theatre scenery. Such material must indeed have appealed to the more economical producers. Therefore a high proportion of the cheap British war dramas included news shots of marching soldiers, or material such as that filmed in an aeroplane factory and used in the Progress film *Democracy*. Borrowed stage scenery was no longer used so widely, however, despite its superficial convenience, and even the one Shakespeare film made in Britain during the war, Broadwest's *The Merchant of Venice*, caused great disappointment by using scenery from the stage production in the manner of so many earlier films. In general, efforts were made to give studio-made interiors a greater degree of realism; the growing use of plywood sets rather than canvas flats contributed to this, although it must be admitted that even in such a spectacular film as *Jane Shore* some of the interior and exterior set construction was flimsy and reminiscent of a village pageant. More convincing, as well as more beautiful, were country location scenes and great use was made of these in so far as the type of stories chosen would allow. It is true that the subjects then in vogue did not, on the whole, encourage filming in the open air. But when they did permit the producer to go out and search for the beauty of nature, his efforts were almost certain to be applauded. Realism, if not beauty, was also found in the London locations which were used so extensively until about 1917 in the Melville type of melodrama[1] and the Embankment, Leicester Square and many other familiar parts of London were used as settings for action. This, however, seems to have been simply a fashionable device to give a film an extra "punch" by claiming that it had actually been filmed on the spot, and by 1917 the novelty of this was disappearing. Greater attention was given by the better companies to ways of securing an equal realism within the more easily controlled studio conditions; the Embankment sequence in *Shopgirls* was made by Turner films in the studio, and *Alone in London* occasioned favourable comment with its shots of Trafalgar Square, which were a "combination of double photography and a stage back cloth."[2]

[1] *The Beggar Girl's Wedding, Girl of My Heart, The Girl Who Took the Wrong Turning, Rogues of London*, etc.
[2] *Kinematograph Monthly Film Record*, July 1915, p. 81.

The paramount importance of visual realism was stressed to an even greater extent in the use of lighting. By 1916 lighting was receiving much more attention and it was being openly recognized that a cameraman's capacity to light the studio set was one of his most important qualities. Dewsbury recalls,[1] for example, that much of the London film's reputation for good mounting was gained by the trouble and money spent on lighting, and cites Frenguelli as a brilliant young cinematographer whose flair for lighting distinguished him from the company's first cameraman, Lomas, much of whose earlier experience had been gained in actuality work and whose knowledge of studio lighting was small. This attention to lighting and the desire to control it led gradually to the disappearance of the old glass stages using both sunlight and lamps. Studios everywhere went "dark," although the important Walton studio, for one, continued to use a mixture of daylight and artificial light. There were various open and enclosed arc lamps, mercury vapour lamps (which were less frequently used), and the recent gas-filled lamps.[2] It was for the cameraman to decide which type of light was best and whether to have permanently installed lighting covering as large an area as possible or smaller portable sources. The best way to obtain diffused or local lighting, or in any particular case to represent daylight, moonlight, firelight, lamplight and so on, was his concern. But on the other hand an interesting series of articles on lighting in the *Bioscope* in 1918 appealed for producers with greater knowledge of technical problems and possibilities; they maintained that selection and composition of light and shade was in truth the art of the cinematographer. Moreover on several occasions it was suggested that the source and type of light required in any particular shot or sequence should be indicated by the script writer. British practice was severely condemned, and it was suggested in these articles that in most British studios the amount, type and position of the light were determined by nothing so much as the personal convenience of the producer. It seems that the most discussed problems were such things as the determination of how the various colours would photograph, or how far it would be possible to control daylight in out-door shooting by the use of portable screens. Little deliberate thought seems to have been given to the use of lighting to

[1] In an interview with the author.
[2] Described in the *Bioscope*, November 29, 1917, p. 46.

Chrissie White, probably in *The Eternal Triangle*, released in 1918, produced by Frank Wilson.

The Bottle

Released in 1915, produced by Cecil Hepworth.

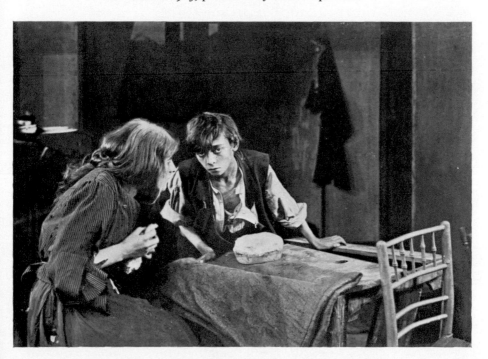

The Elder
Miss Blossom

Released in 1918, produced by Percy Nash, with C. M. Hallard, Isobel Elsom, Owen Nares.

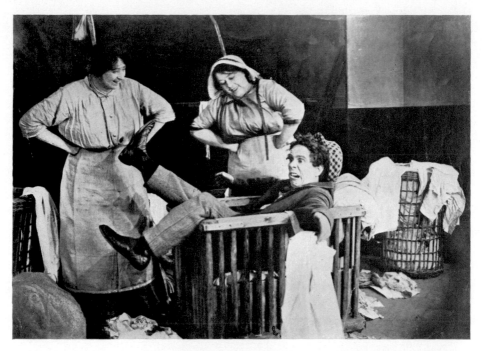

Billy Merson in *The Tale of a Shirt*, released in 1916, produced by W. P. Kellino.

Henry Edwards in *The Hanging Judge*, released in 1918, produced by Henry Edwards.

Towards the Light

Released in 1917.
Produced by Henry Edwards.
With Henry Edwards and Chrissie
White.

Merely
Mrs. Stubbs

Released in 1917.
Produced by Henry Edwards.
With Henry Edwards and Alma
Taylor.

Broken Threads
Released in 1918, produced by Henry Edwards, with Henry Edwards and Chrissie White.

The Second Mrs. Tanqueray

Released in 1916, produced by Fred Paul, with Sir George Alexander and Hilda Moore.

The Ware Case

Released in 1917, produced by Walter West, with Violet Hopson, Matheson Lang, Gregory Scott.

Her Luck in London

Released in 1914–15, produced by Maurice Elvey, with Fred Groves,
A. V. Bramble, and Elizabeth Risdon.

Florence Nightingale

Released in 1915, produced by Maurice Elvey, with Fred Groves, Elizabeth Risdon.

set the mood or heighten the drama of a sequence. How to give a convincing illusion of reality was a sufficiently large problem, and the only elaboration of this straightforward approach was to make the scene beautiful as well as real. The fusion of the two requirements in the following letter from E. S. Palmer, one of the most important cinematographers, is typical:

I do think that if you can get nice, pleasing quality throughout a picture it greatly enhances the value of the subject, for nice quality is pleasing to the eye, and puts the picture audience in a pleasing frame of mind to fully enjoy the subject. This is especially so if one gets suitable surroundings for the scene to be enacted, and if you can add some artistic lighting, that would help the scene. The photographer must study out the story from a photographer's point of view, just as the producer does from his view-point, keeping in mind the scheme of lighting required and light to get the desired effect, as the more realistic and natural the lighting is, the more convincing the scene will be, and if producer and photographer can each work together to make the lighting and atmosphere as natural as possible, the best results will be attained.[1]

This keen appreciation of the need to achieve some sort of illusion of reality is of the utmost importance, and may even be regarded as a clue to the whole theory of film making as it existed in this country at the time. The camera lens was seen not as the mind's eye, with power to apprehend abstractions, but as a veritable window through which the spectator viewed an imagined reality. Whether it opened on to two walls or three of the imaginary world—a point upon which theorists did not speak with one voice—the position of the window itself was naturally taken as fixed.

For, as a stage room is deficient in its fourth wall, so is a cinematograph play deficient in its third and fourth; seldom more than a corner of a room being shown at one time. This is a point that the prospective writer should bear in mind, for his action must be concentrated between two walls of a room set at right angles.[2]

Hepworth, who saw three walls, had unexceptionable ideals:

There is no art in which the concealment of art is of greater importance than in that of film-picture making, and there are very few in which it is so difficult. Unless, as a spectator at a picture show, you are deceived into the subjective belief that you are looking on at an actual happening, not at a conterfeited love

---

[1] *Bioscope*, October 14, 1915, p. 156.
[2] *The Art of Photo-Play Writing*, p. 18.

scene, not an assumed emotion, not, indeed, at acting in any shape or form, but at the real thing, then the picture has failed in its most important point. If your neighbour turns to you and says: "That was well acted!" he has condemned the picture. It is only when you find him affected, as he certainly would be if he were present in real life at the scene which is shown before him, that you can honestly say the picture is a success. In very truth a spectator should feel as though he were peeping through a fourth wall at the happenings between the other three; he should be as a silent invisible witness, right in the very heart of things, feeling, enjoying, suffering, in a sympathy with the people in the picture, and believing—not consciously of course, but subjectively and faithfully —in the reality of the things which he sees.[1]

Nothing, it seemed, would be more upsetting to the peeping spectator than that the window itself should move, and the prime necessity that he should be able to forget completely the intermediary, the camera, was made the excuse for great inelasticity in its use. In so far as it merely demanded that technique should be unobtrusive, this ideal was to remain unchanged. But other implications that were thought to be contained in it restricted the use of the camera more than was necessary, and if followed closely would have checked further development even more than they actually did. Weston's explanation of "the limits" refers only to the actors' need to keep within the vertical edges of the picture:

The "limits" . . . are given a great deal of attention, for should a slovenly producer neglect to mark out these very necessary lines, the characters will appear half on the screen only when they move towards the end of the picture; and thus the illusion of the play will be lost, by the audience being called to present conditions, as the one half of the actor disappears. . . . The "limits," so called because they mark off the outside edges of that artificial stage on which the screen actor plays his part, are achieved in the following manner. The camera expert looks through the view-finder while the producer or his assistant walks along the outside of the scene with a white handkerchief in his hand (white, because it will show up well through the lens); the camera-man signals when the handkerchief shows along the outside of the one side of the angle of view, and on this spot a chalk mark is made; the experiment is repeated on the other side of the stage. And when the chalk marks exactly indicate the angle within which the stage is in view of the lens, a length of white tape is stretched from the front leg of the camera tripod to the scenery at the back, and within these "limits" the actors must move.[2]

[1] Quoted in the *Bioscope*, September 30, 1915, p. 1481.
[2] *The Art of Photo-Play Writing*, pp. 20–21.

There was no difficulty by this date, however, with the fact that the horizontal edges of the picture, also, might exclude half the player's body. Movement to and from the camera and off to right or left of the camera was normal, and it must have been obvious to most producers that reality was not lost by showing only part of the player's body. Indeed, since the world was familiar with the same convention in static pictures there was little reason for such extreme caution. But fear of drawing attention to the camera did succeed in retarding the development of camera mobility and changes of camera angle within a sequence—Weston was doubtful about what he called the "run in method" of using the close-up, a device which, however, he admitted had been used by Fred Paul in *The Dop Doctor* and by Elvey in *The Suicide Club* with unusual success.[1] Even the use of the close-up itself in the middle of a scene had to show exceptional justification, while other changes of camera angle were even less considered. It is easy to understand, for example, that clarity might demand a close-up of, say, a hand slipping poison into a cup. But going into close-up for similar reasons to show the detail of an actor's face might not be thought worth the risk of defeating its own end by drawing attention to the technique. The boredom resulting from an almost unvarying camera angle can be imagined, particularly in long sequences, and is perhaps connected with the development, about this time, of the practice of masking. This, which is clearly inconsistent with attempts to make the audience forget the existence of the camera, was yet described even by Weston as a "welcome rest from the sameness of the shape of the screen."[2]

Nearer to the dramatic construction of the film lies acting, and here the important movement of the time was away from the representation of heroic lay figures to more subtle characterization. The necessarily simplified characters of melodrama needed to indulge only in what one paper summed up contemptuously as "arbitrary attitudinisings."[3] But the shift to film subjects employing character and emotion made greater demands on the players. The work of experienced stage actors was valuable here. Most of them did sufficient film work to learn to adapt their technique to the new medium, and in many cases joined stock companies and devoted all

[1] *The Art of Photo-Play Writing*, p. 40. [2] Ibid.
[3] *Kinematograph Monthly Film Record*, August 1915, p. 75.

their time to it. Visiting performances of top-ranking stage players were received with slightly less adulation than formerly and were sometimes even the subject of controversy; there are plenty of examples, of course, but the search for the type of prestige which such performances had brought shifted to the adaptation of novels or to the film companies' own production of stage plays, and away from the filming of existing stage productions. Nevertheless the majority of regular film players had actually received their training on the stage and contrasted favourably with all but the best of native film players. For this reason they had much to unlearn, as well as much to learn, and the famous Savoyard, Rutland Barrington, was voicing the feelings of many when he said that stage players must learn not to act to the camera, but simply in front of it.[1] Help was forthcoming in the way of close-ups and titles, much character background being packed into introductory titles, while Weston mentioned the spread of the American practice of introducing characters for the first time in close-up.[2] The formula of a close-up flash, a descriptive title and then more of the same close-up was also beginning to be used. But the important trend was the growth of more subtle and restrained mime. The little touches and imaginative allegories or "business" which replaced the earlier crude miming are described below. Here it is sufficient to note that "good looks, ease of movement, and natural deportment" were gradually being given as much emphasis as the "histrionic bag of tricks" and it was suggested that the normal British lack of gesticulation should help rather than hinder in the new ideal mime. In general the appearance of the players was more elegant, and indeed this was very necessary since works by such dramatists as Pinero and Oscar Wilde were now being filmed. More care was taken with make-up (which was still being used fairly sparingly), although young stars who played old people sometimes received biting criticism on this score. But in general the myth of the Amazon film star who fell over the cliff during shooting, and cracked a nonchalant joke as she hung suspended by a twig, was being superseded by the idea of real actors with individual performances to be assessed and compared. By 1916 this can be seen in the much more detailed criticism of individual performances and the importance of screenplays written as

[1] *Kinematograph Weekly*, January 20, 1916, p. 6.
[2] *The Art of Photo-Play Writing*, p. 41.

vehicles for particular players, while the fact that in several cases the permission of film companies was quoted when their stock players were lent to the legitimate stage is a hint of their improved status.[1] The appearance of star teams such as the important romantic partnership of Henry Edwards and Chrissie White, the more rigid "type" casting as in the case of Violet Hopson's "dear delightful villainess" or Henry Edwards's gentle hero, the glamorous appeal which lay behind the praise of Violet Hopson's choice of clothes—all these things were making their appearance as the star system continued to develop.

Acting leads us to a consideration of the film as a dramatic structure and as a form of story-telling. In the latter respect there was certainly considerable development, through the use of emphasized detail and indirect suggestion, frequently described at the time as symbolism. Ambitious allegory appeared in curious instances such as the paper boy's "struggle with the Tree of Knowledge" in *Merely Mrs. Stubbs*, or "Valentine's soul, sheltering in the wide expanse of space and burning with a torchlight flame," which was used as a *leit-motif* in *Flames*.[2] Tableaux were used to embellish or symbolize the main theme, as in a "Rodinesque group" in *The Middleman* entitled "Yet is their strength Labour,"[3] or the opening shot of *The Better 'Ole*, in which a posed group of three musketeers dissolved to a similar group of modern Tommies. An example of true symbolism was the candle in *Daddy*, which flickered and went out as the ailing father died.[4] More frequent was the selection of detail to suggest development in the action or simply the mood or personality of the characters. The work of some of the more important producers provides examples. In Tucker's *The Middleman*, for example:

. . . the most effective scene in the play is that in which the potter's daughter and her splendid young lover meet secretly in the dark garden. The girl is carrying a bunch of pure white lilies, but in surrendering herself to the passionate kisses of the man, the flowers fall to the ground and are there heedlessly trampled under foot by the latter. . . . This simple episode is a method of handling a difficult situation with the utmost force and effectiveness, and yet with complete delicacy.[5]

[1] E.g. *Bioscope*, April 29, 1915, p. 426; May 6, 1915, p. 586.
[2] *Kinematograph Monthly Film Record*, December 1917.
[3] *Bioscope*, February 18, 1915, p. 593.
[4] Ibid., August 2, 1917, p. 489.   [5] Ibid., February 18, 1915, p. 593.

The following much admired incident in Trimble's *My Old Dutch* was very different from the vigorous grief of melodrama:

. . . the scene following the death of their firstborn. They are seated by the glow of the fire in a half-darkened room. The woman is downcast and thinking of the little one she has lost. He tries in his rough way to comfort her; presently his hand strays to the mantle-shelf, and he picks up the kiddie's trumpet. With an impatient gesture he is about to throw it into the fire. She stays his hand, and the scene fades away.[1]

Bentley, too, used similar devices, such as the landlady putting up a notice of "rooms to let" after the father's death in *Daddy*,[2] while in *The Labour Leader* the audience became aware that there had been an accident by the sight of someone running for an ambulance, and the mother's death was indicated by the nurse pulling the blind as the father contemplated his newly born baby.[3] Even the reaction shot was described by Weston:

. . . the climax is reached by the actions of a third person, who is apparently watching the main action. It is through this third person's expression that the climax of suggestion is shown. The interest of the audience being thoroughly aroused by an anticipation of a tragedy; this sudden switching away from the main plot to a "close-up" view of a subsidiary character, who is showing by his expression that he is witnessing what is being withheld from the audience, is singularly effective.[4]

More symbolical was the use of the elements in *Burnt Wings*, in which a storm was cut in to the action to heighten the tragedy, or the shot in Edwards's *Broken Threads* of a "rugged coast with a solitary figure to express an utter loneliness."[5] These examples are given because they happen to have been recorded at the time, but there is every reason to think that some other producers, too, were using similar devices. Theoretically they continued to be regarded as a function of the script, although the amount of alteration and elaboration the latter received while the film was being taken was naturally large and much of the creative work was done by the producer after the script had been written. It was the more sentimental producers who made the greatest use of these subtle

[1] *Kinematograph Monthly Film Record*, August 1915, p. 82.
[2] *Bioscope*, August 2, 1917, p. 489.   [3] Ibid., June 21, 1917, p. 1164.
[4] *The Art of Photo-Play Writing*, p. 61.   [5] *Bioscope*, December 6, 1917, p. 38.

touches, and perhaps the best known example is one from the Edwards film *Towards the Light*, the famous "boot and the beetle" incident which, using a close-up, occupied a key position in the devélopment of the story:

He plays the part of Surly—it would be more truthful to say he lives the cripple, whose fine character has been roughened on the surface by the jeers and taunts of unthinking companions . . . he gains the reputation of hasty, ungovernable temper. . . . Into his life comes Annie. . . . He asks her to marry him. Thinking of his hasty temper, she hesitates, and replies: "If you will be kind to me." At that moment a blackbeetle scampers past Surly's foot. Most would have thoughtlessly crushed the creature, repulsive to the eyes of man, but instinctively he moves aside to avoid hurting an insect which also has the will to live. Annie knows from that minute that her happiness is safe in his hands. This is one of the cleverest touches in the play.[1]

Thus it was in the "little touches" of imaginative producers that there emerged a power of visual suggestion which was a true film alternative to verbal story telling. This empirical approach played its part also in the development of editing, but it was still so difficult to make the film entirely intelligible that comparative little energy was spent on elaboration in this respect. Thus although the camera set-up might be changed for an effect like the ones we have discussed the tendency was to leave it as it was. The scene was shot in long shot or long mid shot even at the cost of boring the audience and missing many an emotional shade which could have been brought out by greater selectivity.

Producers still relied heavily on titles, but there was a growing feeling that it was better to do without them. The use of illustrated titles was spreading, and Tucker gave an example of their deliberate use for dramatic effect when he used the same title twice, the second time in larger letters.[2] But on the whole the title was "the one real weakness of the photo-play, which cannot succeed without borrowing so definite a part of the literary art,"[3] and an Italian film[4] which actually had no titles at all, although a few letters and documents, was much admired.

There was an attempt among better producers to dispense with titles to some extent. But so great was the stress on intelligibility that anything,

[1] *Bioscope*, October 10, 1918, p. 39.   [2] Ibid., February 18, 1915, p. 593.
[3] *The Art of Photo-Play Writing*, p. 30.
[4] Itala's *A Page from Life*, *Bioscope*, July 13, 1916, p. 178.

even the need for cohesion in the film as a whole, could be justified on the grounds that it made the story easier to understand. The question of dramatic balance *per se* was not entirely overlooked, however, even by Weston.[1] In reality several ways of achieving balance occupied a fair amount of attention at the time. The fact that their most ambitious films still appeared to the public in mixed programmes of comics, interest films and so on, forced film makers to realize the importance of a good beginning and a clearly developed dramatic framework, and the structure of the reels was theoretically a matter of very delicate balance. In theory they were planned as acts[2] and Weston's scheme for an ideal balance for the first reel gave careful weight to dramatic factors:

The ideal story will open at a convenient point from which a climax may commence to evolve, it will grow during the first few hundred feet, until it reaches its consummation before the reel is halfway through, and from the moment this first climax has run its course, it will automatically blend into a further series of incidents dependent upon the main plot, which will in turn work towards a further climax, which should conclude the first reel.[3]

Another passage in the same book has more in common with later ideas of film editing, though in an extremely crude form:

By "preserving balance," is meant that not only should the story be well knit together, but that a series of long scenes should be balanced by a short one, before another series of long ones is entered upon. The author must mentally weigh his story, and if he discovers that he has all his short scenes at the beginning, and all his long ones at the end, or vice versa, he should revise them; for his play will be out of balance.[4]

But the fact that there was no clearly expressed idea of the function or possibilities of editing is the most important feature of the film technique which was common during this period. There are indications, too, that it was on this point that the British film makers stumbled more than some of their foreign rivals. A new comparison of the construction of the British and foreign films of the time will never be possible, because extremely

---

[1] Since Weston's views are frequently quoted it should be emphasized that they probably represent those of the average British film makers, and are more advanced than those of cheap and vulgar film adventurers, though not so much as those of Edwards, Tucker, Pearson or Hepworth.   [2] *The Art of Photo-Play Writing*, p. 39.
[3] Ibid., pp. 59–60.   [4] Ibid., p. 25.

few of the British productions have been preserved and these are not sufficiently representative. But it is significant that the very term "editor," which was becoming current by 1918, was regarded as an American importation. Moreover it is suggested both by contemporary reviews and by the recollections of a number of film pioneers that the pace of the ordinary British film compared especially unfavourably with that of the ordinary American film. There was, moreover, no British producer of the stature of D. W. Griffith. Only part of the implication of Griffith's own technique seems to have been appreciated here, and although his reputation was immense his methods were not fully understood. Traces of his influence occasionally come to light—Martin Thornton's style in *Diana and Destiny* was compared to Griffith's and in *The Divine Gift* Bentley experimented with a multiple story on a theme of universal human qualities which had something in common with *Intolerance*; but Martin Thornton's attempts at elaboration were noted only to be deplored for their confusion, while the several strands of Bentley's story were not intercut and in reality it had only the most superficial resemblance to Griffith's film. Although they may admire him, the film makers of the period do not as a rule acknowledge a debt to Griffith except in the case of the flashback, which was treated more or less as a tricky device not essentially related to the question of film structure. Pale reflections of his moral sentiments and the scale on which he worked emulated his success, but his inspired film technique was accepted in silence.

Nevertheless it is hard not to suspect that it was economical cutting which lay behind the "pace" so much admired in many American films :

. . . nothing appears to be rushed, and yet the play is carrying the spectator along at a rate which, if analysed, would indicate that climaxes were being rushed, situations forced and connecting scenes ruthlessly erased.[1]

Reviews of Pearson's *Study in Scarlet* pick it out as a fairly long British film not one scene of which could be discarded as inessential, and there are many indications that Pearson's films were outstanding for their tightly knit and rapid development. But admiration for economy of means in telling a story could be carried too far, and even legitimate continuity passages might be classed as "padding" in the enthusiasm for brevity.

[1] *The Art of Photo-Play Writing*, p. 66.

The fade had become a convention for suggesting that a period was being rounded off, or to indicate a lapse of time. The Edwards film *Broken Threads* was more subtle, with its "symbols of moving clouds to denote passage of time."[1] Nash, too, remembers that it was about this time that producers began to use the shot of an empty ash tray which dissolves to a shot of the same ashtray full of cigarette stubs. On the whole such bridges of time seem to have aroused less antagonism than bridges of space, but in either case their function was all too easily misunderstood:

If a man leaves one place and arrives at another, and nothing happens on the way, it is only padding to show us the journey. Will all producers please note. But there is an excuse for one motor-car ride in the play, as it shows us some lovely Surrey scenery.[2]

The ideal professed by Weston was a set of fairly long time sequences linked by "connecting scenes" which tided over awkward passages and each one of which was necessary to the development of the action.[3] But renters loudly complained of a tendency to puff out slender stories to films several reels too long, and although some producers were at fault here it was unfortunate that many of the "connecting scenes" seemed to the suspicious renter simply part of this tendency:

Repeatedly, for example, you will find every stage in a character's progress from one house to another laboriously reproduced, in spite of the fact that there are no incidents on the road he traverses of the faintest dramatic significance. This elaboration of non-essential details is not only tedious; it weakens the pictorial tension of the whole work. All such "padding" should be rigorously avoided, and no incident should be included unless it possesses definite dramatic value, entitling it to a legitimate place in the plot.[4]

Thus changes of camera set up within a sequence were thought to attract attention to the camera, and continuity bridges with too many cuts were condemned by the renters as padding. Consequently cutting seems to have been very restricted and, apart from the minimum required between sequences, was used chiefly for two things, literally justified close-ups

[1] *Bioscope*, December 6, 1917.
[2] *Kinematograph Monthly Film Record*, March 1916, p. 95.
[3] *The Art of Photo-Play Writing*, pp. 23–32.
[4] *Bioscope*, November 4, 1915, p. 503.

234

and parallel action. The use of parallel action was frequently confused with the flashback or cutback. Both were standard devices. They were like masking, in being deviations from straightforward filming which were recommended for the relief they gave from the tedious single camera angle.[1] In actual fact the case cited by Weston is that of parallel cutting of simultaneous action, although he called it the "flash-back":

I refer to the keeping of two apparently distinct stories running at the same time, and not allowing them to converge until the time is ripe for their being dovetailed.[2]

But there are also examples of the later sense of the term, beginning with a dissolve and giving a sequence earlier in time than the main body of the action. A number of films, too, opened with parallel cutting to point a contrast—a poor family and a rich family (*Auld Lang Syne*) or sinfully gay Society and the sadness of war were the type of contrasts used initially to set the theme of a film.

The close-up was used in several well-defined cases. At the beginning of the period it was a favourite comedy climax. (It may be remembered that the early use of the close-up at the beginning of the century had been largely for comic effect.) With or without titles, it was also found to be a good way of introducing the characters. Close-ups of letters, of course, were frequently used and were a compromise between real close shots and titles. And a complaint that few script writers employed close-ups enough indicates their most important use, which was as a pictorial emphasis of detail otherwise requiring a sub-title:[3]

. . . with the exception of a few scenario writers, the outside contributor seldom even suggests this method of explaining a difficult situation, and falls back instead upon the "sub-title," a much more crude way of expressing his ideas.

In this way the players could remain in the middle distance most of the time as seemed best, and yet subtle acting need not be lost. But whereas the flashback or parallel cutting did not actually move the imagined window in the middle of a scene from one position to another, it was impossible to avoid the conclusion that the close-up did so, and hence the need for literal justification in such cases.

[1] *The Art of Photo-Play Writing*, p. 36.
[2] Ibid., p. 35.
[3] Ibid., p. 38.

But although it can be said that the normal technique consisted of a rather steady use of long or long mid shots, it must be remembered that this is a generalization to which there must have been many exceptions. Henry Edwards, for example, states[1] that he had no objection to changing the camera set-up within a scene from one long shot to another or to a mid or close shot as long as the transition was made by means of a title.[2] But from the films still in existence it seems that such a step would only be taken by the more advanced directors.

It was the more advanced directors, too, who were consciously concerned with another factor in the smoothness of the cutting. According to Edwards neither he nor his colleagues would cut from a dark shot to a light one or *vice versa* without some continuity device such as a title or fade to reduce the optical jar. An extreme belief in smoothness was held by Hepworth. Perceiving that cuts jolted the spectator, he preferred to use a fade or dissolve whenever possible.[3] The limitations of the fade and dissolve are obvious. For example, an instance given by Weston of fading in to a masked close-up of a photograph would not now be considered the best possible way of showing that people were looking at it, a direct cut giving a better idea of the time relation involved, although the fade might be used to suggest that the photograph was in their thoughts.[4] But it has already been suggested that Hepworth, as a photographer and artist, was by training and inclination drawn primarily to beautiful composition rather than to dramatic structure. Both stills and reviews give evidence of the fine photographic quality and composition of his films. And since he was temperamentally inclined towards stories with a gentle, sustained tempo his much-discussed and very individual editing technique was perhaps well suited to his material. But people were probably far less sensitive to these shocks than he thought. Moreover the capacity to jolt the spectator is not merely useful in many dramatic situations which presumably would not have appealed to Hepworth, but part of the basis of film technique. It is hard to avoid the conclusion that his choice meant turning his back on a fundamental element in the nature of the film—a nature in which

[1] In an interview with the author.
[2] He also notes that when a dialogue title was to be used, the player would be filmed beginning the remark and ending it and the title would be cut in between the two parts of the shot.　　　[3] Fading was done in the camera by means of a screen.
[4] *The Art of Photo-Play Writing*, pp. 40–1.

rough cutting was after all merely the complement of smooth cutting. By devoting this much attention to the relations of the pictorial composition of adjacent shots as well as to the relations of their intellectual content he was, of course, far ahead of most producers; for too many who lacked his interest in photography and composition were guided only by the story development in assembling their film. But it is clear from Edwards's remarks that producers with a livelier tempo were also becoming aware of the fact that a cut meant a relation between two images which might itself convey something to the spectator, and should be controlled.

From all this it may be concluded that the fundamental ideas of film editing were beginning to emerge. But the work of cutting and assembling the film was still regarded as a mechanical and rather minor function of the producer, and, although we speak of "editing," the term itself was only just coming into use. The way in which it did so is interesting. For during 1918 such mention as there was of the "editor" usually referred to an employee of a renting company, whose functions were described in this way:

After he has watched the story on the screen, he has the whole of the film on the rewinders and in his fingers as he carefully analyses each scene, considering its bearing on the story and the possibility of reducing, quickening or omitting it. It is a big job, calling for a remarkable gift of visual memory, a keen sense of the relation between celluloid length and "screen length" and a thorough understanding of the things that please the public, to say nothing of a super-journalistic dexterity with scissors and paste; but is religiously performed with every film that goes out under the Phillips' trade mark, and Phillips make no secret of the fact that a great part of their reputation is due to the fact.[1]

The renter was in this way even able to impress a style of his own on the films he handled. It was proudly announced that during 1918 this particular company had discarded some nine thousand feet of the films they handled, including "unnecessary close-ups, slow movements and long-winded titles."[2] Sub-titles were particularly important, for it was frequently deplored that so many of them were badly written and even badly spelt, whilst many Americanisms in imported films were considered unsuitable for English audiences. Thus a primary function of the renter's editor was to improve the titles, aiming simply at clarity and accuracy, and thus in a

[1] *Bioscope*, November, 28, 1918, p. 22.   [2] Ibid.

real sense film editing was similar to the journalists' function from which it took its name.

The duty of the film editor, first, last and all the time, is to make the film so simple and clear that a child can follow it. If he does this he will have done all that is required of him, for a well-constructed story cannot fail to be interesting.[1]

It is ironical that it was through the renters' interference that the artistic importance of editing came into prominence. With the exceptions noted most producers seem to have given it little thought as a specific problem and their strongest feeling in connection with it was fury with the renter for his mutilation of their finished films:

Unfortunately, in England there are many firms of renters who have little or no conception of artistic effect; and who wantonly mutilate a film, because they think it will "rent" better at a less number of reels than it was originally produced for. This astounding thing happened to the author, who produced a film which ran to over four thousand feet, and was "cut" to a little more than three thousand, because the firm at the moment desired a "three-reeler" and not a four; the film was cut by a budding vandal, with the sledge-hammer fist of a prize fighter![2]

"Film editing is not a business man's job"[3] and the renters' activity seems to have stressed the importance of editing from the producers' point of view. When the same writer, in 1917, spoke of " 'cutting,' revising sub-titles, and occasionally suggesting an additional scene or scenes to strengthen the story" it was obviously the producer's editor that he had in mind. And signs of the future can be seen in an isolated expression of faith:

The importance of the film cutter is very seldom appreciated as it deserves to be. The photoplay is no more produced, until it goes into the cutting room to be edited, than a play before it goes into rehearsal. The photoplay is as truly made or unmade in the process of cutting as any stage production in the rehearsal period. Scenario writers, actors, directors may do their utmost, but the success of their work is never assured until the cutter or editor is through.

He may ruin a splendid idea of fine continuity, superb acting. He may take mediocre material and improve it. His is the ultimate work in the motion picture industry. . . .

Quite apart from matters of continuity, which may or may not be properly

---

[1] *Bioscope*, May 31, 1917, p. 811.
[2] *The Art of Photo-Play Writing*, p. 64. [3] *Bioscope*, May 31, 1917, p. 811.

or perfectly adapted in the mind's eye of the writer, the film editor controls that vitally important factor of screen art.

The cutter's work, limited, as it is, physically, is the most fascinating in the studio.[1]

But at this stage the "editor's" creative contribution to the film was certainly less important than that of, for example, the lighting cameraman and final responsibility for the conception of the film was ascribed to either the producer or the writer. The growing tendency was to emphasize the importance of the producer-director, a deliberate policy which insisted on many an apology in the trade press for previously omitting to mention the producer of some film. The phrase "produced under the personal direction of so-and-so," too, was marking the distinction of producer and director. But by many it was still believed, as it had been believed before the war, that the final responsibility was or should be on the writers' shoulders.

Many references to the importance of the scenarist built up a composite picture of a writer, the oft-sought "film Shakespeare," who would indicate everything in his script, including all lighting and movement:

He will mentally "set his scene," draft the movements of his characters that all may blend in harmony, into a complete picture, which shall be pleasing to the eye. He will, ever and again, suggest, during the course of his story, that such and such a character shall be in such and such a position, wherever he deems that the best effect may be achieved; he will not only work to climaxes, which shall be dramatic, but to climaxes which shall have picture value as well.[2]

He was to draw diagrams and make models to facilitate this.[3] He was to think of stories which could only be told in terms of pictures. He was, in fact, to overcome the artificial division between the visual and time elements of the film. The blame for the film's "slow progress" was reported to be laid by the American producer Lasky on the writer,[4] and a somewhat premature fear of exhausting the classics as a source of stories began to haunt people whose view, apparently, extended little further than *East Lynne* and *The Vicar of Wakefield* (both of which continued to be remade every now and then). But reproaches were not accompanied by practical

[1] *Bioscope*, January 24, 1918, p. 65.   [2] *The Art of Photo-Play Writing*, p. 75.
[3] Ibid., p. 74.   [4] *Kinematograph Weekly*, June 29, 1916, p. 11.

encouragement, and writers protested that neither pay, prestige, nor protection against plagiarism were adequate.[1]

Whether creation of the film lay in the writing or directing, however, none would have said that it lay in the cutting, and not even Griffith's work seemed to have drawn attention to the importance of editing—whether contained in the script or not—as the distinctive element in the art of the film. In so far as there was any formulated basis of the film technique then practised it was, instead, the idea of the camera lens as the spectator's window on to the scene. From this followed quite naturally the features we have discussed—a certain inelasticity in the camera set-up, literal continuity, and the search for realism. More imaginative use of the film medium was appearing in the "little touches" given to their story by some producers. But for the more timid or the less skilful, the supposed need for literal treatment acted as a drag on such advance. The excessive care to wipe out the audience's consciousness of the camera, the lack of faith in its ability to follow any but rather laborious continuity, have a parallel in the history of the novel. The careful explanation given by so many early novelists of how they came to know the stories which they were about to tell or why they were telling them shows a similar uncertainty that people would accept their authority, a similar anxiety to justify the use of their medium. Meanwhile the co-operative nature of film making was beginning to cast a shadow on the former happy assumption that the film was an art form. Doubtfully, enthusiasts had to combat the charge that here was no individual creative process, that author, director and players merely pooled their separate talents and produced a more or less mechanical record of their various arts. But although it was still too early for a theory of editing as the film's distinctive quality, it was not too early for the film to have its true believers:

. . . it is to this newest of arts which is given the power of awakening the people's minds from their apathy toward art in general . . . audiences whose inner artistic souls have been touched and awakened by the picture play . . . it has given the pleasures of the highest art to the multitude, in a way that they can understand. It is the greatest democratic factor of the twentieth century.[2]

[1] E.g. *Bioscope*, July 13, 1916, p. 109.
[2] *The Art of Photo-Play Writing*, p. 125.

British Film Studios—1900—1920

A TECHNICAL SURVEY

by BAYNHAM HONRI

Long before entering the business, I went through the schoolboy phase which usually results in some kind of "collecting" craze—tram tickets, conkers, or railway engines. My particular craze was the unusual one of "collecting" film studios and their equipment, and many were the miles I cycled to see and, if possible, to "infiltrate" into, some of these early studios. Cecil Hepworth was something of a god to me, and when, somehow or other, I managed to get into the Walton-on-Thames studio, the great man showed me around the premises himself, including a thorough inspection of his new automatic developing and print plant—which was then the most up-to-date in the country. It is interesting to note that, on that particular day, Alma Taylor and other principals were not playing in a film and were usefully occupying their time spooling up film as it came off the drying machine! My grubby little note-book was filled with sketches and other information of this seventh heaven, and I thereupon determined to be a "film manufacturer" when I grew up instead of a locomotive engine driver. (There was too much competition in the engine driving business, anyway, as the whole of my form IIIb had selected that particular profession.)

Some of these schoolboy notes and memories have enabled me to make some contribution to the Table following this Appendix, in which the technical facilities of all British studios of the period are collated.

A Typical "Glasshouse" Studio

Let us first consider the technical facilities available at an average British film studio of, say, 1913.

The pre-1914 studio premises usually comprised a large glasshouse type of studio with a stage which had approximately the same dimensions as that of a theatrical stage. Indeed, many films were made of stage productions in which the painted canvas theatrical scenery was used. The British Empire Films Studio in the 4-acre grounds of "Woodlands," Whetstone, near Barnet, was typical of one of the lesser important studios of the time, and can be described in detail. This studio was used by Walter and Frederick Melville for making, under the trade name of "British Empire Films," film versions of their bloodcurdling Lyceum melodramas, *The Female Swindler*, *The Bad Girl of the Family*, etc., and by their associated company, Zenith Films Limited, for Oscar Asche's big His Majesty's Theatre productions *Kismet* and Seymour Hicks' *Scrooge*, *Always Tell Your Wife*, etc. The stage scenery from both theatres was accommodated comfortably on the 40 ft. by 45 ft. glasshouse stage, and the large sliding doors opened up to enable the cameraman to set up his camera outside for extreme long shots.

The glass was of muranese or morocco type for diffusing the sunlight and reducing the shadow effects of the sun, and blinds and calico diffusers were also available. Behind the stage was a scene dock and a small workshop. From the roof of the stage were suspended about sixteen Westminster enclosed arcs, and an additional twelve of these lamps were mounted in groups of two or four on mobile floor stands, known as "guillotines." Current was drawn direct from the Finchley Corporation mains at 250 volts, which enabled the lamps to burn a very long violet-coloured arc, highly actinic and quite suitable for the non-red sensitive negative film stock of that time.

At this studio, like many others at the time, developing and printing was carried out, and there was a small laboratory in the basement of the house, which was also used for offices and dressing rooms. Mention should also be made of the extensive ornamental grounds, small lake and various permanent "props," which were used time and time again.

Premises

Studio stages specially built before 1914 all more or less conformed to the same pattern. Following the ideas of R. W. Paul at Southgate and Williamson at Brighton, they were virtually large glass sheds for housing the scenery and enabling a camera to be placed outside the structure to obtain long shots. Forty or fifty feet square was considered adequate stage space, and the floor itself was frequently extended outside the sliding doors to accommodate additional sections of set in the open air. Shooting a set inside the studio with the sliding doors open, so that the exterior view of trees, etc., could be seen through the windows of the set, was a normal procedure—excepting on a windy day. Barker's first two stages at Ealing, M.L.B. at Esher, and British Empire at Whetstone, were examples of this type. Later in this period, it became the practice to build the studio stage on the first floor, with workshops, prop room and sometimes a developing plant underneath. Barker's No. 3. stage was considered a good example of this type, with a stage 80 ft. × 30 ft. and an "apron" above extensive workshop premises, and this plan was also carried out by Cunard (later Broadwest) at Walthamstow, Windsor at Catford, Homeland at Kew Bridge, Herkomer at Bushey, and, of course, at Hepworth's Walton plant.

Lighting

It soon became apparent that the hours of shooting were severely limited with daylight studios, especially in the winter time. In addition, the intensity of light varied a great deal, even from minute to minute, and it was necessary to post an assistant at the studio door to shout when the sun was emerging from behind a cloud.

Artificial lighting was then introduced. By 1900 the Westminster enclosed arc had become the standard unit of lighting, and numbers of these were suspended from the roof and mounted on floor stands. This lamp was an adoption of the long-burning shop-front and street light arc of that period—long before the days of incandescent gas-filled metal filament bulbs. With the negative film stock (non-panchromatic), at that time, the violet-coloured enclosed arc was equal to about three open white arcs.

In 1912 the Cooper-Hewitt mercury vapour tube, extensively used in many American studios, was also introduced. This mixture of daylight and violet-coloured artificial lighting made it extremely difficult to judge exposure accurately, but cameramen became proficient after hard experience.

It will be realized that the intensity of light in these glasshouse studios was high, especially when supplemented by banks of artificial lights. This was necessitated by the low transmission of the kine camera lenses of that time which worked, when full open, at f./3.5 or f./4.5, and the insensitivity of the negative film stock. The f./2 lens of to-day, which transmits three or four times the amount of light, was unheard of. During the summer time, in daylight studios, the lenses were stopped down to f./5.6 or even f./8 on bright days.

Film Stock

Negative and positive emulsions were coated on imported film base at the factories of Kodak, Harrow; Austin Edwards, Warwick; Criterion, Birmingham and Brifco, Ashford. Coated negative and positive stocks were also freely imported from Pathé, Gaumont and Lumière (France) and from Agfa (Berlin). The negative stock was orthochromatic and slow; and quite insensitive to the red end of the spectrum, consequently soldiers' red tunics, pillar boxes and London buses all reproduced as black. Also, this necessitated the use of heavy pale yellow (Leichner No. 5) make-up on the artistes' faces. Film stock was supplied unperforated to studios, who carried out this job themselves.

Camera Equipment

The first commercially successful "professional" cine camera was made by Messrs. J. A. Prestwich of Tottenham, in 1899, and this camera was used by nearly all the early British producers for some years. The Prestwich was followed by the Williamson, the Darling and the Moy cameras,[1] all British-made and all rather cumbersome wooden-box affairs. For a long time the Moy camera was the most popular and large numbers were sold to studios and topical film makers all over the world. Moy also made the two-colour process Kinemacolor cameras for Charles Urban.

Will Barker, always a bold pioneer, was the first producer to fit 1,000 ft. magazines to his cameras, which he did for the filming of long Shakespearian scenes in 1913. The normal capacity of the studio cameras was the rather odd length of 350 ft. Great economy was exercised with negative film, and cameramen were expected to join old sections of spacing on the front, to avoid wastage in threading up. One take per scene was the rule. Even the opening of the camera to check the gate for scratches was frowned upon, owing to the consequent fogging of a few feet of negative.

In 1914 the French Pathé and Debrie cameras were imported. Both cameras were quite revolutionary with the many refinements that were made available. The extreme portability of the "cigar box" Debrie camera, with its 400 ft. magazines side-by-side, its front iris and mask-box in front of the lens, its easily manipulated focusing and fading rods and its automatic reverse, made a big impression and it was immediately adopted by Hepworth, Homeland, and London Film Company. All cameras were hand-turned. Hepworth and others experimented with electric motor drive, but abandoned it as being unreliable. The battery driven camera motor was first introduced by Bell and Howell, and Newman, at the end of the period under review.

It is interesting to note that the catalogue price of the Pathé professional cine camera (without accessories) in 1914 was £70, compared with over £2,000 for a modern studio camera! In these early days, many cameramen owned their own cine camera outfits.

Most of the cameras were fitted with German lenses, the most popular being the Zeiss Tessar f./3.5 and the Voightlander f./4.5. The range of lenses was generally restricted to 3 in. and 2 in. focal length, the latter giving the widest angle then available.

Laboratory

It will be noted that, unlike present day practice, almost every studio perforated, developed and printed its own rushes, and some studio plants also printed release copies. Hepworth and Barker had elaborate automatic developing and printing equipment. The laboratory equipment at most of the studios was rather more primitive, however. Pin frame or rack frames were used in horizontal or vertical developing tanks, respectively, and drying was carried out on huge revolving wooden drums, which, in a few instances, were hand turned!

[1] Moy and Bastie's daylight loading cinematograph camera patented 1900 (No. 4534).

Negatives were usually developed in a pyro-soda bath, and it is therefore not surprising that negatives which were "good" were also called "strong," "robust" or "plucky." Plenty of contrast and everything dead sharp was the exhibitors' demand at the time, and the technicians saw that they got it.

Print densities were considerably lighter than they are now, for light intensities on projectors in the cinemas were extremely low. In 1914 there were still a few small halls and travelling shows using some kind of limelight as an illuminant for their projectors. The term "limelight prints" was used to denote specially light prints long after the final disappearance of this fascinating (if somewhat feeble) type of illumination.

At the Homeland studios, cameraman D. P. Cooper developed all his own negatives in the kitchen sink, on pin frames, and this was by no means an unusual practice! It was considered essential for every cameraman to have a thorough training in the dark rooms before he was allowed to "turn" a camera, and many of them preferred to develop their own negatives.

Excepting at the Hepworth and Barker automatic developing plants, the length of each section of negative which could be printed at a time, was limited by the capacity of the developing frames—about 200 ft. Non-automatic printing machines were of the most elementary type in which the negative was allowed to feed into a box or basket. During the printing process, the operator watched the illumination of the gate of the printer as the negative passed through it and adjusted the light intensity (by means of a mechanical device) according to his "snap judgment" of the density. Some operators became highly skilled at the work, and by means of keeping a finger lightly touching the moving negative above the gate, were able to feel the approach of joins (and probable change in density) and anticipate light changes with great accuracy.

In about 1913 the improved Williamson printing machine was introduced, with the refinement of a take-up for the negative, together with an audible electrical detection device which gave pre-warning of changes of negative density. This warning was operated by a notch made in the edge of the negative.

Nevertheless, in spite of primitive equipment, processing work of a most ambitious order was frequently carried out. Double-printing with two negatives and toning of positives (green, sepia or blue) was a routine job and dye baths for amber, green, blue or red were in everyday use. Night scenes required the blue stain, fire scenes the red and the inevitable "and so we say farewell" sunset was given the double-treatment of "tone blue—tint pink"! Gradual changes from one colour to another were achieved by hand-tinting on a large drum, notable results being achieved in early trick comedy films (e.g. *The Devil to Pay* of J. H. Martin Ltd.) and later in the much more ambitious productions of Welsh-Pearson & Co. at Craven Park Studio, Harlesden.

Indeed, the cameraman whose finger nails were stained yellow with pyro-soda developer was much more likely to get a job than one with lily-white hands.

Viewing Rushes

Review theatre facilities at most British studios prior to 1920 were usually of the most primitive kind. Exceptions were to be found at the Walton Studios, where Cecil Hepworth had a beautifully fitted out miniature kinema in a loft, and at the London Film Company's St. Margaret's studios, where the projection theatre adjoined the huge stage—the largest in England at the time. The Bushey Studio had the use of a small theatre (complete with stage and organ) which had been specially built for Sir Hubert Herkomer, the famous painter, whose residence was later the headquarters and studio of the British Actors Film Company. At most studios, however, a projection machine was set up in a workshop, an office, or even a long corridor, and the use of a fireproof projection booth was dispensed with. Fire regulations were strict at cinemas, where the public paid for admission, and were in themselves a basis for the enforcement of other controls of an entirely different kind—such as the exhibition of uncensored films! But the studios seemed to be outside the scope of either Factory Acts or Regulations covering "Theatrical Performances" and were left to carry on in their own way. Broadwest, for instance, showed rushes under very primitive conditions, and at their Walthamstow studio a screen was set up in a property store, with the machine out in the open in the same room. At the Broadwest Studio at Catford, a canteen was used for viewing. Nevertheless, there seems to be no record of any film studio fire, apart from fires at associated film laboratories. The worst of these occurred in 1918 at the London Film Company's laboratories at St. Margarets, when the negatives of dozens of important British films went up in flames.

Scenery and Properties

Studios carried large numbers of stock flats, painted canvas on wood frames. On open-air stages, these flapped in the breeze but were tightened up by pasting layers of newspaper on the backs. There was little effort in art direction and a stage manager would assemble a number of stock pieces of set in accordance with the producer's requirements.

At Shepherds Bush Studios in 1915 and 1916 George Pearson was directing a lurid series called *Ultus—The Man from the Dead* in which the name part was played by a real "Tarzan-type" he-man. Every time he entered a scene and slammed the door the whole set shook and the door handle usually came off. After this the sets were more solidly built of three-ply on wood framing, with much improved pictorial results.

It was not until the London Film Company was established in 1913 in its converted skating rink at St. Margaret's Twickenham, that the Art Direction side of British film production was taken seriously. Under Dr. Jupp, the Managing Director, a standard of detail and finish was achieved which surpassed even the best American efforts. (The London Film Company was associated with the huge Provincial Cinematograph Theatres which owned sixty of the best cinemas. The first British example of a "vertically integrated combine"?)

The last important film which boasted "entire production and scenery from His Majesty's Theatre" was Matheson Lang's *Merchant of Venice*, which Walter West produced for Broadwest at Walthamstow in 1918. It must be admitted that the painted canvas scenery detracted considerably from what might have been a very fine effort.

During the final phase of the period under review, 1918–1920, a number of pictures were made in the new larger studios, converted from skating rinks and the like, such as St. Margarets, B & C Walthamstow and Clapham Park. All of these studios were "dark" or had their glass roofs blacked out and used artificial light exclusively. Immediately after the war American cameramen came to England and brought with them various American items of equipment, such as Bell and Howell cameras, Wingfield Kerner, Wohl and Kleigl lights and the technique of back-lighting with spot lamps. Blueprints were on the table for the huge new Stoll studios at Cricklewood and the Islington studio of Famous Players-Lasky British Producers Limited, in which facilities in line with the latest Hollywood practice were to be provided. Slowly the technique of camera work improved and more attention was given to lighting effects, modelling and the correct monochrome rendering of various colours. The days of the enclosed arc, the kitchen developing tank and the canvas set were over. The days of the versatile studio worker who could build sets, work the camera or act in a film were numbered. Specialization had arrived and the British film industry had grown up.

	Boreham Wood Elstree	Bushey Lululand, Melbourne Rd.	Croydon Wadden New Road	Whetstone "Woodlands" Great North Road
STUDIO ..				
PRODUCING COMPANIES ..	1913: Neptune Film Co. Ltd. (Percy Nash) 1917: Ideal Films Ltd. (S. Rowson) 1918: British Lion Film Co. (D. Falke) (No connection with present British Lion Films)	1912-13: Herkomer Film Co. 1914-20: British Actors Film Co. Ltd. (G. Malvern)	1910-18: Cricks & Martin Ltd. 1918: Gaiety Productions Syndicate Ltd.	1913: British Empire Films Ltd. & Zenith Films Ltd. 1919: British Famous Films Ltd.
REMARKS ..	The first specially built "dark" stage in England	All-glass studio stage specially built as addition to mansion.	Premises converted to studio. 1923: converted to garage.	Specially built all-glass stage in grounds of large country house
STAGES ..	1 dark stage, 36 ft. × 61 ft.	1 all-glass stage, 30 ft. × 45 ft. (with dark blinds)	1 stage, 65 ft. × 30 ft. with glass roof (side of studio opening to lot, with apron)	1 all-glass stage 40 ft. × 45 ft. with one side opening, with apron stage outdoors
LOT SPACE ..	1 acre	4 acres, garden and estate of late Sir Hubert Herkomer	½ acre	About 3 acres, with gardens and lake
No. OF STAFF ..	60 (including stock company of actors)	30 plus stock company of actors	12	Not known
CAMERAS ..	Pathé, Debrie Later: Bell & Howell	Debrie and Bell & Howell	Moy, Pathé, Prestwich (for titles)	Moy
LIGHTS ..	35 Westminster arcs	15 Westminster arcs 6 Mercury vapour tubes	24 Westminster arcs 6 Mercury vapour tubes	36 Westminster arcs
POWER SUPPLY ..	Generator driven by gas engine	Gas engine driving D.C. generator plus current from mains	Power from Corporation mains plus small rotary converter	250 volts D.C. from Corporation mains
FILM PROCESSING	On premises	On premises	On premises	On premises, in basement of house
No. OF PRINTS ..	30	20-30	20-30	Not known

	Ealing *Ealing Green*	Bayswater *225 Queens Road*	Esher *Portsmouth Road*	Catford *The Hall, Bromley Road*
STUDIO	Barker Motion Photography Ltd.	1912–15: Weston-Finn Feature Film Co. Ltd. 1915–18: Piccadilly Comedies	1913: M.L.B. Productions 1916: Broadwest Films Ltd.	1912: Kent Film Company 1913: Windsor Films Ltd. 1915: N.B. Films Ltd. 1919–22: Broadwest Films Ltd.
PRODUCING COMPANIES				
REMARKS	Specially built all-glass stages in ornamental grounds of large house		Studios stage and work-shops specially built. Other premises existing	Studio stage specially built as extension to large country house
STAGES	3 daylight stages: No. 1: 60 ft. × 20 ft. (with 20 ft. sliding doors) No. 2: 60 ft. × 30 ft. No. 3: 80 ft. × 30 ft. (on first floor with workshops under)	1 stage, part glass roof (25 ft. × 35 ft.)	All-glass stage 60 ft. × 28 ft.	1 all-glass stage on first floor, 100 ft. × 50 ft., with workshops and labs. underneath
LOT SPACE	3¾ acres	None	¼ acre	2 acres
NO. OF STAFF	75 (including stock company of 22)	Not known	Not known	Not known
CAMERAS	Moy and other	Moy	M.L.B.: Moy. Broadwest: Pathé, Debrie	Windsor: Pathé, Darling. Broadwest: Debrie
LIGHTS	24 Westminster arcs 50 Mercury vapour tubes	10 Westminster arcs	18 Westminster arcs	40 Westminster arcs 4 Westminster Spots } Broadwest 6 Kleigl spots } west
POWER SUPPLY	230 volts A.C. from Corporation mains	150 amps from mains	From mains	Gas engine driving generator plus Corporation mains
FILM PROCESSING	On premises. Lab. underneath No. 3 stage	Not known	Cottage adjoining converted to dark room where film processing was done	On premises
NO. OF PRINTS	Up to 25, staged Up to 250, topicals			

	Walthamstow 245 Wood Street	St. Margarets The Barons, E. Twickenham	Merton Park Quentin Avenue	Victoria 115a Ebury Street, S.W.
STUDIO				
PRODUCING COMPANIES ..	1914: Cunard Films Ltd. 1915–22: Broadwest Films Ltd.	1913–21: London Film Co. Ltd. (Associated with Provincial Cinematograph Theatres Ltd.)	1912: J. H. Martin Ltd.	1912–14: British Oak Film Co. Ltd. 1915: New Agency Film Co. Ltd. 1917: Artistic Films Ltd. 1919: Geo. Clarke Productions Ltd.
REMARKS ..	Studio stage specially built	Originally a skating rink	Specially built	Converted from store
STAGES	1 all-glass stage on first floor, 115 ft. × 45 ft., with workshops and labs. under	1 stage 165 ft. × 75 ft., with part glass roof 1916: glass blacked out	2 stages 70 ft. × 40 ft., all glass, with blinds and diffusers	1 stage, 90 ft. × 25 ft., with part glass roof
LOT SPACE ..	½ acre	¾ acre	¼ acre	¼ acre
NO. OF STAFF ..		50–60 plus stock company of actors	15	9
CAMERAS ..	Moy, Debrie	Pathé, Debrie, Moy	Prestwich, Moy	Moy, Debrie (slow motion)
LIGHTS	30 Westminster arcs 1 L.E.C. searchlight	120 Westminster arcs 6 Mercury vapour tubes 8 Boardman "North Lights"	Westminster arcs Mercury vapour tubes	20 Westminster arcs
POWER SUPPLY ..	Corporation mains	300 k.w. rotary converter (from Twickenham mains)	Direct from corporation mains	500 amps. from Corporation mains
FILM PROCESSING	On premises	At firm's own works in Crown Road. (Burned down 1918)	On premises	On premises
NO. OF PRINTS ..		From 12 to 50	35	

	Hackney Tuileries Street	East Finchley Newstead House Great North Road	Eel Pie Island Twickenham	Alexandra Palace N.W. Tower, etc.
STUDIO	Hackney Tuileries Street	East Finchley Newstead House Great North Road	Eel Pie Island Twickenham	Alexandra Palace N.W. Tower, etc.
PRODUCING COMPANIES ..	1913–20: Union Jack Film Co. Ltd. (Lawrence Cowen)	1910(?)–13: British & Colonial Film Co. Ltd. (J. B. MacDowell) (Removed in 1913 to Walthamstow)	1912–15: Phoenix Film Co. Ltd. ("Folly" comedies) 1918: Hagen & Double ("Kinekature" comedies)	1912–14: Union Film Publishing Co. Ltd. ("Big Ben" Film) (Associated with Pathé)
REMARKS ..	Converted from disused gas works	Large private house and grounds	Converted from boat builder's shed	Indoor studio converted from skating rink. (Later reconverted to rink)
STAGES	1 dark stage 75 ft. × 30 ft. × 30 ft. high	1 open-air stage 50 ft. × 30 ft.	1 part-glass stage 30 ft. × 25 ft.	1 dark stage: 70 ft. × 60 ft. 1 open-air stage: 65 ft. × 40 ft.
LOT SPACE ..	None	2 acre grounds		¼ acre, including special open air stage with diffusers
NO. OF STAFF ..	Not known		12 (including 6 at lab. in London)	10
CAMERAS	Moy	Moy	Moy	Moy, Pathé
LIGHTS	20 Westminster arcs	None	6 Westminster arcs 4 Cooper-Hewitt mercury vapour banks	15 Westminster arcs
POWER SUPPLY ..	Corporation mains	Corporation mains	Corporation mains	Generators driven by gas engines
FILM PROCESSING	Not on premises	At firm's own lab. in 33 Endell Street, W.C.	At firm's own lab. in Charlotte Street, W.I.	Not on premises
NO. OF PRINTS ..	Not known	Not known	20–40	Not known

	Shepherd's Bush Lime Grove	Kew Bridge (South Side) Above Boat House Hotel	Kew Bridge (North Side) Prince's Studio	Thames Ditton Portsmouth Road
STUDIO				
PRODUCING COMPANIES	1913: Gaumont Co. Ltd.	1915–19 Homeland Films Syndicate Ltd. (Billy Merson, W. P. Kellino) 1919: Stoll Film Co. Ltd.	1919: Lucky-Cat Films 1920: Lucoque Ltd. 1922–25: Walter West Productions Ltd.	1913: Comedy Combine Co. 1915–18: Climax Film Co. 1920: Standard Kine Laboratories (Later: Dufay-Chromex Ltd.)
REMARKS	Specially built as studio: stage on first floor, with workshops and labs. underneath	Studio formerly a dance hall.	Converted from theatre to studio. (Has since been reconverted into the "Q" Theatre)	Premises used chiefly as a film developing and printing laboratory
STAGES	1 all-glass stage 90 ft. × 40 ft. × 20 ft. high: end section 30 ft. high. Glass blacked out in 1917	1 all-glass stage on first floor 44 ft. × 40 ft. with lights	1 dark stage 90 ft. × 60 ft.	1 glass-roofed stage 35 ft. × 25 ft.
LOT SPACE		Grounds of Boat House Hotel occasionally used	None	None
No. OF STAFF		5	Varied from 6 to 30	6
CAMERAS	Debrie	Debrie	Debrie	
LIGHTS	Westminster arcs Boardman "Northlight" lamps	20 Westminster arcs 2 banks Cooper-Hewitt mercury vapour tubes	24 Westminster arcs 4 Wohl broadsides 2 Kleigl spots } 1924	10 Westminster arcs
POWER SUPPLY	Corporation mains and motor generator set	Corporation mains	Corporation mains	Corporation mains
FILM PROCESSING	On premises	Negatives only developed on premises (Homeland) Printed at Williamson's, Barnet	Not processed on premises	Developing and printing on premises
No. OF PRINTS		20 prints (Homeland comedies)		

	Teddington Weir House	Shoreham, Sussex Bungalow Town	Walton-on-Thames Hurst Grove	Croydon 16 Limes Road
STUDIO				
PRODUCING COMPANIES	Master Film Company	1913: Sunny South Film Co. 1913–18: Progress Film Co. Ltd. (Sidney Morgan)	1910: Hepworth Film Manufacturing Co. Ltd.	Clarendon Film Co. Ltd. Harma & Co. Ltd.
REMARKS	Specially built daylight stage in grounds of mansion	Specially built. Daylight only, no supplementary lighting	Stages specially built on first floor, workshops and labs. underneath	Specially built stages
STAGES	1 all-glass stage 60 ft. × 40 ft.	1 all-glass stage 50 ft. × 30 ft.	Stage 1: 50 ft. × 25 ft. (all glass) Stage 2: 35 ft. × 25 ft. (all glass)	1 stage 60 ft. × 25 ft. (part glass) 1 stage 80 ft. × 35 ft. (all glass) added later
LOT SPACE	3 acres, well wooded, with mansion	None	½ acre	3 acres across road from studio, including 1 acre lake
NO. OF STAFF			40–60	20
CAMERAS	Moy, Debrie	Moy, Pathé	Prestwich, Moy, Debrie	Moy (with external magazines)
LIGHTS	Westminster arcs	No lights used—reflectors, diffusers and blinds only	20 Westminster arcs 16 Open arcs 1 "searchlight"	Westminster arcs
POWER SUPPLY	Not on premises	None	240 D.C. from mains	Corporation mains
FILM PROCESSING	Not on premises	Not on premises	First automatic developing and printing plant in Britain, under stages	On premises
NO. OF PRINTS				50 to 100

STUDIO	Clapham Cranmer Court	Isleworth Worton Hall, Worton Rd.	Surbiton Regent House, Park Road	Leyton 588 Lea Bridge Road
PRODUCING COMPANIES	1913: Cherry Kearton Film Co. 1914–18: Bertram Phillips Productions 1919: Quality Film Plays Ltd.	1913–21: Samuelson Film Manufacturing Co. Ltd. (G. B. Samuelson)	1918–23: Stoll Film Co. Ltd.	I.B. Davidson Film Company
REMARKS	Premises under railway arches	Stages specially built in grounds of country mansion.	Studio stage in ballroom of mansion	Converted from old horse tram shed
STAGES	1 dark stage 45 ft. × 30 ft.	1 all-glass stage 50 ft. × 40 ft. (later enlarged to 65 ft. × 40 ft.) 1 stage 85 ft. × 30 ft., glass roof only	1 dark stage 25 ft. × 60 ft.	1 dark stage 60 ft. × 40 ft.
LOT SPACE	None	Well-wooded grounds and lawns, 5 acres	3 acres ornamental grounds	
NO. OF STAFF		20	35	6
CAMERAS	Pathé, Moy	Pathé	Debrie	Moy, Debrie
LIGHTS	Westminster arcs with Barkay reflectors	30 Westminster arcs 24 Wingfield-Kerner lights	Westminster arcs	35 Westminster arcs
POWER SUPPLY	Corporation mains	From mains	From mains	Corporation mains
FILM PROCESSING	On premises	On premises	Developing and printing (rushes only) on premises	Negatives developed on premises
NO. OF PRINTS				

	Walthamstow Hoe Street	Clapham Park Thornton House	Manchester Rusholme	Torquay Watcombe Hall, Babbacombe
STUDIO				
PRODUCING COMPANIES	British and Colonial Kinematograph Co. Ltd. (J. B. MacDowell)	1919–22: Bertram Phillips Productions	Lancashire Film Studios	1918–20: Raleigh-King Film Co.
REMARKS	Converted from old skating rink	Stage specially built in grounds of house		Specially built in grounds of mansion
STAGES	1 stage 150 ft. × 60 ft. × 12 ft. high (part-glass roof)	1 stage (dark) 130 ft. × 35 ft.	2 stages 50 ft. × 40 ft. and 50 ft. × 30 ft.	2 all-glass stages each 55 ft. × 60 ft. (No. 1 side opened to face sea)
LOT SPACE		1 acre, grounds of house	None	4 acres
NO. OF STAFF			6	
CAMERAS	Moy, Pathé	Pathé	Moy, Williamson	Debrie
LIGHTS	21 Westminster arcs 1 open arc	Westminster arcs	Westminster arcs Whol "broadsides"	Westminster arcs
POWER SUPPLY	Mains	Mains	Mains	100 kVA. from mains
FILM PROCESSING	Processing done at Company's lab., 33 Endell Street, W.C.	Not on premises	At National Film Agency, Victoria Street, Manchester	
NO. OF PRINTS				

STUDIO	*Harlesden* *Craven Park*
PRODUCING COMPANIES ..	1918–30: Welsh, Pearson & Co. Ltd. (Geo. Pearson)
REMARKS	Conversions and additions to old school premises
STAGES	1 dark stage, 100 ft. × 60 ft.
LOT SPACE	None
NO. OF STAFF	12 to 15
CAMERAS	Debrie
LIGHTS	36 Westminster arcs 2 Jupiter sun arcs 6 Digby lamps
POWER SUPPLY	Corporation mains
FILM PROCESSING	On premises
NO. OF PRINTS	

Other Studios of which particulars are not available:

Studio	Producing Companies	Date
TOWERS HALL, Manchester Road, Bradford	Captain Kettle Film Company Pyramid Films Ltd.	1912–1914
CRYSTAL PALACE (section of)	Motograph Film Company	1913
GREAT PORTLAND STREET	Pathé Frères Cinema Ltd.	1912
MANCHESTER	Lama Film Company	1911–1913
WHIPPS CROSS, WALTHAMSTOW	Precision Film Company	1911–1914
HOLMFIRTH, Yorkshire	James Bamforth	1910–1914
PAIGNTON (Drill Hall)	Torquay and Paignton Photoplays Ltd.	1919
ST. ANNES-ON SEA, Lancs. (Old aircraft factory)		1920
KINGSBURY, Herts.	Zodiac Films Ltd. (Walter Forde Comedies)	1919

Early Synopsis of *Ultus and the Three Button Mystery* (originally known as *Ultus and the Cabinet Minister's Overcoat*) by George Pearson. Dated September 15, 1916.

London was seething with excitement. In club and inn, street and shop, the late press had whetted the appetite of the eager palate ready for the latest sensation.

. . . Ultus had escaped from his captors during his trial. Exactly how was not yet known. The fact that the daring personality of The Avenger was free again was news enough.

Rich and poor discussed it; Scotland Yard cursed; the men in the street laughed.

Regret was mingled with interest, for the sentence would probably have been light. After all Ultus had been more sinned against than sinning.

Yet he was at large . . . that was the vital fact. And the stop press news stated that his capture would be a matter of hours only, for he had been followed to a remote corner of slumdom, and every avenue of escape had been closed. . . .

And that night was noteworthy for another reason. Britain's favourite Minister of State was delivering a great speech in the East End of London to a packed audience. The country was passing through a great crisis. With tremendous issues at stake, this Minister, who of all the great names in Britain stood for the Confidence and Hope of the People wrought his eager listeners to a pitch of excitment such as even his eloquence had never before reached.

After this night's work, it was certain that Britain, with this man at the helm, need fear no foreign aggression.

Outside the hall, dense crowds waited for just a glimpse of the statesman. They could cheer if they could not hear his words of guidance. . . .

And away in a frowsy room in a low-down shanty in the slums, a curious gathering of toughs were listening with the utmost attention to a man, to all appearances a gentleman, who was obviously eliciting from them some vital information. "Have you thought of everything . . . is there any part of our plan likely to break down?" . . . And the answers satisfied the questioner, for he smiled appreciatively. With final injunctions, he left, after one ominous caution . . . "Remember, *if you get him here safely*, the Secret Service to which I belong will reward you generously." . . . Whilst at that moment, Ultus darted from corner to corner along the dark alleys, followed by the cleverest of Scotland Yard's plain clothes police. . . .

Alone in the slum room the toughs arranged their separate duties and departed.

And in the mews near the big hall, the statesmen's chauffeur wound up the engine of his big car. A labourer casually strolled up to the chauffeur and asked for a light for his pipe . . . men rushed from the shadows and the chauffeur was knocked down, his coat and cap taken from him, he was thrown into a corner and another chauffeur took his place on the car. . . .

And in the hall the speech ended in a furore of acclamation. The statesman passed to the entrance of the hall amidst the cheers of the audience, and outside he entered his car through a lane of people accompanied by his two detective guards, who entered a second car that drove up as the statesman was driven away. . . .

And right and left through the slums Ultus darted seeking for safety from the police who were closing in upon him. In his hurry he knocked into a man standing by a lamp . . . for a moment Ultus saw the face and rushed away. . . .

The cars from the hall swerved into the main street from a side turning at a good pace, as a man apparently drunk stumbled across the roadway. The man fell . . . the first car was on him . . . there was a cry, a rush of men from some alley . . . the cars stopped . . . the occupants got out . . . the little crowd surrounded the man on the ground . . . the Minister slipped off his coat . . . it was taken by a man to place under the sufferer . . . all was confusion . . . which turned to dismay when the roughs who formed the crowd suddenly changed their tactics and turned on the Minister and his companions. The apparently hurt man got up . . . the Minister was hooded with his own coat . . . the detectives were run off their legs in another direction . . . it was all the work of a couple of minutes . . . the Minister was hurried away to a dirty alley entrance . . . in short, the great Statesman had been kidnapped in the streets of London. . . .

And in the dim passages of the slums, the man who had spoken to the roughs in the shanty, watched the proceedings with relish. . . .

The Minister, who despite his predicament, still kept his dignity, was hurried and almost thrown into a dirty doorway. In the final effort to restrain his captors his coat fell from him, and in the hurry to get inside the building, his captors neglected the coat for a moment, and it lay on the door step . . . as Ultus dashed round the corner, nearly fell over the coat . . . stopped . . . looked at the house . . . picked up the coat . . . dashed away with it, for it formed a good disguise, and once more took up his attempt to outwit the pursuing police.

. . . as in the slum room, the still perfectly calm and dignified statesman stood watching his uncouth captors, one of whom left to get the coat from the doorway. . . .

It was gone . . . the man was terrified . . . the news threw the roughs into a fever of fear . . . the Minister was bundled into a small room . . . and at the door outside all was quietness. Hark . . . someone was knocking at the outer door. . . . It was the man who had watched in the slums . . . his knock was understood—answered . . . and he entered the dirty room with glee . . . glee which was turned to amazement when he heard of the loss of the coat. . . .

And Ultus emerged upon the highway . . . free . . . as the police gave up the chase in the slums, utterly discomfited.

. . . The man in the kitchen gave money and instructions to the roughs, peeped through the door of the statesman's prison . . . and departed.

. . . and in a well-lit study in a house on the outskirts of London, the last confederate of Ultus sat with a paper in his hand reading of the escape of his old chief . . .

. . . whilst through the garden behind, that chief crept from bush to bush towards the window of the study . . . the entry was dramatic . . . the joy of both was great . . . the escaped leader needed money and clothes. He could not stay for the police might think of this one possible hiding place. . . . And the secret service agent passed through his hall in a large house in the West End to his private room, well pleased with his night's work . . . he took up a phone . . . rang up . . . and three men, gentlemen by dress and bearing who were sitting silently in a chamber in a flat in Piccadilly rose at the sound of the bell and crowded to the telephone . . . the news was good . . . the statesman was kidnapped . . . Britain had for the time lost its leader.

. . . And Ultus in a disguise that had even perplexed his confederate left the house as silently as he came. He carried the coat. Though he had come by it strangely he decided to retain it that night.

. . . Whilst in a small private hotel in the vicinity of Euston station, Elsie Meredity, a young girl of about eighteen bewailed her dull existence . . . life without adventure . . . to her old mother. . . . If she could only have adventures like those of Ultus in the paper. . . . Hark . . . the street beli . . . a lodger at that time of night . . . the midnight from the North was just in . . . it was late . . . but even a fresh visitor to the little hotel was an adventure. The door was opened . . . Ultus was admitted . . . he was requiring bed and breakfast . . . he was accommodated . . . shown to his room . . . and on the landing outside Elsie bowed in mock fun to the shut door . . . and was caught by Ultus who opened it suddenly to ask for a paper. . . . The situation was humorous . . . all laughed . . . the mother excused the girl, telling Ultus what a madcap she was, and how she had been grumbling that night about the lack of adventure in her life . . . Ultus retired. . . .

. . . and the morning brought adventure enough for all . . .

. . . In the little sitting room, Ultus had left the coat overnight . . . breakfast was on the table . . . Elsie was very inquisitive . . . she glanced at the papers . . . no news of Ultus . . . it was swamped by another item of tremendous moment . . . the big headlines stared out . . . a Cabinet Minister kidnapped, etc. . . . what news . . . the clothing was described, etc. etc. . . . an overcoat, fur lined . . . M. V. L. . . . initital in the collar . . . etc. . . . At last Elsie got up . . . stopped . . . the lodger's coat was on the door . . . fur lined . . . the collar . . . yes . . . M. V. L. Good God . . . this man knew . . . Elsie nearly fainted. . . .

And Ultus finished his toilet in the bedroom all unconscious of the storm brewing elsewhere. . . .

Elsie did not hear his footsteps . . . he caught her with the coat in her hand . . . an awkward moment, but she got out without betraying herself. . . . Ultus did not realize his danger yet . . . he sat to his meal . . . took up the paper . . . laughed as he read of the failure to catch the adventurer . . . turned to the middle page . . . saw the big headlines of the kidnapping . . . read on . . . started . . . the coat!!! . . . he jumped to rapid conclusions . . . the girl and the coat and the paper . . . yes it was the statesman's overcoat . . . Heavens! how much did she know, what was she doing? . . .

. . . and in the kitchen below Elsie with hat and coat was deciding to act . . . the police were at the corner . . . hark . . . the lodger's bell . . . it took courage . . . but she went to him. . . . They faced each other in the little room . . . it was a tense moment. . . . By sheer magnetism he held her . . . what do you think . . . what do you know . . . what have you done . . .

. . . The girl was brave . . . the man admired her for her courage . . . bold measures were needed. . . ."If I press this bell my mother will call in the policeman who is at this moment at the corner ten yards away!" . . . Ultus never knew quite how he managed it but he compelled her by sheer force of will to listen. . . . "If you act without hearing me you will defeat your own ends. I alone know now that I hold a clue, but I am also the only one who cannot use it" . . . why . . . because I am Ultus. . . . Here was adventure enough for the girl. . . . Ultus had a willing partner . . . his personality swayed her . . . a brief but pregnant talk . . . a hand shake . . . and the two were fellow adventurers committed to the strangest partnership. . . . End of Reel One.

Reel Two . . .

London was still in the throes of unwonted excitement all that day . . . no news . . . no clues either of Ultus or the Minister.

. . . And the girl's mother found a strange note in her daughter's bedroom . . . a note that told briefly that the girl was embarked on the strangest adventure that could befall any person . . . that she was well able to look after herself . . . that she would astonish her mother and perhaps London, etc. etc. . . . the mother was at a loss to understand it.

. . . Whilst in a private room in the Hotel Albert, Ultus, the girl, and Dane were evolving a plan to effect the capture of the Minister's kidnappers. Ultus was thinking of the face of the man he ran into in the slum . . . who was he . . . where had he seen him . . . the face was familiar . . . he racked his brains. . . .

. . . at last it came . . . it was the face of Derwent the notorious Secret Service agent of England's most powerful rival in the nations of Europe. . . . It was all clear . . . it was in the interests of that nation to get the Minister out of the way for a time . . . without his guidance his country was for the moment leaderless . . . it was a bold scheme.

. . . Now for Derwent . . . where did he live . . . the telephone was at hand
. . . his number was found . . . he was rung up . . . by well chosen questions
Ultus learnt that Derwent was at the Crown Hotel. . . . Now for a plan. . . .
Ultus pondered . . . sat . . . scribbled aimlessly on a pad . . . suddenly had an
idea . . . wrote rapidly . . . scrutinized the writing closely . . . was satisfied . . .
turned to his friends . . . showed the note he had written so carefully after
several attempts . . . they read it. . . .

"If you receive any communications from me, always use code 3–6–9–,
etc. . . . Derwent."

. . . this was meaningless to them . . . Ultus laughed . . . then quickly gave
them definite instructions . . . Dane was to go with Ultus. . . . Elsie was to take
the famous coat and lay it at the door where it had been found . . . knock and
go away. Then Ultus very seriously told her that some of his actions might
appear strange, but she was always to trust him . . . Agreed . . . all departed
. . . but first Ultus cut the three buttons from the coat in a knowing way. . . .

. . . The girl wended her way through the streets to her objective. . . . Dane
and Ultus turned towards the Hotel that held Derwent . . . the struggle of wits
was about to begin.

. . . The two men discovered Derwent in the lounge . . . it was easy for Ultus
to strike up a conversation . . . there were plenty of topics that night . . . the
papers were full . . . Dane watched from a corner of the lounge. By degrees a
very dramatic situation was evolved by Ultus putting down the paper containing
the latest news of the kidnapping, that had been under discussion, and giving
Derwent one of the buttons from the coat, as a souvenir that might interest
Derwent.

. . . The man betrayed sufficient surprise to convince Ultus he was on the
right track . . . a quarrel in the hotel was unwise. . . . Derwent rose quickly
. . . walked into the smoking room as Dane moved to Ultus.

Derwent almost ran into the smoking room and burst upon three men at a
table . . . the talk was brief and vital . . . in the lounge there sat a man who
knew something . . . where . . . there behind that paper . . . the men watched
through the glass doors . . . emerged . . . strolled ominously to the man . . .
looked . . . and were amazed at finding the innocent Dane. Ultus had gone
. . . this was startling . . . the three were thunderstruck . . . left . . . watched by
Dane with amusement.

. . . and at the slum, Elsie laid the coat and ran away after knocking loudly.

. . . . The slummers heard . . . were startled . . . one went to the door . . .
found the coat . . . ran back . . . the news was terrifying . . . someone knew
something . . . Derwent must be informed.

. . . and Elsie watched from a corner in the slum.

. . . as one of the men ran from the house to tell Derwent the news . . .

. . . as Derwent entered his hall door and passed to his study.

. . . in the study he stood in meditation by the fire . . . turned . . . switched on the light . . . and almost fell in amazement to find Ultus sitting in the room pointing a revolver at him. . . . "Let us talk," said Ultus. "I had a job to get in, but I have managed it as you see, and I have not wasted my time." . . . It was a tense scene that followed . . . the revolver was very prominent. . . . Forced by Ultus, Derwent writes a strange letter. . . .

"You will take along the bearer to our prisoner. He comes with terms the Minister may consider." Derwent.

. . . this finished, it was placed in Ultus' pocket. . . . Derwent was awed only by the revolver . . . it restrained him from any unwise retaliation. . . . Ultus told him there might be visitors presently . . . a suggestion that did not ease Derwent's mind. . . .

. . . and at that moment Dane joined Elsie in the slums . . .

. . . as the slum messenger arrived at Derwent's house . . . was admitted . . . ushered to the study . . . and faced the two men.

. . . despite reluctance to tell his story before Ultus, the story of the coat was told at the order of Derwent, who acted under the influence of the persistent revolver under the table. . . . Ultus had learnt his second piece of news . . . the coat had drawn the fact he needed. . . .

. . . and in the slum the roughs waited impatiently for the return of their messenger . . .

. . . who was now leaving the study of Derwent, but was recalled to be given that peculiar message Ultus had written in the hotel with his confederates. . . . Ultus had initiated the business by saying to Derwent "You agree to this don't you . . . sign it and give it to the man" . . . and he was obeyed, again due to the revolver. . . . Every move of Derwent was watched by Ultus closely . . . The man left . . . the two were alone . . . and Derwent seemed to be less anxious . . . he began to play his own game . . . suddenly he spoke . . . "You've got me . . . I don't know who you are, but I'll make a clean breast of it. Let me give you the papers I took from the Minister, they are in my safe." . . . Ultus agreed . . . the safe in the wall was opened. . . . Derwent entered . . . it was as big as a man . . . the door shut to . . . click . . . he had gone. . . .

. . . and he emerged into a narrow passage in the wall . . . it was a trick exit . . . Ultus was fooled. . . .

. . . On the other side of the wall the man yelled, "You have got to get up early to fool Derwent . . . when I shut the safe I locked the door of the study and bolted the iron window shutters . . . you will wait my pleasure now, Mr. Spy" . . . and Ultus listened in the study beyond . . .

. . . as the man ran down the narrow stairway to the door below, only to find pinned upon it a paper stating that his visitor had found out all this before and that all was prepared for in regard to the doors and windows . . . etc. . . . and the paper was signed by . . . ULTUS!!! . . .

Ultus laughed . . . Derwent raved . . . the Avenger quietly departed.

. . . and in a short time joined his two friends in the slums . . . all goes well so far. . . .

Dane was given the strange letter written by Derwent in the study, and knocked at the slum door. . . . Elsie watched the door from a distance, whilst Ultus crept to the back of the house and watched the dirty canal that washed by the rear of the house . . . hiding on a barge that lay like a huge slug on the water.

. . . Dane was admitted to the kitchen . . . his letter was of importance . . . the roughs were all nerves that night. . . .

. . . The man who had visited the study looked at the paper that Derwent had given him concerning the code . . . it cast a new light on the matter.

"Take bearer prisoner with Minister. . . . Derwent" . . .

The innocent Dane was cornered . . . but it was not time to act . . . the roughs must be wary . . . one man left the room. . . . Dane was given no clue to the intentions of the men . . . but he knew what he had to do presently if all went well . . .

. . . and Elsie watched the door as Ultus hid at the rear of the barge . . .

. . . a man emerged on the canal . . . whistled . . . and went back to the house . . .

. . . Dane was led by the others quietly through the passage to the canal doorway . . .

. . . in the meantime Ultus had called Elsie and placed her in a small boat and sent her to watch up the river, and he had dived into the water . . .

. . . the men emerged with Dane . . . he was put into a tug that had just come up as if in response to the whistle of a moment ago . . . one man joined Dane . . . the others went back to the house . . . and as the tug turned to retrace its way, Ultus and Elsie slipped into the water and hung on to its rear . . . .

. . . and as Derwent at last emerged from his captivity released by his butler in response to his shouts, the tug tore along to the Minister's hiding place . . . only once stopped by the river police who were searching everywhere for a clue to the lost statesman . . . and behind Ultus and Elsie still clung, and Dane sat smoking on board above them. . . .

End of Reel Two.

Reel Three.

The tug wound its way round the river bends, and reached its goal.

. . . a lonely house by the river side. . . .

. . . Dane got out with his guide and the two men were admitted to the house by another sinister looking rough . . . as Ultus and Elsie emerged from the water and took cover in the bushes. . . .

. . . Inside the house Dane played his part well . . . he was led along the passage to a small kitchen . . . another man was waiting there . . . thus Dane was alone with three toughs . . . there was a little whispering . . . and Dane was led by the men down a dark stairway to a secret room below . . . a room with a steel lined door . . .

. . . now it was time for him to act . . . suddenly he bolted back the way he had come . . . out through the door, followed by three men . . . in their surprise at being forestalled they ran from the door to the open air after him, leaving the door open . . . as Ultus had expected.

. . . Through the undergrowth the roughs tracked Dane, whilst at the open doorway Ultus and Elsie entered the house and slipped into the kitchen, hiding for a moment behind some lumber. . . .

. . . as Dane was caught and dragged back to the house . . .

. . . and away in the slum room in town Derwent revealed to the astonished crooks that the man who was following them was no other than the dreaded Ultus.

. . . as Dane was hurled struggling and shouting into the little room with the steel door that held the captive Minister.

. . . and upstairs in the kitchen, Ultus and Elsie listened and located the whereabouts of the hiding place below.

. . . The men returned to the kitchen well pleased by their work . . . only to receive the surprise of their lives by the reception they got . . . some super-human water demon sprang at them . . . tables and chairs fell about them . . . they seemed to be fighting each other . . . all was chaotic . . . but in a few seconds they found themselves locked in the kitchen, a bewildered trio . . .

. . . as Ultus and Elsie ran to the room below guided by the cries of Dane.
. . . To turn the latch was a moment's work . . . the Minister, too astonished for words, and Dane were free . . . and all the while the rescue was punctuated by the smashing blows on the door of the kitchen above, for the roughs realized the nature of their visitors only too well . . .

. . . whilst down at the secret room a strange scene was enacted . . . just as Ultus was closing the door he called Elsie to him . . . without any warning he pushed her violently into the chamber, and shut the door . . . yelling through the wall . . . "You have served my purpose well, goodbye" . . . The surprise and revulsion of feeling were tremendous . . . the flood gates of the girl's wrath were opened . . . a growing love for the Adventurer was in a second turned to a revolting hate . . . he was a despicable cur . . .

. . . and as Ultus, Dane, and the Minister rushed across country towards London and the house of the confederate where Ultus had changed on the night of his escape . . . the venue agreed upon by all if the plans went right . . .

Derwent and the roughs from the slums sculled madly round the bends of the canal towards the house that had held the Minister. . . .

. . . and the kitchen door at last fell to the blows of the toughs, who rushed in a body to the room below to find the only prisoner now was a young girl dripping wet and furious at her capture. . . .

. . . as Derwent and his men rushed to the house and were admitted by the frightened toughs within. . . .

Explanations were brief and stormy . . . the secret room was examined . . . Elsie was brought up to the dismantled kitchen . . . but below in the room Derwent had found the secret button of the coat in an envelope on the floor . . . he was furious . . . tricked again . . . now for the girl . . . what did she know.

Her revelation astonished all . . . it was the greatest of many surprises that night had witnessed. . . .

. . . she too had been duped . . . and she was a willing turncoat now.

. . . Ultus was her one object of fury . . . she would show him the folly of playing with a woman beyond endurance . . . and Derwent saw in her a tool to aid him . . . she knew where Ultus was going, for he had told her. . . .

. . . 9 o'clock at the confederate's house. . . .

. . . and away in London, Parliament was aroused to intense indignation that as yet no news of the kidnapped Minister was to hand. . . . What were the police doing . . .

. . . and Scotland Yard went mad at their own impotence. . . .

. . . and in London the three men who had escaped from the clutches of the roughs found their way to refuge. . . .

. . . In the study of the house, at eight o'clock they sat down to rest a moment. . . . Ultus asked two things only from the statesman in return for the rescue. . . .

. . . first that he would call at the local police station and report his escape, and that the police were to be in full force in the grounds of the house, well hidden by nine o'clock, but they were not to act until they heard a whistle . . . in this way they would round up the whole gang of roughs. . . .

. . . secondly that he was to deliver a note in an envelope to the Editor of the *Daily Messenger* in person. . . .

. . . the Minister agreed only too glad to repay his rescuer . . .

. . . and as the Minister left the house with Dane . . . Derwent left his riverside haunt with his toughs bent on the recapture of Ultus and the Minister. . . . Elsie was to remain behind as hostage in case she was misleading Derwent, but she had told all she knew. . . .

. . . and Ultus in the big house sat alone making queer shapes out of cardboard with a pair of scissors. . . .

. . . whilst the Minister entered the local police station . . .

. . . and Derwent and his men started from a local garage in two powerful cars . . .

. . . as Ultus still played with his scissors and cardboard . . .

. . . and the Minister left the Station . . .

. . . whilst the cars rushed along the road to London . . .

. . . and a body of police left the station . . .

. . . and Elsie sat brooding over the fickle nature of the adventurer . . .

. . . who was pondering over a paper that bore some notes, viz. . . .

    track the ringleader

    track the gang

    find the Minister

    capture the criminals

    escape myself.

He crossed out slowly the first four items, but sat in deep thought as he stared at the last two . . . will all go well yet . . . it was uncertain . . . but he could try.

End of Reel Three.

Reel Four.

In London the editor of the great paper was like a child in his glee . . . he had the stunt of the century . . . he alone had the news of the Minister's escape . . . and his only condition of payment was that he should phone the Yard and tell his news . . . and headline his papers according to the request of the Minister, viz. . . .

    THE KIDNAPPED STATESMAN . . . SAVED BY A GIRL

. . . this was easy . . . and the machines whirred and screamed in the printing rooms below, as the Minister left the great building for the Houses of Parliament.

. . . Scotland Yard was thunderstruck . . . telephones buzzed . . . all was excitement . . .

. . . and the police crept through the bushes in the grounds of the house that held Ultus alone . . .

. . . as Derwent and his men emerged from the cars and mounted the low walls of the same building. . . . It was 9 o'clock. . . .

. . . Round the house crept the toughs . . . yes . . . there at the window was the silhouette of Ultus . . . he was writing . . . what a fool . . .

. . . the entry was easy . . . the toughs crossed the hall . . . crept up the stairs . . . Derwent with a revolver in hand held the door handle, and quietly entered . . .

. . . and cursed . . . the trick of the cardboard silhouette and the pendulum pen was so simple . . .

. . . and down below the window outside, Ultus whistled loudly . . . the police heard . . . and so did the roughs. . . .

. . . and there on the table in front of Derwent was the third button . . . he was furious . . . he rushed to the window . . . saw the police in the grounds . . . sprang from the window . . . right into the arms of Ultus. . . .

. . . as the toughs fought madly with the police on the stairways and in the passages . . . it was a clear round up. . . .

. . . In the grounds, Ultus and Derwent fought like tigers . . . Derwent escaped . . . Ultus followed . . . it was a chase for life. . . .

. . . and the House of Commons went mad as the Minister entered. . . .

. . . and the police marshalled the discomfited roughs and led them away to the station. . . .

. . . as Ultus took up the long chase of Derwent through the lanes that led back to the riverside house. . . .

. . . where Elsie waited expectantly . . . and to that house the two men ran . . . Derwent tore to the frightened girl . . . down to the secret chamber . . . to break vengeance on the girl he thought had betrayed him . . . and Ultus followed . . . and Elsie saw him . . . the man fell into the secret room . . . and Elsie seized her one chance of revenge . . . she slammed the door on both . . . and ran to the station . . . and down in the secret room the two men fought such a fight as two men have seldom fought. . . . Lit only by a small gas jet the room seemed to contained some phantasmagoria of wild shadows . . . it was confusion . . . down went the gas bracket broken in the furious rush of the combatants . . . the gas permeated the air . . . the fight went on. . . .

. . . Elsie reached the police station with her news. . . .

. . . and Elsie was astonished beyond measure by the questions of the sergeant . . .

. . . You are Elsie Meredith . . . Scotland Yard has just told us of your work in this business . . . you are the girl who has led to the Minister's rescue . . . congratulations . . . and now you have got Ultus . . . Sherlock Holmes is a kid to you. . . .

. . . and Elsie began to realize something that had crept into her understanding during the last few moments. . . .

. . . and the fight went on in the room by the river . . . Derwent was nearly done . . . he was knocked out . . . and as he finally fell almost lifeless, Ultus realized for the first time that the gas was going to end them both . . . he tried to stuff his handkerchief into the pipe . . . ah . . . an idea . . . let it escape. . . .

. . . and Elsie turned her thoughts to that conversation in the hotel . . . Ultus had warned her to trust him no matter how strange his actions might seem . . . it was all clear now . . . he had by his actions led her to aid him in a way that misled the gang as well as it had misled her. . . .

. . . Ultus covered up the body of the unconscious Derwent with the mattress that had served the Statesman for a couch and hid himself under the clothing.

. . . Elsie rushed suddenly from the station . . . she must race the police if she was to undo the error she had committed.

. . . and Ultus struck the match that lit the mixture of gas and air in the

secret room . . . there was an explosion . . . the steel door was blown out-
wards . . . and Ultus staggered into the passage more dead than alive.

. . . as Elsie arrived a short distance ahead of the police.

. . . and met Ultus emerging from the house like a drunken man . . . there
was no time to lose . . . the girl begged for forgiveness. . . .

. . . as the police arrived. . . .

. . . Ultus understood . . . he kissed her . . . they parted.

. . . the police rushed up . . . the girl directed them to the house . . . the half
dead Derwent was made fast . . . the girl ran in to the police after a backward
glance to the river . . . down which Ultus sculled rapidly to safety, his objects
all attained . . . once more the Adventurer free for Adventure.

Part of the Script for *Shadows*, by Harold Weston

Synopsis

Creda, a young modiste, is turned out of her employment for rudeness to a customer, when she is over-tired by the strain of a long day's work. She is driven into the streets, as her salary was barely sufficient to support her when in employment. She meets Sally, a lady of apparently independent means, who sympathizes with her and takes her to her flat, thence to a night club, where she meets Vivian, a young undergraduate, who has just finished his career at a university. Vivian is expected by his parents to marry his cousin Millicent. Vivian falls in love with Creda, and Creda, at the end of her resources and egged on by Sally, lives with Vivian.

The ideality of the union is touched upon, but the power of convention is too strong for such a flower to exist, and Vivian's parents commence to exert their control. Vivian is struck by his father on a visit to the parental home, and Millicent in the meantime (whilst Vivian is lying ill, at home), visits Creda and convinces her that she is ruining her cousin's life. Creda leaves the flat and disappears, and Millicent returns to tell Vivian what she has done. Vivian, ill and distraught, leaves the house with Millicent, who insists on accompanying him, to arrive at Creda's flat to find her gone. Vivian breaks down, and the impression is left that he returns to Millicent. The theme is that convention being too strong to fight, one must merely submit or be broken. Creda's end is symbolized by showing her standing with drooping head in a large query mark. *Shadows* is the play of any young man and any young woman, the one with financial resource, the other without.

Cast

Sir William Rodney: Man of affairs, typifying the middle class in general; a casual husband, fond of his son, if his son is disposed to carry out his wishes. Neither good nor bad, he is what opportunity and circumstance have made him.

Lady Rodney: Weak and inoffensive, giving way to her husband for the sake of a peaceful life; having assisted in making her husband's social life, she is now terrified of his greatness. She is typical of weakness, strong only in her love for her child.

Vivian: A public school boy. Clean, healthy and generous. Understanding as little about the relations of the sexes as does the average youngster.

Sally: A decadent through force of circumstance; a lady whose moral fibres have become warped. Evil only through necessity, whose natural impulses are generous and warm, but whom society has made to blind herself regarding her mode of life.

Creda: This character typifies youth. Optimistic, cheerful, knowing little and caring less about life in general; happy when life is rosy, sad when life becomes drab coloured. Creda might have been ideally happy, married to a parson with a hundred a year. A thoroughly English girl of the lower middle classes.

Furniture

The furniture in Sir William Rodney's house should be typical of the family; an early Victorian atmosphere should reign in the main room, the furniture being for the most part treasured relics of Lady Rodney, coming to her down the ages from her forbears. Here and there should be touches of expensively decorated modern furniture, neither in good taste nor bad, merely uninteresting. Flowers should decorate the tables. The oak settee in the window should be heavy, as should the rest of the furniture used. During the day scenes the light should come from the windows up stage to the left. During the evening scenes from the firelight or the electric bracket above the centre of the room.

The furniture in Creda's flat should be light, bright pictures should be on the walls and flowers in plenty. Dainty cushions be upon the settee and the lightest of carpets used. Light chintz curtains should decorate the windows at the right of the stage, and a bowl of flowers be placed before it. The lighting of the room in daytime should come from the window, whilst for the evening scenes the light should come partly from the electric globes on the walls and partly from the adjoining room.

The remaining scenes will suggest their own furniture.

SHADOWS

Part I

SUB-TITLE: I have a story to tell, Oh ye with feet of clay, and I would carry ye with me into the country of dreams, where my fable was given birth. See ye with my eyes, understand ye with my understanding, and so until my people have passed away into eternal night, shall ye sorrow with their sorrows and joy with their joys. Forget ye that my feet too, are of clay, and imagine that God implanted wings to my heels, that I might soar into the kingdom of dreams, and returning, chain my story to the earth. Come.

SECOND SUB-TITLE: The Street of the Shadows.

SCENE 1. The Street of the Shadows. A mean street, lighted only by the rays from a glaring lamp in a public-house, and the semi-transparent light from a broken luminant in a street lamp. An atmosphere of gloom and discontent pervade the road, which is heightened by a thin drizzling rain. No person is visible, but the shadows of the women of the night are cast upon the wall, which is only broken by a pair of drab doors and a window shaded by an old dark-coloured blanket. Sin is stamped indelibly upon the abode of the foolish virgins.

As the shadows pass and re-pass, a man's figure is cast upon the wall every now and again, until at last the street is empty, desolate and alone. A pause. Another shadow appears at the far end and slowly comes toward the camera, as yet only its shadow is seen, but soon it passes before the lens, pausing a moment, then with a cry of terror is gone. The figure is Creda.

6.30 p.m.
Day Dress

SCENE 2. Room in Sir William's house. Sir William and Lady Rodney are sitting over their tea cups and chatting. Sir William has a newspaper on his knee, and is laying down the law concerning the political outlook. Lady Rodney is dutifully listening. Maid enters and hands letter to Lady Rodney. She takes it and reads.

LETTER ON SCREEN

Tanqueray Lodge.

My dear Auntie,

Of course I will come and dine with you to meet Vivian on his return from Oxford. I have been looking forward to it for so long.

Your affectionate niece,

MILLICENT.

RESUME. Lady Rodney hands the letter across to Sir William, who glances at it and smiles. He desires his son to marry Millicent, as does Lady Rodney. Footman appears carrying a bag, Vivian enters in his overcoat and is carrying his hat and stick. He embraces his mother and shakes hands with his father. Lady Rodney asks him to send his overcoat away, but Vivian says he has an appointment and must leave almost immediately. Lady Rodney presses him to stay.

SUB-TITLE. Vivian: I have promised to meet some of our men at my club for a farewell supper.

He glances at his watch. His mother hands him Millicent's letter, and he smiles in a superior manner and returns it, saying, "Sorry." Sir William tries to persuade him to stay.

271

6.35
Day Dress

SCENE 3. Interior of a cheap city Café. Creda enters, wearily, glances at people, and goes to table, looks at menu, takes purse from pocket and counts coppers.

CLOSE UP OF PURSE AND A FEW COPPERS IN CREDA'S HAND

RESUME. Waitress appears and takes order. Creda wearily looks around her.

6.39
Dress as before.
Millicent in
evening dress

SCENE 4. Room in Sir William's house. Vivian is still chatting while his parents listen. He signifies he must leave room to dress, is about to do so, footman announces Millicent, she is in evening dress. Her first smile is for Vivian. Greetings. She is told Vivian has an appointment, and her face shows her disappointment. Vivian exits to dress. Millicent looks after him. Bus.

SCENE 5. Interior of cheap café. Creda is taking tea from waitress, who also deposits beside her some cakes. Sally enters and looks round for a seat, sees an empty one beside Creda's table, takes it and sits, looking at Creda's soiled clothes a little contemptuously.

CLOSE-UP OF CREDA. BUS

CLOSE-UP OF SALLY. BUS

6.45
Vivian evening
dress; Millicent
evening dress

SCENE 6. Interior of Sir William's Room. It is empty, lights are down, the only illumination comes from the fire, which leaves the background in shadow. Vivian enters, and a flood of light enters door as he opens it. He crosses to fire and stoops to light his cigar. Millicent enters and crosses to him. Bus. Vivian starts and Millicent laughs and lays her hand on his arm affectionately, saying that she saw him enter and wants to talk to him. He says he is in a hurry. Milly appears very disappointed.

SUB-TITLE. Millicent: Must you go?

Vivian assures her that he must, smiles a little patronizingly, and after a quick pat on her arm—for friendship's sake, exits. Millicent, alone, allows her face to express her sorrow; she is very deeply in love with him.

6.50
Dress as before

SCENE 7. Interior of cheap café. Waitress places an egg on toast before Sally, and, in doing so, upsets the salt on to Creda's lap. Waitress laughs and Sally smiles, and after a moment Creda smiles too. Waitress replaces salt, and Creda and Sally fall into conversation.

6.55
All evening dress

SCENE 8. Private room in fashionable Club. Eight or nine men are assembling. Vivian enters and is greeted boisterously. All sit at table. Waiters enter and dinner commences.

272

6.57
Dress as before

SCENE 9. Interior of cheap café. Creda and Sally conversing. Sally very curious as to why Creda is taking tea in such shabby clothes. Sally asks her.

SUB-TITLE. Sally: What are you doing here?

Creda, recollecting her position, buries her face in her hands and almost breaks down. Sally tries to comfort her, and after a while Creda commences her story. Creda speaks:

SUB-TITLE. Creda's story.

Creda is seen speaking a little brokenly.

FADE THIS SCENE THROUGH INTO

Noon
Mannequins
fashionably
attired.
Others day dress

SCENE 10. Modiste's Room in Elegant Milliners. Creda with several girls, in gorgeous dresses, standing talking. Creda looks ill and weary. Customer enters with the head of the department, and gazes insolently at Creda. Creda is called over to show off the dress she is wearing, the customer catches her by the arm and turns her round, the better to see the dress. Creda resents this, and the customer speaks sharply to her. Creda walks away. Customer angrily rises, and, after a few words to head of the department, leaves the room, the head of the department apologizing to her. The girls cluster around Creda asking what has occurred. The head of the department enters with Sir William Rodney, the proprietor of the shop, and after a short, curt explanation Creda is discharged.

FADE THIS SCENE INTO

Noon
Day dress for all

SCENE 11. A Room in a cheap Lodging-house. Creda enters and sits disconsolately upon the bed. The landlady enters and asks for her rent. Creda says she has no money, but points to a paragraph in the paper wherein a girl is wanted.

PARAGRAPH OF PAPER ON SCREEN

Wanted, a young woman of good appearance. Must have good figure for show room. Apply, Daunton and Welham, 22, Ames Street.

RESUME. Landlady sniffs and asks if she is going after the job. Creda nods and landlady allows her to depart. Bus.

FADE THIS SCENE THROUGH INTO

Noon
Day dress for all

SCENE 12. Interior of Office. Manager dictating notes to his typist. Office boy enters with a message. Manager shakes his head.

Office boy exits, returning with Creda, who has insisted on seeing the manager. She asks for the situation.

SUB-TITLE. Manager: Fixed an hour ago.

Manager continued dictating, and Creda is forced to depart. At her exit

FADE THIS SCENE THROUGH INTO

SCENE 13. A Room in a cheap Lodging-house. Landlady tidying up room. Creda appears, and is asked if she has succeeded in getting work. Creda shakes her head. Landlandy tells her she must go, Creda starts to collect her things, but is stopped by the landlady, who claims them for the rent due. Creda slowly exits.

FADE THIS SCENE THROUGH INTO

Time: 7.20 p.m. SCENE 14. Interior of cheap café. Creda ending her story, and Sally listening. There is a short pause while Sally thinks over the story she has heard, then

SUB-TITLE. Sally: What are you going to do?

Creda looks around the room in an endeavour to think out her position, then she shakes her head.

CUT SHARPLY

SCENE 15. Room in Club. All very merry. Waiter enters to ask them to make less noise. Syphon is squirted at him. Bus. Youngster rises to sing a song which no one desires to hear. Bus.

SCENE 16. Interior of cheap café. Sally is speaking to Creda. She leans back in her chair and says a little bitterly.

SUB-TITLE. Sally: Listen to my story.

Sally commences to speak, and little by little the stereotyped smile passes and Sally becomes in earnest.

FADE THIS SCENE THROUGH INTO

Time: 10 a.m.
Factory dresses
for girls
SCENE 16. Factory. Large sewing machines around the room. Girls hard at work. Forewoman inspecting their work. Bus. Sally, at machine at front, is seen to sway; she recovers herself. Forewoman comes toward her and examines the waistcoat she is at work upon. Sally commences again, sways and faints. She is carried out.

FADE THIS SCENE THROUGH INTO

Time: Evening
Nurses in
uniform
SCENE 17. A Ward in a Hospital. Patients in beds, nurses passing along corridor outside. Sally appears, pale and convales-

cent; she is dressed for the street. Nurse crosses stage. Sally bids her good-bye, as she does other patients. Sally exits.

FADE THIS SCENE THROUGH INTO

Time: 7.40 p.m.   SCENE 18. Interior of Cheap Tea Rooms. Sally concludes her story. She tells Creda that she tried to get work but found it impossible, that in the end she was forced to live by any means in her power. Sally realized that she is growing earnest, and suddenly laughs, "Life is like that." She draws out her purse and extracts a five-pound note. She hands it to waitress, who is impressed; then she points to Creda's bag and asks if she has any money. Creda shakes her head. Sally laughs, then seeing Creda is nearly in tears, she leans forward and commences to talk quickly.

SCENE 19. Room at Club. The table is now littered with cigarettes, cigar boxes and bottles. The dinner is over. The men are smoking and drinking. Vivian calls waiter and orders more wine. One of the men suggests that they have had enough, whilst another says:

SUB-TITLE. Guest: Let's go on to a Night Club.

The idea is taken up at once, and the young men troop from the room.

Time: 7.50 p.m.   SCENE 20. Interior of cheap Tea Rooms. Sally is still speaking. Creda, with the light of terror in her eyes, is listening. She lowers her head, reading what lies before her. Sally is suggesting a way out. Creda shakes her head. I can't, I can't. Sally lies back in her chair and asks her what she is going to do. People pass in and out. Creda brokenly tells Sally to go. Sally rises and touches her arm.

SUB-TITLE. Sally: Come with me. You have failed. I'll help you to succeed.

Creda brokenly rises and exits with Sally.

Time . 8.10 p.m.   SCENE 21. Interior of Sally's rooms. Gaudily decorated bed-sitting-room in the worst possible taste. Landlady is looking through the drawers and searching the mattress for odd money. Creda and Sally enter. Landlady sent out. Bus. Sally takes Creda by the shoulders and gazes at her; then she nods, saying, "You'll do," and goes to her wardrobe, taking out an *outré* evening dress, which she places against Creda's dress, looking at the effect. She tosses the evening dress on the bed and starts undoing Creda's frock.

275

Time: 8.20 p.m.

SCENE 22. Exterior of Night Club. Three taxis drive up and Vivian's party exit into night club. Bus with porter.

Time: 8.20 p.m.
Creda and Sally
Evening dress

SCENE 23. Sally's Rooms. Sally is in evening dress and Creda is now dressed in the evening frock. Sally stands a little way off regarding her thoughtfully; she goes to her table and returns with rouge and haresfoot and applies it to Creda's cheeks, then catching her by the arm, she tosses a cloak over her shoulders and they leave the room.

Time: 8.40 p.m.
All evening dress

SCENE 24. Interior of Night Club. Dancing, music. Men and women seated at tables, waiters with beverages. Enter Creda and Sally; they cross to table and sit. Sally calls waiter for drink. Creda shudders. Sally sees man she knows and goes over and talks to him. Creda alone. Vivian and boys from Club burst in; laughter and noise. They rot with girls, bringing them up to table by Creda—and Vivian alone sits opposite Creda; his head is a little dizzy from the alcohol he has taken. The girls and young men run up stage to see dancing taking place in the far room. Creda opposite, Vivian glances up and—

CLOSE-UP CREDA GLANCING AT VIVIAN
CLOSE-UP VIVIAN LOOKING AT CREDA

RESUME. Vivian is very struck by Creda's beauty; he leans a little forward to watch her the better. Creda's eyes again fall on Vivian. Bus. Work scene to point then FADE OUT.

END OF PART I

Film List

The following list includes fiction films of 1,000 ft. or more in length, released between August 1914 and December 1918, with some fifty not released until 1919 but announced before the end of the previous year. It is not complete, but includes all the films on which sufficient reliable information was obtainable to make their inclusion valuable for reference and identification.

In so far as it is possible the following information is given:

1. In the brackets following each title is

   (a) the name of the producing company or brand;
   (b) the length in feet or, failing this, the number of reels or parts;
   (c) the date of the first release; failing this, the date of the first London Trade Show has been given, accompanied by the letters "T.S."

2. Then follow the name of the producer-director, and any other production credits obtainable, and finally the player's names (these are not listed in any particular order).

The sources of this material were:

> *The Bioscope*
> *Kinematograph Weekly*
> *Kinematograph Monthly Film Record*
> Various publicity brochures for individual films.

Abide With Me (T.S. February 1916). With Austen Camp, George Foley.

Ace of Hearts, The (Clarendon, 3 reels, 1916). From a sketch by James Willard.

Adam Bede (International Exclusives, T.S. April 9, 1918). Produced: Maurice Elvey, from the novel by George Eliot, adapted by Kenelm Foss. With Bransby Williams, Ivy Close, Malvina Longfellow, Gerald Ames.

Admirable Crichton, The (Samuelson, 7,000 ft., 1918). Produced: G. B. Samuelson, from the play by J. M. Barrie. With Basil Gill, Lennox Pawle, Mary Dibley, James Lindsay.

Adventures of Deadwood Dick, The (Samuelson, 6 weekly parts of 2,000 ft., released from November 29, 1915). With Fred Paul.

Adventures of Dick Dolan, The (Broadwest, 1,800 ft. January 1, 1918). With Basil Gill, Ivy Close, T. Beaumont, W. McMahon, Violet Hopson, Gerald Ames.

After Dark (Buckland, 3 parts, 1915). With Flora Morris, Harry Royston, Harry Gilbey.

All the Sad World Needs (B.A.F.C., 5,000 ft., January 20, 1919). Produced: Hubert Herrick, by Kenelm Foss. With Lauri de Frece, Joan Legge, Adelaide Grace, Lennox Pawle.

All the World's a Stage (5 reels, T.S. 1917). Produced: Harold Weston, by K. Herbert Everett, artistic adviser John Everett. With Eve Balfour, Esme Beringer, James Lindsay, Judd Green.

Alone in London (Turner, 4,500 ft., August 9, 1915). Produced: Larry Trimble, from the play by Robert Buchanan. With Florence Turner. Cin.: Tom White.

Altar Chains (4,750 ft., August 6, 1917). Produced and written by Bannister Merwin. With Edward O'Neill, Dawson Milward, Heather Thatcher, Fred Volpe, Minna Gray, Philip Hewland.

Always Tell Your Wife (British Empire, 2 reels, 1914). With Seymour Hicks, Ellaline Terriss.

American Heiress, The (Hepworth, 3 reels, T.S. 1917). Produced: C. M. Hepworth, from story by Blanche McIntosh. With Alma Taylor, Violet Hopson, Lionelle Howard, Stewart Rome, John McAndrews.

Annie Laurie (Hepworth, 1916). Produced: C. M. Hepworth, based on the song. With Alma Taylor, Stewart Rome, Lionelle Howard, Elizabeth Herbert.

Another Man's Wife (B. & C., 1915). From the play by Miles Wallerton.

Answer, The (Broadwest, 5 reels, October 2, 1916). Produced: Walter West, adapted from the novel *Is God Dead?* by Newman Flower. With Dora Barton, Muriel Martin Harvey, George Foley, George Bellamy, J. R. Tozer, Arthur Cullin, Gregory Scott.

Anti-Frivolity League, The (Ideal, 2 reels, T.S. September 1916). With George Robey.

Arsene Lupin (London, 1916). Produced: G. L. Tucker, from the play by Leblanc and de Croisset. With Gerald Ames, Douglas Munro, Manora Thew.

As He was Born (Butchers, T.S. January 8, 1919). Produced: Wilfred Noy, from the story by Tom Gallon. With Stanley Logan, Odette Goimbault.

As the Sun went Down (Hepworth, 3,075 ft., March 1919). With Chrissie White, Stewart Rome, Lionelle Howard.

Asthore (Clarendon, 5 reels, October 22, 1917). Produced: Wilfred Noy, based on the song. With Violet Marriott.

As Ye Repent (Turner, 3 reels, August 23, 1915). Produced: Larry Trimble. With Florence Turner, Edward Lingard, Anthony Keith, Tom Powers.

Auld Lang Syne (B & C, 4,400 ft., April 8, 1918). Produced: Sidney Morgan. With Violet Graham, George Bellamy, Henry Baynton, Roy Travers, Jack Buchanan, Elinor Foster, Sydney Fairbrother.

Auld Robin Gray (Ideal, 4,500 ft., April 22, 1918). Produced: Meyrick Milton. With Miss June, Langhorne Burton.

Avenging Hand, The (Cricks, 1915). Produced: Charles Calvert, by W. J. Elliott.

Baby on the Barge (Hepworth, 1915). Produced: C. M. Hepworth, by Blanche McIntosh. Cinematography: Gaston Queribet.

Barnaby Rudge (Hepworth, 5,000 ft., March 1, 1915). Produced and adapted by C. M. Hepworth, from the novel by Charles Dickens, designed by Warwick Buckland. With Harry Royston, Stewart Rome, Chrissie White, Tom Powers, Harry Buss, Harry Gilbey, Henry Vibart, John McAndrews, Lionelle Howard, Violet Hopson. Cinematography: Tom White.

Basilisk, The (Hepworth, 2,500 ft., November 9, 1914). Produced, photographed and written by C. M. Hepworth. With William Felton, Alma Taylor, Tom Powers.

Beau Brocade (Lucoque, 1916). Produced: Thomas Bentley, from the novel by Baroness Orczy. With Mercy Hatton, Cecil Mannering, Charles Rock, Austin Leigh, George Foley, Cecil Morton York. Cinematography: W. Bowden.

Beautiful Jim (B & C, 1914). Produced: Maurice Elvey, from the novel by John Strange Winter. With Elizabeth Risdon, Fred Groves.

Because (Progress, 5 reels, T.S. April 23, 1918). Produced and written by Sidney Morgan, based on the song. With Lilian Braithwaite, Joyce Carey, George Foley, Ben Webster, J. Hastings Batson.

Beggar Girl's Wedding, The (British Empire, 4,500 ft., September 6, 1915). From the play by Walter Melville. With Lauderdale Maitland, Henry Lonsdale, Nina Lynn.

Betta the Gypsy (Famous Pictures, 5 reels, 1919). Produced: Charles Raymo nd from the operetta by Edward Waltyre, cinematography E. L. Groc. With Marga la Rubia, Malvina Longfellow, George Foley, Frank Dane, Edward Combermere, Barbara Gott.

Better 'Ole, The (Welsh-Pearson, 6,600 ft., July 1, 1918). Produced and adapted by George Pearson, from the play by Bruce Bairnsfather and Arthur Eliot, cinematography Lucien Egrot. With Charles Rock, Arthur Cleave, Hugh E. Wright, Mary Dibley, Margaret Blanche, Mercy Hatton, Hayford Hobbs, Lilian Hall-Davis.

Bid for Fortune, A (Unity-Super, 5 reels, September 3, 1917). Produced: Sidney Morgan, from the stories of Dr. Nikola by Guy Boothby. With A. Harding Steerman, Violet Graham, Sydney Vautier.

Bigamist, The (4 parts, 1917). With Hayden Coffin, Ethel Warwick, Arthur Wontner.

Big Money (5,320 ft., March 1919). Produced: Harry Lorraine, adapted by Reuben Gilmer from the novel *A Run for his Money* by May Wynne. With Rose Manners, James Knight, Lionel D'Aragon, Charles Rock, Edward O'Neill.

Billy's Spanish Love Spasm (Homeland, 3 reels, T.S. August 4, 1915). Produced: W. Kellino. With Billy Merson, Teddie Gerrard, Blanche Bella.

Billy's Stormy Courtship (Homeland, 2,200 ft., December 25, 1916). Produced: W. Kellino. With Billy Merson, Winifred Delevanti.

Billy Strikes Oil (Homeland, 2 reels, 1917). Produced: W. Kellino. With Billy Merson.

Billy the Truthful (Homeland, 2 reels, May 7, 1917). Produced: W. Kellino. With Billy Merson.

Black Knight, The (Broadwest, 3 reels, October 16, 1916). From the novel by A. Soutar. With Gregory Scott, J. R. Tozer.

Blackmailers, The (I. B. Davidson, 1916). With Arthur Rooke, Joan Legge.

Blind Boy, The (British Photoplay Company, 5,000 ft., April 22, 1918). Based on the sketch. With G. H. Chirgwin.

Blindness of Fortune, The (Hepworth, 4 reels, April 25, 1918). With Chrissie White, Lionelle Howard, Henry Vibart, John McAndrews, Violet Hopson, William Felton.

Bold Adventuress, A (Broadwest, 3 reels, 1915). Produced and written by Walter West. With Walter West, Nell Emerald.

Bonnie Mary (Master, 5 reels, T.S. December 5, 1918). Produced: A. V. Bramble, scenario by Eliot Stannard from a story by Herbert Pemberton. With Lionel Belcher, Arthur Cullin, Jeff Barlow, Elaine Madison, Miriam Ferris.

Bootle's Baby (London, 3,800 ft., September 7, 1914). Adapted by Bannister Merwin from the novel by John Strange Winter. With Ben Webster.

Bottle, The (Hepworth, 3,000 ft., June 7, 1915). Produced: C. M. Hepworth, by Arthur Shirley. With Albert Chevalier, Alma Taylor, Ivy Millais, Henry Brett. Cinematography: C. Hepworth.

Boundary House (Hepworth, 5 parts, T.S. December 3, 1918). Produced: C. M. Hepworth, from the novel by Peggy Webbling. With Alma Taylor, Gwynne Herbert, William Felton, Gerald Ames, Victor Prout, John McAndrews. Cinematography: C. Hepworth.

Boy Scouts—Be Prepared (Trans-Atlantic, 8 parts of 1 reel, released from October 18, 1917). Produced: Percy Nash, by Bannister Merwin. With Edward O'Neill.

Boys of the Old Brigade (British Oak, 1916). Produced and written by Mr. and Mrs. E. G. Batley, based on the song, cinematography Frank Grainger. With Charles Vane, George Leyton, Dorothy Batley, Stella Brereton, Letty Paxton.

Boys of the Otter Patrol, The (Trans-Atlantic, 6 reels, 1918). Produced: Percy Nash, from the story by E. le Breton-Martin.

Brigadier Gerrard (Barker, T.S. September 17, 1915). Produced: Will Barker, adapted by Rowland Talbot from the novel by Conan Doyle. With Lewis

Waller, Madge Titheradge, A. E. George, Blanche Forsythe, A. Austin Leigh, Fernand Mailly, Frank Cochrane.

Britain's Naval Secret (I. B. Davidson, 1,229 ft., March 18, 1915). With Percy Moran.

Britain's Secret Treaty (I. B. Davidson, 3 reels, 1914). With Thomas Canning.

Broken Doll, A (Homeland, 1917).

Broken Melody, The (Ideal, 5 reels, November 20, 1916). Produced: Cavendish Morton, from the play. With Martin Harvey, Hilda Moore, Courtice Pounds, Edward Sass, Manora Thew, Barbara Hannay, Nelson Ramsay.

Broken Threads (Hepworth-Edwards, 4,700 ft., June 5, 1918). Produced: Henry Edwards, by Harold Bartholomew. With Chrissie White, Henry Edwards, W. G. Saunders, Harry Gilbey, A. V. Bramble, Gwynne Herbert, Fred Johnson. Cinematography: C. Bryce.

Brother Officers (London, T.S.: February 16, 1915). Produced: Harold Shaw, from the play by Leo Trevor. With Henry Ainley, Charles Rock, Gerald Ames, Frank Stanmore, Lettice Fairfax, Wyndham Guise, Gwynne Herbert, Christine Rayner, George Bellamy.

Building a Chicken House (Sunny South, 1,150 ft., T.S. December 1914). With Will Evans, Arthur Conquest.

Bunch of Violets, A (Hepworth, T.S. March 21, 1916). Produced: Frank Wilson, adapted by Victor Montefiore from the play by Sidney Grundy. With Chrissie White, Violet Hopson, Charles Vane. Cinematography: Charles Sanders.

Burnt Wings (Broadwest, 3 reels, 1916). Produced: Walter West, adapted by Byron Webber from the novel by Mrs. Stanley Wrench. With Eve Balfour, J. R. Tozer, Tom Macdonald.

Buttons (Samuelson, 2,000 ft., 1915). Produced: George Pearson. With Fred Paul, Gerald Royston.

By the Kaiser's Orders (Barker, 3,000 ft., 1914).

By the Shortest of Heads (Barker, 5 reels, 1915). By Percy Manton and Jackup. With George Formby.

Called Back (London, 3,600 ft., October 26, 1914). Produced and written by G. L. Tucker, from the novel and play by Hugh Conway. With Henry Ainley, Jane Gail, Charles Rock, George Bellamy.

Called to the Front (Regent, 3 reels, August 1914).

Call of the Drum, The (Cunard, 2 reels, T.S. November 3, 1914). Produced: Harold Weston. With J. R. Tozer, H. G. Shaw, Slaine Mills, Mary Manners, Alice Drummond.

Canker of Jealousy, The (Hepworth, 3 reels, March 22, 1915). Produced: C. M. Hepworth, by Blanche McIntosh. With Alma Taylor, Violet Hopson, Stewart Rome, Tom Powers, Eric Desmond. Cinematography: C. Sanders.

Caste (Turner, 4,500 ft., January 24, 1916), Produced: Larry Trimble, from the play by Tom Robertson. With Sir John Hare, Esme Hubbard, Peggy Hyland, Dawson Milward, Campbell Gullan, Mary Rorke.

Caught in a Kilt (Cricks & Martin, 1,036 ft., July 5, 1915). Produced: Will Kellino, by Reuben Gilmer.

Chance of a Lifetime, The (Holmfirth, T.S. February 1917). Produced: Bertram Phillips, from the novel by Nat Gould. With Queenie Thomas, Austen Camp, Frank Runchman, Fay Temple, H. Agar Lyons.

Charlatan, The (1916). Produced: Sidney Morgan, from the play by Robert Buchanan. With Violet Graham, Anna Mather, E. Dagnall, Eille Norwood.

Chimes, The (Hepworth, 1914). Produced and adapted by Thomas Bentley. With Violet Hopson, Stewart Rome, J. Butt, Harry Royston, Warwick Buckland. Cinematography: Roland Hill.

Christian, The (London, T.S. November 30, 1915). Produced: G. L. Tucker, from the novel by Hall Caine. With Derwent Hall Caine, Elizabeth Risdon, Christine Rayner, Charles Rock, Philip Hewland, Bert Wynne, Gerald Ames, Douglas Munro, Frank Stanmore, George Bellamy, Gwynne Herbert, Mary Dibley.

Christmas Carol, A (London, 1,200 ft., December 10, 1914). Produced: Harold Shaw, from the novel by Charles Dickens. With Charles Rock, George Bellamy, Mary Brough, Edna Flugrath, Edward O'Neill, Assheton Tonge.

Cinema Girl's Romance, The (Samuelson, 1915). Produced: George Pearson, from the story by Ladbrooke Black. With Agnes Glynne, Fred Paul, Alice de Winton.

Cloches de Cornville, Les (B.A.F.C., 6,000 ft, 1918). Produced: Thomas Bentley, adapted by Bannister Merwin from the comic opera by Planquette. With Elsie Craven, Moya Mannering, J. R. Morand, Leslie Stiles, Fred Volpe, Arthur Vezin, Ben Field.

Coal King, The (Neptune, 3,600 ft., January 3, 1916). Produced: Percy Nash, from the play, cinematography Georgio Ricci. With Douglas Cox, May Lynn, Frank Tennant, Daisy Cordell, Gregory Scott, Joan Ritz, Jack Denton.

Cobweb, The (Hepworth, 5 reels, T.S. January 2, 1917). Produced: C. M. Hepworth, from the play by Leon M. Lion and Naunton Davies. With Henry Edwards, Violet Hopson, Alma Taylor, Stewart Rome, Margaret Blanche, John McAndrews. Cinematography: Geoffrey Faithfull.

Comin' Thro' the Rye (Hepworth, 5,000 ft., T.S. October 18, 1916). Produced: C. M. Hepworth, from the novel by Helen Mathers. With Stewart Rome, Alma Taylor, Lionelle Howard, Campbell Gullan, Margaret Blanche.

Comradeship (Stoll, 1919). Produced: Maurice Elvey, by Louis N. Parker. With Gerald Ames, Lily Elsie.

Cost of a Kiss (Mirror, 5 reels, 1917). With Bertram Wallis, Marjorie Day, Thomas Canning.

Crime and the Penalty (Clarendon, 4 reels, 1916). With Betty the chimpanzee, Alesia Leon, Louis Nanten.

Crimson Triangle, The (Martin, 4 reels, 1915).

Curtain's Secret, The (Hepworth, 3,000 ft., 1915). Produced: Frank Wilson, by Kate Murray. With Chrissie White, Stewart Rome, Henry Vibart, Violet Hopson. Cinematography: C. Sanders.

Cynthia in the Wilderness (4 parts, 1916). Produced: Harold Weston, from the novel by Hubert Wales. With Milton Rosmer, Ben Webster, Eve Balfour, Odette Goimbault, Barbara Hannay.

Daddy (B.A.F.C., 5 reels, November 5, 1917). Produced: Thomas Bentley, based on the song. With Langhorne Burton, Peggy Kurton, William Lugg, C. T. Macdona, Audrey Hughes, Eric Barker, M. R. Morand.

Damages for Breach (Windsor, 2 reels, 1919). Produced: A. Bocchi, by Kenelm Foss. With Kenelm Foss, Hayford Hobbs, Bert Wynne, Charles Vane.

Dandy Donovan (Cunard, 2 reels, T.S. November 3, 1914). Produced: Wallett Waller. With Thomas Meighan, Gladys Cooper, Owen Nares.

Darby and Joan (Master, 1918). Produced: Percy Nash, by Hall Caine, cinematography S. L. Eton. With Derwent Hall Caine, Ivy Close, Edward O'Neill, Leal Douglas, Douglas Munro, Herbert Rea, Meggie Albanesi, Edward Craig, Ernest Douglas, Joan Ritz, George Wynn.

Daughter of England, A (British Empire, 4,000 ft., 1915). From the play by Jose D. Levy. With Marga Rubia Levy, Frank Randall, Mme d'Esterre, George Barran, Frank H. Dane, Billy.

Dawn (Lucoque, 5 reels, June 4, 1917). Produced: H. Lisle Lucoque, adapted by Pauline Lewis from the novel by H. Rider Haggard. With Madeline Seymour, Annie Esmond, Madame Karina, Hubert Carter, Capt. Heaton Grey, Edward Combermere, Frank Harris.

Dead Heart, The (Hepworth, 3 reels, 1914). With Harry Gilbey, Alice de Winton.

Deception (Harma, 5,544 ft., 1918). Produced: A. C. Hunter, by Reuben Gilmer. With Charles Rock, Maud Yates, James Knight, Rose Manners.

Democracy (Progress, 6 reels, 1918). Produced and written by Sidney Morgan. With Alice de Winton, Wyndham Guise.

Derelicts (Unity Super, 5 reels, 1917). Produced: Sidney Morgan, from the novel by W. J. Locke. With Violet Graham, Julian Royce, Sydney Vautier, Mona K. Harrison.

Devil's Bondman, The (Trans-Atlantic, 4 reels, April 3, 1916). Produced: Percy Nash, by Rowland Talbot. With Douglas Payne, George Bellamy, Fay Temple, Daisy Cordell, Gregory Scott, J. Hastings Batson.

Devil's Profession, The (Arrow, 3 reels, T.S. May 28, 1915). Produced: F. C. Tudor, from the novel by Gertie de S. Wentworth James' cinematography A. Frenguelli. With Alesia Leon, Nancy Roberts, May Lynn, Rohan Clensy, Sidney Strong.

Diana and Destiny (Windsor, 5 reels, January 15, 1917). Produced: F. Martin Thornton, from the story by Charles Garvice. With Evelyn Boucher, Roy Travers, Wyndham Guise.

Diana of Dobson's (Barker, 1917). From the play by Cicely Hamilton. With Cecilia Loftus.

Dick Carson Wins Through (Hepworth-Edwards, 4,600 ft., March 18, 1918). Produced: Henry Edwards. With Henry Edwards, Chrissie White, Fred Johnson, Lionelle Howard, W. G. Saunders, Charles Vane. Cinematography: C. Bryce.

Disraeli (N.B., 6,000 ft., 1917). Produced: Percy Nash, from the play by Louis N. Parker. With Dennis Eadie, Mary Jerrold, Dorothy Bellew, Daisy Cordell, Arthur Cullin, Fred Morgan, Cecil M. York, A. B. Imeson.

Divine Gift, The (B.A.F.C., 6,000 ft., March 27, 1919). Produced: Thomas Bentley, by Kenelm Foss. With Ernest Hendrie, George Tully, Sydney Paxton, George Shelton, Joyce Dearsley.

Dombey and Son (Ideal, 6 reels, February 25, 1918). Produced: Maurice Elvey, adapted by Eliot Stannard from the novel by Charles Dickens. With Norman McKinnell, Lilian Braithwaite, Hayford Hobbs, Odette Goimbault, Douglas Munro, Jerrold Robertshaw, William Corri, Evelyn Walsh Hall, Fewlass Llewellyn.

Doorsteps (Turner, 4 reels, June 1st, 1916). Produced and adapted by Henry Edwards from his own play. With Florence Turner, Campbell Gullan, Henry Edwards. Cinematography: Tom White.

Dop Doctor, The (Samuelson, 1916). Produced: Fred Paul, from the novel by Richard Dehan. With Booth Conway, Agnes Glynne, Fred Paul, Bertram Burleigh, Minna Gray.

Drink (British Pictures, 6,000 ft., January 27, 1919). From the play based on Zola's novel. With Fred Groves.

Dr. Wake's Patient (Samuelson, T.S. October 12, 1916). From the play by W. Gayer Mackay and Robert Ord. With Phyllis Dare, Dora Barton, Mary Rorke, Gerald McCarthy, James Lindsay, Wyndham Guise.

Dummy, The (Homeland, 2 reels, February 5, 1917). With Lupino Lane.

Dustman's Outing, The (Homeland, 2 reels, March 5, 1917). With the Brothers Egbert.

Earl of Camelot, The (Aurora, 1,250 ft., November 15, 1914). Produced and written by Henry Wilson.

East is East (Turner, 4,750 ft., February 12, 1917). Produced and adapted by Henry Edwards, from the play by Philip E. Hubbard and G. Logan. With Florence Turner, Henry Edwards, Edith Evans, Ruth MacKay, W. G. Saunders. Cinematography: Tom White.

Elder Miss Blossom, The (Samuelson, 5 reels, T.S. September 5, 1918). Produced: Percy Nash, from the play. With Owen Nares, Isobel Elsom,

C. M. Hallard, Minna Gray, Tom Reynolds. Cinematography: J. C. Bee-Mason.

England Expects (London, 2,500 ft., August 31, 1914). Produced and written by G. L. Tucker. With Jane Gail, Charles Rock, George Bellamy.

Enoch Arden (Neptune, T.S. November 24, 1914). Produced: Percy Nash, adapted by Gerald Lawrence from the poem by Lord Tennyson. With Gerald Lawrence, Fay Davis, Ben Webster, May Whitty, John East, Gregory Scott, Douglas Cox.

Esther Redeemed (Renaissance, 3 reels, September 8, 1915). Produced and adapted by Sidney Morgan from the play *The Wolfe Wife* by Arthur Bertram. With Julian Royce, Miss Tittell-Brune, William Brandon, A. Harding Steerman, Cecil Fletcher, Mona K. Harrison.

Eternal Triangle, The (Hepworth, 5 reels, T.S. April 2, 1918). Produced: Frank Wilson, by Percy Gordon Holmes. With Stewart Rome, Lionelle Howard, Chrissie White, Violet Hopson.

Eve Comedies (Gaumont, 1 reel each, 1918). From the drawings by Miss Fish in the *Tatler*. With Eileen Molyneux, Cecil Morton York, Pat Somerset.

Everybody's Business (Western Import, 2 reels, 1917). Produced: Ralph Dewsbury, by Frank Fowell, cinematography Ernest Palmer. With Renee Kelly, Kate Rorke, Gerald du Maurier, Matheson Lang, Norman McKinnel, Gwynne Herbert, Edward O'Neill.

Exploits of Parker, The (Homeland, 2 reels, 1917). Produced: W. P. Kellino, cinematography D. P. Cooper. With Charles Austin.

Fair Imposter, A (Samuelson, 1916). From the novel by Charles Garvice. With Madge Titheradge, Charles Rock, Edward O'Neill, Gerald McCarthy, Lionel d'Aragon, Alice de Winton, Florence Nelson.

Fallen Star, The (Ideal, 4,000 ft., August 14, 1916). With Albert Chevalier, Harry Brett.

Family Solicitor, The (Clarendon, 3 reels, 1914). By the Marchioness of Townshend.

Far from the Madding Crowd (Turner, 4,600 ft., February 28, 1916). Produced and adapted by Larry Trimble, from the novel by Thomas Hardy. With Florence Turner, Henry Edwards, Malcolm Cherry, Campbell Gullan, "Jean." Cinematography: Tom White.

Fatal Fingers (B & C, 5 reels, 1916). Produced: A. V. Bramble, adapted by Eliot Stannard from the story by William le Queux. With Icilma Rae.

Female Swindler, The (British Empire, 5 reels, November 1916). From the play by Walter Melville. With Alice Belmore, Henry Lonsdale, Andrew Emm, Ninette de Valois, Newman Maurice, Ralph Forster, Maude Olmar, Bessie Walters, Charles Grenville, Arthur Poole.

Fisherman's Infatuation, A (Cunard, 3 reels, 1915). Produced: Wallett Waller.

Flames (Butchers, 5,200 ft., February 18, 1918). Produced Maurice Elvey, adapted by Eliot Stannard from the novel by Robert Hichens. With Owen Nares, Margaret Bannerman, Edward O'Neill, Clifford Cobb, Douglas Munro.

Florence Nightingale (B & C, 3,700 ft., March 22, 1915). Produced: Maurice Elvey. With Elizabeth Risdon, A. V. Bramble, Fred Groves.

Footprints in the Snow (Master, 1919). From the novel by Dora Russell.

For all Eternity (I. B. Davidson, 5 reels, March 25, 1918). Produced: Arthur Rooke and A. E. Coleby, based on the song.

For Her People (Turner, 3 reels, 1914). Produced and written by Larry Trimble. With Florence Turner. Cinematography: Roland Hill.

For King and Country (Regent, 1914). Produced: Arthur Finn. With Arthur Finn.

For the Empire (London, 2,100 ft., September 12, 1914). With Douglas Munro, Charles Rock, Wyndham Guise, George Bellamy, Christine Rayner.

Fortune at Stake, A (Broadwest, 6,000 ft., December 2, 1918). Produced Walter West, from the story by Nat Gould. With Violet Hopson, Gerald Ames, James Lindsay, Gwynne Herbert, Wyndham Guise, Edward O'Neill.

Four Feathers, The (Lucoque, 1915).

Frailty (Unity, 1916). Produced: Sidney Morgan. With Joan Morgan.

Fringe of War, The (London, 1914). Produced: G. L. Tucker, by Bannister Merwin. With Jane Gail, Gerald Ames, Lewis Gilbert.

From Shopgirl to Duchess (B & C, 3,600 ft., April 19, 1915). From the play by Charles Darrell. With Elizabeth Risdon.

Gamble for Love, A (Broadwest, 5,500 ft., December 10, 1917). Produced: Harold Weston, adapted by Benedict James from the story by Nat Gould. With Violet Hopson, Gerald Ames, James Lindsay, George Foley, Hubert Willis, J. Hastings Batson.

Gardener's Daughter (Clarendon, 1,460 ft., December 14, 1914). From the poem by Lord Tennyson. With Nora Chaplin.

Gay Lord Quex, The (Ideal, 5 reels, January 28, 1918). Produced: Maurice Elvey, adapted by Eliot Stannard from the play by Sir Arthur Pinero. With Ben Webster, Irene Vanbrugh, Lilian Braithwaite, Donald Calthrop, Hayford Hobbs, Lyston Lyle, Margaret Bannerman.

George Robey's Day Off (2 reels, 1919). Produced: E. P. Kinsella and Henry Morgan. With George Robey.

Girl from Downing Street, The (Butchers, 4,800 ft., T.S. November 5, 1918). Produced and written by Geoffrey Malins. With Ena Beaumont.

Girl of My Heart (British Empire, 4,500 ft., September 20, 1915). Produced: Leedham Bantock, from the play by Herbert Leonard. With Leal Douglas, Herbert Leonard, J. Graeme Campbell, Frank Dane.

Girl Who Didn't Care, The (Neptune, 4 reels, August 7, 1916). With Agnes Paulton, Mercy Hatton, Jerrold Robertshaw, Tom Coventry.

Girl who Loves a Soldier, The (Samuelson, 3 reels, 1916). With Vesta Tilley, Rutland Barrington, James Lindsay.

Girl Who Took the Wrong Turning, The (British Empire, 5 reels, October 11, 1915). From the play by Walter Melville. With Henry Lonsdale, Nina Lynn, Alice Belmore, Andrew Emm, Mercy Hatton.

Girl Who Wrecked His Home, The (British Empire, 5 reels, October 1916). From the play by Walter Melville. With Alice Belmore, Henry Lonsdale, Andrew Emm, Maud Olmar.

God and the Man (Ideal, 7,000 ft., October 7, 1918). Produced: Edwin J. Collins, adapted by Eliot Stannard from the story by Robert Buchanan. With Joyce Carey, Langhorne Burton, E. Vivian Reynolds, Sybil Arundale, Edith Craig, Bert Wynne, Nelson Ramsay, Henry Vibart.

God Bless our Red, White and Blue (Samuelson, 6,000 ft., December 9, 1918). With Isobel Elsom, Owen Nares, Madge Titheradge, J. Fisher White.

Goodbye (Butchers, 5,000 ft., September 30, 1918). Produced: Maurice Elvey, adapted by Eliot Stannard from the novel by John Strange Winter. With Margaret Bannerman, Jessie Winter, Ruth McKay, Donald Calthrop, Douglas Munro, Fewlass Llewellyn, Frank Dane, Edward Arundel.

Grand Babylon Hotel, The (Hepworth, 1917). Produced: Frank Wilson, from the novel by Arnold Bennett. With Fred Wright, Margaret Blanche, Gerald Lawrence, Violet Hopson, Charles Vane, Lionelle Howard, Stewart Rome, Henry Vibart, Alma Taylor. Cinematography: C. Sanders.

Great Adventure, The (Turner, 5,500 ft., March 27, 1916). Produced by Larry Trimble, adapted by Benedict James and Larry Trimble from the play by Arnold Bennett. With Henry Ainley, Esme Hubbard, Arthur Cullin, Rutland Barrington, Amy Lorraine, Hubert Harben.

Greatest Wish in the World, The (International Exclusives, 5 reels, T.S. February 5, 1918). Produced: Maurice Elvey, from the novel by E. Temple Thurston. With Bransby Williams, Jean Alwyn, Ada King, Gwynne Herbert, Odette Goimbault, Edward Combermere, Douglas Munro, Edward Arundel, William Corri.

Great European War, The (Samuelson, 3 reels, 1914). Produced: George Pearson.

Great Game, The (I. B. Davidson, 6 reels, T.S. December 1918). Produced and adapted by A. E. Coleby, from the novel by A. Soutar. With Bombardier Wells.

Great Imposter, The (Harma, 5 reels, December 9, 1918). Produced: F. Martin Thornton, by Reuben Gilmer. With Marie Blanche, Bernard Dudley, Lionel d'Aragon, Harry Lorraine, Edward O'Neill, James Prior, Cecil Stokes, Rupert Stutfield.

Green Orchard, The (Broadwest, 5 reels, November 6, 1916). Produced and adapted by Harold Weston, from the novel by A. Soutar. With Gregory Scott, Dora Barton.

Grim Justice (Turner, 4,250 ft., T.S. August 1, 1916). Produced and adapted by Larry Trimble, from the novel by Rita. With Florence Turner, Henry Edwards, Malcolm Cherry, Maud Williamson, George Moore. Cinematography: Tom White.

Grip (B & C, 1915). Produced: Maurice Elvey, adapted by Eliot Stannard from the novel by John Strange Winter. With Fred Groves, Elizabeth Risdon, M. Gray Murray, Leon M. Lion, E. Compton Coutts, A. V. Bramble, Eliot Stannard, James Nott.

Grit of a Jew, The (Butchers, 5 reels, September 10, 1917). Produced: Maurice Elvey, by Kenelm Foss. With Augustus Yorke, Manora Thew, Hayford Hobbs, Fred Groves, Margaret Blanche, Frank Stanmore.

Hanging Judge, The (Hepworth-Edwards, 5,300 ft., January 6, 1918). Produced and adapted by Henry Edwards, from the play by Tom Gallon and Leon M. Lion. With Hamilton Stewart, Henry Edwards, Chrissie White, Gwynne Herbert, John McAndrews, A. V. Bramble, Randle Ayrton. Cinematography: C. Bryce.

Happy Warrior, The (Harma, 6,200 ft., February 1918). Produced: F. Martin Thornton, from the novel by A. M. Hutchinson. With Minna Grey, Roy Byford, H. Agar Lyons, Harry Lorraine, James Knight.

Harbour Lights (Neptune, 3,000 ft., T.S. October 2, 1914). Produced: Percy Nash, from the play by G. R. Sims and Henry Pettitt, cinematography A. Frenguelli. With Mercy Hatton, Daisy Cordell, Gerald Lawrence, Fred Morgan, Gregory Scott, John East, Douglas Payne, Joan Ritz, May Lynn.

Hard Times (Trans-Atlantic, 4 reels, 1915). Produced: Thomas Bentley, from the novel by Charles Dickens. With Bransby Williams, Leon M. Lion.

Hard Way, The (Broadwest, 1916). Produced: Walter West. With Muriel Martin-Harvey, Lily Saxby, George Bellamy, Tom Macdonald, Owen Francis, J. R. Tozer.

Haunted Hotel, The (Kinekature, 1 reel, T.S. May 16, 1918). Produced: Fred Rains. With Will Asher, Marion Peake.

Her Greatest Performance (Ideal, 6 reels, January 22, 1917). Produced: Fred Paul, by Enid Lorimer and Benedict James. With Ellen Terry, Edith Craig, Dennis Neilson Terry, James Lindsay, Barbara Hannay, Neilson Ramsay, Gladys Mason, E. Vivian Reynolds, Joan Morgan.

Her Lonely Soldier (Barker, 5 reels, 1918). Produced: Percy Nash, by Irene Miller. With Daphne Glenne, Eva Brooke.

Her Luck in London (B & C, 4,000 ft., T.S. November 1914). Produced and adapted by Maurice Elvey, from the play by Charles Darrell. With Elizabeth Risdon, A. V. Bramble, Fred Groves, M. Gray Murray.

Her Marriage Lines (Hepworth, 3,450 ft., T.S. February 1917). With Violet Hopson, Stewart Rome, Chrissie White, Lionelle Howard.

Her Nameless Child (3,500 ft., May 24, 1915). Produced: Maurice Elvey, from the play by Madge Duckworth. With Elizabeth Risdon.

Herself (Trans-Atlantic, 1 reel, 1918). Produced: Percy Nash. With Ella Shields, Henry Vibart, Leslie Styles.

Hidden Hand, The (5 reels, January 20, 1919). Produced and written by Lawrence Cowen, from the play based by him on his film *It is for England*.

Hills are Calling, The (Hepworth, 1,150 ft., October 19, 1914). Produced: C. M. Hepworth. With Henry Vibart. Cinematography: Gaston Queribet.

Hindle Wakes (Samuelson, 5,000 ft., T.S. May 1, 1918). Produced: Maurice Elvey, adapted by Eliot Stannard from the play by Stanley Houghton. With Colette O'Neill, Norman McKinnell, Edward O'Neill, Ada King, Dolly Tree, Hayford Hobbs, Margaret Bannerman, Frank Dane.

His Brother's Wife (M.L.B., 1,912 ft., July 26, 1915). Produced and written by Warwick Buckland. With Warwick Buckland, Flora Morris, J. R. Tozer.

His Dearest Possession (Hepworth-Edwards, T.S. January 1919). Produced: Henry Edwards, by E. Temple Thurston. With Chrissie White, Henry Edwards. Cinematography: C. Bryce.

His Uncle's Heir (Gaiety, 2 reels, 1917). Produced: Dave Aylott. With Bob Reed.

Holy Orders (I. B. Davidson, 6 reels, January 14, 1918). Produced: A. E. Coleby, from the novel by Marie Corelli. With A. E. Coleby, Arthur Rooke, Malvina Longfellow, Olive Bell.

Home (B & C, T.S. September 15, 1915). From the play by Fred Lindo. With Elizabeth Risdon, Fred Groves, M. Gray Murray, A. V. Bramble.

Honeymoon for Three, A (B & C, March 15, 1915). Produced: Maurice Elvey, by Dr. Charles. With Charles Hawtrey, Elizabeth Risdon, Fred Groves, Ruth MacKay, A. V. Bramble.

Honour in Pawn (Broadwest, 4 reels, January 15, 1917). Produced: Harold Weston, from the novel by W. B. Maxwell. With Manora Thew, Hetta Bartlett, Marjorie Compton, Helen Haye, George Bellamy, Ivan Berlyn, Julian Royce.

House of Fortescue, The (Hepworth, April 1917). By Percy Gordon Holmes, With Violet Hopson, Lionelle Howard, Stewart Rome, Charles Vane.

House Opposite, The (Broadwest, 4 reels, September 10, 1917). Produced: Walter West, adapted by Reuben Gilmer from the play by Percival Landon. With Matheson Lang, Ivy Close, Gregory Scott, Violet Hopson, Dora Barton, Dora de Winton.

How Lieut. Rose, R.N., Spiked the Enemy's Guns (Clarendon, 1915).

How Men Love Women (Phoenix, 3 reels, 1916). With Percy Moran.

Idol of Paris, The (B & C, 3,300 ft., February 15, 1915). Produced: Maurice Elvey, from the play by Charles Darrell. With Elizabeth Risdon.

If England were Invaded (Gaumont, 2,380 ft., October 19, 1914). From the story *The Invasion of England* by William le Queux.

If Thou Wert Blind (Clarendon, 5 reels, T.S. December 1917). Produced: F. Martin Thornton, based on the song. With Ben Webster, Evelyn Boucher, Joan Legge, Minna Grey, Clifford Pembroke, Sidney Lewis Ransome, Harry Lorraine.

In Another Girl's Shoes (Samuelson, 1917). Produced: G. B. Samuelson. With Mabel Love, Ruby Miller, Leo Belcher.

Incomparable Bellairs, The (London, T.S. January 28, 1915). Produced: Harold Shaw, from the story *Sweet Kitty Bellairs* by Agnes and Egerton Castle. With Edna Flugrath, Wyndham Guise, Lewis Gilbert, Hubert Willis, Gregory Scott, Florence Wood, Wallace Bosco, Mercy Hatton, Christine Rayner.

Infelice (Samuelson, 6 reels, January 3, 1916). From the novel by Mrs. Augusta J. Evans-Wilson. With Peggy Hyland, Fred Paul.

In Search of a Husband (Clarendon, 3 reels, January 1916). From the story in *Behind the Curtain* by Max Pemberton. With Murray Carrington, Frank Hilton, Barbara Conrad.

In the Blood (Clarendon, 3 reels, 1915). With Ben Webster, Dorothy Bellew.

In the Dear Dead Days. With A. E. Coleby, Malvina Longfellow, Janet Alexander.

In the Grip of Spies (Pathé, 3 reels, October 28, 1914). With Ivy Montford.

In the Ranks (Neptune, T.S. December 16, 1914). Produced: Percy Nash, from the play by G. R. Sims and Henry Pettitt, cinematography Alfonso Frenguelli. With Gregory Scott, James Lindsay, Douglas Payne, Frank Tennant, Daisy Cordell, John East, Edward Sass, Joan Ritz.

In the Shadows of Big Ben (Hepworth, 3,000 ft., 1914). Cinematography: C. Sanders.

Iris (Hepworth, 5,600 ft., March 13, 1916). Produced: C. M. Hepworth, from the play by Sir Arthur Pinero. With Alma Taylor, Henry Ainley, Stewart Rome. Cinematography: C. M. Hepworth.

Iron Justice (Renaissance, 1915). Produced and written by Sidney Morgan. With Miss Tittell-Brune, Sydney Fairbrother, Julian Royce, Alfred Drayton, Cecil Fletcher, A. Harding Steerman, Marguerite Belona, Joan Morgan.

It is for England (10 reels, November 20, 1916). Produced and written by Lawrence Cowen. With Baroness Helene Gingold.

It's a Long Long Way to Tipperary (B & C, 3 reels, T.S. November 13, 1914). Produced: Maurice Elvey. With Elizabeth Risdon, A. C. Ogan, A. V. Bramble, James Russell, H. Gray Murrey, Earnest Cox.

It's Always the Woman (Clarendon, 5 reels, 1916). Produced: Wilfred Noy, from the play by Bryant Adair. With Hayden Coffin.

It's Happiness that Counts (Butchers, 4,900 ft., April 1919). Produced: Bertram Phillips. With Queenie Thomas.

It's Never Too Late to Mend (A. E. Martin, 5,000 ft., March 1918). Produced:

D. Aylott, adapted from the play by Arthur Shirley based on the novel by Charles Reade. With Margaret Hope, Frank Robertson, George Leyton, Sam Jones, George Dewhurst, Maurice Gerard, Charles Vane.

Jade Heart, The (Martin, 3,390 ft., February 14, 1916).

Jane Shore (Barker, 5,500 ft., T.S. March 17, 1915). Produced: B. Haldane and F. Martin Thornton, by Rowland Talbot, designed by P. Mumford and F. Ambrose, cinematography Fred O. Bovill, L. Eveleigh. With Blanche Forsythe, Roy Travers, Robert Purdie, Nelson Phillips, Tom Macdonald, Rolfe Leslie, Tom Coventry, Frank Melrose, Fred Pitt, Dora de Winton, Maud Yates, Rachel de Solla.

Jimmy (B & C, 4 reels, 1916). Produced A. V. Bramble, adapted by Eliot Stannard from the novel by John Strange Winter. With A. V. Bramble, Betty Strange Winter, George Tully, Letty Paxton.

Jockey, The (Sunny South, 1,150 ft., T.S. December 21, 1914). Produced: F. L. Lyndhurst. With Will Evans, Arthur Conquest.

John Halifax, Gentleman (Samuelson, September 6, 1915). Produced by George Pearson, from the novel by Mrs. Craik. With Charles Bennett, Fred Paul, Lafayette Ranney, Harry Paulo, Edna Maude, Peggy Hyland.

Jo, the Crossing Sweeper (Barker, 5 reels, T.S. June 12, 1918). From the novel *Bleak House* by Charles Dickens. With Unity More, Dora de Winton, A. Beaulieu.

Just a Girl (Samuelson, T.S. July 1916). From the story by Charles Garvice. With Daisy Burrell, Owen Nares, J. Hastings Batson.

Just Deception, A (Tiger, 5,600 ft., November 1917). Produced: A. E. Coleby, from the novel *Aaron the Jew* by B. L. Farjeon. With Augustus Yorke, Robert Leonard.

Justice (Ideal, 6 reels, November 19, 1917). Produced: Maurice Elvey, from the play by John Galsworthy. With Gerald du Maurier, Hilda Moore, Lilian Braithwaite, Douglas Munro, Hubert Carter, Hubert Willis, James Carew, Vivian Reynolds.

Kent, the Fighting Man (Tiger, 5,500 ft., November 13, 1916). Produced: A. E. Coleby, adapted by Rowland Talbot from the novel by George Edgar. With Bombardier Billy Wells, Charles Vane.

Key of the World, The (Gaumont-British, 1919). Produced: J. L. V. Leigh, from the novel by Dorin Craig. With Eric Harrison, Eileen Molyneux.

Kiddies in the Ruins, The (Welsh-Pearson, 3 reels, T.S. November 13, 1918). Produced George Pearson, from the play by Poulbot and Paul Gull. With Emmy Lynn, Hugh E. Wright.

Kilties Three, The (Gaiety, 5,819 ft., March 17, 1919). With Bob Reed, Ernest Esdaile, Phyllis Beadon.

King of Crime (3,500 ft., 1914). From the play by Arthur Shirley.

King's Daughter, The (London, 4 reels, December 10, 1917). Produced: Maurice

Elvey, from the novel *Une Fille de Régent* by Alexandre Dumas. With Gerald Ames, Edward O'Neill, Hubert Willis, Janey Ross.

King's Minister, The (London, 3,000 ft., T.S. October 13, 1914). Produced: Harold Shaw, from the play by Cecil Raleigh. With Charles Rock, Edna Flugrath, George Bellamy, Langhorne Burton, Gerald Ames.

King's Outcast, The (London, 3 reels, 1915). Produced: Ralph Dewsbury, from the play by W. Gayer Mackay and Robert Ord, cinematography Gustav Pauli. With Charles Rock, Douglas Munro, Gerald Ames, Philip Hewland, Blanche Bryan, Chappel Dossett.

Kismet (Zenith, 4,000 ft., T.S. December 8, 1914). Produced: Leedham Bantock, from the play by Edward Knoblock, designed by Joseph Harker. With Oscar Asche, Lily Brayton, Herbert Grimwood, Caleb Porter.

Kiss Me (Harma, 2,000 ft., T.S. October 28, 1918). By Reuben Gilmer. With James Reardon, Leal Douglas, Trevor Eaton.

Knut and the Kernel, The (Trans-Atlantic, 1,005 ft., January 24, 1916). With Whimsical Walker.

Labour Leader, The (B.A.F.C., 5 reels, October 15, 1917). Produced: Thomas Bentley, by Kenelm Foss. With Fay Compton, Fred Groves, Christine Silver, Lauri de Frece, Owen Nares, Fred Volpe, Mrs. Macdona.

Lady Windermere's Fan (Ideal, 4,500 ft., August 28, 1916). From the play by Oscar Wilde. With Milton Rosmer, Netta Westcott, Irene Rook, Nigel Playfair, Arthur Wontner, Alice de Winton, Joyce Kerr, Vivian Reynolds, Evan Thomas, Sidney Vautier.

Lancashire Lass, A (Hepworth, 3 reels, 1915). With Alma Taylor, Stewart Rome, William Felton. Cinematography: C. Sanders.

Laughing Cavalier, The (Dreadnought, 5 reels, January 7, 1918). Produced: A. V. Bramble, adapted by Eliot Stannard from the novel by Baroness Orczy. With Mercy Hatton, Edward O'Neill, George Bellamy, A. V. Bramble.

Liberty Hall (London, 3 reels, 1915). Produced: Harold Shaw, adapted by Bannister Merwin from the play by R. C. Carton. With O. B. Clarence, Ben Webster, Langhorne Burton, Douglas Munro, Hubert Willis, Gwynne Herbert, Edna Flugrath, Ranee Brooke.

Lifeguardsman, The (B.A.F.C., 4 reels, August 6, 1917). Produced: Frank G. Bayly, from the play by Walter Howard, With Annie Saker, Alfred Paumier, A. E. Matthews, Alfred Bishop, Paul Arthur, Fred Kerr, Spencer Trevor, Fred Volpe, Leslie Carter, Cecil Ward, Leslie Henson, Sam Livesey, Cecil Humphreys, Charles Daly, Cecil Wynne, Eva Rowland, Ninon Dudley.

Life of Lord Kitchener, The (Windsor, 6,240 ft., January 1918). Produced and written by Rex Wilson, designed by M. Boella.

Life of Lord Roberts, V.C., The (Samuelson, 3 reels, December 14, 1914). Produced: George Pearson. With Hugh Nicholson.

Light (Renaissance, 3 parts, 1915). Produced and written by Sidney Morgan. With Joan Morgan, Julian Royce, A. H. Steerman, Mona K. Harrison.

Lil O' London (London, T.S. January 21, 1915). Produced: Harold Shaw, by Bannister Merwin. With Edna Flugrath, Ben Webster, Douglas Munro.

Little Damozel, The (Clarendon, 5 reels, T.S. September 21, 1916). From the play by Monckton Hoffe. With Barbara Conrad, Nora Chaplin, Geoffrey Wilmer, Roy Byford, J. H. Batson.

Little Minister, The (Neptune, 3 reels, T.S. February 12, 1915). Produced: Percy Nash, from the novel by Sir James Barrie. With Gregory Scott, Henry Vibart, Joan Ritz, John East, Douglas Cox, Brian Daly, Fay Davis, May Whitty, Douglas Payne, Frank Tennant.

Little Women (Samuelson, 5 reels, September 17, 1917). From the novel by L. M. Alcott. With Daisy Burrell, Wyndham Guise, Milton Rosmer, Ruby Miller, Roy Travers.

London's Enemies (5 reels, 1916). With Percy Moran, Lionel D'Aragon.

London's Yellow Peril (B & C, 2,300 ft., 1915). With Elizabeth Risdon, Fred Groves, A. V. Bramble.

Lost and Won (Turner, 4,000 ft., November 8, 1915). Produced Larry Trimble, by Henry Edwards. With Florence Turner, Edward Lingard, Henry Edwards.

Lost Chord, The (Clarendon, T.S. December 1916). Produced: Wilfred Noy, by Reuben Gilmer, based on the song. With Concordia Merril, Barbara Conrad.

Love (4,100 ft., September 11, 1916). Produced: L. C. MacBean, adapted by Rowland Talbot from the novel *When Woman Loves* by Rathmell Wilson. With Eve Balfour, Frank Tennant, Arthur Cullin, J. H. Batson, Dora de Winton.

Love of an Actress, The (Clarendon, 3 reels, 1914). By the Marchioness of Townshend.

Love's Old Sweet Song (Clarendon, 5 reels, December 3, 1917). Produced: F. Martin Thornton, based on the song. With Evelyn Boucher.

Lure of Drink, The (Barker, 3,300 ft., 1915). With A. E. Coleby, Roy Travers, Blanche Forsythe.

Lyons Mail, The (Ideal, 5 parts, 1917). Produced: Fred Paul, designed by Willie Davies. With H. B. Irving, Nancy Price, Wyndham Guise, Tom Reynolds, James Lindsay, Nelson Ramsay, Edward Arundel, Charles Vane, Harry Welchman.

Man and the Moment, The (Windsor, 5,800 ft., February 3, 1919). Produced: A. Bocchi, adapted by Kenelm Foss from the novel by Elinor Glyn. With Hayford Hobbs, Manora Thew, Charles Vane, Peggy Carlisle, Kenelm Foss, Maud Cressall, Jeff Barlow.

Man Behind the Times, The (Hepworth, 4 reels, December 17, 1917). Produced:

Frank Wilson, from the story by Percy Manton. With Stewart Rome, Harry Gilbey, Chrissie White, Lionelle Howard, Charles Vane, Mrs. Bedells.

Man in Possession, The (Homeland, 3 reels, T.S. September 14, 1915). Produced: W. Kellino. With Billy Merson, Blanche Bella, Winifred Delevanti, Lupino Lane.

Man in the Shadows, The (1916). Produced and written by Charles McEvoy. With the Aldbourne Village Players.

Man the Army Made, A (Pathé, 4,089 ft., 1918). Produced: Bertram Phillips. With Queenie Thomas, Cpl. Paul R. Hull.

Man Who Saved the Empire (Ideal, 1918). Produced: Maurice Elvey, by Sir Sidney Low.

Man Who Stayed at Home, The (Hepworth, 3,500 ft., 1915). Produced C. M. Hepworth, from the play. With Dennis Eadie, Henry Edwards, Alma Taylor, Violet Hopson, Chrissie White. Cinematography: C. M. Hepworth.

Man Without a Soul, The (London, 1916). Produced: G. L. Tucker, by Kenelm Foss. With Barbara Everett, Milton Rosmer, Edward O'Neill, Charles Rock, Kitty Cavendish, Hubert Willis.

Man with the Glass Eye, The (British Empire, 3 reels, September 1916). With Henry Lonsdale.

Manxman, The (London, 7,000 ft., September 3, 1917). Produced and adapted by G. L. Tucker, from the story by Hall Caine. With Henry Ainley, Elizabeth Risdon, Fred Groves, Edward O'Neill, John East.

Marked Man, A (London, T.S. May 1917). From the story by W. W. Jacobs. With Frank Stanmore.

Marriage of William Ashe, The (Hepworth, 5 reels, T.S. November 7, 1916). Produced: C. M. Hepworth, from the novel by Mrs. Humphry Ward. With Alma Taylor, Violet Hopson, Mary Rorke, Amy Lorraine, Henry Ainley, Stewart Rome, Henry Vibart, Alice de Winton. Cinematography: C. M. Hepworth.

Married for Money (Neptune, 1915). Produced Leon Bary, by Mrs. Maclean. With Frank Tennant, Gregory Scott, Douglas Payne, C. Morton York, Daisy Cordell, Lawrence Phillips, Douglas Cox, Fred Morgan, Constance Bachner, Louise Maclean.

Mary Girl (Butcher, 4,700 ft., April 22 1918). Produced: Maurice Elvey, adapted by Eliot Stannard from the play by Hope Merrick. With Norman McKinnel, Jessie Winter, Edward O'Neill, Margaret Bannerman, Marsh Allen.

Masks and Faces (Ideal, 6,700 ft., May 14, 1917). Produced: Fred Paul, adapted by Benedict James from the story by Charles Reade, designed by Willie Davies. With Sir George Alexander, Sir H. Forbes-Robertson, Irene Vanbrugh, Gladys Cooper, Dennis Neilson-Terry, Winifred Emery, Lillah McCarthy, Ben Webster, H. B. Irving, Dion Boucicault, Gerald du Maurier,

Matheson Lang, Weedon Grossmith, Gertrude Elliott, Lilian Braithwaite, Ellaline Terriss, Charles Hawtrey, etc.

Master and Man (Neptune, 3 reels, August 9, 1915). Produced: Percy Nash, from the play by G. R. Sims and Henry Pettitt. With Gregory Scott, Bryan Daly, Douglas Payne, Daisy Cordell, Joan Ritz, Frank Tennant.

Master of Men, A (Harma, 5,050 ft., March 11, 1918). Produced: Wilfred Noy, from the novel by E. Phillips-Oppenheim. With Malcolm Keen, Dorothy Bellew, Marie Hemingway.

Master of Merripitt, The (Clarendon, 3 reels, 1915). From the novel by Eden Phillpotts. With Dorothy Bellair.

May Queen, The (Favourite, 2,300 ft., November 2, 1914). From the poem by Lord Tennyson.

Me and My Moke (London, 1916). Produced: Harold Shaw, by Richard Ganthony.

Meg o' the Woods (Holmfirth, 5,464 ft., September 2, 1918). Produced: Bertram Phillips, by Irene Miller. With Queenie Thomas, Alice de Winton.

Merchant of Venice, The (Broadwest, 5 reels, December 11, 1916). Produced: Walter West, from the play by Shakespeare. With Matheson Lang, Hutin Britton, Kathleen Hazel Jones, J. R. Tozer.

Merely Mrs. Stubbs (Hepworth-Edwards, 4,000 ft., December 3, 1917). Produced and written by Henry Edwards. With Alma Taylor, Henry Edwards, Mary Rorke, Lionelle Howard, Charles Vane, W. G. Saunders, Fred Johnson, Molly Hamley Clifford, Ruth Mackay. Cinematography: C. Bryce.

Middleman, The (London, T.S. February 10, 1915). Produced: G. L. Tucker, from the play by Henry Arthur Jones. With Albert Chevalier, Jane Gail, Douglas Munro, Frank Stanmore, Gerald Ames, Hubert Willis, Christine Rayner.

Midshipman Easy (B & C, 2,700 ft., February 8, 1915). Produced: Maurice Elvey, from the novel by Captain Marryat. With Elizabeth Risdon.

Milestones (Samuelson, T.S. December 1916). Produced: Thomas Bentley, from the play by Arnold Bennett and Edward Knoblock. With Campbell Gullan, Isobel Elsom, Esme Hubbard, Owen Nares, Hubert Harben, E. Graham, Mary Lincoln, Minna Grey, Cecil Morton York, Lionel D'Aragon, Roy Travers, Winifred Delevanti, Herbert Daniel.

Missing Link, The (Homeland, 2 reels, July 2, 1917). With Lupino Lane, Winifred Delevanti.

Missing the Tide (Broadwest, 5,000 ft., April 8, 1918). Produced:Walter West, from the serial story. With Violet Hopson, Ivy Close, Basil Gill, Gerald Ames, James Lindsay, Master Hopson.

Mizpah (Magnet, 4,000 ft., July 1915). Produced: Stewart Kinder, from the play. With Kahli Ru.

Molly Bawn (Hepworth, 4 reels, T.S. December 5, 1916). Produced: C. M.

Hepworth, from the novel by Mrs. Hungerford. With Alma Taylor, Stewart Rome, Lionelle Howard, Fred Wright, John McAndrews, Violet Hopson.

Monkey's Paw, The (Magnet, 2,800 ft., March 8, 1915). From the story by W. W. Jacobs. With John Lawson.

Motherhood (Trans-Atlantic, 2,000 ft., July 2, 1917). Produced: Percy Nash, by Dorothea Baird. With Dorothea Baird, Lord Rhondda.

Motherhood (B & C, 4 reels, April 17, 1916). Produced and written by Harold Weston. With Lilian Braithwaite, Fay Temple, A. Caton Woodville, Laura Leycester, A. V. Bramble.

Mother of Dartmoor, The (London, 5 reels, October 22, 1917). Produced: G. L. Tucker, from the novel *The Mother* by Eden Phillpotts. With Elizabeth Risdon, Enid Bell, Hubert Willis, Bertram Burleigh, George Bellamy, Sidney Fairbrother, Frank Stanmore.

Mrs. Cassels' Profession (Neptune, 3 parts, 1916). Produced: Fred W. Durrant, from the novel by Irene Miller. With Margaret Belona.

Munition Girl's Romance, A (Broadwest, 4,500 ft., October 1, 1917). Produced: Walter West, by Charles Barrett. With Violet Hopson, Gregory Scott, George Foley, H. Sykes, Tom Beaumont.

My Lady's Dress (Samuelson, 8,500 ft., January 14, 1918). Produced: Alexander Butler, from the play by Edward Knoblock. With Gladys Cooper, Malcolm Cherry, André Beaulieu, Olive Richardson, Alice de Winton.

My Old Dutch (Turner, 5,600 ft., August 23, 1915). Produced: Larry Trimble, by Albert Chevalier and Arthur Shirley. With Albert Chevalier, Florence Turner. Cinematography: Tom White.

Mystery of a Hansom Cab, The (B & C, 5,500 ft., December 6, 1915). Produced Harold Weston, from the story by Fergus Hume. With Milton Rosmer.

My Sweetheart (Ideal, 5 parts, September 23, 1918). From the play. With Margaret Blanche, Concordia Merrill, Randle Ayrton, Bert Wynne, E. H. Kelly.

My Yorkshire Lass (Pyramid, 4 reels, 1916). By Herbert Pemberton.

Nature of the Beast, The (Hepworth, 1919). Produced: C. M. Hepworth, by E. Temple Thurston. With Alma Taylor, Gerald Ames, James Carew, Gwynne Herbert, Stephen Ewart, Mary Dibley, Victor Prout, Christine Rayner, John McAndrews. Cinematography: C. M. Hepworth.

Nature's Gentlemen (Harma, 5 reels, June 1919). Produced: F. Martin Thornton. With Madge Stuart.

Nearer My God to Thee (Hepworth, 5 reels, March 4, 1918). Produced: C. M. Hepworth, by Herbert Pemberton. With Alma Taylor, Henry Edwards, A. V. Bramble, John McAndrews, Teddy Taylor, Beryl Rhodes.

Nelson (International Exclusives, 7 reels, 1918). Produced Maurice Elvey, by Eliot Stannard. With Malvina Longfellow, Donald Calthrop, Ivy Close, Ernest Thesiger.

New Clown, The (Ideal, 4,500 ft., November 6, 1916). Produced: Fred Paul, from the play. With James Welch, Edward Sass, Manora Thew, Marjorie Day.

Night and Morning (Clarendon, 1915). From the novel by Lord Lytton.

1914 (London, 3 reels, T.S. January 21, 1915). Produced: G. L. Tucker, by Rita. With Jane Gail, Gerald Ames.

Nursie, Nursie (Samuelson, 2 reels, 1916). By Reuben Gilmer. With Clare Mayne.

O.H.M.S. (2,000 ft., 1914). With Percy Moran.

Once Upon a Time (B.A.F.C., 5 reels, November 1918). Produced Thomas Bentley, by Kenelm Foss. With Manora Thew, Joan Legge, Lauri de Frece, Nelson Keys, Charles Macdona, Adelaide Grace, A. E. Matthews, Dorothy Minto, Fred Volpe, Mrs. Macdona, Jeff Barlow, Noel Fisher.

One Summer's Day (B.A.F.C., 4 reels, August 20, 1917). From the play by H. V. Esmond. With Owen Nares, Fay Compton, A. G. Paulton, Roy Royston, Eva Westlake, Caleb Porter, Sam Livesey, Gwendoline Jessen.

On His Majesty's Service (London, 3,000 ft., 1914). Produced G. L. Tucker, by Frank Fowell. With Jane Gail, Douglas Munro, Wyndham Guise.

Only Man, The (Homeland, 3 reels, November 10, 1915). With Billy Merson.

On the Banks of Allan Water (Clarendon, 1917). Produced Wilfred Noy, by Reuben Gilmer based on the song. With Basil Gill, Violet Leicester.

Onward, Christian Soldiers (Samuelson, 1919). Produced: Rex Wilson. With Minna Grey, Isobel Elsom, Owen Nares, Tom Reynolds.

Ora Pro Nobis (Windsor, April 16, 1917). Produced Rex Wilson, by Rowland Talbot, based on the song, cinematography Silvanus Balboni. With Harding Thomas, Henry Victor.

Our Boys (Cherry Kearton, 2,450 ft., June 1915). Produced: J. Payne and Sidney Morgan, from the play by H. J. Byron. With Maitland Marler, W. Compton Coutts, Kathleen Harrison.

Outrage, The (Hepworth, 1915). Produced: C. M. Hepworth, from a story by Albert Chevalier. With Henry Ainley, Alma Taylor, Violet Hopson, Lionelle Howard, John McAndrews.

Pair of Spectacles, A (Samuelson, 3 reels, 1916). From the play by Sidney Grundy.

Pallard, the Punter (Gaumont-British, T.S. January 9, 1919). From the novel by Edgar Wallace. With J. L. V. Leigh, Heather Thatcher.

Parker, P.C. (Homeland, 2 reels, May 22, 1918). Produced: W. P. Kellino. With Charles Austin.

Parker's Weekend (Homeland, 2,300 ft., January 22, 1917). Produced: W. P. Kellino. With Charles Austin.

Parted by the Sword (Phoenix, 3 reels, 1916). With Percy Moran.

Passing of the Third Floor Back (Ideal, T.S. July 25, 1918). From the story by Jerome K. Jerome. With Sir Johnston Forbes-Robertson, Molly Pearson.

Paula (Bamforth, 5 reels, 1916). From the novel by Victoria Cross. With Hettie Payne, Frank McClellan.

Peace, Perfect Peace (Windsor, 2 reels, December 1918). Produced: A. Bocchi, by Kenelm Foss. With Marie Marsh Allen, Charles Vane, Chubby Hobbs, Hayford Hobbs, Bert Wynne, Evelyn Harding, Odette Goimbault, Mme Goimbault.

Peep Behind the Scenes, A (Master, 5 reels, T.S. December 11, 1918). Produced: Geoffrey Malins, from the story by Mrs. O. F. Walton. With Ivy Close, Gerald Ames, Gertrude Bain, Vera Bruger.

Perils of Pork Pie, The (Homeland, 2 reels, February 19, 1917). Produced: W. P. Kellino, by Reuben Gilmer. With Billy Merson.

Persecution of Bob Pretty, The (London, 1,000 ft., November 26, 1917). From the story by W. W. Jacobs. With Frank Stanmore, James Reardon.

Phantom Picture, The (British Empire, 5 reels, November 1916). Produced: Albert Ward, by Harold Simpson. With Violet Cambell, Henry Lonsdale, Arthur Poole, Ivan Berlyn.

Picture of Dorian Gray, The (Neptune, 4 reels, 1916). Produced: Fred W. Durrant. From the novel by Oscar Wilde. With Henry Victor, Sidney Bland, Jack Jordan, A. B. Imeson.

Pimple as Hamlet (2 reels, 1916). With Fred Evans.

Pit Boy's Romance, A (Tiger, 1917). Produced: A. E. Coleby, Arthur H. Rooke. With Jimmy Wilde, Tommy Noble.

Place in the Sun, A (Turner, 4,600 ft., T.S. June 6, 1916). Produced and adapted by Larry Trimble, from the play by Cyril Harcourt. With Reginald Owen, Lyston Lyle, Lydia Bilbrooke, Margaret Blanche, Frances Wetherall, Malcolm Cherry, Campbell Gullan.

Pleydell Mystery, The (British Empire, 5 reels, January 15, 1917). Produced and adapted by Albert Ward, from the novel *Poison* by Alice and Claude Askew. With Christine Silver, Cecil Humphreys, Mrs. Bennett, Richard Lindsay, Frank Randall.

Power to Kill (Union, 2,000 ft., September 6, 1914). Produced and written by L. C. MacBean.

Princess of Happy Chance, The (London, 1916). Produced: Maurice Elvey, from the story by Tom Gallon. With Elizabeth Risdon, Gerald Ames, Hayford Hobbs, Douglas Munro, Dallas Cairns, Gwynne Herbert, Janet Ross.

Prisoner of Zenda, The (London, March 9, 1915). Produced: G. L. Tucker, from the play by Edward Rose of the novel by Anthony Hope. With Henry Ainley, Gerald Ames, Jane Gail, Charles Rock, Arthur Holmes-Gore, Douglas Munro.

Profit—and the Loss (Ideal, 5 reels, March 19, 1917). Produced and adapted by Eliot Stannard, from the play by H. F. Maltby. With James Carew, Margaret Halston, Saba Raleigh.

Profligate, The (5 reels, September 10, 1917). Produced: Meyrick M. Milton, from the play by Sir Arthur Pinero. With Dorothy Bellew, Amy Brandon Thomas, Ben Webster, Fred Volpe, Langhorne Burton, Isabel Jeans, Cecil Humphreys, Geoffrey Kerr, Edith Mellor.

Queen of My Heart (5 reels, December 3, 1917). By Ella Langford Reed based on the song. With Christine Rayner, Charles Vane, Alfred Lugg, Hayden Coffin.

Queen of the Wicked, The (British Empire, 5 reels, September 1916). Produced and adapted by Albert Ward, from the play. With Henry Lonsdale, Nina Lynn.

Quicksands (International, 5 reels, September 24, 1917). Produced: George Bellamy, from the play by Ben Landeck. With George Dewhurst, Vera Cornish, Mercy Hatton, Minna Grey, J. H. Batson, Douglas Munro, George Bellamy, Mrs. Sterling McKinlay, Wyndham Guise, Hayford Hobbs, Nelson Ramsay.

Ragged Messenger, The (Broadwest, 4,025 ft., January 7, 1918). Produced Walter West, from the novel by W. B. Maxwell. With Violet Hopson, Basil Gill, Gerald Ames, George Foley, Marjorie West.

Rations (Ideal, 2 reels, May 1918). With Fred Evans.

Real Thing at Last, The (1916). By Sir James Barrie.

Red Pottage (Ideal, 4850 ft., November 4, 1918). From the novel by Mary Cholmondeley. With C. Aubrey Smith, Gerald Ames, Mary Dibley, Holman Clark, Margaret Hume.

Refugee, The (Hepworth, 2 reels, T.S. September 2, 1918). Produced: C. M. Hepworth, from the story by E. Temple Thurston. With Henry Edwards, Alma Taylor, Chrissie White.

Rogues of London (Barker, 4,500 ft., 1915). With Fred Paul, Blanche Forsythe.

Romany Lass, A (Harma, 6,600 ft., 1918). Produced: F. Martin Thornton, by Reuben Gilmer. With Marjorie Villis, Charles Rock, Bernard Dudley, James Knight, Arthur Cullin, Mrs. Hayden Coffin.

Romany Rye, The (Neptune, 4,000 ft., March 29, 1915). Produced: Percy Nash, from the play by G. R. Sims. With Gerald Lawrence.

Rugged Path, The (Lucoque, 5 reels, February 1919). From the novel by Charles Garvice. With Hayford Hobbs, Marjorie Villis, Ivy Stanborough, Michelin Poteus.

Rupert of Hentzau (London, 1915). Produced: G. L. Tucker. With Henry Ainley, Gerald Ames, Jane Gail, Charles Rock, George Bellamy, Warwick Wellington.

Russia—the Land of Tomorrow (Gaiety). Produced: Maurice Sandground, by Capt. Merivale, research E. Esdaile. With Eve Balfour, A. B. Imeson, Clifford Cobb, Bob Reed.

Sally Bishop (Gaumont-British, 4 reels, December 10, 1917). Produced: George Pearson, from the novel by E. Temple Thurston. With Aurele Sydney, Peggy Hyland, Alice de Winton, J. L. V. Leigh, Hugh Croise, Christine Rayner, Marjorie Villis.

Sally in Our Alley (Turner, 4,500 ft., May 8, 1916). Produced: Larry Trimble. With Hilda Trevelyan, Reginald Owen.

Sanctuary (Claude Harris, 1916). From the playlet by Malcolm Watson. With Sylvia Cavalho, Clifford Pembroke, A. Austin Leigh.

Second Mrs. Tanqueray, The (Ideal, 5 reels, May 22, 1916). Produced: Fred Paul, adapted by Benedict James from the play by Sir Arthur Pinero. With Sir George Alexander, Hilda Moore, Norman Forbes, Marie Hemingway, May Leslie Stuart, Nelson Ramsay, Mary Rorke, Roland Pertwee, James Lindsay, Minna Grey, Bernard Vaughan.

Secret Woman, The (I. B. Davidson, 6,297 ft., October 21, 1918). Produced: A. E. Coleby, from the novel by Eden Phillpotts. With Maud Yates, Janet Alexander, A. E. Coleby, Nicholas Bales, Henry Victor, W. S. Manning, Olive Noble, Humbertson Wright.

Shadows (B & C, 4,000 ft., August 30, 1915). Produced and written by Harold Weston. With Fay Temple, A. V. Bramble, Evelyn Shelley, Una Venning, Henry Hargreaves, M. Gray Murray.

She (Barker, T.S. February 29, 1916). Produced Will Barker, adapted by Nellie E. Lucoque from the novel by H. Rider Haggard, designed by Lancelot Speed. With Alice Delysia, Henry Victor, Sidney Bland, Blanche Forsythe, J. H. Batson, Jack Denton.

Sheffield Blade, The (British Pictures, 5 reels, T.S. November 7, 1918). Produced: Harry Roberts, from the story by A. G. Hales. With George Foley.

Shepherd Lassie of Argyle, The (Turner, 3 reels, 1914). Produced: Larry Trimble, by Hector Dion. With Clifford Pembroke, Florence Turner, Hector Dion, Rex Davis, Isobel Carma. Cinematography: Roland Hill.

Shopgirls (Turner, 3,500 ft., March 1, 1915). Produced: Larry Trimble, by Florence Turner. With Florence Turner, Rhoda Grey. Cinematography: C. Sanders.

Shop Soiled Girl, The (British Empire, 4,050 ft., January 17, 1916). From the play by Walter Melville. With Alice Belmore, Henry Lonsdale, Gladys Williams, Nina Lynn, Frank Randall.

Silence of Jasper Holt, The (Martin, 2,030 ft., January 17, 1916).

Silver Greyhound (Harma, 1919). Produced: F. Martin Thornton, by Bannister Merwin. With Marjorie Villis, James Knight.

£66 13s. 9¾d. *for Every Man, Woman and Child* (Ideal, 1916). With George Robey.

Slave, The (Windsor, 4,707 ft., July 1918). Produced: A. Bocchi, from the novel by Robert Hichens. With Hayford Hobbs, Marie de Lisle, Charles Vane, Hettie Grosman, Paul Courtenay, Earnest Wallace.

Smith (London, 3,440 ft., December 24, 1917). Produced: Maurice Elvey, from the play by Somerset Maugham. With Elizabeth Risdon, Manora Thew, Fred Groves.

Smugglers, The (1915). With Fred Evans.

Smugglers' Cave, The (Cunard, 2 reels, T.S. November 3, 1914). Produced: Wallett Waller. With Harold Easton, Charles Cantley, Mary Manners.

Snare, The (Broadwest, 5 parts, October 14, 1918). With Violet Hopson, George Foley, James Lindsay, Trevor Bland.

Snow in the Desert (Broadwest, 1919). From the serial story by A. Soutar. With Violet Hopson.

Soldier and a Man, A (B & C, 1916). From the play by Ben Landeck.

Somewhere in France (Regal, 3 parts, T.S. July 1915). From the story *None but the Brave*, by Ruby M. Ayres.

Son of David, A (Broadwest, 1919). Produced: E. Hay Plumb, by Charles Barrett. Arthur Walcott, Poppy Wyndham, Vesta Sylva, Constance Backner, Robert Vallis, Joseph Pacey, Ronald Colman.

Son of France, A (Samuelson, 2 reels, December 21, 1914). Produced: George Pearson. With Gerald Royston.

Sorrows of Satan, The (Samuelson, 1917). Produced: Alexander Butler, from the novel by Marie Corelli. With Owen Nares, Gladys Cooper, Cecil Humphreys, Lionel d'Aragon, Minna Grey, Winifred Delevanti, Alice de Winton.

Soul of Guilda Lois, The (Broadwest, 1919). From the story *The Crucifixion* by Newman Flower. With Violet Hopson, Basil Gill, Cameron Carr, Hilda Bayley, J. H. Batson, Clifford Pembroke.

Sowing the Wind (Hepworth, 5 reels, 1916). From the play by Sidney Grundy. With Henry Ainley, Alma Taylor, Violet Hopson, Lionelle Howard, Stewart Rome, Charles Vane. Cinematography: C. Sanders.

Spinner o' Dreams (Butchers, 5,200 ft., February 3, 1919). Produced and adapted by Wilfred Noy from the story by Leon M. Lion and W. Strange Hall. With Basil Gill, James Carew, Stella Mervyn Campbell, Odette Goimbault, Sam Livesey, Jos Boddy, Jeff Barlow, Molly Hamley Clifford.

Splash Me Nicely (Homeland, 2 reels, 1917). With Lupino Lane.

Splendid Coward, The (Harma, 6,000 ft., T.S. February 25, 1918). Produced: F. Martin Thornton, from the novel by Houghton Townley. With James Knight, Joan Legge.

Still Waters Run Deep (Ideal, 4,500 ft., April 10, 1916). Produced: Fred Paul, from the play by Tom Taylor. With Lady Tree, Milton Rosmer, Rutland Barrington, Hilda Bruce-Potter, E. H. Brooke, Sidney Lewis-Ransome.

Stolen Masterpiece, The (Pathé, 3 reels, October 28, 1914). With H. O. Martinek, Ivy Montford.

Stolen Sacrifice, The (4 reels, 1916). With Peggy Richard.

Strange Case of Philip Kent, The (Neptune, 4 reels, August 1916).

Strategy (B & C, 2,330 ft., September 1915). Produced Harold Weston. With A. V. Bramble.

Strong Man's Weakness, A (Tiger, 4,500 ft., October 1918). Produced: A. E. Coleby. With A. E. Coleby, Janet Alexander, Malvina Longfellow, Arthur Rooke.

Study in Scarlet, A (Samuelson, 5,800 ft., December 28, 1914). Produced and adapted by George Pearson, from the novel by A. Conan Doyle. With Fred Paul, Agnes Glynne.

Successful Operation, A (Regal, 2 reels, 1916). Produced and written by Aubrey Fitzmaurice. With Billy Boreham.

Suicide Club, The (B & C, T.S. August 18, 1914). Produced: Maurice Elvey.

Sweater, The (Hepworth, 3 reels, 1915). Produced: Frank Wilson, by W. J. Elliott. With Chrissie White, Lionelle Howard, Stewart Rome.

Sweet Lavender (Hepworth, 5,000 ft., T.S. October 19, 1915). Produced: C. M. Hepworth, from the play by Sir Arthur Pinero. With Alma Taylor, Chrissie White, Henry Ainley, J. V. Bryant, Stewart Rome. Cinematography: C. M. Hepworth.

Tailor of Bond Street, The (Barker, 4 reels, T.S. February 10, 1916). With Augustus Yorke, Robert Leonard, T. H. Macdonald, Peggy Richard.

Tale of a Shirt, The (Homeland, 3,000 ft., 1916). Produced: W. P. Kellino. With Billy Merson.

Tares (Hepworth, 2 reels, T.S. September 2, 1918). Produced: C. M. Hepworth, from the story by E. Temple Thurston. With Alma Taylor, Chrissie White, Henry Edwards. Cinematography: C. M. Hepworth.

Tatterley (Lucoque, T.S. September 1916). Produced: H. Lisle Lucoque, from the novel by Tom Gallon. With Charles Rock, Mercy Hatton, George Foley, Cecil Mannering, Madge Tree, Harry Lofting.

Terrible 'Tec, The (Homeland, T.S. January 18, 1916). Produced: W. P. Kellino. With Billy Merson.

Thelma (I. B. Davidson, 6 reels, August 26, 1918). Produced: A. E. Coleby and Arthur Rooke, adapted by Rowland Talbot from the novel by Marie Corelli. With Malvina Longfellow, Maud Yates, Leal Douglas, Arthur Rooke, A. E. Coleby, Fred Shaw, Judd Green, Harry H. Wright, Marsh Allen.

Thelma, or Saved from the Sea (Cygnet, 2,500 ft., October 12, 1914).

Then You'll Remember Me (4,000 ft., December 1918). Produced: Edward Waltyre. With Lionel D'Aragon, Mabel Hirst.

Thornton Jewel Mystery, The (I. B. Davidson, 3 reels, T.S. November 4, 1915). Produced: I. B. Davidson.

Through the Valley of Shadows (Turner, 3,700 ft., November 9, 1914). Produced: Larry Trimble, by Florence Turner. With Florence Turner, Edward Lingard, "Jean." Cinematography: Gaston Queribet.

Ticket of Leave Man (Barker, 6 reels, February 7, 1919). From the play by Tom Taylor. With Rolfe Leslie, Daphne Glenne, Peggie Maurice, George Foley.

Time and the Hour (M.L.B., T.S. May 18, 1915). Produced: Warwick Buckland. adapted by Muriel Alleyne.

Tinker, Tailor, Soldier, Sailor (Samuelson, 7,000 feet, September 12, 1918). Produced: G. B. Samuelson, by Kenelm Foss. With Isobel Elsom, Owen Nares.

Tom Brown's Schooldays (Windsor, T.S. March 31, 1916). Produced: Rex Wilson. With Dorrie Roberts, Mr. Arundell, Mr. Johnson, Joyce Templeton, Jack Coleman.

Tom Jones (Ideal, 6 reels, May 13, 1918). Produced: Edwin J. Collins, adapted by Eliot Stannard from the novel by Henry Fielding. With Langhorne Burton, Wyndham Guise, Sybil Arundale, June, W. Corri, Bert Wynne, Nelson Ramsay.

Tommy Atkins (Barker, 4 parts, T.S. January 1915). From the play by Arthur Shirley and Ben Landeck.

Top Dog, The (Windsor, 5 reels, March 15, 1919). Produced: A. Bocchi, adapted by Kenelm Foss from the novel by Fergus Hume. With Kenelm Foss, Odette Goimbault, Charles Vane, May Henry, Evelyn Harding, Clive Currie, Hayford Hobbs, Edward O'Neill, Bert Wynne, Douglas Munro.

Touch of the Child, The (Hepworth, 4,800 ft., July 1918). Produced and adapted by C. M. Hepworth, from the playlet by Tom Gallon and Leon M. Lion. With Alma Taylor, Henry Edwards, Stewart Rome. Cinematography: C. Sanders.

Towards the Light (Hepworth-Edwards, 5 reels, T.S. October 1, 1918). Produced and written by Henry Edwards. With Chrissie White, Henry Edwards, Henry Vibart, George Traill, Marsh Allen, A. V. Bramble. Cinematography: C. Bryce.

Traffic (I. B. Davidson, T.S. November 11, 1915). Produced and adapted by Charles Raymond, from the story by E. Temple Thurston. With Charles Vane, Marjorie Villis, Lily Saxby, Alden Lovett, Arthur Rooke.

Trapped by London Sharks (Barker, 4,500 ft., T.S. April 6, 1916). With Maud Yates, Blanche Forsythe.

Treasure of Heaven, The (Tiger, 5 reels, April 26, 1917). Produced and adapted by A. E. Coleby, from the novel by Marie Corelli. With A. E. Coleby, Olive Bell.

Trelawney of the Wells (Hepworth, 4,875 ft., T.S. February 29, 1916). Produced: C. M. Hepworth, from the play by Sir Arthur Pinero. With Alma Taylor, Stewart Rome, Lionelle Howard, Violet Hopson, Chrissie White, Warwick Buckland, John McAndrews, Percy Manton, Elizabeth Herbert.

Trumpet Call, The (Neptune, T.S. April 30, 1915). Produced: Percy Nash, from the play by G. R. Sims and R. Buchanan. With Gregory Scott, Frank Tennant, Cecil Morton York, John M. East, Jack Denton, Douglas Payne,

Douglas Cox, Daisy Cordell, Stella St. Audrie, Agnes Poulton, Biddy de Burgh, Joan Ritz.

Truth and Justice (Brum, 3,000 ft., October 19, 1916). Produced and written by G. Hewitt. With Horatio Bottomley.

Turf Conspiracy, A (Broadwest, 5 reels, T.S. August 23, 1918). Produced: Walter West, adapted by Bannister Merwin from the novel by Nat Gould. With Violet Hopson, Gerald Ames, Joan Legge, Wyndham Guise, Arthur Walcott, Cameron Carr, Tom Coventry, W. R. Harrison.

Two Columbines, The (London, 2,000 ft., December 14, 1914). Produced: Harold Shaw. With Edna Flugrath, Charles Rock, Hubert Willis, Christine Rayner.

Two Lancashire Lasses in London (A. E. Martin, 4,500 ft., T.S. January 10, 1917). Produced Dave Aylott, from the play by Arthur Shirley and Sutton Vane. With Wingold Lawrence, Dave Aylott, Dolly Tree, Letty Paxton.

Two Little Britons (London, November 2, 1914). Produced: Harold Shaw. With Edna Flugrath, Charles Rock.

Ultus and the Grey Lady (Gaumont, 4 reels, October 2, 1916). Produced and written by George Pearson. With Aurele Sydney, Mary Dibley, J. L. V. Leigh, M. Goujet.

Ultus and the Secret of the Night (Gaumont, 4 reels, January 29, 1917). Produced and written by George Pearson. With Aurele Sydney, Mary Dibley, J. L. V. Leigh, Leonard Shepherd, Mary Forbes, Lionel D'Aragon.

Ultus and the Three Button Mystery (Gaumont, 4,650 ft, August 27, 1917). Produced and written by George Pearson. With Aurele Sydney, Manora Thew, Charles Rock.

Ultus: The Man from the Dead (Gaumont, 6,000 ft., March 20, 1916). Produced and written by George Pearson. With Aurele Sydney, J. L. V. Leigh, A. Caton Woodville, Marjorie Dunbar, M. Goujet.

Under the German Yoke (Clarendon, 3,000 ft., 1915).

Under the Red Robe (Clarendon, 1915). Produced: Wilfred Noy, from the novel by Stanley Weyman. With Owen Roughwood, Jackson Wilcox, Sydney Bland, Dorothy Drake.

Unexpected Treasure, The (Kinekature, 2 reels, 1918). Produced: Fred Rains. With Lupino Lane.

Vagabond's Revenge, A (Cunard, 3 reels, October 25, 1915). Produced: Wallett Waller, by Florence Britton. With Lyston Lyle, Sydney Paxton, Alice de Winton, Agnes Glynne, Jack Morrison.

Valley of Fear, The (Samuelson, 6 reels, 1916). From the novel by Sir Arthur Conan Doyle.

V.C. (London, 1914). Produced: Harold Shaw, by Bannister Merwin. With Edna Flugrath, Charles Rock, Ben Webster, Douglas Munro, Gwynne Herbert.

Veiled Woman, The (British Empire, 4 reels, T.S. February 2, 1917). Produced: Leedham Bantock, by Harold Simpson. With Gladys Mason, Cecil Humphries, Frank Randall, Marjorie Chard.

Verdict of the Heart, The (Clarendon, 3 reels, November 15, 1915). From the novel by Charles Garvice. With Barbara Conrad, Frank Royde, Harry Welchman.

Vicar of Wakefield, The (Ideal, 5 parts, February 12, 1916). Produced: Fred Paul, adapted by Benedict James from the novel by Oliver Goldsmith. With Sir John Hare, Laura Cowie, Marie Illington, Ben Webster, Margaret Shelley, Mabel Twemlow, Jess Dorynne, A. E. George, Martin Lewis, Lambert Terry, Frank Wolfe.

Vice and Virtue (Regent, 3,200 ft., June 1915). Produced: C. Weston. With Charles Weston, Lily Saxby.

Village Blacksmith, The (Tiger, 4,000 ft., November 5, 1917). Produced: A. E. Coleby and A. H. Rooke, from the poem by Longfellow. With C. Arundale, Arthur H. Rooke, A. E. Coleby, Joyce Templeton, Janet Alexander.

Wages of Sin, The (Windsor, 5 reels, May 1919). Produced: A. Bocchi, adapted by Kenelm Foss from the novel by Lucas Malet. With Kenelm Foss, Odette Goimbault, Marie Marsh Allen, Charles Vane, Hayford Hobbs, Edward O'Neill, Bert Wynne, Arthur Walcott, Harry Lofting, Judd Green.

Wake Up! Or a Dream of Tomorrow (Wake Up Exclusives, 3,500 ft., 1914). By Lawrence Cowen.

Walrus Gang, The (Gaiety, 2 reels, 1917). Produced: Dave Aylott. With Bob Reed.

Ware Case, The (Broadwest, 5 reels, June 11, 1917). Produced: Walter West, from the play based on the novel by George Pleydell. With Matheson Lang, Ivy Close, Gregory Scott, George Foley, Violet Hopson.

War is Hell (Burlingham, 2,300 ft., 1915). Produced: Mrs. Ethyle Batley.

Way of an Eagle, The (6,500 ft., T.S. May 9, 1918). Produced: G. B. Samuelson, from the novel by Ethel M. Dell. With Mary Dibley, Isobel Elsom, André Beaulieu, Annie Desmond, Odette Goimbault.

Welsh Singer, A (Turner, 4,600 ft., T.S. December 1, 1915). Produced: Henry Edwards, from the story by Allen Raine. With Henry Edwards, Florence Turner, Campbell Gullan, Malcolm Cherry, Una Venning, Fred Rains, Edith Evans. Cinematography: Tom White.

What a Life (Harma, 2,000 ft., T.S. October 28, 1918). By Reuben Gilmer. With James Reardon, Leal Douglas, Maxine Hunter, R. Adkins, Peggy Paterson, Nellie Jackson, Maude Harris, Trevor Eaton.

What Every Woman Knows (Neptune, 1917). Produced: F. W. Durrants, from the play by Sir James Barrie. With Hilda Trevelyan.

What's Bred in the Bone Comes out in the Flesh (4 reels, 1916). From the story by Grant Allen. With Janet Alexander, Lauderdale Maitland.

What Would a Gentleman Do? (Butchers, 5,000 ft., September 1918). Produced: Wilfred Noy, from the play by Gilbert Daylis. With Queenie Thomas, Stanley Logan, Mabel Bunyea, Jean Cavendish, Dora de Winton, Rupert Stutfield, Jeff Barlow, Cooper Middleton, Harry Drummond, Will Corri, A. B. Imeson.

When East Meets West (Clarendon, 3,000 ft., 1915). By the Marchioness of Townshend.

When Knights Were Bold (London, 4 reels, T.S. August 1916). Produced: Maurice Elvey, from the play by Charles Marlowe. With James Welch, Gerald Ames, Douglas Munro, Janet Ross, Marjorie Day.

When London Sleeps (B & C, 3,400 ft., October 26, 1914). From the play by Charles Darrell.

When Paris Sleeps (B & C, T.S. February 12, 1917). From the play by Charles Darrell.

When Passions Rise (Clarendon, 3 reels, January 13, 1916).

When the Heart is Young (Gaiety, 2 reels, 1917). Produced: Dave Aylott. With Bob Reed.

When Woman Hates (British Empire, 5 reels, September 1916). Produced and adapted by Albert Ward, from the play.

Where's Watling? (Harma, 1918). By Reuben Gilmer. With Hugh E. Wright, Mr. and Mrs. Lawrence Layton, Maud Yates, E. G. Thurstans.

White Hope, The (Hepworth, T.S. November 16, 1915). Produced: Frank Wilson, by Victor Montefiore from the novel by W. R. H. Trowbridge. With Stewart Rome, Violet Hopson, George Gunther.

White Star (3 reels, 1915).

Whosoever Shall Offend (Windsor, 1918). Produced: A. Bocchi, adapted by Kenelm Foss from the novel by Marion Crawford. With Kenelm Foss, Charles Vane, Barbara Everest, Joyce Templeton, Evelyn Harding, Philip Hewland, Hayford Hobbs, Mary Marsh Allen, Maud Cressall, Odette Goimbault.

Whoso is Without Sin (Ideal, 4,700 ft., February 7, 1916). Produced Fred Paul, adapted by Fred Paul and Benedict James from the scenario by May Sherman. With Hilda Moore, Milton Rosmer, Arthur M. Cullin, Ronald Squire, Flora Morris, Lawrence Leyton.

Why Not Speak Out? (Ideal, 4 parts, April 2, 1917). With H. B. Irving.

Woman Who Dared, The (Trans-Atlantic, 3 reels, T.S. December 22, 1915). Produced: Thomas Bentley, by Rowland Talbot. With Austen Camp.

Woman Who Did, The (Broadwest, 1915). Produced: Walter West, from the novel by Grant Allen. With Eve Balfour, T. H. Macdonald, George Foley, W. Brandon, Joan Morgan, Thelma Giddens.

Woman Who was Nothing, The (Butchers, 4 reels, November 5, 1917). Produced: Maurice Elvey, adapted by Eliot Stannard, from a story by Tom Gallon.

With Lilian Braithwaite, Ruth Mackay, Marjorie Day, Madge Titheradge, George Tully, Leon M. Lion, Lyston Lyle, Douglas Munro.

Woman Wins, The (Broadwest, 5 reels, May 1919). From the story by Cecil H. Bullivant. With Violet Hopson, Gerald Ames, Trevor Bland, Arthur Walcott.

Women Who Win (5 reels, 1919). Produced: Percy Nash and Fred Durrant, by E. Alma Stout, cinematography J. C. Bee-Mason. With Minna Grey, Phillis Villiers, Mme d'Esterre, Unity Moore, Mary Forbes, Lloyd Morgan, Frank Gwyn Richardson, Alice de Winton, Rachel de Solla, Stanley T. Barrie, Frank Adair.

Women's Land Army, The (Broadwest, T.S. August 14, 1917). Produced: Walter West. With Ivy Close, Violet Hopson.

Won by Losing (3 reels, 1916). With Queenie Thomas, Frank McClellan.

World of Sin, A (British Empire, 4,400 ft., February 7, 1916). From the play by Walter Melville.

World Power or Downfall (I. B. Davidson, 5 reels, T.S. November 1918). Produced A. E. Coleby, "edited" by Frederic William Wile.

World's Desire, The (B & C, 3,300 ft., May 10, 1915). Produced and written by Sidney Morgan. With Lilian Braithwaite, Joan Morgan, Fred Groves, A. V. Bramble, Kathleen Warwick, M. Gray Murray.

Wreck and Ruin (Clarendon, 3 reels, 1914). By the Marchioness of Townshend.

Ye Wooing of Peggy (Holmfirth, 2 reels, T.S. May 1917). Produced and written by Bertram Phillips. With Queenie Thomas, Frank Petley, H. Agar Lyons.

Yoke, The (International Cinematograph, 1916). From the novel by Hubert Wales.

You (London, 1,300 ft., 1916). With Charles Rock, Douglas Munro, Gerald Ames, Edna Flugrath.

1. *Books and Brochures*

Art of Photo-Play Writing, The, by Harold Weston.
Published by McBride, Nast & Co. Ltd., London. 1916.
Art of the Moving Picture, The (Revised Edition), by Vachel Lindsay.
Published by The Macmillan Co., New York, U.S.A. 1922.
Cinema, The, Its Present Position and Future Possibilities.
(Special Cinema Trade Edition.)
Being the Report of the Chief Evidence taken by the Cinema Commission of
Inquiry instituted by the National Council of Public Morals.
Published by Williams & Norgate, London, 1917.
Cinema Plays, How to Write Them, How to Sell Them, by E. H. Ball.
Published by Stanley Paul & Co., London, 1917.
Film Game, The, by Low Warren.
Published by T. Werner Laurie Ltd., London, 1937.
How I Filmed the War, by G. H. Malins.
Published by Herbert Jenkins Ltd., York Street, London, 1920.
How to Write for the Movies, by Louella O. Parsons.
Published by A. C. McClurg & Co., Chicago, U.S.A., 1915.
Motion Picture Making and Exhibiting, by John A. Rathbun.
Published by T. Werner Laurie Ltd., 8 Essex Street, London.
Moving Pictures, How they are Made and Worked, by F. A. Talbot.
(Revised Edition).
Published by William Heinemann, London, 1912.
National Film Library Catalogue.
(2nd Edition).
Published by the British Film Institute, London, 1938.
Picture Play Photography, by H. M. Lomas.
Published by Ganes Ltd., 85 Shaftesbury Avenue, London, 1914.
Playwriting for the Cinema, by Ernest A. Dench.
Published by Adam and Charles Black, London, 1914.
Practical Cinematography and its Applications, by F. A. Talbot.
Published by William Heinemann, London, 1913.
World Film Encyclopedia, The, edited by Clarence Winchester.
Published by The Amalgamated Press Ltd., London, 1933.

The publicity brochures of many individual films were lent by: James
Anderson, W. G. Barker, British Film Institute, Maurice Elvey, Cecil Hepworth,
Will P. Kellino, Percy Nash, George Pearson.

2. *Trade Periodicals*

The Bioscope.
Published by Ganes Ltd., 85 Shaftesbury Avenue, W.1.
Bioscope Annual and Trades Directory.
Published by Ganes Ltd., 85 Shaftesbury Avenue, W.1.
Kinematograph and Lantern Weekly.
Published by E. T. Heron & Co., 9–11 Tottenham Street, W.1, until April 1917, and then by Odhams Ltd., 93 Long Acre, W.C.2.
Kinematograph Year Book.
Published by E. T. Heron & Co., 9–11 Tottenham Street, W.1, until the 1918 edition, which was published by Odhams Ltd., 93 Long Acre, W.C.2.
The "Kinematograph Weekly" Monthly Alphabetical Film Record.
Published by E. T. Heron & Co., 9–11 Tottenham Street, W.1, until July 1917.
The Monthly Film Record.
Published by E. T. Heron & Co., 9–11 Tottenham Street, W.1, between August 1917 and May 1918.
The Monthly Film Record.
Published by Odhams Ltd., 93 Long Acre, W.C.2, between June 1918 and December 1918.
Pictures and the Picturegoer, Volume VIII, April 1915 to September 1915.
Published by Odhams Ltd., 93 Long Acre, W.C.2.

3. *Interviews.*

Information was obtained by interviews and correspondence, mainly the former, with the following: Ray Allister, Dave Aylott, W. G. Barker, Joseph Best, Adrian Brunel, R. H. Cricks, Ralph Dewsbury, J. D. Anson Dyer, Maurice Elvey, Henry Edwards, Jympson Harman, Frank Hauser, L. J. Hibbert, Baynham Honri, A. T. Jones, Will Kellino, Gerald Malvern, J. H. Martin, Percy Nash, George Pearson, I. Roseman, Sam Simmonds, Theodore Thumwood, Walter West, Chrissie White, Tom White, D. J. Williams.

I